MW00582687

The Complete Celebrant Handbook

Han Hills

The Complete Celebrant Handbook:
How to Officiate Weddings, Memorials, and more,
from Beginner to Professional
Copyright Hypathian Books 2016
ISBN-10: 0692634738
ISBN-13: 978-0692634738 (Hypathian)

Disclaimer: Although every effort is made to ensure the information contained in this volume is correct at the time of publication, laws, and public information, are subject to regular change, and every reader is encouraged to pay attention to any changes made within their state or area. The author accepts no responsibility for discrepancies between the information contained within, and that held, or adopted, by any jurisdiction.

The author is in no way responsible for the actions of any party taken as a result of the advice contained within this publication. The opinions given with regards to third party companies, organizations, or vendors, are entirely those of the author. No payments, or other incentives, were received to recommend any organization over any other.

Cover picture and author picture by Kristin Frey (kristinfreystudios.com)
Back cover picture by J Jones Photography (joshjonesphoto.com)

I would like to very gratefully acknowledge the help of the following individuals in the creation of this book: Wyndi Hills, The Society of Celebrations, The Humanist Institute, Louis Shackleton, David Ptasnik, Ellen Sutliff, Laura Cannon, Brenda Cadman, Josh Withers, Bethel Nathan, Marie Burns Holzer, and all the amazing individuals from whom I have learned so much on my Celebrant journey.

The Complete Celebrant brings you a growing and regularly updates set of guides, handbooks, and references for everyone creating and participating in modern ceremonies in the twenty-first century.

Visit us today at hanhills.com/complete-celebrant/ to sign up free to receive critical updates, extra content, and exclusive offers. For further details, see the section on extra content at the end of the book.

Contents

Introduction

Welcome to the fully revised and updated edition of the Complete Celebrant's Handbook. Since the publication of the first edition, we have spent a great deal of time refining and updating every section, as well as adding whole new sections created for this volume.

Since the previous edition, there has been a continuing growth in the demand and performance of modern ceremonies of all kinds. A modern ceremony is one which is created unrestrained by inflexible religious rules and traditions, and where the core emphasis is on the life and emotions of the participants, rather than on supernatural references. As the table below shows, in many western countries there is a significant and sustained growth in the number of people identifying as removed from organized religion. This change is most pronounced in "Millennials", defined as those born after 1980. For this increasing percentage of the population, a modern, personalized ceremony is often preferred. Continuing growth in demand for the sorts of ceremony described in this book therefore seems assured.

Table: Trends in self-ascribed non-religious behavior.

United States: Those self-described as unaffiliated with a particular faith.			
2007	16.1% (36.6M)	2014	22.8% (55.8M)
Source: Pew Research Center, Religious Landscape Study, 2014			
United Kingdom: Those stating they have 'no religion'.			
2001	14.8% (8.8M)	2011	25.1% (14.1M)
Source: Office for National Statistics Census			
Australia: Those categorized as having 'no religion'.			
2006	18.7% (3.7M)	2011	22.3% (4.8M)
Source: Australian Bureau of Statistics Census			

One of the most important social events in the U.S. during 2015 was the landmark decision made by the Supreme Court that same-sex marriages must be acknowledged and available across the nation. Although there are still some pockets of dissent on this issue, the wonderful acceptance of marriage equality is now with us to stay. From this author's perspective, that is an overwhelming cause for celebration.

Similarly, in Ireland, 2015 saw the passing of the Marriage Equality Act, that allows for weddings across the country to take place regardless of sex. This was the first time that a country legalized same-sex marriage through a popular vote. All appeals have now been dismissed, and this principle is now firmly established in Irish law.

I hope that other countries, especially Australia, will quickly follow suit and fully embrace and establish marriage equality. When I next write an introduction to an edition of this book, it is my fondest hope to report they have done so. Because of these changes in marriage equality law, those relevant sections of this book have been revised, and the sections of appendices that specify same-sex legality for each U.S. state removed.

Throughout this book, I have worked to make each section applicable to both same-sex and different-sex occasions, but apologize if any hints of 'different-sex bias' remain, even if only as afterthoughts. The use of the terms 'bride' and 'groom' is still heavily entrenched in popular culture. As the amazing Australian Celebrant Josh Withers has pointed out so well, it is now possible across the entire U.S. to have a wedding without a bride, or a wedding without a groom. I found, in revising this text, I had a problem with the use of gender-neutral terms such as 'partner' or 'party,' with the addition of a letter (A or B) or number (1 or 2) to differentiate. These monikers seem impersonal. Therefore, at times throughout this book I may still refer to brides and grooms, but I promise I mean no bias or offense. Where possible, I use the joint term "couple". Of course, as a Celebrant we should never forget that very best way to refer to each party in a marriage is by their given names. The mark of a powerful modern ceremony is that it stays personal in every moment.

I should also say a few words about how I have referred to clients in the parts of this book dealing with funerals and memorials. In some cases, such as when preplanning a memorial with an individual, I will refer to them as the 'client,' as it is they I am working with directly. When referring to planning with friends and family members, or when implementing the plans that were discussed before death with a client, I have referred to that individual as the 'deceased', the standard term used by professionals for such occasions. Deceased is preferable to use in modern celebration, as it does not carry with it any implied religious or spiritual subtext.

There is still no doubt in my mind that the demand for Celebrants, particularly those specializing in Humanist and Non-religious ceremonies, outweighs the number of Celebrants practicing, particularly those doing so at a professional level. The industry of Celebration, if we can refer to it by such a cold title, has entered a period of increasing maturity in the last few years. Professional organizations, such as The International Association of Professional Wedding Officiants, are helping to organize the Celebrant community, and encourage higher standards of practice among those who market themselves in this role on a professional basis.

Despite the increase in the demand for celebration professionals, there is still a trend for couples to choose friends, family members, or well-spoken acquaintances to act as their Celebrant. This is especially true in the United States, where the requirements for an individual to legally perform a wedding ceremony are often low.

At the time of writing, there is still a disparity in the legal rights of Humanist Celebrants within the U.K. Although Humanist weddings have been fully legal in Scotland since 2005, they are still not recognized in England. A Humanist ceremony may be held in the latter location, but for the marriage to be legal a registry office ceremony must also take place. Further details about current marriage law in the United Kingdom, and elsewhere, can be found in the appendices of this book.

There appears to be a current, troubling trend among wedding industry professionals for understating the importance of the Celebrant in the wedding process. Photographers, when posting their record of an event on their business blog, frequently omit reference or credit to the individual who performed the ceremony. Additionally, Celebrants remain among the lowest paid types of ceremony professional, although they are uniquely indispensable to the process. I hope that as the number of professional modern Celebrants increases and professional organizations continue to promote understanding of the value that we bring to the ceremony, the dedicated hard work of the thousands of devoted Celebrants will be better recognized and acknowledged.

In recent years, there has been a growth, albeit still a slow one, in the availability of training for Celebrants outside of organized religion. In Australia, where training and certification are mandatory, this requirement ensures that all Celebrants must meet a basic professional standard. However, training in the United States, however, remains optional, and there are unlikely to become any uniform standards of qualification unless there is uniformity of the requirements to perform a marriage across all 50 states. At this point, the imposition of such a uniform standard in the U.S. seems highly unlikely, as the confusion in statutes receives very little attention, and most traditional religious organizations would heavily oppose any initiative by the government to standardize requirements for clergy.

If you are reading this as you embark on a Celebrant career, I wish you the very best, and hope you find the deep, personal satisfaction and rewards that this author has over the last decade. If you are reading this as an established Celebrant, I hope you find the material useful and thought-provoking, and I would welcome any feedback and suggestions you may have for improving this book in forthcoming editions. Thank you, and happy reading.

Who this Book is For

I have tried to make this book useful, and relevant, to all Celebrants, whatever the stage of their career.

If you are just beginning, this book can provide you with a complete course of instruction, and contains all the information you need to get you started with your Celebrant practice.

If you are already performing ceremonies, and looking for further instruction and direction, this book will take you deeper into the process, and guide you towards mastering your role.

If you are a Celebrant with many years of experience, I hope the following pages will provide you with some new and interesting perspectives that will enable you to gain a fresh outlook on your role, and perhaps encourage you to try new approaches.

If you are involved in the leadership of a group that is looking to add ceremony to your activities, I hope you will find this a handy guidebook full of advice and ideas to get you started, and then help you master successful ceremonies of all kinds.

If you are not a Celebrant, I hope this book will give you some fascinating insights into our profession, as well as demonstrating the many skills and techniques that a professional brings to any ceremonial occasion. Many of the skills used in performing a ceremony translate with surprising effectiveness to other areas of life.

How to Use this Book

This book was designed to work as a course of instruction, as well as a reference book to keep handy, and to dip into for ideas and information whenever needed.

If read from cover to cover, you will be armed with enough information to take you from planning and performing your first ceremony, through to establishing your professional Celebrant business.

Each section stands alone, as its own reference to a particular topic, easy to locate the first time you encounter a particular issue, or when you need to revisit a subject to refresh your thoughts.

The later sections and appendices contain many useful references and resources, including sample contracts and question sheets, as well as guides to local rules and procedures. You will also find links to obtain many of these sample documents, as well as information on a host of further resources online.

Part One
The Role of the Celebrant

1.1 What is a Celebrant?

A professional Celebrant is a qualified and experienced person who helps individuals, couples, families, and communities create and perform ceremonies that recognize and celebrate significant events, milestones, and values.

A traditional Celebrant is most likely employed exclusively by a religious body or institution. The nature and content of the ceremonies such an individual is allowed or required to perform is likely to be heavily regulated. There may also be strict constraints placed by the employing institution on the types of persons to which that Celebrant was able to offer services. One example would be the position of Catholic Priest, where the content of ceremonies is very carefully and explicitly outlined, and the clergy are strictly prohibited from performing services for persons outside their faith, or for proscribed social groups such as same-sex couples.

A modern Celebrant, though often trained and ordained by an official body, is usually given a wide degree of latitude and discretion in the types of ceremony they can perform, the content they can choose to include, and the community they can elect to serve. Such freedom necessitates a different approach and skill set to their traditional counterparts. Most modern Celebrants administer and regulate their own practice, and, therefore, require a mature personal ethic, as well as a degree of entrepreneurial skill. It is up to the modern Celebrant to establish their own style and create their own ceremonial content, and such a role requires a high degree of creative effort. Although the modern Celebrant may borrow the practices of his or her traditional counterparts, they have the freedom to expand and adapt conventional forms and structures in an almost infinite number of ways.

It is important to remember that a professional Celebrant will pass through a process of education. This training may be partly academic or entirely experiential, but their abilities and skills will develop over time. Although the barriers to performing ceremonies are very few, the path to mastery of the craft of celebration takes dedication. The development process can last many years.

1.2 Which Title to Use

If you attend a significant number of ceremonies, you will hear Celebrants addressed in many different ways. The titles adopted by, and given to, Celebrants are hugely varied, and often have overlapping and ambiguous meanings and definitions. There are, however, three main monikers that have been adopted by modern Celebrants practicing in Western, English-speaking, countries: Celebrant, Officiant, and Minister. Let us take a moment to examine the distinctions between these three titles. Each can be defined thus:

Celebrant. A person who performs, or leads, a ceremony.

Officiant. One (as a priest) who officiates at a rite.

Minister. A person whose job involves leading church services, performing religious ceremonies (such as marriages), and providing spiritual or religious guidance to others.

Consider the following diagram.

Figure: The relationship of professional Celebrant terms.

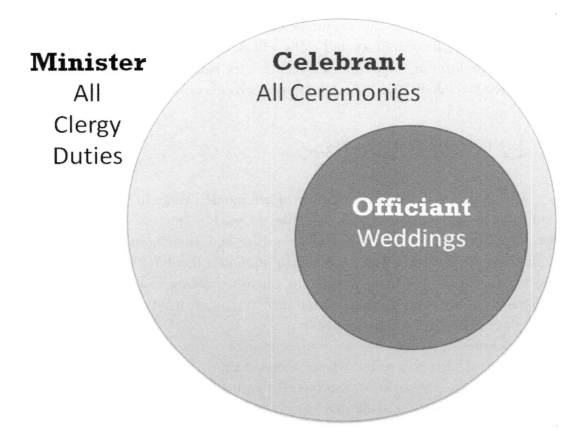

Minister
All
Clergy
Duties

Celebrant
All Ceremonies

Officiant
Weddings

As you can see, the term Minister covers the broadest range of duties and obligations. These are not limited to ceremonies, but may also include giving sermons, teaching, and pastoral care. Seen as a subset within that category, the term Celebrant applies only to those duties involving ceremony, though this can include rituals of many different types. In using the term Officiant, we need to make a geographical distinction. In the United States, this term is commonly used as the standard designation for the official performing a marriage. However, in English-speaking countries outside the United States, most particularly the United Kingdom and Australia, the term Celebrant is usually adopted for this purpose. These are of course general guides. Even among Ceremony professionals, such as wedding planners and funeral specialists, you may hear the titles used interchangeably, with others such as Pastor or Reverend also mentioned.

For the purposes of this book, and the professional roles addressed, the term Celebrant is the most appropriate, and is, therefore, used throughout the text when referring to the professional job title.

The choice of your own title, to be known by in general or for a particular event, is ultimately at your discretion. However, it is important that you do not mislead others in any way as to your professional or educational status. You should also undertake your duties in a manner that carefully and consistently honors and respects the honorific you use.

It is worth saying a few notes about qualifying modifiers that may be used with a Celebrant title. The base title is often narrowed by placing another noun or pronoun before it, to denote membership of a group(i.e. Mormon Minister), allegiance to a particular creed or ideology (i.e. Humanist Officiant), or that the only duties undertaken by that individual are highly specific (i.e. Funeral Celebrant). When conferring ordination, many organizations may have rules regarding the use of such modifiers, similar to the rules about the types of service you will be allowed to perform under their license. You should consider these rules before deciding how to refer to yourself publicly, and especially before sending your business card design to the printer.

1.3 Types of Ceremony

As a practicing Celebrant, you should expect the majority of your duties to involve the preparation and performing of wedding ceremonies. This role, also known as the solemnizing of marriage, is one of the few ceremonial functions in the United States for which there are specific legal requirements. These can vary widely between states. In the United Kingdom, the rules vary between England and Scotland. In all places, the laws are often subject to change or redefinition. Appendix A of this volume lists the current marriage Celebrant requirements for each state of the U.S. It is important that you become very familiar with the rules for the regions in which you practice. You should also stay alert for any changes to local laws.

In addition to weddings, there are many other types of ceremony you may be asked to perform. The actual scope of celebration is limited only by the imagination and desires of individuals and communities. It is important to note that you are free to choose which of these ceremony types you wish to participate or specialize in. A modern Celebrant should never be obliged to perform any kind of service, as is often the case with their traditional counterparts.

1.4 Characteristics of a Modern Ceremony

Modern ceremonies, which are primarily humanistic and non-religious in nature, already make up a significant percentage of those taking place in Northern Europe, and this trend is fast taking hold across the United States. Let's take a moment to review what sets such occasions apart from traditional celebrations. Traditionally, ceremonial practices were restricted by the policies and rules of a particular faith or denomination. A Celebrant was explicitly required to devote considerable amounts of a ceremony to prayers and scripture. Such additions were frequently unrelated to, irrelevant to, or at odds with the personal values and experiences of participants and witnesses. These rules and traditions often became a hindrance to creating a ceremony which addressed the needs and hopes of a young couple or bereaved community.

A modern ceremony, which is essentially humanistic in nature, does away with these restrictions as far as possible. There should be no requirements to reference particular ancient texts, nor should there be demands to subordinate the wishes of a couple to the arbitrary rules of a distant governing body. This leaves the Celebrant, couple, family, or community free to give full creative expression to the powerful and special emotions of the occasion.

However, although modern ceremonies are free from the demands of dogma and scripture, and in many cases free of any supernatural references whatsoever, they often incorporate core traditions from the cultural backgrounds of the participants. This can be readily observed in the structure of modern wedding ceremonies. Almost all will contain a statement of vows and the majority will incorporate the exchanging of rings. Couples from distinct cultural traditions may choose to include symbolic customs unique to theirs. One example of this would be a secular Jewish couple choosing to include the glass breaking ritual, or 'Mazel Tov,' at the close of their wedding ceremony.

Most importantly, A humanistic ceremony is a celebration of life, even when recognizing the legitimate issues of death. Services are focused clearly on the lives of those at their center. This may be a couple entering wedlock, a person whose life has recently ended, or one whose life is just beginning. The focus, as with

many modern invocations, could just as easily be on a group of people who are making a difference within their community. It is also critical for a modern ceremony that it make an effort to connect and resonate with *all* those attending at a very human and emotional level.

Table: Comparing modern and traditional ceremony Characteristics.

Traditional/Religious	Modern/Humanistic
Formal, prescribed format	Freedom to choose the format
Emphasizes the supernatural/eternal	Emphasizes the natural/human
Addressed to a divine power	Addressed to participants and witnesses
References sin and punishment	References choice and personal accountability
Limited creative freedom & fun	Unlimited creative freedom & fun

If you choose to define yourself as a Humanist Celebrant, you may encounter a degree of uncertainty in the community as to the meaning and values associated with that title. Although Humanism is fast entering common, everyday vocabulary and usage in the United Kingdom, this is not yet true in the United States, where the 'brand recognition' is still at a much earlier stage. Additionally, in the U.S., the confusion may be compounded due to misleading and negative propaganda created by conservative religious groups. You should expect to be asked for explanations of Humanist ideas and practices. It is important that you have a comfortable familiarity with the key points of Humanism. You should be able to convey these quickly and clearly to individuals and groups. I encourage you to read the 'Humanism and Its Aspirations' document, published by the American Humanist Association, and freely available on its website, AmericanHumanist.org. You will also find a great deal of other helpful information there, as well as on the websites of the British Humanist Association, humanism.org.uk, and the International Humanist and Ethical Union, iheu.org. You may wish to practice your quick explanations, often referred to as your elevator speeches, as they should take no longer than it might be to deliver on a short elevator ride with a stranger. Friends and family can be useful in helping you hone these skills. As with every aspect of ceremony preparation, those close to you can often give you valuable, unexpected feedback on how your words and performance may be perceived.

1.5 Practical Considerations

Much has been written about the 'philosophy' of modern, humanistic ceremonies, especially when debating on the cultural role of religion. It is vital to understand that the role of the Celebrant is primarily a practical one. If you are considering any type of Celebrant duties, and especially if you plan to practice at a professional level, you should first consider the practical skills you will need and be expected to demonstrate every time you accept that role. In the following sections, I will discuss some of the skills you should evaluate in yourself that are critical to creating and performing any modern ceremony.

1.6 Your Writing Skills

Although many Celebrants rely heavily on material taken from other sources, such as books or websites, the creation of a truly unique and personalized ceremony absolutely requires some composition ability. However, you do not have to be a Pulitzer caliber author to create an occasion all those attending will remember fondly.

When starting out on your career in celebration, I recommend reading as many ceremonies as you can. There are a great number of examples available in book form, as well as online. You will find a wide variation in writing styles, but you should notice that the best writing comes from genuine sincerity. As you compose your first ceremonies, write in a style which feels comfortable, but never lose sight of the respect and personal formality that should be present in every event you are creating.

Most importantly, when composing a ceremony, you should remember that you are writing text to be spoken. Keep your sentences clear and concise. Use simpler and shorter words where possible. Read your work aloud to yourself or a friend, and change anything which sounds clumsy or overly-complicated. Become familiar with the language of ceremonies. Included in this book are glossaries for both weddings and memorials.

When composing each ceremony, it is also important to consider your audience. There are some groups for which simpler language might be more appropriate. Others may prefer something a little more formal in construction. If you can adapt to the needs of each occasion, you will please your clients far more than if you stick to a uniform style and tone.

1.7 Your Public Speaking Skills

Performance is central to the role of every Celebrant. You will be expected to speak in front of large groups, and you should be comfortable doing so. It is important to develop a clear and strong speaking voice. Although some locations will provide microphone amplification, many will not do so.

If a DJ is contracted for the ceremony, they will often provide amplification equipment. Many Celebrants have found that a wireless lapel microphone, or Lavalier, provides the best solution, as this attaches discretely to the clothing. These also allow freedom of movement and leave both hands available for holding a ceremony script or other ritual items.

An Important Note on Microphones

In my experience, it is always better to have a microphone rather than not. If you have to exert to increase the volume of your voice in any way, this detracts from your ability to express nuance and subtle emotion, which are important in the spoken words of a wedding ceremony. You may wish to consider the purchase of your own personal amplification system, if your budget, and the number of events you are performing, make this a financially sensible decision. There are several systems available that are effective for this purpose. A popular choice among Celebrants in the United States is manufactured by Happie Amp (happieamp.com) though I advise you to read reviews, seek advice from colleagues, and carefully consider your budget before making any purchase for your Celebrant business.

There are many practical and entertaining written guides to help you improve your public speaking. However, there is no substitute for practice and receiving honest personal feedback. You may decide to try out your skills on family and friends whose opinion you trust. You might also offer to give a talk or presentation to a local social group or club. If the opportunity arises, and if you are brave enough, you may be able to watch video playback of yourself speaking in public, or review audio recordings. Although this can sometimes be an uncomfortable experience, it is by far the best way to help iron out any unwanted vocal mannerisms or habits of gesture.

Breathing technique is essential for producing proper voice projection. Whereas, in ordinary everyday speech, one may only use air from the top of the lungs, a correctly projected voice uses air flowing from the expansion of the diaphragm. Well-balanced respiration is critical to maintaining strong vocal projection. The goal of clear speaking is to isolate and relax the muscles controlling the vocal folds, leaving these unimpaired by tension.

Before each event, you should try to put a short time aside to warm up your voice. A cold start, after a period of vocal inactivity, could cause you to strain your voice and begin to sound croaky. A quick way to do this is to practice exaggerated facial expressions and yawning, followed by a short selection of tongue twisters. Be careful where you perform these pre-ceremony rituals. For a couple to catch the Celebrant yawning or speaking to themselves directly before a wedding ceremony may cause anxiety.

It is also important to stay hydrated at all times. Many Celebrants pack a bottle of water or tea to keep them refreshed directly before a ceremony.

I have included some recommended guides to improving your public speaking skills at the back of this book. However, there is absolutely no substitute for practice.

1.8 Celebrant Dress and Clothing

For the Celebrant in a modern ceremony, there are no established traditional or mandatory dress requirements. Many choose simply to dress smartly and in a way that best fits the occasion. This is one issue where it can be helpful to consult the client. An individual, couple, or family, may have strong opinions as to what they expect you to wear. Some may be uncomfortable with any garments which seem traditionally 'religious'. In contrast, others may prefer a costume which is overtly ceremonial, perhaps to fulfill the conventional expectations of notable guests who will be attending the event.

For men, a suit and tie is often the standard, perhaps with the addition of a vest (waistcoat). For women, a tasteful dress or gown is often appropriate. Maintaining a clean, respectable appearance is important at all times. You should also take care not to choose a style, or color, that might distract from the atmosphere, gravity, or focus of the occasion.

If you are representing a particular group or philosophy, you may wish to add a subtle symbol representing this to your clothing. However, it is wise to confirm, in advance, that any such symbol is acceptable to your client.

A simple item of ceremonial attire might be the addition of a neutral colored stole, a strip of fabric worn over the shoulders that hangs down to the knee or ankle. The color may be selected to suit the nature of the occasion. Such items can also help to establish the authority of the Celebrant in the ceremonial proceedings. Plain and tasteful stoles are readily available, at a reasonable price, from websites such as Etsy.

TIP: Ascertain which colors the clients have chosen for their event. You can then be sure not to wear clothing that may clash with these.

1.9 Location and Travel

If you live in an area of high population density, such as a major city, you may find you need to travel only a few minutes to reach most ceremony locations. However, most Celebrants are asked to commute significant distances to perform their services.

It is important to consider the availability of transportation, and how far you are willing, and able, to travel on any particular day. Long drives, in addition to the performing of a ceremony, can be tiring. You may also have reservations about traveling at night, or driving in twilight conditions. It is important to account for these factors before deciding if you should accept a ceremony booking.

When starting your Celebrant practice, you should consult a map of the region surrounding your 'base of operations'. Decide on the areas, and distances, you will be happy to cover. Not only will this affect your decisions on which bookings to accept, but it will also have a significant impact on the methods and locations for marketing your services.

TIP: If you operate a vehicle, keep a simple mileage log with you as you travel, record the starting value of your odometer before departing, and the new figure when you return. This information will help you calculate your business expenses. In many cases, the miles you travel for business will be tax deductible.

1.10 Seasonal Factors

Weddings will likely make up the majority of the ceremonies you perform. It is important to realize that booking volumes for these are often highly seasonal. Regional climate, as well as the dates of public holidays, will profoundly affect your work calendar.

The peak months for wedding ceremonies are usually between April and October in the Northern Hemisphere, though this is reversed if you practice in Australia.

In warmer climates, your busy season can extend further towards the winter months. In particularly hot regions, you may find a slight dip in bookings in the peak summer months, most especially where most clients are planning an outdoor ceremony. The reason for this drop is that extended periods in the sun can be uncomfortable, especially if dressed in formal wear. Heat can also take an extra toll on the very young or old.

There are also times throughout the year when more couples begin to plan their wedding day. Many Celebrants expect a rise in inquiries just after New Year, and again around Valentine's Day.

For other types of ceremony, there is no season to speak of. You may receive requests for memorials, or new life celebrations, at any time of the year.

1.11 Keeping a Calendar

When working as a Celebrant, your calendar immediately becomes an indispensable tool. It is used not only for recording the bookings you accept but also for anticipating your own important life events and commitments. Many of these will be scheduled several months in advance.

It is important to record every forthcoming event as soon as possible, even if the booking is still provisional. This is essential to avoid any possibility of a double booking. It will also help you to decide how to balance your work, and avoid overload. Busy Wedding Celebrants also find they often have to plan their vacations for the off-season or to set aside particular personal dates as much as a year in advance.

Ideally, you should keep a calendar handy, perhaps installed on your telephone. This will give you constant access to answer any questions about your availability.

An excellent tool is Google Calendar, which is available free with any Gmail account. This can be synchronized automatically between your computer and telephone, allows for multiple users, and can store a great deal of additional information about any event, such as location, contact details, and even a copy of your booking contract and ceremony! You can also share the calendar and any attachments with colleagues and family. This can give family members advance information to help them plan activities in which they would like you included.

TIP: When recording a booking on your calendar, be sure to allow for time needed for preparation and travel, mark off appropriate safety margins for unexpected delays such as traffic difficulties. When considering more than one booking on a single day, it is vital to know if the transition from one ceremony to the next is both practical and desirable.

1.12 Your Boundaries and Comfort Zone

If a modern Celebrant is selected for a ceremonial occasion, it is reasonable to assume that the main parties involved wish it to have a modern format and style. A couple, or family, may be intentionally seeking a wholly non-religious and humanistic ceremony. This position may be held *despite* the expectations and opinions of others attending. However, there may be occasions where you are expected to include spiritual, or traditional, elements in the ceremony. This often happens to pacify more conservative family members who are attending the event.

Whether you agree to officiate on such an occasion can often be a matter of boundaries. Many Humanist Celebrants are uncomfortable with, and unwilling to participate in, references to the supernatural, spiritual, or religious. Others may allow minor references, providing these do not misrepresent or distort the core message and principles of the occasion.

A reliable rule of thumb is to never participate in any ritual that is insincere or hypocritical to your own beliefs and values. If you are faithful to, and honest about, your own principles you will not go far wrong. If you find yourself uncomfortable with the wording of a particular reading, or uneasy about leading those attending in a moment of spiritual contemplation, it is perfectly acceptable to explain this to your client, and suggest that a guest, family member, or friend whose outlook is better fitted, read that section of the script. Most couples and families will be understanding in such matters and respect your honesty and integrity.

It is important to carefully consider your personal boundaries and limits before you begin practicing as a Celebrant. These questions will almost certainly arrive sooner than you expect.

1.13 Maintaining your Reputation

As a respected figure at any event, and as an ambassador for your profession, it is crucial that you seek to protect your reputation at all times. Only through having an excellent public reputation will you successfully build your Celebrant business. It is a widely accepted statistic that 95% of couples choosing a wedding professional online do so primarily according to reviews and testimonials. A single poor review can undo the impressive work of a hundred excellent ones, so actively cultivate and encourage feedback when you feel you have given good service. If you believe your performance fell short of excellence, you should consider practical steps you can take to improve, and to avoid the recurrence of any pitfalls on your part.

1.14 Your Professional Ethic

The role and responsibilities of a professional Celebrant requires a strong professional ethic. In my own work, I have created a set of rules I try to follow. You may wish to adopt some, or all, of these:

1. **Treat everyone with dignity, respect, and politeness at all times.**

2. **Do not drink alcohol.** Many ceremonial occasions involve the consumption of alcohol, often with regrettable consequences. As the Celebrant, you are acting in a professional capacity, and are expected to maintain decorum at all times. There is no harm in a polite refusal. In fact, that is always the very best policy.

3. **Moderate your language.** The use of vulgarity is not only offensive to many, but insults the dignity of your position.

4. **Do not 'fraternize'.** Although it is important to be friendly, always be aware of the social boundaries which exist between yourself and clients, their guests, and other professionals. As a figure of authority, there may be occasions where you receive personal advances from those you encounter. Days of celebration are, after all, emotional times. Any amorous attentions, or intimate suggestions, you receive should always be politely, but firmly, declined.

5. **Do not smoke.** Strangely, this is a rule some Celebrants of my acquaintance have contested. This is, of course, a matter of personal choice. However, smoking is now a minority practice that many consider unpleasant and undignified. The dignity of your position is never something you should sacrifice. For Celebrants who smoke, I strongly recommend waiting until you have completely finished your duties, and left the ceremony venue for the final time, before lighting your first cigarette.

6. **Do not discuss politics.** Political opinions vary widely, and they can often be extremely emotive. Discussion of such topics too often leads to conflict. As a professional, hired to oversee an important ceremony in a dignified manner, you should avoid engaging in such debates, or being seen to express any personal opinion that some may find offensive. This is, of course, a proper rule for any workplace outside the twenty-four-hour newsroom. It is entirely acceptable to politely decline such a conversation, explaining that it is not appropriate to engage in such a topic while acting in your professional capacity. Unless an individual is deliberately obtuse and provocative, which is sometimes the case, they will have respect for your honesty, integrity, and professionalism.

7. **Do not debate religion.** Because of the historical traditions of ceremonies, and the assumptions made by participants, topics of faith will inevitably arise at some point once you begin to practice. These are dangerous waters where passions often run high. As with politics, it is perfectly acceptable to politely

decline to discuss your personal faith position. Where you decide it is important to explain a concept, such as the meaning of Humanism, do so with care and empathy. Many people you encounter at events will hold a different spiritual outlook to yourself. It should always be a primary concern not to cause offense while acting in your professional capacity as a Celebrant, however much you may find yourself appalled by any viewpoint you hear expressed.

8. **Ensure you are always punctual.** Most ceremonies are carefully timed, and you are essential to proceedings. Arriving when you have agreed is indispensable to facilitate a smooth and successful day. I consider it good practice to plan to arrive slightly earlier than is needed. This allows for any unexpected delays while traveling, and also gives a cushion of time to address any unexpected problems that may have occurred at the venue during the final preparations.

9. **There is no such thing as 'Off Duty'.** From the time you arrive at the site to the time you depart, you should be acting in a professional capacity. Particularly at weddings, you may be enthusiastically encouraged to relax. To do so can easily place you in danger of acting in an unprofessional manner. We live in an age of Facebook, Twitter, Instagram, and many other means by which bad news and pictures can quickly spread beyond all control. One indiscretion can damage a Celebrant's reputation in a way that it may never fully recover. Be always mindful of your behavior, and maintain a clear separation between the professional and the personal areas of your life.

10. **Discretion is critical.** Publishing sensitive information about your clients, or their ceremony, is unprofessional. Where you share details of an event, either with other Celebrants, friends, or online, you should not reveal real names and dates unless you have explicit written permission to do so. Some wedding ceremonies are held in a private manner for sensitive, personal reasons. It is an essential aspect of your professional integrity to respect your client's confidences at all times.

11. **Keep a smart appearance.** Your personal image is key to your professionalism, and it should be carefully maintained at all times. You should ensure that your garments are clean, and that you have excellent standards of personal hygiene and grooming. In my own practice, I do not loosen my tie, or adjust my clothes for comfort, until I have left the venue. Clients will hugely respect this sort of professional behavior, and it will have a high impact on the types of testimonial you receive following the event.

12. **Do not overstep your role.** In your capacity as a Celebrant, you will have many different duties to perform. However, it is important not to impede the functions or the other professionals you work beside. Remain aware of who has been hired to perform specific tasks, and allow them to do so without criticism or instruction. You should resist the temptation to 'step in' if you feel another vendor is not performing as you would choose or expect. To intervene in such a way rarely results in the best resolution to any problem situation. Initiative and willingness are significant and valuable skills, but only when used with discretion, understanding, and care for the feelings of everyone involved.

13. **Do not proselytize.** You should never use your position as Celebrant as a platform to promote your own personal viewpoints or agenda.

Always remember that your reputation is your greatest business asset. Your behavior will make, or break, that reputation. This is something it can take many years to build, but only a single moment to destroy.

1.15 Assessing your Celebrant Skills

When starting out as a Celebrant, it is important to understand your personal strengths and weaknesses as they relate to that role. With honest self-assessment, you should be able to highlight areas for growth and improvement. You should also examine, then nurture, the special and unique qualities that you bring to the job, and those that could be powerful assets in building, and promoting, your business and practice.

What follows is a set of questions addressing the skills most required to practice and succeed as a modern Celebrant. There are no right or wrong answers to these. This is an exercise to aid you in understanding your strengths and weaknesses. Following these questions, I have given a commentary on each to help you understand their importance. Please circle your own self-assessed rating, based on a number from one to ten. If you have the opportunity, you might like to have a trusted friend or family member review your ratings. When seeking to evaluate our personal qualities, the perspective of a knowledgeable and sincere third party can be invaluable.

1.16 Celebrant Skills Questionnaire

Question 1. Have you any previous experience as a Celebrant?
(1 - No experience | 10 - Extensive experience)
1 2 3 4 5 6 7 8 9 10

Question 2. Have you any previous experience as a Public Speaker?
(1 - No experience | 10 - Extensive experience)
1 2 3 4 5 6 7 8 9 10

Question 3. Are you nervous speaking in front of large groups?
(1 - Very nervous | 10 - Very comfortable)
1 2 3 4 5 6 7 8 9 10

Question 4. Do you have a strong and clear speaking voice?
(1 - Not at all | 10 - Professionally trained)
1 2 3 4 5 6 7 8 9 10

Question 5. Do you have good writing skills?
(1 - Very limited | 10 - Professional writing experience)
1 2 3 4 5 6 7 8 9 10

Question 6. Do you have a clean and smart appearance?
(1 - Scruffy and unwashed | 10 - Extremely smart at all times)
1 2 3 4 5 6 7 8 9 10

Question 7. Can you remain standing for several hours at a time?
(1 - Poor physical condition | 10. Excellent physical condition)
1 2 3 4 5 6 7 8 9 10

Question 8. Are you comfortable traveling?
(1 - Regularly avoid traveling | 10 - Very comfortable)
1 2 3 4 5 6 7 8 9 10

Question 9. Are you comfortable among large groups of strangers?

(1 - Highly uncomfortable | 10 - Highly relaxed)
1 2 3 4 5 6 7 8 9 10

Question 10. Can you remain composed in a crisis?
(1 - Easily panicked | 10 - Consistently calm)
1 2 3 4 5 6 7 8 9 10

Question 11. Are you methodical and organized?
(1 - Chaotic and disorganized | 10 - Fastidious and highly organized)
1 2 3 4 5 6 7 8 9 10

Question 12. Are you able to work flexible hours and weekends?
(1 - Very restricted timetable | 10 - Great flexibility and availability)
1 2 3 4 5 6 7 8 9 10

Question 13. Can you commit to bookings months in advance?
(1 - Cannot pre-plan | 10 - Can plan over a year in advance)
1 2 3 4 5 6 7 8 9 10

Question 14. Do you have any small business or bookkeeping experience?
(1 - No experience | 10 - Extensive experience)
1 2 3 4 5 6 7 8 9 10

Question 15. How familiar are you with web design or creation?
(1 - No experience | 10 - Extensive experience)
1 2 3 4 5 6 7 8 9 10

Question 16. How familiar are you with online social networking?
(1 - No experience | 10 - Extensive experience)
1 2 3 4 5 6 7 8 9 10

Question 17. Are you comfortable speaking on the telephone?
(1 - Dislike telephones | 10 - Very comfortable)
1 2 3 4 5 6 7 8 9 10

Question 18. Have you attended many weddings?

(1 - Have attended none | 10 - Have attended dozens)
1 2 3 4 5 6 7 8 9 10

Question 19. Have you attended many funerals or memorials?
(1 - Have attended none | 10 - have attended dozens)
1 2 3 4 5 6 7 8 9 10

Question 20. How large do you plan on building your Celebrant business?
(1 – One ceremony only | 10 – Full-time professional)
1 2 3 4 5 6 7 8 9 10

1.17 Evaluating your Questionnaire Answers

Question 1. Have you any previous experience as a Celebrant?

You may have already performed ceremonies, perhaps for friends, or informally for a local social group, and may be reading this with the desire to take your skills and practice to the next level. If so, you have already taken the first steps towards one of the most emotionally rewarding jobs available.

It is important to remember that every ceremony will present new challenges. The nature of modern ceremonies is that they are responsive to the needs of the couple, individual, family, or community. Just as each of those is unique, so no ceremony is ever the same.

Like all professions, mastering celebrancy requires a degree of continuing study and practice. However many ceremonies you perform throughout your career, there will always be something new and unexpected just a few steps ahead. That is one of the exciting challenges and joys of becoming a modern Celebrant. For this reason, even I only score myself a nine on this scale. I know I could perform ten thousand ceremonies, and still have new experiences waiting for me at the next venue.

Question 2. Have you any previous experience as a Public Speaker?

The ability to speak in public is the core skill for any Celebrant. It requires practice, but this can be attained in many ways. Clubs and discussion groups are terrific places to grow and refine your public presentation skills. I have listed some recommended reading on this topic later in this book.

Public speaking is often referred to as an art. It is a creative performance experience much like Theater and Dance. If you embrace the challenge, and nurture your abilities, the rewards for success can be as uplifting as any curtain call on the Broadway stage. Few things beat the exhilaration of walking out of the spotlight knowing you have just given a terrific show. This is also true of the Celebrant role. Leaving a venue knowing that you have moved a group to happy emotion, and given them an experience they will remember for life is always hugely satisfying. The more experience you have, the more you will be able to achieve that goal at a deeper level.

If you scored yourself high on this question, you already have a tremendous advantage to becoming an outstanding Celebrant. However, if your public speaking skills are limited, do not lose heart. If it is something you enjoy, and you embrace the challenge, you can very quickly rise up the curve of public speaking mastery.

Question 3. Are you nervous speaking in front of large groups?

The phenomenon of stage fright is a very real one, and it can affect even the most seasoned and gifted performers. However, a little nervousness before each event can be a good thing, as it stops us becoming complacent, and keeps us mindful and concentrating on the moment.

If nerves are a serious problem for you when addressing crowds, there are many ways to combat this. Relaxation and visualization techniques, which I discuss later in this book, are highly useful in steadying and centering your mind before you walk into a venue.

If you gave yourself a low (nervous) score on this question, why not brainstorm a list of the reasons you feel you have this anxiety. Fears that can seem looming and unconquerable in our heads shrink, and lose their power, when laid bare on paper.

If you gave yourself a high (confident) score on this question, it is important never to become so relaxed that you allow your focus to drift. The moment you do, you will begin to make mistakes, and with ceremonies, there is no such thing as a second take or a "do-over". Treat every occasion with the gravity it deserves, but never allow it to overwhelm you.

Question 4. Do you have a strong and clear speaking voice?

As a Celebrant, you may perform many events with attendance numbers well into double, or triple, figures. Many venues chosen for ceremonies were not designed with public speaking in mind. This is especially true of beaches, gardens, and other recreational locations. In some cases, especially when an event takes place outdoors, you may not have the benefit of microphone amplification. It is advisable to practice your vocal skills and build the strength of your voice. Theatrical techniques to help breathing and projection can make a significant difference to the power of your voice.

One of the most helpful things to show you how your voice can improve is to record yourself speaking, on audio to evaluate the sound alone, or on video, to evaluate your entire performance. We all have ticks or quirks particular to our everyday speech, such as saying 'umm' or 'right' far too frequently. Listening to ourselves, though always a little unsettling, teaches us quickly and easily where to work to remove bad vocal habits as we go about our daily activities.

TIP: When planning to perform, it is important to consider whether you will need the aid of a microphone. The larger the audience, the more volume you will need. In places such as beaches, you may be competing with a significant amount of 'ambient' noise, such as waves, seagulls, traffic, aircraft, and the wind. Such situations will greatly tax even the strongest voice and best projection skills. A good rule is to try to arrange for a microphone if you have even the smallest anticipation that one may be needed. It is usual for the client to provide these, although some Celebrants choose to purchase a personal amplification system. I address this question further in the section on your Celebrant 'kit.'

Question 5. Do you have good writing skills?

A core aspect of modern ceremonies is that they do not adhere to a rigid, or prescribed, format or text. Even if you primarily take the text of your ceremonies from other sources, there will be many times when you have to adapt these materials, or write additional new sections. Understanding the difference between good and bad writing, and having the confidence in your written voice, can become highly important. You should also remember that you are creating and building written passages to be spoken, rather than read silently from the page. This makes it vital to keep your writing clear and simple, and to maintain a relaxed and comfortable rhythm to your words.

If you rate yourself highly on this question, you should still need to take care that each ceremony you craft matches the needs of that specific occasion. Although it can be tempting to use a ceremony to showcase our linguistic talents and specialties, we should never subordinate the meaning or focus of the event to our style.

If you rated yourself low on this scale, do not lose heart. Read and listen to as many ceremonies as you can. There are thousands of examples available online and in book form. Additionally, there are many online groups and networks to where you can share scripts. Although this might sound daunting, the vast majority of your Celebrant colleagues will be more than happy to offer a helpful review or advice.

You may wish to find an experienced Celebrant to act as a mentor for your first few ceremonies. Many in our community are happy to answer questions by email and telephone, and in some cases may even be willing to accompany you to your first booking as a support. If doing so, they will usually act in the guise of an 'assistant', so as not to undermine your authority in any way.

Question 6. Do you have a clean and smart appearance?

There is a definite and reasonable expectation that a Celebrant will have an excellent standard of appearance. Personal hygiene, neat and tidy hair and nails, clean and pressed clothing, often dry cleaned, and polished shoes, are expected and important. Elaborate personal adornment can be an unwanted distraction during a ceremony, and jewelry should ideally be kept to a minimum. It is important always to keep in mind that you should not be the primary focus of the occasion. That privilege belongs to the clients for whom you are performing the ceremony, whether that is a marrying couple, a bereaved family, or a community organization.

With regards to tattooing, which has seen a massive growth in popularity and mainstream acceptance as an art form in recent years, many designs are beautiful, and in no way represent a poor personal appearance. However, during ceremonial occasions you should be acutely aware of the perceptions and opinions of those you will be serving. Body art, however subtle or artistic, may still be a distraction from the focus of the occasion. Where possible and practical, I would recommend covering tattoos, and removing piercings.

If you have marked yourself poorly on this question, make a list of what steps you should take immediately to improve this rating. If your daily style is naturally unkempt, you will want to set aside extra preparation time before the ceremony to ensure your appearance reaches the expected standards.

Question 7. Can you remain standing for several hours at a time?

This may sound a strange question. However, a Celebrant can find themselves standing for several hours at a time, with very few opportunities to rest. This may take place in warm surroundings, or perhaps in constant, direct sunlight. If this is a potential problem, you should consider these factors when choosing whether to accept a booking. This should also be an important consideration when selecting your footwear. It is possible to obtain shoes built for beauty, comfort, and endurance.

Question 8. Are you comfortable traveling?

Many ceremonies may be held far from your home base. You should be realistic about the distance you can travel to an event and still give an excellent performance. Many people are uncomfortable driving in the twilight, or at night. For ceremonies held later in the day, although the journey to the venue may take place in daylight, you may find yourself traveling home after nightfall.

For particularly distant ceremonies, that require an overnight stay, the client should be willing to lodge you in suitable conditions.

In all circumstances where you incur noticeable travel expenses, you should look for reimbursement. The United States I.R.S. specifies a per-mile rate as an allowance for businesses travel. This is the best guide to use when calculating how much you should add to that portion of your invoice. They adjust this rate annually, and the standard business rate is $0.54 per mile in 2016. You can find information regarding this rate at:
http://www.irs.gov/Tax-Professionals/Standard-Mileage-Rates

Question 9. Are you comfortable with large groups of strangers?

Many people are uncomfortable mingling in crowds, though they may be perfectly content addressing them. There is a difference between the performance barrier and the social one. Before and after most ceremonies, you will likely find yourself surrounded by large groups of people. If this is something with which you have difficulty, the good news is that it usually becomes easier with practice. Try to breathe slowly, talk only about neutral topics, and try to keep gently smiling. If you are uncomfortable shaking hands, you may choose to carry a small bottle of hand sanitizer to use with discretion.

Question 10. Can you remain composed in a crisis?

Events such as weddings and memorials can be both complex and emotional. The unexpected will happen, and often the Celebrant, perceived as an experienced professional and leader, may be requested or required to take charge and resolve problems. At such times, the ability to remain calm is an important skill. You can improve your ability to do so by mentally preparing yourself for as many eventualities as you can, and visualizing a positive outcome to any situation before it takes place. I discuss these techniques later in the book.

It is also important to understand that immediately assuming control of a situation may not always be the correct, or appropriate, course. In some cases, perhaps where another professional is far better positioned to handle the crisis, it is better to allow others to focus on an issue, and concentrate on your own duties and priorities.

Question 11. Are you methodical and organized?

For a Celebrant, organizational skills are essential. They become more so the more bookings you accept. You should ensure that your calendar is kept accurate, and updated immediately any changes occur. You will need to create files and folders for each event, and store these in a location easy to access. You will need to plan to have your clothing, and other essential items, ready for the day, and to always leave home in excellent time to reach the venue early.

If you score low on this question, it might be helpful to ask assistance from a reliable friend or family member to create a system of processes, checklists, and reminders.

Question 12. Are you able to work flexible hours and weekends?

You may be asked to perform ceremonies at any time, and on any day of the week. Weekends are especially popular for weddings, and memorials are often planned adjacent to meal times. If you have other employment, or family obligations, it is important to consider these carefully when building your Celebrant business, and deciding which bookings to accept.

Being a Wedding Celebrant often necessitates a sustained seasonal commitment. This high workload in the summer months may have a significant impact on your ability to take vacations, and other extended trips, during that period.

Question 13. Can you commit to bookings months in advance?

Although funerals and memorials usually take place within a short number of days of the booking, weddings may be planned as much as a year in advance. Although events that far in the future can be unpredictable, it is important to consider other factors that may affect your life over that period. If you are planning to move house, have a child, or take retirement, you may want to consider a 'cut-off date' or 'temporary pause' for bookings.

Question 14. Do you have any small business or bookkeeping experience?

As a professional Celebrant, you will be working in a business capacity. You will be contracting for work, taking payments, and incurring expenses. You should ensure that you fulfill all the legal obligations required of you, and observe best business practices. It is especially important to understand your responsibilities regarding taxation. If you have limited experience in accounting, you may want to seek some friendly, professional advice. There are many reasonably priced accountants located in every city, and a little of their time could save you many hours of frustration, worry, and cost.

Part Five of this book deals with the business aspects of becoming a professional Celebrant.

Question 15. How familiar are you with web design or creation?

If you plan on any form of marketing, an online presence is essential. A website, which showcases your services and skills, and makes your contact information easily available, can be relatively easy to create. With a domain name, hosting account, and a tool such as WordPress, which is a user-friendly system for creating and organizing content, you can be up and running in a couple of hours.

If the Internet and Social Media are not areas you are comfortable with, there are many reasonably priced designers and consultants you may turn to for advice. When seeking a professional, such as an accountant or web designer, an excellent way to begin is to ask friends and associates for their recommendations.

When choosing a name for your business, you should also consider the 'domain name', or Internet address, that you might use for your online presence. Check that the domain name is available by searching on a site such as GoDaddy.com. You will be a 'for profit' entity, so the suffix .com is more appropriate than .org, the latter being used almost exclusively by non-profit organizations.

Question 16. How familiar are you with online social networking?

In addition to your website, it is useful to become familiar with online social networks, such as Facebook and LinkedIn. Not only are these proven, and highly affordable, ways to promote your business, but they are also a way to network with other Celebrants, for the purpose of sharing ideas, information, and experience.

Question 17. Are you comfortable speaking on the telephone?

Along with email, you will almost certainly take inquiries by telephone. This can be vital to making a positive first impression. Your vocal qualities are one of the key factors that clients will consider before booking your services. To ensure you collect all necessary information about the event, you might keep a short questionnaire by the phone. I have included sample forms and questionnaires later in this book.

Question 18. Have you attended many weddings?

The best way to learn about weddings is to attend them. In watching how the various roles fit together, and witnessing the emotions and reactions of those involved, you will find yourself far more prepared for the experiences you will encounter when officiating. Although I strongly advise against becoming a 'wedding crasher,' I suggest you stay alert for family, friends, and colleagues who may be happy for you to attend their ceremony. You can also find many wedding videos available online, and these allow you to observe without intruding, dressing formally, or having to eat unevenly catered dinners.

Ceremonies differ radically in style. As you watch the differences unfold, you will begin to get a much clearer vision of your own style, and the aspects of celebrancy that you wish to develop. You may also witness some surprising variations, and wonderful ideas that may not have occurred to you otherwise.

Question 19. Have you attended many funerals or memorials?

As with weddings, you cannot fully appreciate funerals or memorials until you have some personal experience of the emotions and conventions involved. I do not, of course, hope you gain this experience from your own grief! Unlike weddings, memorials can sometimes be easier to attend without an invitation. Many ceremonies make allowances for some unexpected 'walk in' mourners. You should, of course, exercise caution and discretion in attending any event uninvited, and never fail to have respect for the occasion and those emotionally involved. As a substitute for attending in person, there are also videos and documentaries on this subject available online.

Question 20. How large do you plan on building your Celebrant business?

How extensively you intend to develop your business is entirely your decision. Some Celebrants only practice a single ceremony, while others may limit themselves to just a few ceremonies in any year, and then for only family or friends.

For those looking to build a professional celebrancy business, you can quickly begin making an income, particularly in the summer months. You should expect, at least for the first year or two, for this to be secondary income only. As with every business, you will need time to establish yourself, and to build your contacts, reputation, and future bookings. This is not a venture for anyone looking to 'get rich quick'. However, like other businesses, if you stay focused and committed, you can do well. Success is there for you to find if you plan carefully and enjoy your work.

Some of the greatest rewards in becoming a Celebrant are the ways it changes your work day. Instead of a cubicle, you 'go to work' at some of the most beautiful places in your region. Instead of dull and sad Monday morning faces, you are surrounded by waves of positive emotion. Instead of meeting your clients on an average and forgettable day, you are playing a pivotal role in one of the most important days in their lives. Few jobs offer those sorts of benefits.

1.18 Part One Conclusion

You should now have a good general idea of the duties and skills involved in the daily life of a Celebrant. I hope you will also have a clearer understanding of your strengths and weaknesses, as they relate to this role, and what you can do to develop and improve, thereby increasing your chances of overwhelming success. As with any profession, there is always more to learn, and new directions to grow. Even after a decade, I still learn one new useful fact or skill almost every week, and am always refining my techniques, both in the ceremonies I perform, and how I run my business. I hope you are still excited to move forward on your path, helping others to create some of the most memorable moments in their lives.

Part Two
Weddings

2.1 Introducing Modern Weddings

As a Celebrant, weddings will likely make up the majority of the ceremonies you perform. Mirroring notable trends in Northern Europe, the demand for modern marriage ceremonies is now growing at an accelerated rate across the United States. This is particularly true among the younger generations, many of whom now consider themselves unaffiliated with any particular church or denomination, and often identify as non-believers.

From a demographic perspective, the majority of couples seeking this sort of ceremony will be professionals in their twenties, though you will be asked to serve a fascinating variety of brides and grooms.

Couples today are seeking out modern, humanistic ceremonies and Celebrants because they can best offer a hugely personal touch to their special day. A modern wedding ceremony offers great freedom of expression, and a chance to build an occasion that reflects their personality and story. These are celebrations where every word and gesture can reflect their love, their lives, their history, and their dreams.

Officiating a modern wedding is a hugely positive and rewarding experience, and will leave you with memories you will treasure long after the event.

A modern wedding is, above all else, a celebration of love, life, caring, and hope. The primary focus of this type of ceremony is the couple. The is no requirement, and often no desire, to reference supernatural forces or mythological entities. These are often considered a distraction from the couple, and the vows they are making.

As modern weddings are performed apart from any particular religion, there are no prescribed ceremonial edicts we must obey. They demand no specific forms or structures. Because of this, each occasion can be, and should be, beautifully unique. A ceremony may indeed reflect the cultural background(s) of a couple and their community, but the real mark of a modern wedding ceremony is that it is guided, formed, and created first by the personality and stories of the couple. The ceremony should be a reflection of their wishes rather than forcing them to obey a set of mandated forms or formulas.

An important characteristic of the majority of modern wedding ceremonies is that they are fun. Although the vows taken are both earnest and sincere, a wedding is a time for celebration and joy. You may be asked to include jokes to amuse the family and guests, and this is in no way disrespectful. If we create and perform a ceremony with genuine love and hope, even the more religious among the guests may find themselves moved in a way that could be described as spiritual. This is the human spirit, and the spirit of a natural Humanism at its very best. Positivity is at the core of, and the driving force behind, a truly modern, humanistic wedding ceremony.

In summary, a modern wedding is:

- Focused on the couple, their love, hopes, and commitment.
- Based on a natural viewpoint of a treasured, finite, earthly life.
- Unconstrained by tradition or dogma.
- Flexible to the wishes of the couple.
- A fun celebration, rather than a somber, solemn occasion.
- Focused on values of compassion, equality, responsibility, and human potential, and not on the tenets of a religion.
- The vows are made to each other, and not to, or in front of, any supernatural authority.

2.2 The Role of the Modern Wedding Celebrant

At a modern wedding, the role of the Celebrant, more commonly referred to as the Officiant in the United States, is to preside and facilitate rather than restrain or dictate. As the one chosen for that role, you are there to work with, and for, the couple. Your job is to give them a ceremony that reflects their wishes, hopes, and their personalities, both individually and together. You will also be using your knowledge and experience to mold the ceremony around other factors, such as the venue, the number of guests, and the time of day it is planned to take place.

Many modern couples meet their Celebrant for the first time armed only with the knowledge that they want to marry. They may have booked a venue, and hired other vendors, but the actual process of building a ceremony may be a mystery to them. The Celebrant's job, at this time, is to introduce them to the many possibilities, the usual and successful elements that others have chosen, and all the options and additions they might consider incorporating into their day. Together, you will build something truly personal and satisfying.

2.3 Your First Contact with a Couple

The process will often start with an initial contact from one of the couple though this may come through a parent or wedding planner. If you connect, regarding availability and interest, you will then need to arrange a more extensive consultation.

Often, the first contact may come in the form of a telephone call. There are certain fundamental facts you should seek to establish as quickly as possible:

- If you are available on that date, and at that time.
- If a separate rehearsal is required, and if you are available for that (see the section on rehearsals later in this book).
- If your price, including any travel expenses, is acceptable.
- If your style of ceremony is in harmony with their vision, and their spiritual outlook.

You should also be willing to answer any questions, not just about yourself, but also about ceremonies in general, and about the license processes in their region. You should give out such information freely and eagerly. This generosity and enthusiasm will help to impress prospective clients with your passion and integrity. The rapport you build at the first point of contact is vital to closing the booking, as well as establishing an excellent working relationship going forward. You should be frank and honest about the types of ceremony you create, the prices you charge, and the limits of the services you provide.

There are a number of critical pieces of information to collect in a relatively short period. It is useful to keep a question list by the phone, to guide your conversation and quickly show you what you still need to discover. I have included a sample inquiry form later in this book, as well as in the companion downloads available online (see the Appendices and Resources sections).

When discussing any topic, you should be positive, and seek to put the client at their ease. It is likely that a bride or groom is already becoming a little overwhelmed by the organizational stresses of wedding planning. If they feel you are already working, with confidence, authority, and positivity, to ease their burden, you will be taking a significant step towards securing the booking.

If you are available, your price is acceptable, and you are a good match, you should look to:

- Collect their full contact details.
- Secure the booking with a deposit payment.
- Establish a time to meet, either in person or via a program such as Skype, to discuss their plans in much greater detail.

Be sure to let the clients know that you are available at any reasonable time to answer any questions they may have, or to be a sounding board for ideas they have for the ceremony. From day one, each client you work with should feel confident that they are in the hands of a trustworthy and friendly professional.

2.4 The Consultation Meeting

Ideally, primary consultation meetings will take place in person with couples. Where this is not possible, perhaps for reasons of time or distance, an online call using a service such as Skype or Google Hangouts can make an effective alternative. A teleconference can also be sufficient for talking through ceremony plans.

The relationship between the Celebrant and the couple should develop into one of trust and friendship. I believe we create the best ceremonies when a bond of understanding becomes well established. For this reason, I think it inadvisable to carry out the entire process of creating the ceremony only through email or a third party. When working to create a modern, humanistic wedding ceremony, there is no substitute for genuine human contact.

If you can meet with a couple in person, it is wise to choose a venue that offers the right atmosphere. You may elect to interview the couple in your home, or in theirs. However, many prefer to meet at a café or restaurant. It is best to pick a spacious venue, with tables of a size large enough to spread out your notes and paperwork. Although chain coffee shops may seem a good choice, many are often crowded, noisy, and have tables barely larger than a dinner plate. It is far better to pick a venue that has booths, as these are better suited to comfort and privacy.

You will often be asked to meet outside regular business hours, as many couples have day jobs with inflexible working hours. You should consider whether your chosen meeting venue will remain open, and comfortable, during such times.

Begin the session by asking how their plans are coming along in general, and if they have been having any particular problems. If they have, offer positive suggestions and advice where you are able, but always consider that another professional may be working on that aspect of their plans. You should never undermine the authority of another vendor involved in the creation of the ceremony. When discussing, the wedding plans of any couple, an excellent maxim to keep in mind is to 'first do no harm.' A couple may already be noticeably stressed about the many aspects of the day. Aim to put their minds at ease, and explain the complexities of the day in a clear manner. Listen *first* to the needs and concerns of the couple, and then offer solutions where you are able.

Once you have settled into the conversation, establish that all the necessary details of the ceremony, and the rehearsal if required, have remained as previously stated.

TIP: It is common for a couple to adjust the start time of their ceremony slightly and it can easily slip their minds to inform the Celebrant. For this reason, it is wise to make a strong habit of starting each conversation with a bride or groom by quickly establishing that time and location remains unchanged.

As early as possible in the process, you should formalize the booking and have the couple fill out the contract for your services. Later in this book, I have created a sample contract for you to use as a guide. However, I recommend that you seek professional legal advice when creating any contract for your business that you wish to be confident will be fully binding in, and meet the requirements of, your particular region. I also strongly advise you take a deposit for services to secure the date on your calendar. For more information on contracts, deposits, and collecting final payments see section 5.10 later in this book.

It is then wise to move forward by discussing the license, and answering any questions a couple has about the legal requirements of the wedding. Of course, you can skip this part in the case of vow renewals, or 'cosmetic' ceremonies (see that section a little further on). You will need to ensure they also meet your own requirements for the day. If microphone amplification is required, and it is better to have it rather than not, then you need to ensure that this is ordered from the DJ or venue, or will be provided in some other way. If you will need special transport to a site, such as ferry tickets or a helicopter ride (it could happen!) you need to ensure this is arranged. It is a good idea to note special travel requirements in your contract.

You should then discuss the 'key players' in the ceremony (see the next section). This is particularly important for children, as their age and abilities may limit what they can be reasonably expected to perform on the day. For example, a very young ring bearer, aged below five years, should not usually be trusted to hold the rings themselves, but should rather act only as a symbolic courier. This is particularly true if a wedding takes place on sand or over water, where a dropped ring can present a far bigger problem. There is a whole section on children and weddings later in this book, and it is wise to cover these important issues with a couple at the first meeting, if they plan to have young children in the wedding party or among the guests.

You should continue by going through each potential core element of the ceremony, and listening to the thoughts, ideas, and concerns of the couple, before offering suggestions, possibilities, and solutions.

It is helpful to have a questionnaire to guide you during your discussion, and to help ensure that you do not miss a vital aspect of the ceremony. Such a document is also useful in bringing a conversation back on track, should the energy and enthusiasm of the discussion cause it to stray from practical topics. To help you, I have included a sample questionnaire later in the book.

As you discuss each aspect of the ceremony with the couple, you will often find yourself acting in the role of an 'educator.' As such, you should have patience with any couple that has significantly less ceremony experience than yourself. You should also be able to illustrate each point you make with a short story, often from your experience. Be wary of telling too many 'wedding catastrophe' stories, as these can often only serve to increase the nervousness of a couple. Each story you use in illustration should have direct relevance and a positive conclusion.

Although you will almost certainly not be the vendor providing the music, it is a good idea to go over how this will be used before, during, and after the ceremony. There are certain aspects of the ceremony, such as the procession and recession, in which music can play a pivotal role. I discuss this at more length in a later section.

You should aim to leave the consultation meeting with sufficient notes to enable you to produce a rough ceremony outline and a list of practical action points for both yourself and the couple. It is a helpful and courteous practice to write these up, and pass a copy to the bride and groom at some point in the following days. You should also create a prioritized list of things they must do, and decisions they must make, to help the project forward.

TIP: After meeting many happy couples in succession over an extended period, it can be hard to have immediate recall of faces to match names. Here is an idea that might help. At the end of the first meeting, provided everything is going well, ask them if you can take their photo (or if they have one handy). You can then attach the photo to their file. This gives you a quick and simple way to identify them at the second meeting, and on the wedding day.

2.5 The Key Participants in a Wedding Ceremony

Other than the Celebrant, here are the other roles you may encounter in a creating a wedding ceremony.

The Wedding Party and Supporters

Groom. The man, or the term used for the first partner to enter, and who then "receives" the second partner.

Bride. The woman, or the term used for the last partner to enter, often escorted, and presented at the commencement of the ceremony.

Escort(s). The primary escort, although sometimes there may be two or more, accompany the bride during the processional portion of the ceremony. For the bride, this is most often a parent or sibling. Of course, a bride may decide to enter alone and unescorted. Secondary escorts may be tasked with formally accompanying family members, such as mothers and grandmothers, to their seats just before, or during, the processional. Although the bridal escort is almost always a one-way job, escorts for other members of the wedding party may be tasked with formally escorting their charge out of the ceremony during the recessional.

The Bride's Parents/Grandparents. Though often acting as escorts, the bride's parents can sometimes enter jointly during the processional. Assigning the grandparents a place in the processional lineup is also common, when they are attending.

The Groom's Parents/Grandparents. Often, the groom's parents and grandparents, if attending, are given a place in the formal procession and seating.

Groomsmen. This is a selection of (usually) men, chosen to represent the groom's support during the ceremony. It is not uncommon for a female, such as a sister, friend, or colleague or the groom, to act as a 'groomswoman'.

Best Man. This is a specially nominated groomsman, or attendant, who usually stands beside the groom during the ceremony. He (or she) may typically be given special duties, such as holding the rings until the part of the ceremony where they are exchanged.

Bridesmaids. A selection of (usually) women, chosen to represent the bride's support during the ceremony. Unlike women, it is less common for a man to take on the role of a bride's attendant, though this is perfectly acceptable.

Maid/Matron of Honor. A specially nominated bridesmaid, or attendant, who usually stands beside the bride during the ceremony. She (or he) may typically be given special duties, such as holding the bride's bouquet during the ceremony, or adjusting the dress once the bride has reached her final position. The distinction 'Maid' is used for those who are unwed, while the title 'Matron' is applied if the individual is married.

Junior Bridesmaids. Where a bridesmaid is under the age of eighteen, they are often referred to as a 'junior' bridesmaid. The age range is usually between 11 and 17. This is a way to include female friends or relatives who are perhaps too old to act as flower girls, but too young to be considered adult, or of marrying age.

Flower Girls. Typically aged ten or under, these are female relatives, or the children of friends, who immediately precede the entrance of the bride. They are often tasked with spreading flower petals, or other small items, onto the path along which the bride will enter, and around the ceremony center.

Ring Bearers. Typically aged ten or under, these are male relatives, or the children of friends, who act as part of the processional and are tasked with bearing both rings into the ceremony. Often, the rings are carried in a box, or on an ornamental pillow. Where a ring bearer is particularly young, perhaps under five years of age, it is common to make them a 'symbolic' ring bearer only. The actual rings carried safely into the ceremony by the best man or another responsible adult party. In modern wedding ceremonies, it is surprisingly common to see a beloved pet dog appointed an honorary ring bearer, and escorted into the ceremony by a trusted friend or relative.

Ushers. The helpful people who watch out for the little things that need doing before, and after, a ceremony. These are individuals tasked with making sure guests find their seats, programs are handed out, doors are opened and closed at the right times, and communicate any special instructions to guests. This role is also a good way to include family members, or friends, if no positions remain for bridesmaids or groomsmen. Ushers are sometimes given special matching attire, though this is usually less formal than that required of the primary attendants. At smaller ceremonies, groomsmen may take on some of the ushering duties until it is time to take their place in the line-up.

It can be useful to have ushers attend the rehearsal, especially if the venue has a complicated layout for them to help others navigate, or if they are to undertake other special duties on the day.

Readers. These are friends or family tasked with performing a pre-selected reading at a particular point during the ceremony.

A Note on Relationships: While many in the wedding party will have long established ties and friendships, for others this will be the first meeting. Additionally, in situations where there has been divorce and remarriage, there may be multiple sets of parents and accompanying partners. You should always be careful to employ tact and discretion in such situations, as there may remain complicated emotions between the divorced parties.

The Professionals

Event Planners. These are, usually, experienced professionals charged with coordinating and advising the couple throughout the period of planning and preparation. Their job is to oversee the logistics of the day. In some cases, a friend, or family member, may have been appointed to this position, and will be less experienced in the role. Where a planner lacks experience, it is important always to be patient and helpful without interfering with their activities. For weddings where no planner exists, a Celebrant may find the scope of their duties expanded to include other organizational roles, though it is more usual for the bride and bridesmaids to assume the planning responsibilities in such a situation. However, if you undertake noticeable extra duties beyond your contracted Celebrant role, it is important to ensure you are properly compensated for your time and expertise.

'Day of' Coordinators. These are professionals hired only to coordinate the activities on the day of the ceremony, though this may on occasion also include the rehearsal.

Venue Coordinators. These are usually employees of a particular venue, and their job is to explain and operate the facilities in that location only. They can be extremely useful, particularly if they are available for the rehearsal, as they will have detailed knowledge, and extensive experience, of the best practices specific to that space. As with event planners, these are critical professionals to network with, as they are often asked to give recommendations to couples on which vendors should be hired.

Photographers. These may be a single individual or a professional team or duo. Although most wedding photographers have years of experience, you may encounter talented amateurs entrusted with recording the event. It is important to be patient and courteous, and offer advice only when requested and useful. It is important to network with photographers, as they may be able to provide pictures for your portfolio or blog, and this can be to your mutual advantage, as it showcases both your talents simultaneously. I have included a more extensive section on working with photographers later in the book.

Videographers. Much like photographers, these will be an individual, or team, tasked with recording the wedding day, and producing a final finished movie. They may ask you to wear a wireless microphone during the ceremony to capture audio for their recording. This is often additional to any microphone equipment provided to amplify your voice. Once the finished version is available, you should try to get permission to use the ceremony video as part of your Internet marketing. However, the final film can take several months to produce. A video is a terrific way to showcase your ceremonial style and abilities, and most couples and videographers will be happy for you to use it in that way. You should always secure written permission before publicly posting any record of a ceremony you have performed.

DJ Tasked with providing the music, and often the vocal amplification, for the ceremony. For smaller ceremonies, especially those taking place outdoors, the couple may choose to do without hiring a professional for this service. They may have decided to have no music, and no amplification. These factors are important to you, as the coordination of music and procession/recession is important, but, more urgently, because you will need to be sure you have microphone facilities where needed. You should discuss the plans for music and microphones early on with your clients. In some cases, a friend or family member will be tasked with providing the music, perhaps on an iPod or laptop. In such situations, it is important to be as patient and helpful as possible with that individual, and make sure they have clear instructions and are comfortable with the equipment.

Musicians. When not provided by the DJ, ceremony music may often be performed by a musician or group of musicians. Many will be highly experienced professionals, who will readily understand their cues, and how to adapt to the unexpected. Much like the DJ, it is important to coordinate with any ceremony musicians before the ceremony, so that you are all working from the same set of expectations.

Caterers. Tasked with providing the food and beverages, you will likely not have much involvement with these vendors, as they will focus primarily on events that follow the completion of the ceremony. However, you should cultivate a habit of greeting and thanking *all* the other vendors for their help on the day. Networking is a core skill and practice for wedding professionals, and politeness and gratitude are marks of quality and true professionalism.

Florists. Even more so than caterers, your activities will rarely intersect with the persons providing the flower decorations. However, as with all the professionals you encounter, networking is essential, and, where you do encounter them, a greeting and sincere appreciation for their art will mark you out as a high-quality professional. In the wedding business, your reputation is your greatest asset, among other professionals as much as among your clients.

A Note on 'Friendors'

Sometimes, perhaps because of budget constraints, the couple may choose a friend to act in a role more usually occupied by an experienced professional. Some may be highly talented, and carry out their job with great skill and effectiveness. All too often, however, the friendor (the word is an uncomfortable union of friend and vendor) may find they are out of their depth. Worse, they may cause more problems than they solve. Friendor musicians may fail with the technology, or miss their cues. Friendor caterers may produce a cake that was far from the design the bride had envisioned. A friendor photographer may have no idea how to shoot a wedding day. Where you can, assist with advice if requested, but never compromise your role to help compensate for the failings of another vendor. The very best way to salvage a situation caused by one aspect of the day failing is for you to raise the standard by doing an impeccable job for your clients.

For a discussion of processional and recessional orders and options, please refer to that section later in the book.

2.6 Legal Wedding Ceremonies

It is vitally important to know the legal status of the ceremony you will be performing. If a couple is already legally married, and you will be performing a 'cosmetic' ceremony only (see that section), be sure to ascertain who, among their family and friends, is aware of this situation. Occasionally, secondary ceremonies are held so as not to offend relatives who were not present at, or aware of, the original legal solemnizing. When talking with those individuals, it will, therefore, be important to maintain discretion. More often, a cosmetic ceremony is held to fulfill the dream of a 'grand' celebration, although a small, legal ceremony may previously have taken place for practical purposes.

On a very rare occasion, you may be asked to perform a purely theatrical ceremony for a couple, one or both of whom are still married to other persons. Under no circumstances should you accept such a booking. In doing so, you would be leaving yourself open to adverse potential legal consequences, as well as extreme damage to your professional reputation.

2.7 Same Sex Weddings

It is with great pleasure that I rewrite this section for the 2016 edition, to recognize the historic changes that have taken place in the last year. In the United States, same-sex marriage has been legal nationwide since June 26, 2015, when the United States Supreme Court ruled in, Obergefell v. Hodges, that state-level bans on same-sex marriage are unconstitutional. At the time of writing, there are still a very few unprofessional local officers violating the trust of their position, and refusing to issue licenses to same-sex couples.

As a modern, professional Celebrant, you should not allow your actions or decisions to be shaped by personal prejudices. If you find that you are unable to perform in a professional capacity, based on private convictions, or unable to hold with concepts such as universal marriage equality and the primacy of the rule of law, you should strongly consider whether a role as a Celebrant is right for you. If you choose to continue, only offering your services selectively, you should make this clear in all your marketing materials. You should also be aware that such behavior will likely exclude your membership of many professional organizations. Many ordaining bodies may well revoke your status if they become aware that you actively deny services based on sexual orientation, creed, or race.

There are, unsurprisingly, few differences between a same-sex wedding ceremony and its different-sex counterpart. For a Celebrant, the most important difference to understand is one of terminology. Although, in this book, I have used the words 'bride' and 'groom' for convenience, these may not be preferred by a couple in a same-sex ceremony. The simplest way to determine the correct terminology for any occasion is simply to discuss with a couple the terms they prefer. This is also true in deciding which side they might prefer to stand, as well as which order they choose to enter, and with who escorting.

2.8 Cosmetic Wedding Ceremonies

Cosmetic ceremonies occur when a couple has already participated in a legal marriage ceremony, but wishes to have a public celebration, perhaps as a way of announcing their marriage to family or friends, or sometimes for better photographs. Where the first ceremony is a guarded secret, you should take great care in discussing the situation with, or in the presence of, anyone outside the couple.

Where possible, ask the couple to repeat the vows they gave in their original ceremony.

On rare occasions, you may be requested to provide 'fake' or 'dummy' paperwork as part of the subterfuge of concealing the prior ceremony. Under no circumstances should you do so, as this would be the forgery of government legal documents, even if only meant as harmless fun.

It is wise to avoid all mention of any previous legal solemnization during any words you speak during the cosmetic ceremony. To do so only diminishes the value of the current occasion.

2.9 Wedding Vow Renewals

Many couples are now choosing to celebrate milestones in their marriage by renewing their vows. A renewal ceremony is often similar to a first wedding ceremony, in that it is both formal, orchestrated, and contains many of the same core elements. However, there is rarely a procession but rather a request, or summoning, of the couple to stand before their guests.

In some cases, one partner may choose to surprise the other by presenting them with an opportunity for a vow renewal. As the Celebrant, you should always be aware of the background, and initiating circumstances, of any ceremony you are asked to perform.

If possible, you should ask a couple to repeat the vows they gave in their first ceremony, though they may wish to add a few short lines to reflect the passage of time, and to acknowledge all they have accomplished together.

If you are asked to write the opening, or closing, remarks, it can be useful to interview friends and family members beforehand.

The majority of vow renewals take place in settings that are more informal than those of a first wedding ceremony. Settings such as private gardens, or restaurant function rooms, are often chosen.

Although there are no legal requirements for the renewal of vows, this should not prevent you from treating them with the full dignity you would accord any wedding.

2.10 Template Wedding Ceremonies

Although one of the core characteristics of a modern wedding ceremony is personalization, such a unique, and tailor written, text may not always be possible or desired. There will be occasions, such as last minute bookings, that call for a more generic script. Many Celebrants are also, quite understandably, unwilling to write a completely unique ceremony for every couple they provide service, especially those seeking a budget option.

For these, and other reasons, many Celebrants choose to create and maintain a portfolio of ceremonies, that they are then able to offer to a prospective couple.

Each of these would then have the names, and other appropriate information, replaced before the event is performed. A word of warning in such cases. Take the greatest care to replace ALL instances of a name throughout the text. Even if you have proofread several times, you should still be acutely alert for any slip-ups in this regard as you perform. During my own wedding, the Celebrant referred to me as 'William' in the introduction to the vows. It was clearly a typographical error, and, after a few moments of genuine uncertainty, we were able to laugh it off. I am sure, and would hope, that he was mortified at the slip. In my practice, getting a name wrong is almost on a par with forgetting my script as the stuff of Celebrant nightmares.

I would suggest that where you keep 'template' files of a ceremony, you use the insert '[Groom]' instead of an actual name. This not only makes missed replacements easy to spot but also makes for a good element to use in automated 'Find and Replace' functions, such as those available in MS Word.

For Celebrants who build up a back catalog of ceremonies, there is absolutely no harm in reworking some of your 'greatest hits' for new clients, though you should be wary of lapsing into using the same jokes or signature lines for every occasion. Where you have a couple who are passionate about travel, for example, it may be appropriate to adapt a paragraph used previously for a couple similarly inclined. After several dozen ceremonies, it becomes near impossible to create every new script completely from scratch. Refining your best ceremony language is just as natural as refining your best performance techniques, or your pre-ceremony warm-up ritual.

2.11 Elopements

There may be occasions where you are contacted to perform a basic ceremony at very short notice. For such requests, you may wish to keep a 'standard ceremony' script in your kit, or perhaps stored on your smartphone, along with scans of your credentials, in case these are also required.

Many Celebrants offer a significantly discounted fee for elopements, to reflect the reduced preparation time. Where you choose to do so, it is important to define clearly the difference between your standard and your elopement 'package'. A core characteristic of an elopement is that it is spontaneous. In my practice I only offer this package, and the reduced rate, for couples who will marry within 48 hours of the booking. I am still, however, regularly contacted by couples who are 'planning to elope in a couple of months'. This is not an elopement in the recognized sense and is most likely a couple trying to obtain full Celebrant services at bargain rate. Similarly, elopements do not involve a large number of guests or elaborate seating arrangements.

In the case of a true elopement, you may find yourself on the courthouse steps, or in another public venue, without friends or relatives accompanying the couple. In such cases, it is perfectly acceptable to ask passing strangers if they would mind acting as witnesses, and many will be delighted to do so. When seeking those to ask, it is wise to watch for tourists, or retired couples, as they will more likely have more time to spare. A hurried office employee, perhaps on a short lunch break, is less likely to have the inclination. Do not be offended if a passer-by refuses. Simply thank them kindly for considering, and move on. Do not offer payment to potential witnesses, and do not agree to a fee if requested Such rude opportunists have no place in a romantic moment.

Even with the simplest ceremony, you should still ensure you strive for the highest standards of excellence and professionalism, and that you complete the paperwork, and other formalities, with care.

2.12 Relationship Biographies

When working with a couple to build a personalized ceremony that reflects their history, personalities, and hopes, it is essential to know something of their life together. It is obviously impractical to become intimate friends with every couple with whom we work. Therefore, we need a shortcut to understanding their story.

During the consulting interview, you will collect many details of a couple's history, and have the opportunity to observe their personalities, style, and humor. However, there will be many important details that are not conveyed in so short a time.

One method to easily and efficiently solve this problem is to ask each of the couple to produce a 'relationship biography.' This is a short document that details their recollections and perspectives of the courtship from its beginning to the present. It is most enlightening to have a couple produce theirs separately, and in whichever format and style they are most comfortable. Some may choose merely to offer a few bullet points. More often, they will find this a hugely enjoyable experience, and the floodgates of storytelling will open. You may frequently receive heartfelt, and deeply moving, tales of some length. The longest narrative I have personally received was over six thousand words! For many, this becomes an opportunity to revisit the highlights of their romance, and the writing itself can be a hugely motivating part of the ceremony process.

These biographies offer us two important types of information. First, they give us insight into the style and personalities of the couple. Second, they highlight significant themes and events that have shaped their time together. If a particular item appears in both narratives, we know it is of special importance.

This process provides an excellent starting point for crafting the text of a ceremony, particularly when writing sections such as the opening address and closing remarks. We can also avoid statements that will be noticeably at odds with their story. For example, where a couple was friends for some years before their romance began, it would be pointless to include an effusive statement on 'love at first sight'.

TIP: You may also wish to ask generally about their hopes for their life together in the future, particularly any plans for children. A few couples will have already decided they do not wish to have children, or perhaps have already discovered they are unable to do so. In such cases, the addition of lines about 'starting a family' would be, at best, inappropriate. In the latter case, such words could even be emotionally damaging. Knowledge and understanding are the key to giving your clients the very best personalization.

2.13 Core Elements of a Wedding Ceremony

Although a modern wedding ceremony is not required to follow a mandated structure, there are many traditional elements that couples very often choose to incorporate. In the following section, I detail the core elements of most ceremonies in the order that they frequently occur. However, creativity and expression should always be encouraged, and each of these elements can be adapted, or omitted, as desired. We are limited only by our imaginations, and the practicalities and budgets of the day.

2.13a Gathering

The assembling of guests usually starts around half an hour before the ceremony is scheduled to begin. Ushers, if available, help guests find their seats, as well as passing out printed ceremony programs, and safely storing any gifts the guests may have brought. Ushers are also useful for ensuring that no over-enthusiastic guests accidentally take special seating reserved for the wedding party.

It is usual to arrange for a light musical accompaniment for the guests taking their seat, as this sets and appropriate mood, and heralds the events to come.

There has been a traditional practice of allotting guest seating by 'bride's side' or 'groom's side', although many modern couples are now forgoing this, and allowing guests to spread comfortably and evenly. Where one of the couple expects significantly fewer attendees from among their friends or family, it makes greater sense to have such general seating rather than unbalanced allocated areas. Photographs particularly will not make it then seem as though one of the couple came unsupported in comparison to their partner.

When escorting a female guest, it is traditional for a male usher to offer his right arm. Where several female guests arrive at once, the usher should offer his arm to the most senior, and ask the remaining ladies to follow. For a male guest, a male usher would simply walk at their side. In the case of female ushers, these gender traditions can easily be reversed. An usher should wait at the end of the row until these guests have fully taken their seats, bid them enjoy the ceremony, and then return to their starting position for the next escorting duty.

It is useful to have one or two extra ushers available if possible, in case you need one to undertake a quick errand or gather dallying guests as the start time fast approaches.

Ushers should be instructed to help make space for wheelchairs if required and possible, and to seat any elderly guests in the comfort and shade, where available on a hot summer day. Parents with small children should also be encouraged to sit at the ends of rows, and ushers should let these new families know that it is acceptable to exit mid-ceremony, should their young child become distressed. Most parents will be completely understanding about these instructions.

TIP: At some weddings, the ushers and staff may have surprising difficulty encouraging guests to take their seats. If those are attending are unmoved by the first announcement, have the team circulate and inform each small group that '*the Minister* has asked that everyone take their seats.' The addition of those words of authority can make a surprising difference, particularly in those conditioned from a young age to follow the instructions of clergymen.

A Note on Runners: 'Runners' are cloth, or similar material, laid down a wedding aisle. Many runners are of a light material that easily rips, or gets caught in every gust of wind. If placed before the guests enter, it will be difficult to prevent them stepping on, and possibly disrupting it. In my experience, runners are best avoided altogether. Do not try to get over these difficulties by laying the runner during the procession, as that will almost always become a clumsy mess.

The arrival of the guests will be another key factor in determining the exact start time of the ceremony. If a significant portion of guests, or a few particularly important persons, have not yet arrived, the bride or planner may decide to delay for a few minutes. Starting delays also happen because the couples need a few more minutes for preparation, and they should be allowed this, within reason.

On rare occasions, there may be a significant delay in proceedings. If so, it may become your duty to make a short announcement to guests. When doing so, it is important to remain calm. You should apologize for the delay in a friendly manner without giving away any embarrassing details about the exact cause. You should not embarrass individuals by singling them out as the problem, nor should you attempt to entertain the guests while they wait. A simple, short announcement is all that is required.

2.13b The Processional

Once the wedding party, the planner/coordinator, if one is present, and yourself agree that everyone important is ready, it is time to start the show. The formal entrance of the participants is known as the procession. Several factors will determine the structure and style of the procession (and its counterpart, the recessional, which takes place at the end of the ceremony.

I would like to recommend a handy starting technique the processional, based on my experience. While gathering, many guests will now likely be deep in conversation. They will have encountered family members, and acquaintances, with whom they are now catching up on news. Alternatively, they may have already made new friends, with whom they are sharing information. A few guests may even be busy with social media on their smart phones. With this in mind, it is wise to mark clearly the moment where the ceremony begins. I have found the most effective method is to walk out ahead of the wedding party, though sometimes accompanied by the groom and groomsmen, and make a very short informal statement of welcome. This is also an excellent opportunity to convey some important instructions and information to the guests. I almost always offer the following guidance:

Silence cell phones. Better still, turn off all devices.

If guests plan to take photographs, they should do so with careful consideration for the professionals also doing so, and not obstruct their view. Many couples ask that guests not take pictures during their ceremony, as it can look undignified if guests are waving their phones and cameras, and if unflattering pictures are posted online immediately following the wedding. Professional photographers will be very grateful for you curtailing cell phone use in this way.

I instruct any parents of small children that, should any younger guests become 'distressed', or behave inappropriately, they should immediately remove them to another location out of earshot. The deafening howls of children have ruined too many ceremonies months in the planning, and many parents can be oblivious to the disruption and annoyance their offspring can cause.

With those guidelines in place, I then give the cue for the formal procession to start. Often this is accomplished with a discrete nod to the musicians, and the simple words '…and so, let us begin.'

I will now discuss each of the following factors in turn: cultural background, the size of wedding party, the layout of venue, preference of the couple.

Cultural Background

When deciding the processional order, there are some cultural traditions that a couple may wish to observe.

In Christian tradition, the procession is most often arranged as shown in the figure below. You will notice that the groom and groomsmen enter first, and thus symbolically 'greet' the others as they enter. They are then followed by family, bridesmaids, flower girls, ring bearers, and finally the bride and escort.

In Jewish tradition, the grandparents of the couple enter before the groom. Both his parents then accompany him. Bridesmaids follow them, and finally the bride enters, accompanied by her mother and father.

In a modern ceremony, these traditions are a useful guide, but ultimately the order of entry should be a decision for the couple.

Figures: Traditional Christian & Jewish Ceremonial Orders

Traditional Christian Ceremony Order

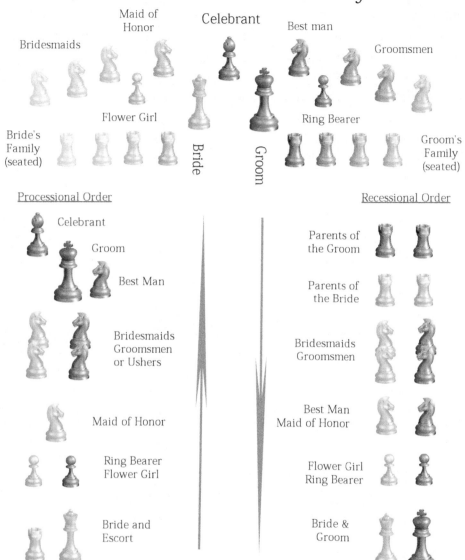

Maid of Honor

Bridesmaids

Celebrant

Best man

Groomsmen

Flower Girl

Ring Bearer

Bride's Family (seated)

Bride

Groom

Groom's Family (seated)

Processional Order

Celebrant

Groom

Best Man

Bridesmaids Groomsmen or Ushers

Maid of Honor

Ring Bearer Flower Girl

Bride and Escort

Recessional Order

Parents of the Groom

Parents of the Bride

Bridesmaids Groomsmen

Best Man Maid of Honor

Flower Girl Ring Bearer

Bride & Groom

Adapted Jewish Ceremony Order

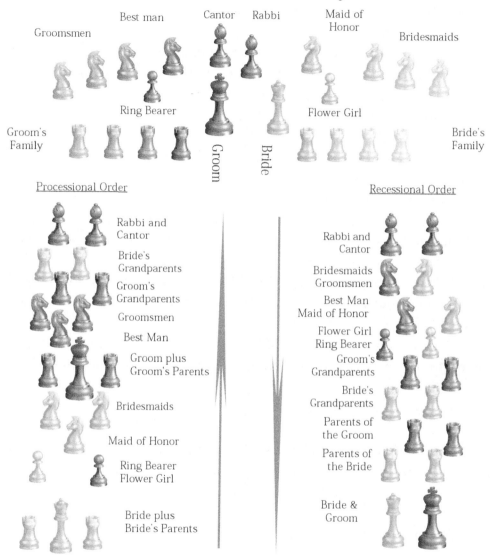

Best man   **Cantor**   **Rabbi**   **Maid of Honor**

Groomsmen   **Bridesmaids**

Ring Bearer   **Flower Girl**

Groom's Family   **Bride's Family**

Groom   **Bride**

Processional Order

- Rabbi and Cantor
- Bride's Grandparents
- Groom's Grandparents
- Groomsmen
- Best Man
- Groom plus Groom's Parents
- Bridesmaids
- Maid of Honor
- Ring Bearer Flower Girl
- Bride plus Bride's Parents

Recessional Order

- Rabbi and Cantor
- Bridesmaids Groomsmen
- Best Man Maid of Honor
- Flower Girl Ring Bearer
- Groom's Grandparents
- Bride's Grandparents
- Parents of the Groom
- Parents of the Bride
- Bride & Groom

Size of Wedding Party

The larger the wedding party, the more complicated the procession can become. Some couples choose to include parents and grandparents, ushers and escorts, a parade of their friends, a running of children throwing glitter, and perhaps even their pets, costumed and accompanied by a trusted friend. The larger the procession, the more crucial a formal rehearsal becomes (See the later section on rehearsals).

For small ceremonies, with perhaps only five or ten guests, it may be enough to assemble and then have the bride enter simply, escorted or alone.

Layout of Venue

In many cases, the design of the chosen venue will shape and limit the procession.

In a natural location, such as a beach or lakefront, it may be impractical to have a large, formal, procession. Sand, especially, makes a long procession more difficult, and can be challenging for older family members. In such circumstances, the best advice is to keep a procession short and simple.

Where a venue has a complicated layout, such as the interior of an old house, or in an elaborate garden, you may need to arrange a system of cues and timing to make a larger procession work.

If a venue was not designed primarily as a location for ceremonies, it will often present extra challenges during the planning of the procession.

Preference of the Couple

In a modern ceremony, the wishes of the couple should be the first concern, and every reasonable effort should be made to accommodate these. For each of the possible participants there are also specific considerations:

Parents and Grandparents

Where they are living and attending the wedding ceremony, it is usual to include the parents of the bride and groom in the procession. It is common for the groom's parents to enter first, followed by those of the bride. This is because, in a traditional Christian ceremony, the mother of the bride would be the last person seated.

Where the parents of either party have divorced, you are presented with some additional possibilities. Divorced parents may still wish to enter together, as a show of solidarity in support of their child. However, it is more likely that they will want to enter accompanied by their new partner. Where one parent has remarried, or is accompanied by a significant other, and the other parent remains single, it is usual to supply an escort. For a mother, this might be a male family member, such as an uncle or brother, or one of the groomsmen. See the note below on how Escorts a dual role. For a father, the couple might consider appointing a female family member, such as an aunt or sister, or one of the bridesmaids.

Although some couples choose to include grandparents in the procession, it is more often appropriate to have them pre-seated, especially if they have difficulty walking.

Groomsmen and Bridesmaids

It is usual for the groomsmen to enter before the bridesmaids though some couples may wish for them to process in pairs. I recommend sending them in individually, as they will most likely be departing in pairs, arm in arm, during the recessional (see that section below). I prefer this for two reasons. First, this gives a greater variety of to the photographers, and many bridesmaids or groomsman may want a photograph of themselves alone, as well as with an appointed partner. Second, entering separately and later leaving in pairs adds to the symbolism of the couple entering as single persons and later leaving joined in matrimony.

It is usual for groomsmen to enter from the far end of the lineup, starting with the groomsman who stands furthest from the couple, and ending with the best man, or the groomsman who will stand directly at the groom's side.

Ring Bearers and Flower Girls

Ring Bearers and Flower Girls, where appointed, are often the last to enter before the bride. Where they are four years of age or younger, it can be wise to arrange for them to have a parental escort. A grandparent, or an older sibling, can also work in this capacity. Many very young children, who may behave extremely well in rehearsal, have overwhelming anxiety when faced with a room full of strange faces turned toward them, and dressed in new clothing. In all wedding situations involving children, designate a 'child wrangler' as the responsible person to take charge immediately any signals of distress occur.

In all cases when involving a pet as a ring bearer or flower girl, the animal should be escorted down the aisle by a handler with whom it is familiar and comfortable..

Escorts

Where any participant is unaccompanied during the processional, they may require an escort to accompany them to their seat. An usher, or attendant, can make an excellent choice.

Where an Escort also has a second role, it is acceptable for them to double gracefully back to fulfill that duty later in the line-up. For instance, the father of the bride may wish to escort his wife to her seat, and then double back to act as the escort for the bride. It is usually preferable that they walk back down the side of the guest seats, rather than returning up the aisle, and thus blocking the next entrant.

The Bride (plus Escort)

Brides may choose to enter on their own, escorted by a family member, or perhaps by both parents.

It is usual for there to be a slight pause before the entrance of the bride, during which the music may change, and you should ask the guests to stand. Do not forget to ask them to sit again before beginning the introduction to the ceremony.

Processional Music

The number and order of the persons in the procession will significantly dictate the use of music during that part of the ceremony. Almost all brides will want a special tune played for their entrance. However, it makes sense to have a second tune for the rest of the bridal party only where a significant number will be processing. If a segment of music lasts under forty-five seconds, it may feel rushed and 'shoehorned in.' However, if there are many senior relatives, and a great number of bridesmaids and groomsmen, all of whom have a significant distance to walk from the first entrance to the final position, it may be appropriate to break up the processional into several short pieces of music. Processional music works best when all the selections are from a similar genre.

Some Example Processional Orders

Below are three example procession orders from start to finish, along with notes on musical accompaniment. All are valid, dependant on the factors discussed above.

		Example One		Example Two		Example Three	
START	No Music	Officiant	Musical Selection One	Officiant	No Music	Officiant + Groom & Groomsmen	
	Musical Selection One	Grandparents	Music One (cont.)	Groom	Musical Selection One	Groom's G'father plus Bridesmaid (double back)	
	Music One (cont.)	Groom's Parents	Music One (cont.)	Both Mothers Arm-In-Arm	Music One (cont.)	Groom's Father plus Partner	
	Musical Selection Two	Groom	Music One (cont.)	Groomsmen	Music One (cont.)	Groom's Mother plus Partner	
	Music Two (cont.)	Groomsmen	Music One (cont.)	Bridesmaids	Music One (cont.)	Bride's Parents	
	Music Two (cont.)	Ring Bearer	Music One (cont.)	Dog as Ring Bearer	Musical Selection Two	Bridesmaids	
	Music Two (cont.)	Bridesmaids	Music One (cont.)	Flower Girl	Music Two (cont.)	Flower Girls	
FINISH	Musical Selection Three	Bride plus Both Parents	Musical Selection Two	Bride and Escort	Musical Selection Three	Bride Alone	

It is important for everyone taking part in the processional to know their final position for the ceremony, whether stood beside the couple or seated in a particular row.

As the Celebrant, part of your role will be to advise on what is appropriate, examining all the above factors, explaining what you have seen work best in practice, and warning of pitfalls there may be to any plans the couple is considering.

TIP: In the first few moments of a bride's entrance, she may need to pause for gown or veil adjustment. It is a good idea for the groom to remain facing the Officiant until the bride has reached the ideal moment for that first sight. Photographers will also appreciate this opportunity for a memorable reaction shot.

2.13c The Handing Off of the Bride

A handing off of the bride, traditionally called the 'giving away,' is an optional element some couples may choose, and that takes place at the moment when the bride and her escort, if she has one, come to stand before the Celebrant. Although this is not required, it can be a charming way to represent familial love and commitment.

The options most often chosen are:

1. The escort may simply hug the bride, and then hug or shake the hand of the groom. The Celebrant would then thank the escort and ask them to be seated (along with the guests, if they stood for the bride's entrance).

2. The Celebrant may offer a question to the escort. Options for the wording include to:

'Who gives this bride in marriage?' (Many now feel the word 'gives' to be outdated.)

'Who presents this woman in marriage?'

'Who brings this woman to marriage?'

'Who supports this bride in marriage today?'

Where they stand alone, an escort may just respond, 'I do', 'Her mother (father and I do', or 'On behalf of her family, I do.'

3. The couple may request a second parent, or grandparent, to step forward and join the escort before any question is asked. They may then both reply, or the

escort may respond on behalf of them.

4. Where a bride has entered alone, you may offer the words 'Do you come here freely, and of your own will?', to which she should respond 'I do.'

5. It is possible to expand the handing off by officially asking the parents, or families, of *both* the bride and the groom for their approval or 'blessing.' This can be asked of each family in turn, or of both together in a single question. It is worth noting that the term 'blessing,' as used here, is a secular one, as you are asking for the approval of persons, rather than requesting it from a supernatural entity.

6. Should a couple wish to expand this part of the ceremony to its ultimate, they may choose to have you request the blessing of all those assembled. In my practice, I usually advise against this, as I have found it can cause confusion. This option also offers an unfortunate opportunity for any 'comedians' among the guests to call out something 'amusing' and inappropriate. For this same reason, asking for formal objections, often referred to as the 'speak now, or forever hold your peace' option, has fallen out of fashion in recent years.

After this element is complete, if you had previously indicated for guests to stand, it is important to remember to ask them to be seated again.

2.13d Opening Statement

Once all the participants are in position, and the guests seated, it is time for the Celebrant to offer some opening remarks. This statement should formally welcome everyone, and explain why the couple has chosen to stand before them and perform the rite of marriage. In addition to conveying the essence of the couple's story, you may wish to discuss the importance of vows, commitment, and the tradition of celebrating important milestones as a community.

At this point in the ceremony, relationship biographies, as described above, can become most useful. Below this section, I have given an example of the process of adapting two biographies into an opening statement. In writing your ceremonies, you should seek to write in your personal style.

During the interview process, it is helpful to ask the couple if there are any people, or events they specifically wish referenced in your opening address. For example, they might wish to include recently deceased grandparents, if they had a strong influence on the couple's relationship. The couple may also want you to mention a beloved pet. For some couples, the raising of a first pet can be as significant a milestone as the purchase of their first home.

It is equally important to ensure that you do not mention any aspect of their lives that they do not wish discussed. This might include past romantic relationships, or the fact that the bride is pregnant, should this be the case. For this reason, it is important to encourage frank, open discussion during the interview process.

Couples may wish you to reference children they each bring to their new family, if such exist, or those they have already parented together. Alternatively, a couple may want to exclude all references to 'family building', and this is usual where they have already chosen not to have children, or are unable to have them.

The more you learn about, and understand, a couple, the easier it will be to know which topics should work well in your opening address.

You should be careful to ask which name each partner wishes to use during the ceremony, and check your pronunciation by repeating this back to them. Although a person may be known by one name, informally or in public, they may wish to be addressed differently, perhaps more formally, for their wedding ceremony. For example, a woman known as Liz in daily conversation may choose to be called Elizabeth during her marriage vows.

For any Celebrant not keen on writing, there are many sample openings available online, or in books. By altering a few words or phrases, these can be adapted to give personalization to an opening address.

However, I strongly recommend every Celebrant take time to develop their writing skills, as your own voice will give your performance the strongest impact.

Before each ceremony, you should carefully read through each passage you intend to speak. Ideally, you will have an opportunity to practice aloud to a trusted friend or family member, who should then be able to give you useful, and perhaps unexpected, feedback. Even the most experienced Celebrant should regularly take time to assess their skills, possibly by watching video recordings of recent ceremonies, to see where they can polish, and perhaps freshen, their delivery.

It is important not to bore the wedding party and guests. An ideal length for your opening words should be between two hundred to three hundred words. An appropriate length will also vary in response to the duration of the other sections of the ceremony. Where a wedding contains many readings, lengthy vows, a unity ritual, or an elaborate procession, you may wish to keep your opening comments brief.

2.13e From Biography to Text – An Example

While relationship biographies are hugely informative, they should always be used in concert with meeting the couple, and after discussing their needs and hopes. Here is some background context to the biographies below. They are both white, American, and at the time of the marriage he was 35 years of age, and she was 31. They are both college graduates, and now reside on the East Coast of the United States. They requested an entirely non-religious ceremony, with vows suggested by the Celebrant. The vows were to contain a section of repeated lines, followed by a formal question. They wanted a single reading, which they would choose and provide, to be spoken by the Celebrant. With those facts in mind, below are the biographies they wrote. They did so approximately two months before the ceremony, and they are reproduced precisely as they arrived in my Inbox.

Note: I have changed the names of the couple to protect their identities. It is important to respect the confidences of our clients at all times and not to disclose personal information linked to them unless they grant written permission.

From Anthony:

'I hardly ever go to the beach during the summer, too crowded for me, but one year I was asked by my roommate at the time if I wanted to go and meet some other friends. I decided to go and it just so happens that Amy had recently meet the same group of friends and was at the beach that day.. We talked and got a long well and a few days later we hung out again. The fourth of July was a few weeks later and I remember walking downtown to see the fireworks and holding Amy's hand and it feeling like the most natural thing to do. I've never been one for card games but Amy and I would hang out at night on her front porch and play cards and talk.

Moving forward: The Dogs.

In the beginning Amy wouldn't let Arrow, my dog, inside her house. Amy was never really a dog person. Slowly that changed. I had to travel for a short work trip and my roommate was going to watch Arrow but instead Amy asked if she could watch her. Arrow stayed with her and Amy walked her and they bonded. It was a pretty amazing gesture that Amy knew how much Arrow means to me and wanted to learn how to take care of her. After we had moved in together it was Amy who suggested we get a second dog and would send me puppies she had found on Pet Finder. We fell for a skittish pup who had had a rough start to life. Pita the puppy was quite a lot of work and I was working a late shift at the time but we made it work. Pita has taught us a lot about patience and partnership.

Welcome Home

Early on, Amy went away to see her family and I put up a welcome home sign over one the doorways. She loved it and we decided to keep it up so every day when we get home we see the sign. This stands out to me because Amy and I have truly built a home together and that sign always makes me smile. She also allowed me to hang up an inflatable tiger head I received as gift in the dining room so you know it's true love.

Thank You

Amy and I have gotten through surgeries, sickness, health related life changes and some other tough times. We have been there for each other through it all and have helped each other grow. One thing that I love about us is that we try and never forget to say thank you. Whether it's something mundane or something special we do for one another we try and remember to say thank you. I could write more but I think the above highlights our relationship and is just a few of many reasons why I want to continue to share my life with Amy.'

From Amy:

'Anthony and I met on June 20, 2010. We both ended up at the beach with mutual friends. I have a fear of swimming in the waves but did swim with Anthony that day. This happens to be the same date that my sister met her husband and the same day they married. It's Summer solstice after all. I ran into Anthony several days later after riding a bike, which I hadn't done in years, to a local bar. He asked me out to see a band that weekend and we spent Fri. and Sat. night together. We spent Sunday afternoon over mimosas getting to know each other better. Anthony and I have spent the last almost 5 years together.

I think our greatest strengths are our ability to thank each other for the little things and forgive each other for the big things. We are both creative. Anthony is an artist and I am a 'chef' in the kitchen. Anthony and I love music. Anthony collects CDs. I grew up singing in a Mennonite family. I think we both want to celebrate music in our wedding ceremony.

We have encountered some hard times. I was diagnosed with Celiac disease in

66

2011 after years of stomach pains and discomfort. Anthony had surgery in 2012 which kept him out of work and put me in a nurse's role. I think the both of us have valued having the other stand by us. Times have been hard but we are strong.

I never considered myself a dog person and initially didn't invite Arrow (Anthony's dog) to the house. After attempting to take in a stray that ran off, our dog Pita has been a shining light between. She is a mess. Seriously, I think at some points that a child would be easier. Haha. Pita really has shown both of us what we need to be as a couple. No more sleeping until noon. This pup gets up at 7am daily and sleeping in until 9 is a treat now.

I can't wait to marry Anthony. I have looking forward to this moment! Anthony is the best part of me and I hope I can be the same for him. We are looking forward to starting family soon. *fingers crossed.'

Key Facts from Their Biographies

When I have received both biographies, I take a piece of notepaper and create two columns, one for each of the couple. I then list the key points I select from the text they have sent me. Below, I have reproduced my notes for Anthony and Amy:

From Amy	From Anthony
Met on a beach	**Met at the beach**
Swam with him	Played cards at night
It was a summer solstice	**They have dogs ('Arrow' and 'Pita')**
They thank each other every day	'Welcome Home' is important
Music is important to them both	**They helped each other through tough times**
They have grown strong together in hardship	**They always remember to say 'thank you'**
They have dogs but also want a family	

When events, ideas, facts, or themes show up in *both* stories, you know that these are of particular significance. In the lists above, I have highlighted the shared important points in bold. Be sure, however, to watch for useful facts that only show up one biography, as these can often provide a personal flavor to highlight in your text.

The Opening Words of the Ceremony

I have reproduced below the opening of the ceremony exactly as it was performed on the day. As you read, see if you can spot how I have integrated information from the biographies into my text:

'We have come here to mark a very special day in the lives of Anthony and Amy. This is the moment when their two paths, which have already traveled many years side by side, will now and forever move forward always as one.

We can never know when that special person will come into our lives, that one encounter that will change our life forever. It can happen on any day, on any shoreline. It is vital that, when this hour finally arrives, when the first glance touches us deep inside, that we seize that moment, and not let it slip away.

You did grasp that opportunity and every wonderful day since has led you here.

As much as passion and attraction, true friendship is at the very heart of love, and key to the greatest of beginnings. The very center of their love, as they have shown, is that they found each other to be true and constant best of friends.

As they talk about each other, you cannot mistake the vast and unshakable trust between Anthony and Amy. There is no more important foundation for a life together. They will always give each other the gift of sharing. They will always stand beside each other, as they do here with us today. They will always be there to welcome each other home.

Nothing of great worth comes easily. We can face struggles, stresses and hard times, but when two bring the strength Amy and Anthony already have, we know they will always prevail. We know they have found the power to adapt, a power that comes from pure love given and received. Understanding that you have the right person at your side means you know that you can both adapt to each other, and, standing at each other's side, meet and overcome any change and any challenge. You always know in your heart, and as now you look into each other's eyes, that you can trust and depend on each other whatever may come.

When two are joined they also bring together two families, two circles of *friends, two communities. Each of us here today also now finds our lives joined in new ways as a result of the love Anthony and Amy share. From today, and for the rest of your days, you each accept and pledge a responsibility to each other. You will learn from the example of love you see in Anthony and Amy, and they will learn from watching you. This is a sharing of life and friendship, of love that builds a legacy that will sound for generations to come. We will watch them build their family, of which Arrow and Pita are simply the first additions.*

As they walk away together in a few minutes, they take steps that will never be apart and know that all the time they have will now be theirs. We come today to wish them all our hopes in building a home, finding their dreams, and life forever full of smiles.

I ask you each to challenge yourselves, and the other, to love you both more all the days of your life, to thank each other for all the happiness you give and receive with each sunrise and each sunset. With that, you will find the greatest reward of all. A lifetime at each other's side.'

2.13f Remembrances and Acknowledgments

For many couples, certain special individuals helped shape and define their relationship. These may have been a role model, or simply friends or relations who offered words of advice or approval. In some cases, perhaps through illness, or because they have already passed away, these people cannot be with the bride and groom on their wedding day. A couple may then choose to acknowledge their importance by either asking their Celebrant to make reference to them, or by taking a moment to personally mention and thank them.

A couple may also choose to openly and explicitly acknowledge individuals who are present, if they have had a defining impact on their path to the big day. This is often done for parents, or grandparents, who have been especially supportive, either emotionally or in offering financial help with the wedding day.

If asked to include this section, first discover if it is a section the couple would like you to speak, or if they would prefer you to introduce them to read a short address. If they choose that you give the statement, keep it short and clear, and begin with an explanation of your words, before focusing on any individuals you have been instructed to mention.

Where a couple chooses to speak this portion directly, have them write it out in advance, and prepare them a card exactly as you would do for a reading or personal statement of vows (see those sections). Caution all couples against trying to improvise this statement, as the emotion of the moment will almost certainly overcome them, and cause them to speak less effectively than if they had prepared in advance.

Example Remembrance and Acknowledgment Text

At this time, [Bride] and [Groom] would like us to give special thoughts to those who could not be with us today. [Relative's Name] helped to shape their story, and was always there with a smile, and trusted words of wisdom. Their memory will always be held close to these two hearts, and anchor and nourish their love on the journey to come. This is also a reminder to cherish those who help us become the people we are.

[Bride] and [Groom] would like to give a very special thanks to [Person's Name] for helping to make today possible. They will always treasure what you done, and will carry that gratitude in their hearts as they go forward through the years to come.

[Groom] and [Bride] would now like to say a few special thank yous in their own words, to those who have made today possible, and those who could not be with them today.

2.13g Vows

Vows are the center of the wedding ceremony. They are the ritual around which all other aspects revolve, and they set the tone of the occasion. They are the opportunity for each of the couple to look into the other's eyes, and make the most significant pledge of their relationship. In a modern, humanistic ceremony, marriage vows are not made to, or under the patriarchal eye of, a supernatural deity. Rather, they are spoken directly from one heart, and life, to another. They are not secured by damnation, but by love, kindness, trust, and honesty.

Before a couple makes their vows to each other, it is wise to say a few short words about the meaning of this ritual. These should impress upon all present that this is the critical moment of choice for the couple, and that they should not speak such words lightly.

In general terms, wedding vows are created in three distinct, but not exclusive, types: recited statements (which are often self-written), repeated lines, and responses to questions.

Recited Statements and Promises

Many modern couples are now choosing to write their own vows, that they then read to their spouse during the ceremony. In many cases, they may prefer to keep their text secret from their partner until it is read on the day, and this is a terrific way to maximize the emotional impact of the promises made.

Below is the advice I offer a couple to help them prepare their statements to each other:

'Your vows are the center of your ceremony. These are the words around which everything else revolves. As you speak your lines, it should be that moment when your heart knows that you are now joined to the one you love in the deepest way. There is no better feeling than watching the words that came directly from your heart light up the eyes of your true love. Here are a few tips to get you ready and excited to create your own vows.

Tip 1: Keep your words secret until the big moment!
Many couples choose to keep their vows secret from each other until the day. It can be both moving and fun to watch your partner react with laughter and heart-melting surprise as they hear for the first time what you have prepared. You may be tempted to slip in a few surprises to catch them off guard and to aim your words directly at their funny bone. My advice is to 'go for it'!

Tip 2: Agree on a target length for your vows.
Officiants are often asked what makes a good length for a statement of personal vows. As with every part of your ceremony, you should be guided first by your heart. Be sure you take the opportunity to say everything that you want to. If a sentence is

important to you, do not cut your words simply for the sake of keeping things short. A rule of thumb would be to make your statement around one hundred and fifty words in length, give or take fifty. Any shorter and you may sound insincere and uncommitted. Any longer and you may run the risk of repetition and reducing the power of what you say. Keep your sentences short, and make each point clearly. One hundred and fifty words may sound like a lot, but it goes by very quickly. It is precisely the number of words I have used in this tip!

Tip 3: Agree on the style.

As much as having a similar length, it is important that you both use a writing style that matches. It is worth deciding on how poetic or silly you plan to be before you each put pen to paper. If one of you chooses to write verses in the style of Oscar Wilde, and the other makes jokes about the Netflix queue and leaving the toilet seat up, you may both end up feeling awkward. Set a few common ground rules, but don't let these stop your personality shining through.

Tip 4: Get your thoughts down on paper.

You should start writing down your ideas for vows as early as possible. However, a blank page can be quite intimidating. Why not try this exercise. Make a list of six traits that you love about the other person, and six successes that you hope you will have together in the future. Now think of the items in your list as promises. If you have written that you love their smile, why not promise always to do so, and that you will do all you can to keep them smiling every day. If you hope to have children, why not promise always to raise them together with love and respect. An important part of marriage vows is promising to work hard for the things you want to share in the years to come.

Tip 5: Keep it personal, but not too personal.

Let your words come from the heart. It is easy to think of statements about love which could apply to anyone, but the best will be those that specially and particularly apply to you. If you describe openly and honestly how you feel, your partner will feel those words far more deeply. However, I offer a small word of caution. Keep in mind that the words you use will be public. Too many private jokes or intimate suggestions could leave your guests a little confused or uncomfortable. If you have something deeply private and personal to say to your partner, why not consider smuggling them a letter before the ceremony that contains those thoughts. Knowing they have read that note, as you stand across from each other, could be just as thrilling.

Tip 6: Keep it FUN!

A wedding can never have too many smiles, or too much laughter. The more fun you have throughout the day, the better your memories will be, and the more the experience will cement your future together. Don't be afraid to have a little fun with your vows. Think of what it was about your partner that you first attracted you to them. Odds are strong that it involved something that made you chuckle or grin. Why not incorporate that into your promises? Why not also do something a little unexpected, that you know will have your partner laugh out loud. Perhaps you could include a long running joke you share, especially if this is also well known to family and friends. You might also try introducing an unexpected action. Recently I watched a bride pause during her vows to take a surprise 'selfie' with her groom and attendants. She even had her bridesmaids smuggle in a 'selfie stick'. It brought the house down in laughter and gave everyone something to remember for a lifetime! (Note: If you choose to do something unexpected with your partner, be sure to warn your Celebrant and planner. They can keep a secret.)

Tip 7: Watch out for clichés.

Most words of love have been said before at some point, but some a lot more than others. Once you have your first draft, read through to see if any line sounds particularly unoriginal. If you find such a phrase, ask yourself two questions: What is it about that line that makes it important to you, and how can you reword it so it sounds like something you would say in everyday life? A line such as 'My love for you is like the stars. It will last forever.' can be transformed with a sprinkle of personalization into something fun, such as 'I'll forever be the star that guides you home to hugs and barbecue.'

Tip 8: Practice your vows out loud.

When you have a new draft of your vows, read them to yourself aloud. Perhaps use your phone to record yourself. What looks elegant on paper can sometimes be an awkward mouthful to pronounce. Even the best public speaker has a short list of words they struggle to say. If you find a line that causes you to grind to a halt, or makes it sound like you have a speech impediment, consider how you might word the same idea more simply. A thesaurus can come in very handy. Your vows should flow naturally with the way you breathe and sound similar to the types of sentences you use on any normal day.

Tip 9: Try your vows on a friend.

A trusted friend can be perfect for supplying feedback on your vows. They will be able to tell you if anything sounds unclear, if a line might cause unintended laughs, or if something sounds awkward. Why not invite your best friend over for a glass of wine, and make a fun game out of practicing and refining your vows? Always remember, however, that the most important voice in your vows is your own. If a line you have written is of particular importance to you, resist pressure to drop it.

Tip 10: Print up a card to read from on the day.

Do not try to memorize your vows. The emotion of the moment would almost certainly cause you to forget a line. Instead, print up your vows on a beautiful piece of card. Use a large, clear font. Write the lines out phrase by phrase rather than in a paragraph. This will help you pause naturally, as you read along. During the ceremony, you will need your hands for many other things. Have a friend, or your Officiant, give you your printed vows at the appropriate time. Cardstock is especially useful for outdoor ceremonies, as it will not flap in the wind.

Bonus Tip! Remember your vows are for each other.

When you reach the moment for your vows, remember that these are first and foremost for the ears of your partner. Don't worry whether your voice is carrying to the back of the room. If it is natural for you to speak softly, that is fine. The secret of personal vows is that they are in your voice from start to finish, and that they travel from your heart directly to the heart of the one you love. I hope you enjoy creating, and speaking, words you will remember and treasure for a lifetime.'

Where couples decide to write their vows in this way, it is important that the Celebrant reviews both texts before the day. This ensures that they balance each other well and that they both have good readability.

It is also useful, and thoughtful, for the Celebrant to provide printed cards for the couple to read from at the critical moments. You should print these in a large font, and in a way that is easy to scan with the eye. Under no circumstances should you encourage a couple to try to memorize their vows. Such attempts will always end in disaster due to the intense emotions of the moment.

A few couples may choose to express their vows in dialogue format. This is where they each take it in turn to make single statements or promises, which the other then reciprocates. This can be a fun, and intimate, way of exchanging personal vows.

Repeated Lines

A more conventional type of vow is when each of a couple takes turns in repeating lines offered to them by the Celebrant. Although the couple may choose to write and prepare these, it is common for the Celebrant to suggest the text. Before doing so, it can be helpful to ask a couple to list the things they wish to promise to each other.

There are many thousands of examples of vows of this type available online, and in reference books. An example of a modern text of this kind, which I have used on several occasions, is:

I take you to be my best friend,
My lifelong partner and my love.
I vow to help you love life.
I promise I will always try my best
To have the patience, and understanding, that love demands.
I vow to be open with you.
I promise to encourage you,
And truly appreciate you,
And the happiness you bring me every day.
I promise to love you through good times and bad.
I will forever be there to laugh with you,
To lift you up when you are down,
And to love you unconditionally

Through all of our adventures in life together.

Question and Response

In the simplest option for the couple, the Celebrant poses a set of questions, regarding the obligations of love and marriage, to which the expected answer is 'I Do.' For couples who are especially nervous about public speaking, this style of vows can be a popular choice.

An example of modern responsive vows that I have used in practice is:

Do you take [Bride or Groom],
To love with all your heart,
To live together and laugh together,
To work by your side,
To seek the best in them,
And give the best of yourself,
To always comfort and understand them,
To grow together all your days,
As long as you both shall live?

An Important Note on the Declaration of Intent

The entire wedding ceremony is embodied in the 'Declaration of Intent', which is expressed in the form of a question and response. In some states, such as New York, the inclusion of a question and response is mandated by law. In the U.S., there are no stipulations as to the exact wording of this exchange. For this reason, all Celebrants should include this section, in some form acceptable to the couple, in every ceremony they perform. Most couples and their guests will not feel the ceremony is complete unless both the bride and groom have each spoken those two simple words, 'I do.'

Many couples choose a combination of vow types, based on the above three options. They may elect to make a personal statement, or to repeat a given set of lines, followed by responding to the question of intent. In a few cases, I have helped couples combine all three types into their vows. They may have felt that, as this was a once in a lifetime event, they ought to sample the entire menu of possibilities while they had the chance!

The Celebrant's job is to help each couple discover, and then craft, the option that best fits their styles and personalities.

Combined Vows and Ring Exchange

Some couples will choose to combine their statement of vows with the exchange of rings (see that section below). This is easily achieved. As each takes his or her turn in placing the ring on the other's finger, you can have them pause and hold position to recite a few lines, or give a response to the question of intent.

2.13h Exchange of Rings

Not all couples choose to exchange rings, although it has perhaps become the most enduring symbol of marriage in Western civilization. For members of some professions, such as farming and medicine, rings are impractical on a daily basis. Others may have a dislike of jewelry of any kind. Some couples, who are perhaps more brave and artistic, may choose to have their rings tattooed before the ceremony. For obvious reasons, tattooing during a ceremony is highly impractical.

The exchange of rings is usually quite straightforward, and can be performed without words if requested. However, it is often desirable for the Celebrant to offer a few short comments explaining the meaning of this ritual. As well as being a traditional symbol of eternity, rings have also been seen historically as representing the exchange of property, and as symbols of ownership. I have had several couples request a playful mention of the latter to inject a little humor into the ceremony, and I am always happy to oblige.

It is usual for the groom to begin by placing the ring on the third finger of the bride's left hand. As this can take a few moments, you may suggest that he recite a few short lines to fill this time, and this also add to the feeling of the ceremony. The bride then mirrors these actions.

An example of repeated lines used during a recent ring exchange is:

I give you this ring
As a token and pledge
Of our constant trust
And abiding love.

It is important to decide who will hold the rings until the moment of exchange. In many cases, if one is appointed, the best man is the ideal choice for this task. Unlike the Maid/Matron of Honor, the Best Man's clothing often has pockets. Additionally, she may be required to hold a bouquet, as well as monitoring adjusting the bridal outfit, Where there are no attendants, it is quite common for the Celebrant to hold the rings until they are needed. If you have not already done so, it may be useful to review the section on ring bearers. This will help you understand the ways rings may be carried into the ceremony.

TIP: Warn a couple that, should a ring be dropped accidentally during the exchange, YOU will be the one to retrieve it. This will avoid them both bending in unison, and violently cracking their skulls against each other. A concussion is never a good way to begin married life! Note: If you are unable to bend down, perhaps because of a back injury, appoint a proxy beforehand. Groomsmen are useful for such tasks.

A Note on Engagement Rings

There is a tradition that the wedding ring is placed 'closest to the heart', by which is meant closest to the knuckle of the bride's third finger. This practice has its origins in Egyptian superstitions, and their ancient conceptions of human anatomy. In practice today, should a couple wish to embrace this custom, any engagement ring should be held elsewhere until the wedding ring in place. Many brides choose to keep their engagement ring on their right hand, and then slip it on below the wedding ring once that has been placed. Some brides choose to leave the engagement ring off completely for the duration of the ceremony. Another option is to have a jeweler fix both rings together before the ceremony, and some ring combinations are designed specially to wear in that way.

As with all traditions, there is no requirement to follow any particular rules or formats. The Celebrant's role is to make the couple aware of all their options, pay close attention to their wishes, and facilitate whichever they may choose.

The Tradition of Ring Warming

Before the ring exchange, a couple may wish to pass the rings around among the guests. The concept is that each guest transfers his or her hopes, thoughts, and blessings to the rings as they are handled. It also gives everyone an opportunity to view the rings up close, and admire the craftsmanship and stone size. As this can take some time, it should ideally be initiated at the start of the ceremony, to give time for everyone to participate before the rings are needed in the ceremony. For this reason, a ring warming may not be practical for ceremonies with a large number of guests. Where a couple is worried about the safety of the rings, they might be affixed to a beautiful pillow. I advise against using this ritual in outdoor ceremonies, particularly those taking place on a beach, as rings can easily be dropped and lost.

A 'speed ring warming' can be achieved by placing the rings on a string, or a colored ribbon, and passing them down the aisle for those seated close enough to reach out and nudge them forward.

2.13i Closing Words

The closing words a Celebrant speaks provide a counterpart to those in the opening section. Whereas an opening might address the events that brought the couple together, closing words may address the obligations, hopes, and wishes for the many years to come.

Example Closing Words

'*We cannot know what the future may bring for the lives of [Groom] and [Bride], but we know that together they will be equal to the needs of all their tomorrows.*

We know they will find patience in times of stress,
Strength in times of weakness,
Courage in times of discouragement,
Vision in time of doubt
Moreover, at all times, a growing love.
We who are here present, and those absent,
thinking of these two people,
Know that the inspiration of this hour will not be forgotten.
May they continue to love one another forever.
Before I pronounce you married partners,
I have just one more thing I want you to do.
Your wedding day is one that seems to fly.
It is a day filled with emotion, friends, rings and dances.
Many people remember how fleeting their wedding day was.
So I want you to take a few seconds to look into each others' eyes.
Think about the happiness that you are feeling in this place, at this moment.
Let that feeling register in your heart and your mind.
Now, I want you to think about your life together in the years to come.
Where are you going? What will you accomplish?
Your visions of the future are not identical, but will always be complimentary.
It has been said, 'a dream you dream alone is only a dream,
a dream you dream together, THAT is reality.' That new reality starts now.'

2.13j Pronouncement and Presentation

At the close of the ceremony, it is usual for the Celebrant to formally pronounce a couple married, and to then present them to those gathered.

For the pronouncement, it is usual and traditional for a Celebrant to employ words such as 'By the power vested in me by...' Although ceremonies sometimes break with this tradition, this statement is often expected by couples, families, and guests.

An important question for any modern Celebrant is the authority they choose to name as granting such 'power'. Some Celebrants may wish to recognize their body of ordination, and adopt words such as '... by the Society of Celebrations.' Far more frequently, a Celebrant will name the state, or principality, in which they are performing the ceremony. In my opinion, the latter makes the greatest sense in the United States, as it is ultimately those authorities who create the rules for the solemnization of marriage, and which therefore grant the privilege of doing so. These bodies also have the advantage of being 'spiritually neutral', and thus can meet the expectations of all attending without provoking a controversy by emphasizing one faith or denomination over another.

For the words of presentation, if giving the couple a title, there are many possibilities a bride and groom may choose from. Most couples will not have considered this question until you mention it, and their options include (using John and Jane Smith as an example):

Mr. And Mrs. John Smith

Mr. John and Mrs. Jane Smith

Mr. And Mrs. Smith

Jane and John

John and Jane

Husband and Wife

The Smiths

The version they choose should be the one that best suits their style, and with which they feel most comfortable. When presented with the above options, most couples will know quickly which they prefer.

Most couples choose to close their ceremony with a kiss. It is always a little uncomfortable on the day if a couple chooses not to do so. For the benefit of photography, you might advise a couple to hold their kiss for at least six seconds, as this gives any professional ample time to record the moment.

Although there is a strong tradition of ordering this part of the ceremony as a pronouncement, kiss, presentation, I believe this makes it unclear when guests should cheer and applaud. It is natural for those assembled to want to cheer the kiss, partly because this is a moment of minor embarrassment, but also because of its mildly bawdy nature. Most importantly, a kiss feels as though it should be the natural climax of events. If a Celebrant waits until the kiss is over before speaking the presentation, they may find themselves trying to talk over spontaneous celebrations, or having to signal intentionally for the guests to quiet. In my experience, the most satisfying endings are created by building up to a triumphant moment of the kiss. This makes for one enthusiastic peak and gives a clear cue for both cheering and recessional music. Ultimately, this is a decision for every Celebrant and their clients to make. A sample wording you might use is:

'By the power vested in me by the great state of [Insert State], it is with true honor that I now pronounce you husband and wife, and present to all here, [Insert Title]. Congratulations, you may now seal this moment with a kiss.'

Many couples are curious as to the exact moment they become legally married. At least in the United States, the time of pronouncement is that moment. This is why the witness signatures may usually be safely and legally obtained before a ceremony. You should never, however, file the documents before the ceremony takes place. The signatures form part of the official recording process.

TIP: When the couple moves to give their final kiss, it is wise to take a step back and to the side, if you have the room to do so. This prevents you 'photo-bombing' an important moment in their wedding album. If you are a male Celebrant, you may like to step to the groom's side. If female, you may choose the bride's side. Wherever you choose to stand at this point, be sure to inform the professional photographers of your intentions privately before the ceremony begins.

2.13k Recessional

A counterpoint to the processional, the recessional is the way the wedding party makes their formal departure at the conclusion of the ceremony. In many cases, apart from the joint exit together of the bride and groom, the recessional is often a reversal of the processional order.

During the recessional, you may find that part of your role is to give signals to the participants as to when they should begin their exit walk. In doing so, you should take into consideration the time needed for the photographer(s) to capture all the pictures they require, as well as the distance each must travel to leave the ceremony space. It is important not to rush these events. Members of the wedding party, perhaps still nervous of making an error, are likely eager to complete their closing duties, and may try to hurry. Your goal should be to keep the pace steady and dignified.

At the end of many ceremonies, you will likely be the last person to leave the space. You may decide to exit along a different path to the bride and groom. For instance, you may choose to walk out through a side door, rather than to process down the aisle. This is symbolic of the fact that, now your ceremonial duties are complete, you are not required to accompany the couple into their new era of married life.

TIP: When you are helping the couple to plan their processional and recessional, you may wish to have the groomsmen and bridesmaids enter separately, and have them follow the couple out in pairs at the end of the ceremony. This offers the photographer a greater variety of shot opportunities, and also adds a further note of symbolism to the 'uniting' of the couple.

2.13l Dispersal

The final act of the ceremony is for the guests to depart. Once the wedding party has completely exited the ceremonial space, you may find it useful to have any music lowered, and briefly say a few words of instruction.

First, be sure to thank the guests once again for attending. It can then be helpful to inform everyone where to go for the next part of the event. If there are to be cocktails, it is useful to explain this, and which path or doorway everyone should take. Where there are a large number of guests, I have found it helpful to instruct them to leave by rows, starting with those seated at the front. On some occasions, you may need to ask the immediate family to stay seated, or take a separate exit, to make them available for post-ceremony photographs.

At the first appropriate opportunity, you should also take the time to thank the other professionals involved for their work. Personally, I have also made it a habit of congratulating the wedding party, especially the children, on a marvelous job (even if there were minor errors). This helps put everyone at ease, as they move into the celebration portion of the day.

2.14 The 'Through Line' of the Ceremony

You will notice two patterns within the structure of most wedding ceremonies.

First, the earlier parts of the ceremony are most usually associated with the events, and emotions, which brought the couple to the day. The later elements more often reflect their dreams, hopes, and obligations of the future.

Second, the components of the ceremony bring the couple progressively closer in physical proximity. The bride approaches and is presented. The couple faces each other for their vows. They must touch during the exchanging of rings. Finally, they come together for the marriage kiss. An understanding of these patterns is a great advantage in creating a meaningful, and coherently structured, wedding ceremony.

2.15 Ceremonial Music

Music is often an important part of a marriage ceremony. The majority of weddings, whether they employ live music or a DJ, usually have four core musical selections:

1. A medley, or 'prelude', to accompany the arrival and seating of guests.
2. A chosen theme to accompany the entrance of the main wedding party, before the entry of the bride.
3. A special theme for the entry of the bride and her escort (if accompanied).
4. An upbeat theme for the exit of the newlyweds, and the main wedding party.

At some ceremonies, you may find it necessary to provide subtle cues for the musician, or DJ, to start, stop, and transition between tunes. This is essential where musicians are physically unable to see the wedding party enter. Before the ceremony takes place, it is wise to converse briefly with the individual(s) providing any musical accompaniment, and establish what cues may be needed. A dignified method of signaling might be a firm nod, or a clear, subtle motion of the hand, rather than thumbs up or a cheeky wink.

For the musical elements, that precede the ceremony, it is usually better to recommend instrumental renditions. These allow greater flexibility for fading in and out if the timing of accompanying activities, such as the bride's walk to the aisle, take a longer or shorter time than expected.

It is also a good practice to have the three opening elements come from a similar musical genre, as this gives a feeling of continuity to proceedings.

For the fourth major musical element, that accompanies the recessional, encourage a couple to choose something upbeat, and gives their personal expression and creativity a free rein. Indeed, many couples decide to dance and joke their way back down the aisle, and in a modern ceremony this is perfectly acceptable.

Musical Interludes during the Ceremony

In the early stages of planning, many couples consider a pause during the ceremony to play of a favorite song. Although the wishes of every couple should be paramount, it is also an essential task of the Celebrant to counsel on such decisions.

It is a sad, but unavoidable, truth that musical 'interludes' during a wedding ceremony are almost always an obstruction. Placing a song between the different spoken sections, with no accompanying visual activities, creates a disruptive hiatus. The guests will most likely become bored, and you will lose energy and momentum you have been working hard to build. It is far better to save a favorite song for the reception.

One occasional exception to this caution on mid-ceremony music is where it is used to accompany activities, such as the lighting of candles or the pouring of sand. A very light instrumental accompaniment may be a pleasant addition at such times. However, you should ensure that the activity will be of sufficient length, perhaps forty-five seconds or more, to justify the time taken to introduce a tune. The instructions to musicians should be clear about the signals to begin and end. I would advise that where you are in any doubt that the music can be introduced smoothly and without error, it is wisest to leave it out. Mid-ceremony music played at the wrong volume, or queued at the wrong time, can disrupt the entire flow and emotion of the occasion.

2.16 Wedding Photography

Photography is an important part of almost all modern weddings. Many couples hire a professional photographer, and sometimes an entire team, to cover the day. In the last decade, it has also become more common to employ a videographer working separately to provide a vivid, musical, high-quality film of the event.

As the Celebrant, it is helpful to take a moment to confer with all photographic professionals before the ceremony. They will appreciate knowing how the bridal party will enter, and what will be the cues for critical moments, such as the final kiss. You should ensure they know the format of the proceedings, where and how the members of the wedding party will stand, and if any parts of the ceremony might require special positioning.

If you have arranged a Unity Ritual (see that section later in the book), the photographer should be told how, and when, this will take place, and how close they will be able to get to record it in detail.

TIP: Why not have the bride and group face the guests for the early parts of the ceremony, perhaps up until the point where they turn to face each other and make their vows. This positioning makes for some beautiful photographic opportunities, and gives a more interesting view for their friends and family.

It is vital to understand how important the visual record of the day is to a couple and their family. It is often a significant portion of the cost of a wedding, and many elements will be designed with great care to how they will look in photographs. For this reason, you should try hard to give these professionals every latitude to get the shots the need. You should accept that they may need to use flash, and may need members of the wedding party to pause at key points to ensure beyond any doubt that these moments are captured for posterity. Some photographers may have suggestions about where to stand to get the best light. Videographers will often ask you to wear a dedicated microphone, which will usually be separate from the microphone you will use to amplify your voice. The bride and groom will, quite understandably, expect you to make every effort to comply with these requests.

If you give a brief welcome to the guests before the ceremony, you may wish to say a few words about cell phone photography. Many couples and photographers will strongly prefer that guests not take cell phone pictures during the ceremony, though it is usually acceptable at the reception. There are several reasons for these choices. First, the presence of raised hands holding cell phones can easily be distracting and undignified in the photographic record. Second, if a photographer has carefully lined up an important shot, and a guest then intrudes to capture their photograph, a crucial, and unrepeatable, moment may be missed. There are no second takes in a wedding ceremony, and in the time it takes to move to a better position, or ask a guest to step aside, the moment is lost forever. Lastly, many modern couples are keen to prevent guests posting amateur, and often deeply unflattering, pictures on Social Media, directly after the ceremony. Couples are often extremely particular about the way their day is presented to the public. I always prefer guests to have the cell phones completely switched off during a ceremony.

Consideration for the photographic record also plays an important part in the choice of clothing that should be worn for the ceremony. Avoid bright colors, as these will be a distraction in pictures. This is especially true of anything colored red, as these items are particularly arresting to the eye. Always to remember that the bride and groom are the focus of the day.

TIP: At the moment a couple seals their ceremony with a kiss, take two steps back and to the side. This will prevent you from 'photo-bombing the kiss shots', and most photographers will be hugely grateful for your doing so. Be sure to inform the photographer and videographer which direction you plan to step.

2.17 Wedding Readings

There is a long tradition of having significant passages of text read during a wedding ceremony. Historically, these would primarily come from scripture. An advantage of modern ceremonies is that readings may be from any source. The most appropriate and meaningful texts are those that resonate the lives, personalities, and love of the bride and groom. Modern readings can include poems, prose fiction, song lyrics, theatrical speeches, or letters. They can be from sources as diverse as Dante, Winnie the Pooh, and Bob Dylan.

In some ceremonies, the bride and groom may wish to 'gift' a reading to one another. This can be a hugely romantic gesture. There are also readings written for two voices, which is highly appropriate to a union of two hearts.

The choice of reader is as important as the selection of text. Where a couple is acquainted with keen public speakers, or have theatrical friends, asking such individuals to take part in a reading can be a marvelous way of involving them in the wedding process. Just as often, however, the Celebrant is asked to perform the reading, or weave an extended quotation into the text of their opening or closing words.

If you are asked to read from a source of authorship other than your own, you should try to adjust your tone slightly from that used in the rest of the proceedings. To underline the fact that you are 'reading,' you may decide to pronounce those parts in a slightly more deliberate, or poetic, manner. You should be careful, though, to avoid any unwanted decent into a pantomime of overacting.

It is important for every reader to give a varied tone to their words, and not to give a flat, staccato delivery. A wedding is an emotional time, and the best reading will fully express the emotion intended by the author in a natural and genuine manner.

The scripts each reader uses on the day are critical components to performance. I very strongly advise against anyone, however experienced, attempting to memorize the text. Without exception, readers have stumbled in every case where I have seen memorization attempted. This is understandable, given the emotional stresses of the day.

Although guest readers may provide their scripts, too often these will be folded sheets of copy paper, and printed in a tiny font. Working from such a sheet can look unattractive, and gives the impression that the preparations for the reading were rushed. Font size is an especially important issue. If a reader has to strain to see small words, this will reduce the strength of their performance. In an outdoor ceremony, copy paper flaps in even the slightest breeze, and this can distract both reader and audience.

The best scripts are provided on card stock, perhaps colored to match the style of the wedding, and printed in a large, dark font. If possible, the entire text of a reading should be kept to a single side. It is also easier to read and perform a text if it is laid out phrase by phrase, rather than in regular paragraphs.

As a Celebrant, it can be useful to acquire a stock of neutral, pastel colored card, and prepare the reading cards for everyone performing in the ceremony. This small gesture will be seen as impressively attentive and professional by the clients.

Some Suggested Readings

Below is a list of fifty readings that I have seen work well in practice, with the opening lines to give you a flavor of the style. In order to save space, the full texts are not reproduced here but are available online. No list of wedding readings will ever be definitive. I encourage you and the couple you are working with to be creative, and to pick passages that reflect their style, personality, and story. Never be afraid to inject a little humor into this part of the ceremony. Smiles are always welcome guests at a wedding.

1. 'I Fell in Love with Her Courage' by F. Scott Fitzgerald
'I fell in love with her courage, her sincerity and her flaming self respect. And if it's these things I'd believe in, even if the whole world in wild suspicions that she wasn't all she should be. I love her and that is the beginning of everything.' [full text of a short reading]

2. 'The Awakened Heart' by Gerald May
'There is a desire within each of us, in the deep center of ourselves that we call our heart. We were born with it, it is never completely satisfied, and it never dies. We are often unaware of it, but it is always awake…'

3. 'The Laws of Wellness' by Greg Anderson
'The greatest pursuit is not good health, unsurpassed wisdom, economic surplus, political freedom, or even faith that can move mountains. It is the daily

practice of unconditional loving. Unconditional, nonjudgmental loving. This is our aim, life's single highest and most rewarding pursuit…'

4. 'Ever After' by C.S. Lewis
'We believe and hope in 'ever after' It implies that every day we feel a perfect love. Is a great love made from only happiness? From continuous unending excitement? No…'

5. 'Let Love be Stronger than Your Anger' by Jane Wells
'Let love be stronger than your anger
Learn the wisdom of compromise
For it is better to bend than to break…'

6. 'A Small Poem of Happiness' by Neil Gaiman
'This for you, for both of you,
a small poem of happiness
filled with small glories and little triumphs…'

7. 'Soul Mates' by Lang Leav
'I don't know how it is you are so familiar to me –
or why it feels less that I'm getting to know you
and more as though I am remembering who you are…'

8. 'The Road Not Taken' by Robert Frost
'Two roads diverged in a yellow wood,
And sorry I could not travel both
And be one traveler, long I stood…'

9. 'To Love is Not to Possess' by James Kavanaugh
'To love is not to possess,
To own or imprison,
Nor to lose one's self in another…'

10. The Traditional Apache Marriage Blessing
'Now you will feel no rain,

for each of you will be the shelter for each other.

Now you will feel no cold,

for each of you will be the warmth for the other...'

11. 'Blessing for a Marriage' by James Dillet Freeman

'May your marriage bring you all the exquisite excitements a marriage should bring,

and may life grant you also patience, tolerance, and understanding.

May you always need one another –

not so much to fill your emptiness as to help you to know your fullness...'

12. 'How Do I Love Thee' by Elizabeth Barrett Browning

'How do I love thee?

Let me count the ways.

I love thee to the depth and breadth and height...'

13. First Corinthians, Chapter 13 (A biblical verse without supernatural references)

'1 If I speak in human and angelic tongues but do not have love, I am a resounding gong or a clashing cymbal.

2 And if I have the gift of prophecy and comprehend all mysteries and all knowledge; if I have all faith so as to move mountains but do not have love, I am nothing...'

14. 'Union from the Beginning to End' by Robert Fulghum

'You have known each other from the first glance of acquaintance to this point of commitment. At some point you decided to marry. From that moment of yes to this moment of yes, you have been making promises and agreements in an informal way...'

15. 'The Point of Marriage' by Rene Maria Rilke

'The point of marriage is not to create a quick commonality by tearing down all boundaries; on the contrary, a good marriage is one in which each partner appoints the other to be the guardian of their solitude, and thus they show each other the greatest possible trust...'

16. 'Yes, I'll Marry You' by Pam Ayres
'Yes, I'll marry you, my dear,
And here's the reason why;
So I can push you out of bed…'

17. 'The Art of Marriage' by Wilford A. Peterson
'Happiness in marriage is not something that just happens.
A good marriage must be created.
In the art of marriage the little things are the big things…'

18. 'Now We Are Six' by A. A. Milne
'A Soul Mate is someone who has locks that fit our keys
And Keys to fit our locks.
When we feel safe enough to open the locks
Our truest selves step out…'

19. 'I love you means…' by Jonathan Safran Foer
''I love you' means that I accept you for the person that you are, and that I do
not wish to change you into someone else. It means that I will love you and stand
by you through the worst of times…'

20. 'Marriage Joins Two People in the Circle of its Love' by Edmund O'Neill
'Marriage is a commitment to life, the best that two people can find and bring
out in each other. It offers opportunities for sharing and growth that no other
relationship can equal. It is a physical and an emotional joining that is promised
for a lifetime…'

21. 'Never Marry But For Love' by William Penn
'Never marry but for love; but see that thou lovest what is lovely. If love be
not the chiefest motive, thou wilt soon grow weary of a married state and stray
from thy promise, to search out thy pleasures in forbidden places…'

22. 'The Confirmation' by Edwin Muir
'Yes, yours, my love, is the right human face.

I in my mind had waited for this long,
Seeing the false and searching for the true…'

23. 'He Never Leaves the Seat Up' by Unknown
'He never leaves the seat up
Or wet towels upon the floor
The toothpaste has the lid on
And he always shuts the door!…'

24. 'Oh The Places You'll Go' by Dr. Seuss
'Congratulations! Today is your day.
You're off to Great Places! You're off and away!
You have brains in your head. You have feet in your shoes.
You can steer yourself any direction you choose…'

25. 'Corelli's Mandolin' by Louis De Bernieres
'Love is a temporary madness, it erupts like volcanoes and then subsides. And when it subsides you have to make a decision. You have to work out whether your roots have so entwined together that it is inconceivable that you should ever part…'

26. Traditional Hindu Marriage Poem
'You have become mine forever.
Yes, we have become partners.
I have become yours.
Hereafter, I cannot live without you…'

27. 'Falling in Love is like Owning a Dog' by Taylor Mali
'First of all, it's a big responsibility,
especially in a city like New York.
So think long and hard before deciding on love.
On the other hand, love gives you a sense of security…'

28. 'A Natural History of Love' by Diane Ackerman
'Love. What a small word we use for an idea so immense and powerful. It has

altered the flow of history, calmed monsters, kindled works of art, cheered the forlorn, turned tough guys to mush, consoled the enslaved, driven strong women mad, glorified the humble, fueled national scandals, bankrupted robber barons, and made mincemeat of kings…'

29. 'Gift from the Sea' by Anne Morrow Lindbergh
'When you love someone, you do not love them all the time, in exactly the same way, from moment to moment. It is an impossibility. It is even a lie to pretend to. And yet this is exactly what most of us demand. We have so little faith in the ebb and flow of life, of love, of relationships…'

30. 'The Key to Love' by Anon, First Century China
'The key to love is understanding …
The ability to comprehend not only the spoken word,
but those unspoken gestures,
the little things that say so much by themselves.
The key to love is forgiveness…'

31. 'Sooner or Later' by Unknown
'Sooner or later we begin to understand that love is more than verses on valentines
and romance in the movies. We begin to know that love is here and now, real and true, the most important thing in our lives…'

32. 'The Passionate Shepherd to his Love' by Christopher Marlowe
'Come live with me, and be my love,
And we will all the pleasures prove
That valleys, groves, hills and fields,
Woods, or steepy mountain yields…'

33. 'The Irrational Season' by Madeleine L'Engle
'But ultimately there comes a moment when a decision must be made. Ultimately two people who love each other must ask themselves how much they hope for as their love grows and deepens, and how much risk they are willing to take…'

34. 'A Lovely Love Story' by Edward Monkton
'The fierce Dinosaur was trapped inside his cage of ice.
Although it was cold he was happy in there. It was, after all, his cage.
Then along came the Lovely Other Dinosaur.
The Lovely Other Dinosaur melted the Dinosaur's cage with kind words and loving thoughts...'

35. 'A Love Knot' by Anonymous
The French actress Simone Signoret said 'Chains do not hold a marriage together. It is threads, hundreds of tiny threads which sew people together through the years.'
Picture hundreds, thousands, of threads, as long as love is...'

36. 'I'll be There for You' by Louise Cuddon
'I'll be there my darling, through thick and through thin
When your mind's in a mess and your head's in a spin
When your plane's been delayed, and you've missed the last train.
When life is just threatening to drive you insane...'

37. 'I Like You' by Sandol Stoddard Warburg
'I like you and I know why
I like you because you are a good person to like
I like you because when I tell you something special, you know it's special
And you remember it a long, long time...'

38. 'I Rely on You' by Hovis Presley
'I rely on you
like a camera needs a shutter
like a gambler needs a flutter
like a golfer needs a putter
like a buttered scone involves some butter...'

39. 'I Wanna be Yours' by John Cooper-Clarke
'I wanna be your vacuum cleaner

breathing in your dust
I wanna be your Ford Cortina
I will never rust...'

40. 'Recipe for Love' by Unknown
'Put the love, good looks and sweet temper into a well furnished house.
Beat the butter of youth to a cream, and mix well together with the blindness
of faults...'

41. 'The Owl and the Pussycat' by Edward Lear
'The Owl and the Pussy-cat went to sea
In a beautiful pea green boat,
They took some honey, and plenty of money,
Wrapped up in a five pound note...'

42. 'The House at Pooh Corner' by A. A. Milne
'Pooh, promise you won't forget about me, ever. Not even when I'm a
hundred.'
Pooh thought for a little. 'How old shall I be then?'
'Ninety-nine.' Pooh nodded.
'I promise,' he said...'

43. 'Untitled' by Bee Rawlinson
'Love me when I'm old and shocking
Peel off my elastic stockings
Swing me from the chandeliers
Let's be randy bad old dears...'

44. 'Weddings' by Unknown
'If you go to a wedding, here's what it means
No one wears trainers and no one wears jeans
Your best new clothes are all that you wear
And everyone in your whole family is there...'

45. 'A Farewell to Arms' by Ernest Hemingway

'At night, there was the feeling that we had come home, feeling no longer alone, waking in the night to find the other one there, and not gone away; all other things were unreal…'

46. 'A History of Love' by Nicole Krauss
'Once upon a time, there was a boy. He lived in a village that no longer exists, in a house that no longer exists, on the edge of a field that no longer exists, where everything was discovered, and everything was possible…'

47. 'Love' by Roy Croft
'I love you
Not only for what you are,
But for what I am
When I am with you…'

48. 'The Awakened Heart' by Gerald May
'There is a desire within each of us, in the deep center of ourselves that we call our heart. We were born with it, it is never completely satisfied, and it never dies…'

49. 'Dao de Jing' by Laozi
'Explore and discover that which is within.
When we find ourselves, we are more easily found by others.
Without words, without even understanding,
lovers find each other…'

50. 'Why Marriage?' by Mari Nichols-Haining
'Because to the depths of me,
I long to love one person,
With all my heart,
my soul, my mind, my body…'

2.18 Wedding Unity Rituals

A Unity Ritual often makes an impressive addition to a wedding ceremony. They make for excellent theater, and also give the guests a break from listening to the Celebrant. Most importantly, they are a way to have the couple visibly participate in the events.

There are no strict rules as to the point in the ceremony where a Unity Ritual may take place. This is ultimately at the discretion of the couple. However, the rituals are usually located after the making of the vows and exchanging of rings. Performing a ritual together, especially one that involves exchanges or gifts, re-enforces the vows, and adds a 'theater of commitment.'

Although there are many types of ritual listed in this book, and more ideas appearing online each year (see especially the excellent website offbeatbride.com), there is no harm at all in encouraging creative couples to invent their own. This can be especially fun where the ritual obviously reflects the particular passions of the couple. One couple, both cattle farmers, chose to brand their initials into a large piece of wood as part of their ceremony. This was then kept as an ornament for their home. Another couple, both long-time fans of Penn and Teller, decided to learn and practice a magic trick. The groom took the traditional role of the assistant.

Modern weddings thrive on creativity, personal expression, and smiles. Where a Unity Ritual contains all these things, it should be a success.

What makes an effective Unity Ritual?

If you are considering creating a new and innovative Unity Ritual with a couple, here are a few recommendations to make it work wonderfully as part of the ceremony:

1. It should be simple to perform.

A unity ritual must be performed quickly, in front of an audience, and often without rehearsal. The more complex the activity, the more likely something will go wrong, or mistakes will be made. An ideal ritual involves minimal movement, and simple physical actions, such as pouring motions or lighting a candle. Where a more complex task is planned, such as tying a knot, mixing a cocktail, or making a sandwich, the couple should be encouraged to put in a few hours practice. Practicing a ritual can be a fun, bonding experience, and also raise their confidence about the ceremony as a whole.

2. It should have a clear start point and a definite end point.

All rituals, like all good stories, need a distinct beginning and end. A candle starts unlit and then is ignited. A rope is straight, and then a knot is tied. Sand is separate, and then different colors are mixed. This reflects the fact that the entire ceremony has its journey from unmarried to married. The best unity activities are those impossible, or very difficult, to reverse. Just as vows cannot be unsaid, so a candle cannot be unburned, a glass of wine cannot be 'undrunk', and sands cannot be unmixed (at least not without an enormous amount of patience!). The action of these rituals has changed the physical state of these objects forever, just as the act of marriage should forever change the couple.

3. It should suit the style of the couple.

The best ceremonies are those that seem natural to the lives and personalities of the bride and groom. Where a couple leads simple lifestyles, an elaborate and lavish ceremony can seem forced and uncomfortable. Similarly, where a couple enjoys the comforts of city and technology, a wedding in the wild can often be unsatisfying, despite initially appearing a romantic notion. This principle applies well in creating a unity ritual. It is best to choose themes that reflect a couple's shared passions, pastimes, or professions. For sporting partners, a more physical activity may suit their natures. For a couple known for quirky humor, something more shocking could be appropriate. Where a couple is both quiet and gentle natured, a simple ceremony of giving can best reflect their story.

4. It should be suitable for the venue.

Any plans for a ritual should consider the space in which the ceremony will be performed. Certain activities will be difficult, or impossible, in particular locations. The obvious example is the candle ceremony, when attempted outdoors, even a small breeze can extinguish a flame. Just as importantly, some venues do not allow open flame. Activities that require tables or support for physical objects, such as the easel in a painting ritual, become much harder if the ceremony takes place on a beach. Some ritual elements can be messy, such as the earth used in a tree planting. Items that can cause marks and stains, such as wine and chocolate, should be used with care around delicate clothing and makeup.

5. It should make good 'theater'.

A great unity ritual is interesting to watch. There is a good reason we say that a couple 'perform' their ceremony. Although a wedding is first about the couple, the guests have been invited to watch and witness. They have also, in most cases, been asked to observe some distance from where the couple is positioned. It is a much more engaging experience for attendees if they can see clearly what is going on. Where 'props' are used in a ritual, they should be large enough for everyone to see and easy to recognize. Planting trees, jumping a broom, painting a canvas, and knot-tying all make terrific theater. Where any ritual uses colored substances, such as sand or wine, it makes for a better visual effect if the receptacles holding these are transparent.

6. It should contain symbols.

Every ritual is a metaphor for life, and the objects used should symbolize a wider concept. There are two major types of symbol used in ritual, symbolic objects and symbolic actions. The most obvious symbolic object used in weddings is, of course, the wedding ring, the 'unbroken symbol of never-ending love.' When seeking the symbolic meaning of an object in a wedding ritual, look for the positive qualities it represents. A tree represents life; a book can represent shared knowledge and experience; a knot represents the strong bonds between a couple. Many objects have multiple symbolic meanings. A fire represents cleansing, warmth, and light, and irreversible change. When looking for the symbolic significance of an action in a wedding ritual, examine how what is taking represents both joining and commitment. A mixing of sand has both these, in that the sands are mingled, and this is an act that cannot be undone.

7. It should represent joining and acting in harmony.

The best unity rituals are those which are carried out together. In doing so, a couple demonstrates that they are more effective together than alone. This also shows a unified purpose and mutual trust. In jumping the broom, or taking the 'seven steps', a couple are acting together. In making a sandwich, a very fun and modern idea for a ritual, they are not only working together but are adding different ingredients to create a greater whole.

8. It should have a clear, easy to describe meaning.

Although it is usual, and polite, for the Celebrant to say a few words explaining the meaning of any unity ritual, this should be straightforward and easy to convey. The meaning of a knot tying, for example, is simple and readily understood. Some activities, such as the exchange of salt or coins, may require a little more explanation. Everyday items, particularly those already associated with love and the home, come pre-loaded with significance that translates to a wedding. Most people already associate wine and chocolate with romance, and objects such as brooms and salt are very frequently shown to represent home life. The more obvious the meaning of any ritual the more appropriate it will seem, and the easier it will be to integrate into the ceremony.

9. It should be ethically, and environmentally, responsible.

Any ritual should be performed with care and responsibility. In addition to their symbolic meaning, ceremonies are also about setting an example and demonstrating the values a couple deems important. Rituals should ideally not involve destruction or waste. No harm should be caused by the ritual to any person during the performance, even if this is only implied. It would be in extremely poor taste, for example, to burn effigies of ex-husbands or ex-wives. No ritual should ever harm the environment, or damage the ceremony venue. Care should always be taken to assess the impact of a ritual for adverse consequences.

One example might be the case of a balloon release. Balloons may seem harmless and cute as they float into the sky. However, there are many documented cases of them falling back to earth in the ocean and choking turtles that mistake them for jellyfish. I have written a special section below about responsible behavior toward animals during ceremonies and rituals.

10. It should be FUN.

Above all, any ritual should be a cause for smiles and celebration. The best ceremonies offer a single triumphant climax, at which point the guests should instinctively feel an urge to cheer or applaud. One of the greatest strengths of a modern wedding ceremony is that it does not have to be a somber and serious affair. It can be a true celebration, and should involve laughter and joy and happiness. The more a couple laughs together on their wedding day, the happier their memories of it will be. Excitement and humor add a tremendous value and enjoyment for both the couple and their guests.

As you read through the unity rituals in this book, consider how each of these above points relates to what is taking place, and perhaps consider how you might personalize the ceremony to give it even more energy and impact.

Animal Based Rituals

Wedding Celebrants are often asked about rituals that involve animals. The two most common are the dove release and the butterfly release. It is my opinion that using animals as props in a wedding ceremony is unethical, and in my practice I very strongly discourage this. There is a big difference between dressing a family pet as a ring bearer and purchasing small animals wholesale to use for a visual stunt.

Although many vendors use a species of dove that is technically a form of homing pigeon, you are still advocating the raising and transporting of animals for your own amusement, and there is no guarantee that any animal bred in captivity, and then released into the wild will survive for long.

Butterflies, bred in captivity and transported in an artificially induced state of hibernation, will all die very shortly after the release into the wild. What may seem like a romantic gesture actually provides an expensive and colorful meal for the local spider and bird population.

With so many harmless alternatives available, the use of any animals as fun props for a wedding is outdated and indefensible. This is, ultimately, a choice for the couple, but both you and they should be fully aware of the realities that accompany such plans.

Ritual Colors

Many rituals use symbolic colors. It is helpful to consider the meaning of the colors in relation to weddings and married life:

Red represents a passion for life, physical energy, and health. It is also representative of physical love, and the ties of blood and family. These meanings have particular importance regarding marriage. In some Eastern cultures, red is associated with luck. It is important to note that red is the color that most draws the eye in any scene or photograph.

Pink is the color of tenderness and femininity. It is also most classically associated with romantic love. Pink and white mix especially well together, but better still with a third dark accent. Hues of pink work along an interesting continuum, with lighter pinks evoking tenderness, and deeper pinks symbolizing the more passionate and sensual.

Orange emphasizes sweetness, trust, and creativity. It is also representative of warmth and a compassionate heart. Orange tones are very popular in fall (autumn) weddings. Orange can also represent the healing of a wounded heart, or overcoming disappointment.

Yellow evokes respect, personal power, and spontaneity. In the right shade, it can bring warmth and the feelings of summer. Light and sunshine are popular themes in romance and marriage. Weaker shades of yellow work best to offset other colors, particularly blue.

Green. Compassion, unconditional love, and balance are represented by green. It is the color of nature, life, and healing. It can also be used to represent financial success.

Light Blue is the color of communication, contentedness, harmony, and self-expression. This is also the color that represents honesty. Blue is traditionally associated with the masculine, as pink is with the feminine.

Dark Blue represents intuition, wisdom, emotional intelligence, and charisma. This is also the color of the ocean and the sky, themes that can symbolize the unknown future of adventure that lays ahead for all newlyweds.

Purple represents peace, spirituality, and selflessness. When used in a wedding, this color evokes royalty and riches, a notion which stems from a time when purple dyes were an expensive luxury. Lighter purples have a more feminine quality, and bring to mind thoughts of flowers and womanhood. Purple and gold work especially well together.

White is commonly used to evoke thoughts of purity, and a connection with the spiritual. For a wedding ceremony, white represents a new beginning, goodness, safety, honesty, and perfection. It is the color of blank pages, upon which a couple will now write their story.

Black does not only represent evil, corruption, and death (hardly appropriate wedding themes). It can also represent mystery, strength, seriousness, power, and authority. It also has strong associations with sex and sophistication. Those who have embraced the 'goth' fashion trend may also wish to use a strong black theme or motif.

Adobe has a useful tool for experimenting with color combinations at: https://color.adobe.com/create/color-wheel/

2.18a Book Gifting Rituals

Many couples exchange books at some point in their courtship, often with inscriptions lovingly placed inside the covers. Many couples meet for the first time at college, or bond discussing their favorite authors. Books are also symbols of the story of life, and the lessons we learn along the way.

A bride and groom for whom books have particular meaning might like to select a volume, and present this to each other as part of their ceremony. They may like to read the inscription they have written aloud for all to hear, and could even incorporate this as part of their vows. They may like to choose a favorite passage from the selected book as a reading.

First edition hardbacks are easily obtained from online retailers, and can even be inscribed by the author.

In the last few years, self-publishing has become easy and inexpensive, using services such as 'Amazon Createspace'. An especially creative couple might choose to create and gift a collection of photographs, poems, or perhaps even short stories!

Books could be placed on a table, or held by 'book pages' until they are needed.

Another possibility might be for a couple to create a single book that will become the journal, or scrapbook, of their adventures. They might sign their names on the first page, and pledge to record the significant events in their lives, including the births and milestones of children and family. In this way, they are perhaps creating a modern equivalent of the traditional family bible.

Example Book Gifting Text

The words of love are the way we convey our most delicate feelings and meaning to each other. For [Bride] and [Groom], the words they have shared have been important from the first in building the wonderful bond and understanding they have come to share.

In our world, the words with the greatest power are often captured and held as written text, printed and shared. As such, they make up the record of our lives, the history of our days, and a legacy that lasts long after we have ceased to speak them.

[Groom] and [Bride] have each chosen a book with special meaning, which they will now give to each other. On the first page, each has inscribed a special message that expresses how they feel now, and captures that feeling for all time. They offer these today in the hope that the message will always be there, carried in those words, so that the beauty of this day will never be forgotten, but travel with them wherever these books are taken.

[Groom], will you please now offer your book to [Bride], and read the inscription you have written within.

(Groom reads)

[Bride], will you please now offer your book to [Groom], and read the inscription you have written within.

(Bride reads)

They will now place these books together on a shelf within their home, or take them with them if they travel far. Each time they read the words they have shared, they will remember this day they heard them first, and the love they share will be written anew.

2.18b Bread Breaking Rituals

The tradition of 'breaking bread' during a wedding comes from Eastern Europe. In this ritual, each of the couple takes a bite, or a chunk, from a loaf, and the one who manages to remove the biggest portion is proclaimed the 'leader' of the new household. Occasionally, the bread may be dipped in a substance such as honey, and then offered to one's partner to taste. Doing so symbolizes the sweetness and nourishment each brings to the union.

This ritual can easily be performed without the need for the competition element.

Bread, broken and then offered, can symbolize many aspects of the wedding ceremony. It may represent the coming together of the different qualities, or 'ingredients', each partner brings to the marriage. That analogy can be extended to the qualities of the two families that have raised the couple. Bread has also long been seen as symbolic of the home. Baking is considered a core 'homemaking' activity in many cultures. Lastly, of course, bread is symbolic of financial income and security. In several English-speaking countries, the word 'bread' is used as a slang term for money.

There are several ways a couple might customize a bread ritual. First, they might choose a type of bread particular to their culture, or region, of birth. Second, they may ask the mothers to share the cooking of the ritual loaf, and then present it during the ceremony.

Example Bread Breaking Text

I now ask the couple to join me at this table.

Under this cloth (removes cloth) is a loaf of bread, baked for you both by your mothers today. They each brought ingredients; just as you both bring different ingredients to your love. They mixed these together and gave the dough time to rise into something new and nourishing. In a moment, I will ask each of you to take a chunk, and offer it to the other.

For those who do not know, the breaking of bread at a wedding is a tradition that comes to us from Eastern Europe. Those cultures held that the bread symbolized the home, and that whoever managed to tear off the greatest chunk of the loaf was thenceforth the leader of the household, or the 'bread winner.' Today we hope that you will both work each day to ensure that, in your life together, you are both winners equally. Therefore, I ask you to offer the other the bread you take. This is your gift, of worth, home, and sustenance, that you bring each day forward to keep you and all you love, safe, secure, nourished, and whole. To sweeten this gift we have also placed a small bowl of honey. May your love always taste sweet to the other.

I ask you then now, starting with [Groom], to take bread and offer it to the other.

[The couple breaks off some bread]

[Improvised, after breaking: 'I believe we have a winner!']

[They offer, dip, and take a bite. Napkins are available for mess.]

To thank you all for coming today, you will each receive a small pot of the same honey. [Bride] and [Groom] hope you will always find some of the sweetness in your lives that they have found with each other.

Please join me again at the center.

2.18c Broom Jumping Rituals

Jumping the broom is a time-honored tradition at African-American weddings. The broom is placed on the floor in front of the couple, and they jump it together. This usually takes place at the start of the recessional. This act symbolizes a new beginning, and a 'sweeping away' of the problems and burdens of the past. It can also signify the joining of two families, and offers a respectful nod to the couple's ancestors. The broom itself is often beautifully ornamental, and may be kept afterward as a keepsake of the day.

It is useful for the Celebrant to say a few words of explanation regarding this ritual and its significance, so that all the guests understand what is taking place. It is usual for the guests to cheer after the couple has made the jump, and so it is helpful to inform them that they should do so.

The couple may wish to appoint a younger member of the family to act as a 'broom bearer,' not only to carry it into the ceremony but also to lay it down in the appropriate position when the time is right.

Example Broom Jumping Text

Sharing a life with another person requires many 'leaps of faith.' The leap they take together over the broom is also symbolic. By making the leap, they make a gesture of dedication to working together through the tough times ahead, as well as the easy times. They leave behind the past and jump into the future together secure in their love.

Now, after I pronounce [Bride] and [Groom] married, I ask them to take that leap, and when they do, I want you all to give them the biggest cheer you can!

And so… [pronouncement]

[Couple turn]

One, Two, Three, JUMP!

[Cheers. Cue triumphal recessional music.]

2.18d Candle Lighting Rituals

Although the Unity Candle has somewhat gained a reputation as the 'classic' unity ritual, it is a relatively new tradition. Its popularity has declined slightly in recent years, as many venues now have fire regulations prohibiting open flames, and it is impractical for most outdoor locations.

This ritual most often involves two taper candles with a large pillar candle between them. At the beginning of the ceremony, representatives from each family, usually the mothers of the bride and groom, step forward to light each of the taper candles. This symbolizes the contribution and guidance that the families have given to the lives of the couple.

Later in the ceremony, usually after the vows, the bride and groom will use these taper candles simultaneously to light the center pillar candle. This represents the light of their love, and the beacon of welcome they will always hold for each other.

The table on which these candles stand is often decorated, perhaps with the wedding invitation, or a photograph of the couple, and the center candle itself may be inscribed with the couple's names and the date of the wedding. The candles selected for this ritual are almost always white. A special musical selection may also accompany the ritual. The Celebrant may wish to suggest that the couple saves this candle, and relight it on their anniversary each year to remind them of the events and emotions of their wedding day.

Example Candle Lighting Text

(At the beginning of the ceremony)

'*At this time I invite both mothers to come forward representing the families who raised and nurtured [Bride] and [Groom]. They light the candles representing not only the love and support of the families who brought us to this moment, but also the two unique individuals pledging themselves to one another in the bond of marriage.*'

(After the exchange of rings)

'[Groom] and [Bride], will you please join me at the candles, and take your places each side of those your mothers have already given light.

[Bride] and [Groom], the two outside candles burning here represent your lives at this moment. Each light is distinct, each able to go its separate way. I invite you to take your candles and together light the center one. To bring strength and happiness to your home, there must be the merging of these two lights into one light, just as two people come together to support one another in a healthy partnership.

[[Groom] and [Bride] light the candle]

This pillar represents the coming together of these two lives in a marriage relationship. [Bride] and [Groom] acknowledge that, although they remain separate individuals with their unique strengths and weaknesses, they now accept the other as their highest priority. The decisions they make will be shared, and the consequences affect them both. A marriage neither results in two distinct personalities nor the complete surrender of individuals into a partnership. Rather it is a relationship that strengthens the individual through love, honor, and respect. As this one light cannot be divided, [Groom] and [Bride] will be united from this day forward, and go forward into a shining lifetime together.'

2.18e Chocolate Rituals

The gift of chocolates in a box is one of the most recognizable emblems of courtship. A box of chocolates may also be a symbol of life, which offers many flavors of experience, some of which are bitter and some sweet. There may also be times when we encounter unexpected nuts.

Exchanging chocolates during a wedding ceremony, usually after the vows, makes an excellent ritual for a number of reasons. Chocolates are light and manageable, and can be placed on a table before the couple. They might be presented by a 'chocolate page', perhaps a junior relative acting in a role similar to that of a ring bearer. There are a vast number of types of chocolate to choose from. A couple may choose their favorites or those that made up a memorable gift during their time dating. They may choose chocolates that are traditional to their culture or region, or which have a particular significance to their families. The act of consuming chocolate is quickly performed, and the smiles and expressions provoked by the taste make great theater. Lastly, a couple may choose to add a small chocolate offering to their guests, so that they can share in the experience.

It is worth sounding a little note of warning, and reminding any couple considering this option that chocolates can be messy. Brown smudges will not look beautiful on a white dress or a beautifully made-up face. Additionally, if a ceremony is to take place outside in summer, it should be remembered that chocolate does not react well to heat.

Example Chocolate Ritual Text

Please join me at the table.

Chocolate is well known for giving moments of pleasure. It has a direct line to the parts of our brain that make us feel good, just as you have for each other. However, like life, chocolate can also be bitter. On the table in front of you, you will see a selection of chocolates, some dark and bitter, some light and sweet, some filled with hidden surprises. I invite you now to take one of the bitter. Savor the unique flavors, just as you will always savor each other.

[Bride and groom select and eat a dark chocolate]

Now select and offer one of the sweet, just as you will always try to bring sweetness into their life from this day forward.

[Bride and groom select and feed each other a milk chocolate]

Ladies and gentlemen, I am sure some of you are sitting and feeling quite jealous right now. Not to worry! When you sit down tonight, you will find on your table a selection of chocolates to enjoy. [Bride] and [Groom] hope that, as you do, you will take a moment to remember how important it is always to try to bring sweetness into the lives of others.

Please join me again in the center.

2.18f Cocktail Mixing Rituals

The mixing of cocktails could be a fun and stylish ritual to add to a wedding ceremony, and there are a nearly endless number of recipes to choose from. The most meaningful selection will be one that has particular meaning and significance to a couple. Particularly adventurous couples might like to invent a cocktail recipe to commemorate the day.

Although cocktail mixing can make great theater, it is quite a complicated process, and will require a significant amount of practice for the couple to perform comfortably. Additionally, you will need a venue where you can set up a small bar table for the ritual ingredients. If some ingredients require a low temperature, you may have to provide ice.

If there are only a small number of guests, you may like to offer everyone attending a chance to sample the recipe, though this is probably best saved for after the ceremony.

Once prepared, the couple should each take a short sip of the finished drink, and then leave the glass to one side. It is not a good idea for either of them to hold it for the remainder of the ceremony, though you may like to joke about them wishing to do so.

As with other food rituals, there is a potential for mess, spillage, and staining, and so care should be taken.

Example Cocktail Mixing Text

I ask the couple to take their places either side of the small table we have arranged.

Today [Bride] and [Groom] have something special to perform together. To honor this day they have invented their own cocktail, one they will mix and share.

[Describe cocktail ingredients and why each represents something about the couple]

And so, now the two of you may begin.

[Note: The couple may wish to describe the process and ingredients to their guests as they mix.]

Well done! So now, we say to them as they take that sip of married life, Cheers!
[Couple drink and all cheer]

If you like the sound of this new drink, we have arranged it so you can try one yourself, on the house, at the bar this evening. We all hope you enjoy it as much as they do, and perhaps try inventing a cocktail of your own.

Please join me again in the center.

2.18g Coin Rituals

The custom of giving wedding coins originated in Spain. Thirteen gold coins, or 'arras', are presented to the bride by the bridegroom. This signifies his willingness to support her. The coins are often contained in ornate boxes or gift trays. Coins may also be used to represent a bride's dowry.

When introducing a ritual of this type, a Celebrant will usually make special mention of the wishes everyone attending has for the couple's prosperity. Where coins are combined, they also symbolize a joining of two incomes into a greater whole.

Example Coin Ritual Text

[Bride] and [Groom] you have just sealed your vows by the giving of rings. To represent the prosperity you will bring to each other's lives I now ask you to make an exchange of coins, or as they are known in Spanish custom, 'Arras.'

Traditionally, cultures embraced the concept of a husband as 'bread winner', and wife as 'homemaker' so the coins were given and received not in a spirit of reciprocation but more of supporting and being supported. In modern times, the coins are a reminder of the financial wisdom needed by all couples; that they will mutually support each other, their family and children, and the world around them. These coins also carry all our hopes and wishes that you will both always know security, and never suffer hardship and want.

(Groom please offer your coins read the words as you give)

(Bride/Groom) I offer you this first coin in the hope that we will always be blessed with an abundance of resources and comforts, and be helpful to one another in all ways.

(Bride/Groom) I offer you this second coin in the hope that we will always be strong and complement one another.

(Bride/Groom) I offer you this third coin in the hope that we will always be blessed with prosperity and riches on all levels.

(Bride/Groom) I offer you this fourth coin in the hope that we will always be

eternally happy.

(Bride/Groom) I offer you this fifth coin in the hope that we will always be blessed with a happy family life.

(Bride/Groom) I offer you this sixth coin in the hope that we will always be faithful to our personal values, and our promises.

(Bride/Groom) I offer you this last coin in the hope that we will always be the best of friends.

(Groom/Bride), I gratefully accept them and make this same pledge to you.

(Groom/Bride repeats the ritual)

Please join me again in the center.

2.18h Circling Rituals

Often, but not exclusively, from Jewish traditions, circling ceremonies come in wide varieties, and can be interpreted as symbolizing many aspects of life, marriage, and family, as well as the creation or protection of a new family unit.

It is common for the couple to circle each other three times. This should be preceded by words of explanation, and may be accompanied by vows or oaths spoken by the bride or groom. A variation on this is for a couple to offer each other questions and responses as they circle. They might have these written down, or be prompted by the Celebrant, as it's hard to memorize words and repeat them correctly under the emotional strains of a wedding ceremony. Once each has circled the other three times, it can be a beautiful gesture to have the couple walk a final circle together.

Although rituals such as this have a strong basis in tradition, modern couples should be encouraged to contribute their style and ideas, and to create something that is unique and meaningful to their relationship and story.

Example Circling Ritual Text

In many cultures, it is an ancient tradition for each partner to circle the other, as a way of sealing the vows they have made. [Bride] and [Groom] have chosen do so today and offer these statements on the promises they are making.

[Groom circles a first time]

I circle you now to create the first seal of our love, that I will always be true.

[Groom circles a second time]

I circle you again to form the second seal of our love, that I will always act with kindness.

[Groom circles a third time]

I circle this last time to create the third seal of our love, that I will always listen with understanding.

[Bride circles a first time]

I circle you now to create the first seal of our love, that I will always be true.

[Bride circles a second time]

I circle you again to form the second seal of our love, that I will always act with kindness.

[Bride circles a third time]

I circle this last time to create the third seal of our love, that I will always listen with understanding.

Finally, you circle together, as you will travel the circle of life together the rest of your days, side by side, hand in hand, hearts joined as one.

2.18i Cup Rituals

Cups have often been used in rituals to symbolize love, giving, and the taking of oaths. Several traditions link wedding ceremonies and cups. However, a couple may also wish to create their own drinking ritual, perhaps with accompanying vows, with a cup, glass, or container that has special meaning for their story.

German Cup Ritual

As with so many rituals from Germany, the cup ritual tradition begins with a legend.

Centuries ago, in old Nuremberg, the Lady Kunigunde fell in love with a young and ambitious goldsmith. Although Kunigunde's wealthy father did not approve of this pair, it was clear that she only wanted the goldsmith to be her husband as she refused many titled and rich suitors who asked for her hand in marriage. Her father became so enraged that he had the young goldsmith thrown into the darkest dungeon. It did not end their love, and the father created what he thought to be an impossible task: 'If your goldsmith can make a chalice from which two people can drink at the same time without spilling one single drop, I will free him, and you shall become his bride.' The young goldsmith created the image of a girl whose skirt was hollowed to serve as a cup, and her raised arms held a 'much smaller cup' that swivels so that it could be filled and then swung towards a second drinker. The 'Bridal' or 'Wedding Cup' remains a symbol; love, faithfulness, and good luck await the couple who drink from this cup!

Many people choose to read the story of the bridal cup to their guests as it is an inspiring story of love. Others prefer to use their own toasts. If you want to add some extra fun to your text, you can use the 'Who Rules the Nest' toast explained below.

Fill the large skirt end with champagne. If you are going to read the story of the bridal cup to your guests, then you should have someone else fill the cup as you read. After the large skirt end of the bridal cup is filled, the smaller swiveling cup needs to be filled. Because the smaller top cup swivels, it will already be upright. Carefully fill the small cup. Now that you have both cups filled, you are ready to perform the bridal cup toast!

The bride and groom must stand closely together facing each other with just enough space for the cup between them. The bride takes the smaller cup in hand while the groom holds the larger cup.

At the same time, the wedding couple raises the cup to their lips to drink.

Find out more by visiting: www.german-toasting-glasses.com, where these wonderful cups are for sale.

Acknowledgments:

Hayley's Wedding Tips 101, https://weddingtips101.wordpress.com/ (accessed December 24, 2015).

Nuernberg Bridal cup - Blissful Tales of Professional Socialites, http://blissfultalesofps.blogspot.com/2009/12/legend-of-nuernberg-bridal-cup.htm (accessed December 24, 2015).

Scottish Cup Rituals

A 'quaich' is a particular kind of shallow cup found in Scotland and has traditionally been used in rituals involving celebration, prize-giving, and victory. Some quaichs' bottoms are made of glass, allegedly so that the drinker could keep watch on his companions. A more romantic quaich had a double glass bottom in which was kept a lock of hair so that the owner could drink from his quaich to his lady love, and in 1589, King James VI of Scotland gave Anne of Denmark a Quaich, or 'loving cup', as a wedding gift.

A couple may wish to have their cup engraved with the date of their wedding day. They may also want to use whiskey instead of more traditional champagne, being more appropriate to the Scottish origins of this ritual.

Example Cup Ritual Text

As part of their ceremony today, [Bride] and [Groom] have chosen to recognize, and yet make their own, the ancient European tradition of the loving cup.

On the table before them is a specially made German wedding cup, a design that solves the riddle of how two can sip from one cup at the same time. [Bride] and [Groom] will now show us how it is done.

[Bride and Groom take up the cup. The best man pours Champagne into each section, and they drink.]

They drink now as they will from life every day from this forward. They will share their experiences, their fortunes, the flavors of their lives. They will know that there is always another who will not take rest or sustenance until the other's is secure. These are the actions that will build a love to last a lifetime, a cup that will truly never run dry.

2.18j Fire Rituals

Fire has ancient symbolic value and meaning. It can stand for a cleansing and renewal, and also the warmth of the home or heart. A fire can represent a beacon of life, the signal each sends the other that marks his or her way home.

For obvious reasons, a fire ritual of any size can only be performed outdoors, and then only in a space where the owner or authority have given approval. Unless a fire pit has been installed, few venues will allow one to be created on their site. Many parks and beaches have very strict regulations to this effect.

If the practical obstacles to a fire ritual can be overcome, it can make terrific theater, and provide for some marvelous photographic moments in an outdoor setting.

Native American wedding traditions sometimes include fire rituals. Two fires, representing the individual lives of the couple, may be joined during the ceremony, sometimes to a third which symbolizes wider universal, or spiritual, concepts.

Symbolism, meaning, and theater may be added to the ritual through the choice of wood that is burned, or through the casting of particular objects into the flames as the ceremony is performed. Any object being burned should have a positive significance. The casting of incense or flowers into the flame can work well. The burning of effigies of former spouses should be avoided.

It is most important that any ritual is performed safely, and that every precaution is taken against accident. You should certainly practice what is to happen, and have a designated safety individual on hand, carrying appropriate equipment.

Example Fire Ritual Text

[Bride] and [Groom], along with their fathers and brothers, have created this fire pit today. It represents the light, warmth, and energy that we know they will always find at the heart of their marriage. The wood used was cut from a tree on the farm where the bride was born, and would play as a child. It grew alongside her, and now brings her light, warmth, and hope, on her wedding day. [Groom] and [Bride] will now stand each side and read their personal statements of vows to each other. They will then cast these words into the fire, so that they may be scattered to the winds, and spread the news of their love high into the air and across the world.

2.18k Flower Rituals

Flowers have long been associated with weddings, both as a symbol of love and in the traditions surrounding the bridal bouquet. Aside from their beauty, they can have great symbolic meaning in the context of a marriage ceremony. By virtue of having roots, and being inclined to grow, plants make excellent metaphors for the growth of a relationship and a family. Flowers are not only symbolic of fertility, but also represent the beauty of natural life. They represent a potential that flourishes in the light.

In less enlightened times, carrying flowers may also have been seen as a way to ward off evil spirits. They were also hugely effective in times when bathing was less frequent than it is today (thus they were used as 'nosegays')

An exchange of garlands is popular in both Hawaiian and Hindu culture. On the Hawaiian islands, the giving or exchange of leis often takes place near the beginning of the ceremony. In Hindu tradition, it is more usual for the bride and groom to offer each other garlands as gifts at a later point in the ceremony, perhaps as an accompaniment to the exchange of vows.

Exchanging flowers is also a great way to involve parents or children in a wedding ceremony. Whether they are the ones who carry or place garlands of flowers, or whether they come together with the couple to arrange flowers in a display, flowers make light, versatile props, and colorful adornment.

Particular species of flower have special meaning:

Calla Lilies	Great beauty
Hydrangeas	Vanity
Peonies	Bashfulness/shyness
Ranunculi	Dazzling charm
Roses	Beauty and love
Stephanotis	Marital happiness
Sweet peas	Lasting pleasure
Tulips	Consuming and lasting love

Example Flower Ritual Text
(Courtesy of Rev. Ann Fuller - brevardminister.com)

At this time, I would like to invite (Bride and Groom's) mothers, (Name) and (Name), to come forward to represent their respective families as we acknowledge these two previously separate circles of love are being united in a new and wider circle. The flower born of the tiniest of seeds symbolizes both the beauty and the potential of love that blooms and grows through time. It is born of a plant with roots that remind us of the families who nurtured (Bride and Groom) to become the one person in the world each holds most dear, families whose love and support is essential to the strength of this new union.

(Bride's Mother) has chosen a pink tulip symbolizing the mutual care and concern needed in a healthy marriage. (Groom's Mother) has chosen a pink rose symbolizing friendship because today (Bride and Groom) each marry their best friend. (Mother) and (Mother) please hand your flower to your child.

I am presenting (Bride and Groom) with Ivy to weave through their flowers symbolizing the fidelity you pledge to one another this day.

(Bride and Groom), I ask you to please place these flowers together in this vase representing your hopes for your marriage as you cultivate a union with strong, deep roots, taking pleasure in the effort that entails. Every time you see a flower, may it remind you of the joy you feel this day and your commitment to bring life and beauty to one another, now and forever.

2.18l Four Directions Rituals

With its origins in Native American culture, a ritual that recognizes the four directions is an excellent way to show reverence for the natural world during a ceremony. Traditionally, the four directions (North, South, East, West) are associated with the four 'classical elements' of earth, fire, air, and water.

When performing a ritual that recognizes the four points of the compasses, it is usual to start with the East, as this is associated with the sunrise and, therefore, the beginning of the day. One would then typically move clockwise through the other directions.

The Celebrant starts by explaining why the couple has chosen this ritual, and the importance of understanding your relationship to the world and the directions you have traveled, as well as knowing your path ahead. The couple would then be guided to turn in the appropriate direction for each stage, and a corresponding text read each time they have done so.

If you are looking to perform this ritual in a literal sense, it is wise to obtain a compass, or a smartphone application, that gives accurate directions.

Example Four Directions Ritual Text

As we travel through life, it is important to know which direction we travel, to understand our place in the world, and the path we follow.

Since ancient times, all peoples have recognized the meaning of the four great directions. They have each been celebrated and revered for the unique qualities and pace in our lives.

As [Bride] and [Groom] begin their new journey today, one they will walk together for the rest of their lives, they choose to recognize each direction, and so center and locate themselves within the universe in which they will create their new life.

I ask you both to turn now to the East [signify which way is East]. In the East we find the light of new beginnings, the hope within the darkness, the dawn of new ideas. In the morning of our lives, we start our journey. With each new sunset, let us know all things are possible.

I ask you to turn now clockwise towards the South. May you build a fire in your hearts that can never die, and may it keep you warm throughout even the longest of nights and the coldest of seasons. May the flame of your love always light the way through the darkness and remind each other to remember the dawn.

I ask you to turn now once again to face the West. With each sunset, may your thirsts be quenched, and may you celebrate the successes and triumphs you have made together. May you always welcome each other home, and be a shelter for each other from all storms.

Finally, I ask you to turn now towards the North. May you find grounding in your days, and sure footing on your daily journey. May the earth of your life and your labors together give fruit and treasures in abundance, and may the path beneath your feet be ever warmed by the sun.

Hold these directions in your heart, and steer a true course together in all things.

Please turn again now to face each other.

2.18m Four Elements Rituals

Adapted from a Yoruba (Nigerian) tradition, tasting the four elements is said to represent the promise to love your partner 'for better or worse, for richer or poorer, in sickness and health.' Vinegar, lemon, cayenne pepper, and honey are traditional choices used to represent the bitter, sour, hot, and sweet aspects of married life.

This ritual can make great theater, and can easily be adapted to suit the personal tastes and style of the couple. Possible substitutes might be:

Bitter	Coffee, bitter melon, beer, unsweetened cocoa, citrus peels.
Sour	Orange, grape, melon, wine and sour milk.
Hot	Garlic, curry, jalapeno, chili.
Sweet	Sugar, milk chocolate, strawberries, ice cream.

Example Four Elements Tasting Ritual Text

Please join me at the table.

[Bride] and [Groom], before you are four glasses, and four bowls. These represent the different flavors of life, the bitter, the sour, the hot, and the sweet. From now on, you will savor the sensations of life together. You have chosen to show this as part of your ceremony today so that you always have a reminder of things it is important to remember: that for each displeasure in life, there is always something wonderful elsewhere to be grateful for, and that every sensation, good or bad, is only fleeting. What matters most is that you experience all life has to offer with the one you love beside you.

Please now each take and taste from the first two glasses. These contain a very bitter coffee. Every life knows setback and dark times. As you drink now, think of those and please always to give each other love and support when these arise.

Please now each take and taste from the second two glasses. These contain a sour wine. Every life knows difficult choices and decisions. As you drink now, think of those and offer always to give each other guidance and patience when these arise.

Please now each take and taste from the first two bowls. These contain a hot and spicy pepper. As you taste it, think of the passions and excitements you will experience together. Promise always to share your thrilling moments, and relish them together.

Please now each take and taste from the last two bowls. These contain a delicious ice cream. As you eat, think of the pleasures and happiness that you will bring and share with each other. Promise always that you will find and give your greatest sweetness in the eyes and arms of the one you love.

Remember to savor every experience in your years to come, be it bitter, or sour, hot, or spicy, as all things are too soon passed away into memory, and never come again.

Join me again now in the center.

2.18n Glass Breaking Rituals

Although strongly associated with Jewish customs, the origins of the glass breaking ritual are somewhat of a mystery. Many associate it with the fall of Jerusalem, although it has a much happier meaning when used in the context of a wedding.

My text below outlines some possible meanings, and is useful in explaining to the guests what is about to take place, and preparing them to give a rousing cheer!

TIP: To achieve the best combination of easy breaking and satisfying crunch, instead of a glass wrap up an old style incandescent light bulb. These are often easier, and cheaper, than using a champagne flute.

Example of a Modern 'Mazel Tov' Ritual

One of the oldest and most traditional symbols of marriage is the breaking of the glass. It teaches us that, in times of joy, we must also realize life brings sadness and sorrow. The sound of the breaking glass is said to frighten away evil spirits, who might spoil this joyous occasion with their mischief. It also warns us that love, like glass, is fragile and must be protected. The promises made by the bride and groom, like the broken glass, are irrevocable. One interpretation of the custom is that even in the happiest times, we must remember there is still much suffering in the world, and it is our duty to reduce that suffering wherever we can. I would now ask [Glass Bearer], to place the glass for us.

For the bride and the groom, the shattering of this glass also symbolizes the breaking down of barriers between people of different cultures and faiths, as you are today.

On a lighter note, this is thought by some to be the last time the groom ever gets to put his foot down. As the groom breaks the glass, I invite everyone to shout, 'Mazel Tov' which means 'Congratulations and Good Luck!'

[Groom], whenever you are ready.

(Groom crushes the glass)

2.18o Knot Rituals

The ceremonial tying of knots is another addition to the wedding that has become popular and fashionable in recent years. It often features in fictional portrayals of historical or fantasy weddings in books, film, and television. Most knot rituals are performed later in the ceremony. The knot, in addition to the ring, is seen as a symbolic reinforcement of the vows the couple has just made.

Handfasting

In this ritual, a couple reaches for and joins their hands, sometimes one but usually both. A cord is loosely draped or tied around these, as either the Celebrant recites a few important words, or as the couple makes vows to each other. The combining of the cord binding with the vows gives additional theatrical impact to the promise making. It is important that any cord is removed before any rings are exchanged, in the event this is planned for after the tying.

There are also variations where one of the couple, usually the groom, ties a knot around the hand of the other. They may even take turns doing this. This is a hugely versatile ritual, and every couple should be encouraged to be as creative as possible in making it unique to their style and story.

What Makes a Good Handfasting Cord?

A handfasting cord is typically around six feet in length. This allows it to be looped twice over the wrists of a couple and still have enough length remaining to tie a loose knot. A cord can be made from light rope, wool, cloth, or embroidered material. It should be light enough to be easily manipulated, but have enough weight that it falls quickly into place when each loop is made. For lighter cord material, or as decoration, you may want to add beading at either end. This extra weight will make the knot hang well once it is tied.

Should the Knot be Untied?

It is often uncomfortable for a couple to recess while still tied together. For this reason, it can be nice to add a few lines about the knot being merely representative, and that the actual ties and bonds made in this ritual have now been made in the hearts and minds of the couple. This then makes it acceptable to gently remove the cord and leave the couple's hands fully free for whatever remains.

Fisherman's Knot

A Fisherman's Knot is a beautiful interpretation of this ceremony, and has seen a tremendous growth in popularity over the last couple of years. In this variation, the couple ties the knot themselves. Each takes a cord, often of similar material but of a different, symbolic, color, and they perform a tying that binds the two together. The best version for a wedding ceremony is the 'Double Fisherman's Knot'. Here is how it is tied:

1. Lay the ends of two lines parallel to each other.

2. Coil the free end of one rope twice around the second rope, and pass it back through the inside of the coils.

3. Repeat with second rope in opposite direction. Pull the free ends to tighten

the knots, then slide knots together.

Tying of the Braid

As with the other knot ritual variations, the tying of a braid represents the joining of lives. However, this version uses a third cord to complete the braid. This third cord can represent family, community, history, or perhaps a spiritual concept. Some Christians, for example, interpret this as representing a holy trinity.

Three cords are hung from a binding at one end. The couple takes turn in looping the outermost cord around the inner. Once the braid is formed, it is tied off at the bottom end. Such a finished braid can make a beautiful keepsake to display in the home.

TIP: If you need to put down your script, for a few moments to perform a handfasting or knot tying, it can be useful to have a music stand set just to the side for this purpose. This is more dignified than placing your book on the floor, or having to walk to a more distant ledge or table. Portable music stands are very easily and cheaply obtained online, and can be folded up quickly to add to your kit.

Image: Tying a Double Fisherman's Knot

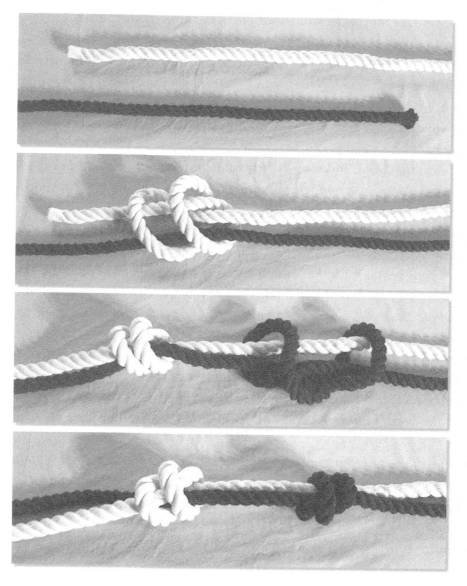

Example Handfasting Ritual

Will you please take each other's hands.

[Bride] and [Groom] have chosen to perform a handfasting in their wedding ceremony, to emphasize their eternal bond, and reinforce the feeling that they never wish to be parted from one another.

Handfasting is an ancient tradition, symbolizing the binding together of two people in love. This may indeed be the origin of the term 'tying the knot'.

This cord was created to represent the hopes, well wishes, and blessings of friends and family for [Groom] and [Bride] as they begin their union as husband and wife. It will bind them together with the strong bonds of love. With the creation of this knot, I tie all the desires and dreams, love and prayers, and happiness wished for you in your lives.

[Place cord on wrists] [Tie cord]

These are the hands of your best friend, young and strong and full of love for you, that are holding yours on your wedding day, as you promise to love each other today, tomorrow, and forever.

These are the hands that will work alongside yours, and together you will build your future. These are the hands that will love you passionately, and cherish you through all your years. With the gentlest touch, they will comfort you like no other.

These are the hands that will hold you when fear or grief fills your mind. These are the hands that will, countless times, wipe the tears from your eyes; tears of sorrow, and tears of joy.

These are the hands that will give you strength when it is needed. These are the hands that, even when wrinkled and aged, will still be reaching for yours, still giving you the same real tenderness with just a touch.

With this cord, I bind [Groom] and [Bride] to the vows they have made to each other.

The ties of your love are not formed by this cord, but by your vows. You hold in your hands and hearts the making or breaking of your lives. May your days and nights be filled with patience and dedication, forgiveness and respect, love and understanding.

[Remove cord]

2.18p Oathing Stone Rituals

During the reading and reciting of the wedding vows, a couple may choose to hold an Oathing Stone in their hands. It was traditionally believed that holding the stone at this time 'casts the words into the stone.' In modern variations, the stone might be engraved with the couple's initials, and possibly the date of the ceremony. The source of the stone, the minerals it contains, its color, or other characteristics may be chosen because they have a special significance for the couple, or the stone may be natural to the region the couple comes from. Although the type of stone is significant, the words spoken over it during the ceremony are of greater importance. As with all kinds of wedding vow, the more personal the oaths are to the couple the more meaningful and memorable they will be.

Before it is needed, the stone may be placed on a table to the side of the ceremony center. Alternatively, it might be carried into the ceremony by a 'stone bearer', perhaps a younger male relative acting in a similar role to that of one who carries rings.

After the wedding, the oathing stone can be kept in the couple's home, as an ornament or keepsake. Alternatively, in keeping with Celtic tradition, the couple may choose to 'release the stone back into nature' perhaps tossing it together into a river, or leaving it in a place of natural beauty, such as on a mountainside.

Example Oathing Stone Text

As [Bride] and [Groom] make their vows today, they have chosen to do so over a ceremonial oathing stone. This is a tradition that comes down to us from the Celtic lands, and the most ancient of times. Please bring forth the stone.

[The Best Man presents the stone laid on a ceremonial pillow.]

The stone today is made of granite. It too is strong and ancient. It has been carved with the names of these two who are now to make their eternal vows, and this date. Just as this is so, let the words they now speak forever be carved with great beauty into each of their hearts.

[Groom] and [Bride], please now each place your hand on the stone and repeat your vows as I instruct you.

[Exchange of vows]

[Bride] and [Groom] will now take this stone and give it a place of honor within their home. There let it stand, just as these words will stand, as a constant and real reminder of the strength of their commitment, and that their love will forever be a rock upon which they can rely.

2.18q Painting Rituals

A blank canvas represents a new beginning. During a painting ritual, the couple pours, or daubs, different colors onto the canvas. Doing so symbolizes the mingling of their ideas, expressions, and styles. This is an especially appropriate ceremony for couples with a strong artistic inclination or background. If a couple has children, or each brings children to the new family unit, this can be a fun way to include them. I have given a sample text (see below) where the painting is used to symbolize the uniting of two familiess.

For couples who wish a more recognizable pattern to their picture, an outline can be drawn on the canvas to be used as a guide. The choice of colors used is perhaps more important in this version than in any other unity ritual (see the notes on color at the start of this section).

Even with great care, this ritual can be extremely messy to perform, and is often best suited to an outdoor setting. A small bowl of water, and cloth to wipe any paint from the hands, can be useful to place alongside the ritual objects.

After the wedding has taken place, and the paint has dried, it can make a fun keepsake to hang in the home.

Example Painting Ritual Text

(Note: The couple each has two children from previous marriages)

I now ask the couple and the four children to join me either side of this table.
(We move across to the painting table)
Every marriage starts out as a blank canvas, and every day is a splash of color.
This blank canvas represents the day of the wedding, and a new beginning.
The paint colors in front of you signify the experiences that lie ahead; colors of joys and sorrows, blessings and heartache.
The two main colors represent [Bride]'s and [Groom]'s milestones, their celebrations, tribulations, passions, and dreams. They are the moments that become the days that make up the years.
Thinking of those moments to come, I ask both of you to take up your paint and apply it to the canvas. Don't be sparing. Be bold. Be fun. Never be afraid to

express yourself.

([Groom] and [Bride] apply their paint)

There will be places on the canvas where the colors blend and mix, flowing together, creating a new pattern of experiences shared. There will be places when the colors stay separate, and stand out alone and independent... yet, still a compliment to the other colors around.

Thank you!

I now ask each of the next generation to step forward and add your own distinct colors to this painting.

(The children begin taking turns adding paint)

You do this just as you will always add new shades, and shapes, and colors to the lives of [Groom] and [Bride]. There may be places of contrast. Parts of the canvas that look dark, or messy, and not at all to the couple's liking, While other spots remain blank and bare. However, when you step back, and look at the canvas in its entirety, you will see that it clearly is 'An Original Masterpiece' unlike anything you've ever seen before. Each color, contrast, shadow, blends as unique and beautiful as [Bride] and [Groom]. You will now take this painting and hang it in a place to view. Let it remind you always of the lives you all share, and the shapes and colors you will always add to each other's lives.

Now please join me again in the center.

2.18r Red String of Destiny Rituals

The tradition of the red string has its roots in Chinese legend. The story is told of a couple whose destinies were joined by a red string; However far they were apart over the years, they would always come together one day and be inseparable from then on. They were seen as soul mates. One tradition has red string tied around the little finger of each of the couple.

From a practical point of view, tying a couple together by their fingers limits their movement for the remainder of the ceremony, and this should be factored into any plans to incorporate this ritual into a wedding.

You will also note the similarity in theatrical impact to the handfasting, with a material used to bind the couple's extremities. You may wish to create a hybrid of these two types of ritual, especially if you have a couple where one is a Celtic descendant and the other Chinese.

In my example below, I have tried to create a ritual involving keepsakes, theater, and the symbolic notion that the couple is fated to be joined for all time.

Example Red String of Destiny Text

There is a legend, in ancient China, of two children bound by a mythological red string. It would start deep in each other's hearts and spread down through their hands. However far apart, that string would always exist between them, unfelt and unseen across the miles and years. It created a life-long joining, an unbreakable bond. It meant they were soul mates. Wherever life took them, it was their destiny one day to reunite, and then to be together for all time.

[Bride] and [Groom] have chosen to show this connection between them today by gifting each other a red bracelet. Red is not only the color of love but, in Eastern tradition, it is also the color of good fortune. Will the bearer step forward.

[Bearer steps forward with two red bracelets. They have clasps, and each a short cord with a charm attached]

[Bride] will you please take a bracelet and place it on [Groom]'s wrist.

[Groom] will you please take a bracelet and place it on [Bride]'s wrist.

The sharp-eyed will have noticed that each bracelet has a cord attached. This is the cord that spreads from their hearts. Wherever [Bride] and [Groom] travel, they will always have that connection, and it will always lead them home to each other. It is a bond that can never be broken. You will see, as I lift each cord and bring them closer together, that they have a natural attraction. Just like [Bride] and [Groom], they long always to be together.

[Move the two end charms closer together, where we discover they are magnetic and seemingly of their own will leap to be touching. They can, however, be separated, so that the couple has full freedom of movement for the remainder of the ceremony.]

[Bride] and [Groom] will keep these bracelets always, as reminders that this bond, of love, of luck, of two spirits, is always with them, and can never be broken.

2.18s Rose Giving Rituals

Roses have long been seen as symbols of love. A simple exchange ritual can be added to a ceremony, in which the couple offers the gift of a single rose. Where the couple wishes to publicly acknowledge their love for family members publicly, this giving can be extended as needed, as in the example text that follows.

Example Rose Giving Text

A great and constant symbol of love is the beauty of the red rose. Many poems have been written, and battles fought, under this image. It was the family emblem of the British King Henry the Eighth, who was, himself, rather fond of marriage, though not always successfully. In this case, however, we know that success is assured, and each has their head firmly on their shoulders as they make their vows today.

I now ask the Rose Bearer to step forward. You will notice that he carries not two, but four roses. This is because [Groom] and [Bride] have also chosen to honor two unique and wonderful women who, with boundless love and care, have made them the people they are today.

Will the groom's mother please step forward.

[Groom's mother steps up, and is presented with a rose by the couple, who also make a short statement, spoken by the bride.]

Will the bride's mother please step forward.

[Bride's mother steps up, and is presented with a rose by the couple, who also make a short statement, spoken by the groom.]

[Groom] please now take a rose and hand it to [Bride], and as you do so will you repeat these words after me.

[Groom gives repeated line vows]

[Bride] please now take a rose and hand it to [Groom], and as you do so will you repeat these words after me.

[Bride gives repeated line vows]

Please now place these together in the vase you see before you on the table. This has been inscribed with your names and this very special date. Place the vase in your home, and each year put two more roses within on this date, that your vows and your hearts will again be renewed with beauty anew.

2.18t Salt Rituals

In both performance and meaning, the salt ritual is similar to wedding rituals involving sand. Each of the couple holds a container of salt, and they take it in turns to pour a few grains onto the hands of the other, or directly into a larger container. This conveys the notion that the couple is joined until the day when one can separate their grains from those the other has offered. This is, of course, virtually impossible.

Indian Salt Rituals

Indian weddings often include a salt ceremony. It is carried out by the bride passing a handful of salt to her groom, during which she attempts not to spill any. He then passes this same amount of salt back to her with equal care. This is repeated three times. The exchange can be used to symbolize many important aspects of married life, as in the example text below.

Example Salt Ritual Text

Please now join me at the table.
You see before you a bowl containing pure salt.
In the most ancient wedding traditions, it was considered important for a couple to perform a public exchange of salt.
Salt has many qualities that reflect the essential qualities we hope for in this union, and throughout life. Salt preserves, without a need for coldness. Salt gives flavor to food that has none. Salt is carried in every sea, adding richness, and yet remains unseen. Salt is precious. We cannot live without a little consumed each day,

and yet it must be treated with care, never overused, or squandered.

I ask [Bride] now to take up a measure of salt in her hands, and place this carefully into [Groom]'s hands, trying not to spill a single grain. [Groom], I ask you then to repeat this exchange. Each does this three times. Take care with each grain of salt you pass, but if any is lost, let all our spills be forgiven. Let these simply remind us to cherish those precious grains that remain.

2.18u Sand Rituals

Sand rituals have become increasingly popular in recent years, especially for ceremonies that take place in coastal regions. Key to their popularity is that they are simple to perform, but very easy to adapt and personalize to the needs of a couple. The ritual can be extended to include family members, especially children. The colors, and types, of sand used can also be varied to provide extra symbolic meaning. Below are some common variations a couple might consider.

Three Vessels

In the most commonly used variation of this ritual, the bride and groom are each provided with a small container of sand. Each vessel is usually made of glass, or another transparent material. Taking turns, or perhaps together, they pour these sands together into a third vessel of greater size. The best visible results are achieved if each has a different color of sand, and these are poured in multiple layers, on top of each other, thus creating a sedimentary effect. The colors can be chosen for particular symbolic significance, or merely because they are those favored by each party.

Complete kits for these rituals are widely available online, and also in many larger craft stores.

The receiving vessel can make a beautiful ornamental keepsake, that can then be displayed in the couple's home.

Family Sand Ritual

By adding additional vessels, other participants can easily be introduced to a sand ritual. This can be a fun way to include children in the wedding ceremony. Where many parties are involved, it is best to have them stand in a circle around the receiving vessel, and each take turns pouring a small amount of their color, moving around the circle repeatedly until all the sand has been used. The resulting glass container will then give a beautiful multi-colored rainbow effect. Kits are available online which can provide for as many as six participants.

Where children are involved, it is important to ensure that all the containers are arranged on a table low enough to provide easy access for those still short in stature.

Beach Sand Ritual

On a beach, where sand is usually plentiful, a couple may choose to scoop handfuls of sand from around the other's feet, and then mingle these together in a large bowl. For a truly improvised sand ritual, where no prop or container is available, they may merely wish to let the sand trickle gently through the fingers of their partner.

Hourglass Ritual

An especially meaningful variation on the sand ritual is to pour the sands directly into an hourglass. This can then be sealed, kept, and perhaps turned on the couple's wedding anniversary.

Hometown Earth Ritual

If a couple wishes to acknowledge their individual histories and backgrounds, they may want to use earth, or sand, obtained from their place of birth or childhood. Where they do so, be sure to mention this in the text of the ritual, perhaps in conjunction with referencing their families, or the contribution of their parents to their life and happiness.

Example Sand Ritual Text   Couple Only

I would now like you both to join me at the table.

(We move to the table)

Today, [Bride] and [Groom] have chosen to represent their love for each other in a special sand ceremony.

[Bride], In front of you is a glass containing white sand. This represents purity, and a connection with the deepest essence of the universe.

[Groom], your glass holds blue sand. This is the color of communication, contentment, harmony, and self-expression.

You will note this third glass is empty. Glass, itself, is made from sand, and the sands of time have come together, melting into one piece to make this vessel.

The sands of time should remind us all of our eternal love and our mortality.

Please [Bride] and [Groom], take your separate glass of sand, and alternately pour into this vessel, and together repeat after me:

You are my love for eternity.

I blend with you.

My heart is like these grains of sand,

merging with yours.

I am yours.

You are mine.

We are together forever

like the sand, like the wind.

We are one.

Please join me again in the center, and take each other's hands.

Example Sand Ritual Text   Including Family

At this time, I would like to ask the groom's mother, and the bride's daughters, to join us at the table.

Marriage is a mingling of two lives, of two stories, of two families, of two futures. Just as the sands mingle, so new people enter our lives and our hearts. Our number becomes greater just as our families grow. It is truly fitting, as we stand here in this coastal location, that we symbolize this permanent union by the mingling of sand. Once mixed, the sands can never be separated. They become part of a new and greater whole, something fresh and unique, committed and joined for all time.

I would like to ask you to go around the circle of your family, each adding to the sand poured by the last, and creating something beautiful and new.

(Pouring of the sand)

You will now take this new creation of sand and place it in your home to always remind you of this hour, the vows and dreams that you share, and the very special and unique way that all your lives, your histories, and your futures are now joined in a truly beautiful way for all time.

Please join me again in the center.

2.18v Sandwich Making Rituals

A fun, and truly modern, ritual that can make for excellent theater, is to put on a show of food preparation. A simple way of doing this is for a couple to share the process of preparing a sandwich. Food preparation rituals might be particularly appropriate for a couple working in the catering industry, or whose first meeting took place in a restaurant, perhaps with one serving the other on that fateful day.

A recipe can easily be made to symbolize marriage. Each of the couple brings their ingredients to the mix, and uses their particular skills and experience to adapt them to fit the whole. Out of many items and qualities, they then create a synergy of tastes and flavors that becomes far more than the sum of its parts.

You may want to set up a table to the side of where the couple stands to make their vows, and arrange it so that both the couple will stand behind it, facing their assembled guests. At the appropriate moment, usually toward the end of the ceremony, and certainly after the vows, the Celebrant could instruct the couple to move to these positions to begin the ritual.

Although the Celebrant might like to say a few words about the symbols and significance of the ritual in general, a couple choosing this type of performance may be keen to explain their choice of recipe directly to the audience, and perhaps put on a little show by way of preparation. To add to the surprise and theater, they may want the ingredients kept out of sight until the last moment, and then brought on by either appointed 'food bearers', or by the venue waiting staff.

An especially nice touch can be if the couple invents a sandwich recipe and names it for the day. They may also like to have samples available for the guests to try after the ceremony.

It will be obvious that, far more than most rituals, sandwich theater requires a significant amount of rehearsal and preparation, and will only appeal to the few couples who are comfortable with a high level of public performance.

Example Sandwich Making Ritual Text

Love is food for our heart, and the very best meals come from unusual combinations of ingredients. Those who know [Bride] and [Groom] know that not only did they meet in a cafe, but that they love to have fun experimenting in the kitchen! Today they are going to perform something very special for us. We are going to get a private cookery demonstration, as [Groom] and [Bride] are going to demonstrate the making of a new sandwich for us. Please bring on the ingredients.

[Ingredients are brought on. Bride and Groom help each other on with aprons]

[Bride] and [Groom], over to you.

[Bride and Groom make their sandwich, having lots of fun and explaining their choice of fillings.]

If you think that sounds too delicious not to try at home, [Groom] and [Bride] have put the recipe on the back of your program today.

And now, the important moment of truth!

[Bride and Groom each take an enormous bite of the sandwich]

Delicious! Please quickly wash your hands, and then join me again in the center.

2.18w Seven Steps Rituals

Based in Hindu tradition, this ritual requires the bride and groom to circle a fire, or another symbolic object, seven times. Each revolution is used to focus on a single hope for the future. Where a fire is used, a couple may choose to throw rice, or tea leaves, into the flames to begin each step.

Example Seven Steps Ritual Text

At this time, we will celebrate and perform the seven vows of marriage. These seal the marriage bond with seven final steps. The bride and groom will make seven circles around this ceremonial fire. Holding hands, they take the seven steps symbolic of their shared journey through life. Before each new turn, I will speak one of the seven high hopes we have for their marriage. I ask you, [Bride] and [Groom], to hear and consider these seven wishes as you take these steps together.

1. May this couple be blessed with an abundance of resources and comforts, and be helpful to one another in all ways.
2. May this couple be strong and complement one another.
3. May this couple be blessed with prosperity and riches on all levels.
4. May this couple be eternally happy.
5. May this couple be blessed with a happy family life.
6. May this couple live in perfect harmony, and be true to their personal values, and their mutual promises.
7. May this couple always be the best of friends.

As you have walked the seven steps with each other, your love and friendship have become inseparable and sealed for all time. Your promises are witnessed by all those here. May they sound in your hearts each day of your lives.

2.18x Tea Rituals

Although often performed before, or after, the wedding ceremony itself, the couple may wish to perform a tea ceremony as part of their main event.

Taken from Chinese traditions, the offering of tea is meant as a symbolic and formal introduction of the bride and groom to one another's families, as well as a form of exchange.

Because this is one of the more complex unity rituals, it is perhaps most effective when performed at ceremonies with a smaller number of guests.

Where the grandparents are present, it is polite that they also are offered tea.

The family members are invited to sit in chairs while the newlyweds stand (or sometimes kneel) before them and serve the tea. It is served in a particular order, starting with the groom's parents, then proceeding from the oldest family members to the youngest. In return, the newlyweds may receive lucky red envelopes containing money, or other special gifts.

The bride and groom may choose to serve each other's families, as a form of formal introduction, or to serve their own, by way of offering thanks and gratitude.

If they wish to add a little British flavor to the ceremony, they may choose to offer biscuits (cookies) along with the tea.

Example Tea Ritual Text

There is an ancient Chinese tradition that a couple should offer tea, on the day of their wedding, to those they honor and cherish, by way of thanks for all they have received and learned.

I ask now that the parents of the bride and groom come forth and take their seats around this table.

[Bride] and [Groom] will now serve them tea.

We must never forget, as we move through the days and years of our lives, to keep gratitude in our hearts, and to act with dignity and respect to those who have given us so much. The family should be at the center of every home, and the simple tasks of each day should always be a reflection of the dignity and care with which we approach all things. These are the skills and lessons we, in turn, make it our pledge to pass on, so that the important values and lessons of our lives can never fade.

[Tea serving is finished]

Thank you. Please now return to your seats, and I ask [Bride] and [Groom] to join me again in the center.

2.18y Tile Breaking Rituals

The tradition of tile breaking originates in Asia, but is similar to the Jewish ritual of 'Mazel Tov', the breaking of a wrapped glass to conclude the marriage ceremony. The central concept, in both rituals, is that what is broken cannot be unbroken, just as the vows that are made during the ceremony cannot be unspoken.

It is wise to choose a tile made of a brittle substance, such as terracotta, and to make sure that it is wrapped securely. In some Asian traditions, the woman breaks the tile as a supposed aid to her fertility.

Example Tile Breaking Text

Finally, to symbolize what has taken place here today, I ask everyone here to witness one final ritual.

(Picks up Tile)

Here we have a red cloth, the traditional color of good fortune. With such tiles, we build our home and the roof over our heads. I will now place this before [Groom] and [Bride], and in a moment, I will ask them both to break this tile in front of us all. Once broken, this tile can never be unbroken. As this is so, your vows cannot be unsaid. What you do today must last forever. This is a beautiful moment, a shared new beginning, and one we all wish will bring you both a lifetime of joy, happiness, and prosperity.

(Places Tile)

Friends and Family, as they do so, I would ask you all to give a loud cheer that will resound from this moment into all the many years ahead. [Bride] and [Groom], will you please now seal this new beginning.

([Groom] and [Bride] crush the tile – everybody cheers)

2.18z Time Capsule Rituals

The wedding 'time capsule' is a beautiful idea, which has gained increased popularity in recent years. A box, or other sturdy container, is placed on a table in the ceremony space. Alongside it, the Celebrant arranges the items that the couple wishes to gift, or send, to their future selves. This might include copies of their vows, a bottle of wine, keepsakes, letters to each other, and sometimes letters to their future children or grandchildren.

At the appropriate time, usually following the vows, the couple places the items into the container and then seals it, perhaps with a padlock. They may have decided to seal it for a particular period, such as until their five year anniversary. Alternatively, they may have decided to keep it until a time of stress or hardship, when they might open it to remember, and regain, the positive energy and emotions of their wedding day. In such cases, it is sometimes referred to as a 'row box'.

A touching gesture can be to have an older relative complete the action of sealing the capsule. This adds another fond memory, that will also be revived when the box is opened.

Example Time Capsule Ritual Text

When we travel the days, months, and years of our lives, we gather moments and memories. These always remind us of the milestones we pass, why we have turned the corners and taken steps we have, and the joys and special moments we have shared along the way.

Today marks a very special passage and celebration and [Groom] and [Bride] have chosen to capture this moment in time and seal it together. In the future, they will reopen these memories, and share again the love and dreams they have for each other today.

I ask you both to step forward and consign the words to this chest, this capsule of time, just as you are fixing them in your hearts. In future years, you will sit together and break open these memories, and once again relive the joys and emotions you have shared here today. On that day, you will know again why time has given you so much together.

Please now seal the box and its treasures until that day in years to come when this moment returns to you again.

([Bride] and [Groom] seal the time capsule, and are invited to go back to their positions hand in hand)

2.18aa Tree Planting Rituals

A tree planting can be especially meaningful for couples who feel a particular bond with nature. It is also especially useful in symbolizing the uniting of two families, cultures, and histories.

A table is placed in the ceremony space, and on it are placed the following objects: a potted tree or sapling, two small containers of soil, two gardening trowels, and a small watering can. For extra meaning, the soil used could be acquired from the region native to each of the couple. Where family is given special reference, the couple might like the parents to step forward and place the earth around the sapling, and then jointly water the plant.

Where a particular species of tree is used, it is useful to say a few words about the meaning and significance of this, and the reasons it was chosen. In the sample below, I have used a Camellia.

This ritual, which involves soil and tools, does have the potential for mess. It can, therefore, be wise to have moist towels placed discretely, in case they are needed to wipe the hands before continuing with the ceremony.

Example Tree Planting Text

It is truly fitting that [Groom] and [Bride] have chosen to symbolize their union today by the planting of a tree.

Like our lives, each tree has roots that feed it life, and set the course it will grow. These are fed by the ground we are born on, and the people who tend our early years. When the place and people we are born to are strong, and our families give us food and love for our minds, our hearts, our bodies, and our spirits, we grow strong, resilient, and beautiful.

The tree planted today is a Camellia. For centuries, its flowers have been seen across the world as symbols of young love, new beginnings, and the deepest commitment between two hearts.

With each new season, and each new flower this tree creates, we hope the love [Bride] and [Groom] feel will find its roots deeper, filled with life and energy, and bound by the strength and beauty they give and find in each other.

At this time, I would like to ask the parents of the groom to step forward and place the Earth around this new tree, as they have nurtured [Groom] all the days of his life.

(Groom's parents step forward and add soil).

I would now ask [Bride]'s parents to step forward and add their soil, as they have nurtured her through her life to this day.

(Bride's parents step forward and add soil).

Thank you.

[Groom] and [Bride], will you please join me at the tree.

Love is the essence of human experience and emotion. It is the root of everything we, as humans, do. Love enriches our experience, and fills our lives with meaning. It gives us a firm base from which to grow, to learn, and to change. Let your relationship and your love for each other be like this tree you plant today. Let it grow tall and strong. Let it stand tall during the harsh winds, rains, and storms, and come through unscathed. Like a tree, your marriage must be resilient. It must weather the challenges of daily life, and the passage of time. Moreover, just like the tree you are planting, marriage requires constant nurturing and nourishment. [Bride] and [Groom], would you please water the sapling?

(Bride and Groom water the Camellia)

Remember to nourish each other, with words of encouragement, trust, and love. This is needed on a daily basis, so you each can grow and reach your fullest potential – just like this tree. The Bride and Groom will plant this tree in their backyard to always be a symbol of their love for each other.

[Groom] and [Bride], will you please now join me again at the center.

2.18ab Truce Bell Rituals

This ritual is a beautiful way to recognize, and celebrate, the realities of married life. During the wedding ceremony, the couple is presented with a small bell. They are instructed to ring it once together, and pay attention to the sound. They are then told to keep the bell close at hand in married life. Should a dispute occur, one partner can choose to ring the bell, and so call for a truce and reconciliation. That they rang the bell during their ceremony also enables them to recall the happy feelings of that day easily, at times when those memories are most needed. Other items, such as a whistle, horn, or gong, could be used in place of a bell.

The couple may like to appoint a junior member of the family to carry the bell into the ceremony during the processional. Such a 'bell page', or 'bell maiden', could then be asked to step forward at the appropriate time.

Example Truce Bell Text

[Bride] and [Groom] have a realistic understanding of married life. They express this today by creating a bell of truce. Bells have long been associated with weddings, as their sounds call to mind good tidings and great news.

Would the Bell Page please step forward, and hand the bell to [Bride] and GROOM], and will you hold it together.

I now ask you to give the bell a hardy ring. As you do so, let the sound fix itself forever to the love you feel in your heart today.

(They ring the bell)

[Bride] and [Groom], keep this bell in your home to remind you of your wedding day. When arguments arise, put this signal to use. One of you should ring the bell to call a truce. The sound will remind you of your wedding vows, conjure up the happiest memories from this day, and help you resolve your differences with love, compassion, and understanding.

2.18ac Volcano Rituals

Although I have yet to find a couple willing to perform this ritual, I hope I will get to see a Volcano ritual at first hand before I retire. The concept of this ritual echoes the school science fairs many American children participate in, and will particularly appeal to those of a proudly nerd-like attitude.

Before the ceremony, a couple crafts a model volcano. Several chemical reactions produce a 'volcanic' effect:

1. Combining baking soda and vinegar.

Although the least dangerous of the possible methods, the reaction is small, and, therefore, may make disappointing theater for all but the smallest number of guests.

2. Combining liquid nitrogen and water.

This creates an impressive explosion but requires that everyone stand quite a distance away. The mess created is also extreme. For a dignified occasion, where you would like guests seated close to where the action takes place, this is not at all practical.

3. Combining yeast mixture with hydrogen peroxide.

This is perhaps the best level of reaction for a ceremony, and the 'lava' can be colored with food coloring to match the scheme of the wedding.

For full instructions, see the following link:

http://www.wikihow.com/Make-a-Volcano

If you are involved in creating a ritual of this kind, please do email me and let me know, so I can send special congratulations. Be sure to get plenty of pictures for your website or blog.

In every case, proper safety precautions should be observed, and gloves and goggles provided for all participants.

It should be obvious that this ritual is perhaps best performed at an outdoor venue, as many clubs, ballrooms, and chapels will undoubtedly have significant concerns about the mess.

This ritual makes excellent theater, and could also be a fun way to involve children in both preparing for and performing the wedding ceremony.

Example Volcano Ritual Text

[Bride] and [Groom] have a very special treat in store for us today, and to give them a truly explosive start into married life. In the spirit of science, they have created this model volcano. In a few moments, they will begin a reaction, and we will witness our own wedding eruption. Our first feelings of love and many moments of married life can feel volcanic in many ways. Like the mixing of these chemicals, two seemingly harmless substances can come together to create a reaction that astonishes the world.

I now invite [Groom] and [Bride] to put on their safety goggles, and show us all what happens when they bring everything together. I invite everyone here to gasp, applaud, and enjoy the show!

[Bride and Groom set off the volcano!]

Let these memories always remind us to have a little fun together every day, and never let life become boring. May their love always be, in the very best of ways, volcanic in its passion, and exciting to behold.

2.18ad Water Rituals

This is performed much like a liquid sand ritual. Two containers of water, typically of different colors, are poured together into a third container to create a new blend or mixture. The colors chosen may reflect a particular meaning (see the notes on color meaning at the start of this section). For couples interested in science or illusion, they may wish to use special chemicals that transform the liquid in unexpected ways, such as turning a darker liquid clear. Doing so could make for terrific theater, and should elicit gasps, and applause, from the guests.

An entirely different ritual concept involves each couple sprinkling water over the hands of the other. This represents a clean start in life, as well as symbolizing trust and support. In one variation of this, the sprinkling may be performed by parents or grandparents, representing the flow of life between the generations.

In all ceremonies involving liquids, there is a danger of spillage, so it is wise to have towels placed discretely near the ritual area in case these are needed.

Example Water Ritual Text

Water is the symbol of life. We need it each day to survive. It is the blood that feeds our world, but also washes away the dust of the past. It is soft and gentle to the touch, and yet with time can carve great valleys in even the strongest stone.

Please bring forward the bowl.

As they speak the words of their bonding today, they will each sprinkle and cleanse the hands of the other. In this way, they offer each other life renewed, and demonstrate to all the world this beautiful new beginning.

[Groom], will you please now dip your hands into the bowl, and wash the hands of your beloved as you repeat these words after me.

[Groom repeats vows]

[Bride], will you please now dip your hands into the bowl, and wash the hands of your beloved as you repeat these words after me.

[Bride repeats vows]

2.18ae Wine Rituals

Wine has often been used for toasting and celebration. It may have a particular significance for the couple, as they may have a variety they shared early on in their relationship, or they may have a wine collection. For couples from different locations, they may wish to select wine from their country or region. Wine, and the grapes from which it originates, often has a strong and well-recorded history. As such, the use of this ritual reflects the rich and subtle backgrounds and natures each brings to the marriage.

Although this is often performed as an exchange, a couple may alternatively choose to drink from the same cup. Such an item is often referred to as a loving cup, and typically has two handles.

In some cases, it can be best for the Celebrant to pour the wine for the couple, as the experienced Officiant may have the steadiest hand.

It is, of course, possible to perform this ceremony with beer, though I would suggest using a rare and expensive type, and only doing this if it has a very special significance to the couple. The ceremony could also be performed with a non-alcoholic beverage, or even perhaps with small glasses of spirits.

In some instances, this ritual may be performed with the addition of chocolates. The idea, which can be explained to the guests, is that these represent both the sour and the sweet aspects of married life. In celebrating all favors, the couple is demonstrating to the world that they will stand beside each other whatever the future may bring.

It should be noted that bottles and glasses are easily knocked over, and care should be taken to ensure they are placed firmly. This is particularly true of outdoor ceremonies, where a strong gust of wind is quite capable of knocking over a wine bottle.

For red wines, you should uncork the bottle in advance of the ceremony to allow the wine to breathe, and thus have the flavor at its peak for the ritual. For white wine, particularly if the ceremony will take place in a warm setting, you may like to place the bottles in ice to maintain an ideal temperature.

Example Wine Ritual Text

At this time, I would like to ask you both to join me at the table.

(Officiant and couple move to wine table)

In front of you, you will see two carafes containing wine you have selected for each other. Like these wines, you have each been shaped by the family you came from, and the land you grew on. You have each grown and developed your own unique and wonderful qualities.

Each wine matures until it is ready to share. It waits patiently until that perfect moment when it is finally right to be savored and shared. So it is with each of us.

For you both today, we celebrate those unique journeys, and that the time of sharing has finally arrived.

I ask you each now to pour a glass for the other and present it to them to toast what has come before, and what is about to begin.

([Bride] and [Groom] pour a glass and hand it to each other)

As with these wines you give to each other, so you savor the wonderful flavors and qualities you find and discover. The best in life passes all too quickly. It is right that we acknowledge each moment, and truly appreciate the pleasure it brings. I ask you both, as you sip of this wine, to appreciate the qualities you see in the other, and that they give to you today.

Now will you please join me again in the center.

Example Combined Wine and Chocolate Ritual

There will come in your life days of great sweetness, and days of bitter sorrow. There will be celebrations, just as there will be tears. There will be triumphs, just as there will be tragedies. Life holds an adventure of happiness in store for you both. And so to symbolize embracing this reality, today you will share both the bitter and the sweet, just as you will share them in the many years to come.

Please start by both taking a drink of this bitter red wine.

(Bride and groom drink)

Taste in it the darker moments that will rock your marriage, and test the strength of your love. Know that these hard times will come, and with them, the opportunity to deepen your bond as husband and wife.

Now, take and eat a piece of this sweet chocolate.

(Bride and groom eat)

Taste in it the sweetness and light that will make your married life filled with joy. Savor it, just as you will savor every happiness that you bring each other. Delight in it, as you will delight in one another all the days of your lives.

2.19 A Moment of Prayer or Contemplation

Although the focus of this book is on less religious ceremonies, some couples may wish to offer a time for their more religious relatives and friends to contemplate the service in their own way.

It is important with this, as with any spiritual or religious addition to the ceremony, that you are comfortable with your part in its performance. It is also crucial that any addition does not disrupt or distort the message and meaning of the ceremony.

Where a couple requests such an addition, take the time to listen to their reasons for doing so. I have often found that couples are under pressure from relatives to make their ceremony more religious than they would prefer. In such cases, they may be looking to you for validation that their own wishes for a less religious occasion are acceptable. Seek to understand what needs they are looking to serve by adding this element, and then to offer the solution that will bring them the most happiness on the day.

Where you are asked to include these types of religious moment, it is vital that they be made as inclusive as possible. A wedding gathering of any significant size will undoubtedly include individuals from all parts of the religious spectrum. Although it is sadly too often true that those with conservative religious positions believe theirs should be exclusive and exclusionary, such a negative ideology conflicts hugely with the spirit of modern weddings, which should be about love, generosity, and welcoming at their core.

It is wise to use the most general wording possible when suggesting a moment of silent contemplation. Make it clear to those assembled that they are sincerely invited to use such a time in their own way, or not at all. In the language you use, always remain positive, focused on the core values of love, hope, and commitment. Under no circumstances should you reference negative religious concepts, such as sin or damnation.

Once you have made the brief explanation and invitation, allow a short moment of silence before firmly resuming the ceremony. A good length of silence is around fifteen seconds. You may wish to practice counting this out silently before they day. It is important to give a clear signal, at the end of the silence, that the ceremony will now resume. This is especially useful for those who have chosen to lower their heads or close their eyes. A simple 'thank you' is often quite sufficient.

It may be that a couple chooses the text of a prayer they wish read during this section. It is important that you be comfortable reading this, if you are asked to do so. If you find that the text of such an addition is in conflict with your own spiritual position to the extent that you would rather not present it, you may wish to request that a friend or family member step forward to lead this part of the ceremony.

These moments and questions demonstrate why it is important to be honest with every couple from the start about your own position, and the types of ceremony you are willing to perform. You have every right to the position you hold, as long as you do not seek to restrict the rights and opinions of others, and any reasonable couple should admire and respect your honesty on these issues.

The two most important guides in helping you craft this part of the ceremony should always be first, the wishes of the couple; and second, your own position, honesty, and integrity.

Example Modern Invitation to Contemplation

'At this time, [Bride] and [Groom] would like to invite you to take a few moments to pause and give your own thoughts on what we are sharing and witnessing today. I encourage you all to think about the love you share each day in your own lives, the commitments you have made, and the examples you set for those close to you. A wonderful day of celebration such as this should remind us all to celebrate each day the people we cherish, to be grateful for all we have, and to face each sunrise with a hope renewed. Please now take a short moment of silence.'

2.20 Understanding and Responding to Spiritual Differences

It is exceedingly rare for any Celebrant to preside at a ceremony where all those attending are of the same spiritual or theological position. More commonly, there will be an array of religious viewpoints, and some attending may be devout in their supernatural beliefs.

It is important to understand, and be confident in, your own spirituality. Just as important is respect for the rights of others to their beliefs. You will find that, if you always act according to humanistic values of empathy, positivity, love, and respect for life, believers of all types should find the words and ideas you offer meaningful and fulfilling.

The sentiments expressed in every ceremony you oversee should be positive, without exception. If you strive to make every wedding resonate with the love of the couple, even the hardest heart should find they warm to the day, rather than becoming angry because their faith positions were not fully referenced or elevated.

You may often find you are asked to mediate a compromise between family members, and sometimes the couple themselves, as to the spiritual content and direction of the ceremony. Just as often, you will encounter couples who have been conditioned to expect a high degree of religiosity in every wedding, but are looking for validation that it is acceptable to break free of those traditions. In a modern ceremony, the wishes of the couple always take precedence over tradition, and it is wonderful to watch a couple smile as you explain this. They should not have to include a single word or gesture in their ceremony that is in conflict with their beliefs or positions.

When I am asked to include spiritual elements in a wedding ceremony, it is very often to recognize, and respect, the religious beliefs of older relatives. Although it is admirable for any couple to show such consideration for their family, I have found that it is always best to build a ceremony closer to the outlook, and viewpoint, of the couple. A loving parent should understand, respect, and appreciate this. Where there is a difference of opinion, your role is to listen to the needs of each party, and try to often the simplest, most inclusive solution available. You are the guide and facilitator, offering the couple and their family your knowledge and experience. Ultimately, however, the final decision of what to include should always be theirs.

2.21 Understanding your Legal Obligations

In addition to performing the ceremony, it is vital that you understand your legal obligations as the wedding Celebrant. An important part of this role is guiding the couple through the process of obtaining their marriage license, ensuring this is filled out correctly, and that it is returned as stipulated by the relevant authority.

In the United States, marriage licenses and registrations are administered by government officers, such as City Clerks or Registers of Deeds, who are either elected or appointed. They are almost always helpful and willing to provide guidance, and most have informative websites.

Before you begin practicing as a wedding Officiant, you should make yourself completely familiar with the licensing process for each region that you intend to serve. You should be aware of which documents should be filed in areas where you are required to register. You should know which documents a couple will be asked to present, how much a license will cost, any waiting period between application and receiving a license, and how each document must be completed and returned. In many locations, it is the legal responsibility of the Officiant to ensure the documents are returned to the government offices within a stipulated time frame. Failure to comply could leave you facing a prosecution and subsequent fine, as well as losing your Celebrant business.

Later in this book, you will find outlines of the current rules and practices for each U.S. State, and you should read these through carefully. You should also make a habit of monitoring local marriage laws, and the prices for a couple to obtain their license, as these often change from year to year.

TIP: It can be more efficient to obtain witness signatures before the ceremony. At that time, there are often a few minutes of waiting time that can easily be utilized. Following the ceremony, a wedding party is often far more busy with photography and celebrations, and this can make it harder to find a moment with the necessary individuals. From a legal point of view, in the U.S., it makes no difference whether the witness signatures are obtained before or after the ceremony. However, the couple may have a preference, and they may also wish their photographer to record the signing. You should check on both these things before the day.

In some regions, you are required to keep records of each marriage you perform. You may wish to purchase a record book, in which you note the date, location, and couple's names for each ceremony you perform. You may also want to take a photocopy of the completed license before you return it to the local government office. This is useful in case the originals are misplaced, or you need a complete reference of what was submitted.

2.22 Wedding Cancellations

On rare occasions, a wedding booking may be canceled before the date of the ceremony. From a business perspective, this is the main reason for taking a deposit. Doing so offers you, at least, partial compensation for other work you may have turned down, and for the planning you have already put in working with the couple. All wedding professionals should follow this practice, and all deposits should be non-refundable where the cancellation is initiated by the client.

The breakdown of an engagement, and the subsequent reversal of wedding plans, is a painful and emotional time. You may be placed under pressure to make a 'special case', and return a deposit despite your policy and the terms of your contract. I strongly advise you not to do this, as it would be unprofessional, and damaging to your reputation and confidence. The correct response is to express your condolences, and only offer advice on matters relating to the ceremony.

When informed of a cancelation, you should act with kindness and sympathy, but a Celebrant should not try to act as a mediator for a couple. Unless you are a qualified relationship counselor, you absolutely must not offer such advice or services. Even if you have such counseling qualifications, you should not act in that role unless it is specifically requested. It is important to maintain a clear and firm line between your professional and personal lives, and also between your job as a Celebrant and any other professional capacities you may have.

On some occasions, I have found it useful to hold a canceled booking as 'provisional' on my books for a week following the first notification that the wedding has been called off. It is not unknown for a couple to have merely hit a 'rough moment', and to quickly come to you again with the news that all is now well, and the wedding plans are back on track. It such a situation it can feel harsh to charge a second booking fee. Ultimately, however, you must set your own policy for such situations, and make this clear in every case. When you act according to the rules you have set yourself, you will feel positive and confident about your actions, and will find you are respected as a professional.

If you act with empathy, kindness, and professionalism, you will manage to find the best outcome in even the most difficult and emotionally challenging situations you encounter. Most importantly, never put your reputation at risk by placing yourself in a compromising situation with a client or a couple.

2.23 Pre−marital Education

In many churches, it is normal for a couple to undergo a short pre-marital education course. If you are qualified, and you decide it makes sound business sense, you may choose to offer such services. You could do so as part of your Celebrant packages, or as regular stand-alone sessions for small groups of couples.

It is critical to understand that such services are different from marital and relationship counseling. You are offering only to provide education and guidance on a set of life skills, rather than resolve relationship issues through therapy.

To obtain information and resources for marriage educators visit the website of the National Healthy Marriage Resource Center (www.healthymarriageinfo.org)

2.24 Producing Your Draft Ceremony

You should produce your ceremony draft electronically using word processing software of some kind. Later in this book, I recommend different software you might consider for all areas of your Celebrant business.

Note: A few Celebrants prefer to work from cue cards, rather than a ceremony that is written word for word. If they can do so successfully, they have my admiration, but I have never been brave enough to extemporize in that manner, even though improvising, when faced with the unexpected, is very much an important Celebrant skill. For this section, I am assuming that you wish to type up a draft, which you will also send to the couple for review.

It is important that your ceremony draft has all the information needed clearly stated, and be designed for maximum readability. Each page should contain, in its heading, the name of the client, the date, time, and location of the ceremony, and the page number. This information ensures that no ceremony will be accidentally mixed with another, and that the pages will not become muddled. Each section of the ceremony should be clearly titled, along with information about who is to speak the lines in that part. Where you need to place instructions for movement or action, as in the case of a unity ritual, you should make sure that these are clearly differentiated, perhaps with the use of italics. The next page shows an example page from a fictional ceremony, as an example of the layout you might consider.

Celebrant - Words of Explanation

Laying out your script is about making your performance as easy as possible. A clear font is important. This is Arial, but Tahoma, Garamond, or even Times New Roman might work just as well.

The directions for this document are written in Courier New.
By keeping your typeface large, you can hold the pages further from your face, which looks better in photographs.

Adding extra line breaks is a great way to add simple reminders on where to best pause to give a natural voice.

Varying your <u>tone</u> as you read is **important**.

You may want to put emphasized words in **bold type** or perhaps <u>underline</u> them. If it is the punch line to a joke, you may wish to do <u>**both**</u>.

I would now like to ask Sid James, the Uncle of the Bride, to read to us the lyrics of "*Four Thirty-Three*", by John Cage.

Sid James (Uncle) - First Reading

I differentiate words that others are reading by making them a lighter shade, but it is useful to have them in your script, so you can follow along, and know where they end. *I also italicize quoted text, to remind me to vary my tone from normal speech.*

Celebrant - Closing Words

Thank you.

For hard to pronounce words or names, such as St. John (sin-jin), you may want to put a phonetic spelling in brackets. If you have templates, mark [BRIDE] or [GROOM] with square brackets for easy replacement. Experiment with ways of making your scripts easier.

2.25 Your Celebrant Wedding Kit

As you start to work professionally, you should begin to create a Celebrant 'kit'. This is a collection of items and tools that you carry with you to events. The size and scope of your kit is entirely a matter of personal choice. Some Celebrants prefer to travel with just the essentials, while others maintain a suitcase filled with items to cover almost any problem or situation. Below is a list of items you might consider, with the more essential items starred for reference.

Items to include in your Celebrant Kit

Notebook	Pens (x3)
Receipt Book	Tissues (Kleenex)
E-card reader (for payments)	Business Cards (x25)
A Copy of your Ordination Certificate	Blank Questionnaires
Blank Contracts	Breath Mints
Duct Tape	Small, foldaway music stand.
Portable Sewing Kit	Trash Bags
Zip Lock Bags	Lighter
Glue	Scissors
Comb	Lint Roller
Generic Handfasting Cord	Generic Sand Ceremony Kit
Blank Commemorative Certificates	Parking Change
Bug Spray	Emergency Tire Inflater Can
First Aid Kit	This Handbook (of course!)

2.26 Getting Paid for your Services

Perhaps the least romantic part of your professional Celebrant life is the act of receiving payment. Asking a couple for a check immediately before or after a ceremony is often an uncomfortable experience for all concerned. It is much better to ensure that all outstanding payments are made before the wedding day, and to have this stipulation clearly stated in your business contract.

Many couples will also prefer to have the financial aspects covered before the day of the ceremony, perhaps for budgeting reasons, but also, because it is one less thing to distract them from enjoying the occasion. For every wedding professional, knowing that payment has been taken care of leaves us free to give our complete concentration to the job in hand the whole time we are on site.

It is a good practice to offer your clients as many payment methods as possible. In addition to cash and check, for which you may want to keep a receipt book handy, you may also wish to put a payment link on your website. Services such as PayPal (paypal.com) offer a solution where they take a small percentage of each payment as their processing fee. Other services, such as Authorize.net (authorize.net), will have payment functions that easily integrate fully into a website. You may also wish to ask your bank if they have an online business payment solution, as many offer this, and the rates can be better than going directly to third party payment services.

Services such as Square (square.com) and PayPal also provide small card readers that plug into a smartphone and allow you to take swipe payments through an associated phone application.

When using any service to process your payments, you should always be careful to factor in the cost to your business budget. Although the percentage you pay per transaction may be small, it will make an impact on your profit margin for every job where the service is used.

Receiving a Tip

In addition to the contracted payment, a Celebrant may also receive a gratuity, and this is always a welcome bonus. Tipping practices and customs vary regionally, and personal generosity will also vary between couples. The best practice is never to expect a tip, but treat it as a happy, unexpected addition to your day. Even the smallest gratuity should be received with warm thanks and appreciation, and you should never express dissatisfaction if a tip is not forthcoming.

When received, you should, in all cases, record your tips as additional income for tax purposes. You will notice all wedding vendors follow this practice without exception, as to not do so is an unthinkable breach of conduct. You will also observe that wedding professionals never employ sarcasm in their written language.

TIP: Always make a point, where possible, to say thank you and farewell to the parents of the couple, just before you leave. These are often the most likely participants to offer a tip, and this is most probable time for them to do so. If you skip on this because you are in a hurry to exit, you could be missing out on a tidy bonus!

2.27 Children and Wedding Ceremonies

Many couples, particularly those who already have children, or who are close to their nieces or nephews, may be eager to include these young ones in the ceremony. This can make for some of the most heartwarming, and beautiful, moments you will witness in your time celebrating weddings. However, it is of vital importance to be fully aware of the limitations inherent in the younger age groups. Particularly below the age of five, children can find the events of a ceremony confusing, and perhaps even frightening.

2.27a Children as Wedding Participants

Where a young child is given a role in the procession, there are a few precautions that can help ensure success. If it is possible for the child to walk with an older sibling or family member, this can be a great help in guiding them in their role, as well as giving them confidence when the gaze of a large group is upon them. If the child must walk or perform the task alone, it is wise to have an appointed 'child wrangler' sat with easy access to the place the child will be walking or standing. For such an adult, that should ideally be their only task; knowing that they are appointed to act immediately if the child becomes confused or distressed. Parents and grandparents always make the best choice for these roles.

2.27b Children as Wedding Guests

Very young children sometimes present more challenges as guests than as participants. Wedding venues, and the emotion of ceremonies, can be unsettling for children under three years of age. They are not yet old enough to understand the significance of the day, or the etiquette involved in the events taking place around them. Most Celebrants have seen ceremonies disrupted, and occasionally ruined, by the continuous screams and shouts of a child or baby. Where children are invited to attend a wedding ceremony, it is wise to request that they are seated near the rear of the guests, or on an aisle seat. Parents can be politely instructed to remove the child to a different part of the venue, out of earshot, if they become in any way disruptive. Any reasonable parent will understand this request if it is phrased respectfully, and they should be happy to comply promptly if the need arises. If the still decide to remain in place, and the disruption continues, it is perfectly acceptable to pause the ceremony, and again politely request that the problem is addressed, and the couple's right to have their ceremony in peace is respected. Children are wonderful in many ways, but their presence should never be allowed to impede or harm the experience for which the couple has long planned and hoped.

There is an increasing trend among couples toward 'adult only weddings', at which children are specifically prohibited. A wedding day is a highly emotionally charged environment, often involving adult intoxication, loud noises, bright lights, and late hours. As such they are often inappropriate occasions for very young children.

TIP: If any small children are expected to attend, encourage the couple to consider hiring a babysitter for the hour around the ceremony. Many venues, even private houses, have a room that could be allocated for a professional to watch the younger children. A qualified babysitter, with certification, can be hired for a small fee, and could save the derailing of a ceremony. Alternatively, the couple may have a younger relative or friend who would is happy to skip the ceremony and serve in this role, perhaps in exchange for payment or a small gift.

2.28 Adapting to the Wedding Venue

The venue, or location, of any ceremony is often a deciding factor in many structural plans for the ceremony. Obviously, the distance you have to travel to and from any location will affect the amount of time you have to set aside for that booking, and your subsequent availability for the rest of that day. There are some other factors about the venue that will affect your plans. Although a couple, along with their event planner if one is hired, should consider these issues, you will likely be consulted about them on a regular basis, and you should be aware of the potential problems, and best practices and strategies to avoid them.

Outdoor vs. Indoor

An important factor in your plans will be whether a wedding is planned to take place outdoors or indoors. Increasingly, couples are seeking to plan their ceremonies outside, on beaches, in parks, and in private gardens. Outdoor venues present some additional factors for you, and your clients, to consider. In case of bad weather, all outdoor ceremonies should have a backup plan. Rain can fall even in the warmest of climates, and weddings are usually planned much too far in advance to offer any certainty of a dry day. A couple may wish to plan to have a tent available to protect guests or an alternate ceremony location that can be used at relatively short notice.

Another important factor for outdoor venues is the lighting. Many couples will want to plan their ceremony so that they have plenty of time for pictures in good light. In warmer climates, there is often a 'sweet spot' between the part of the day where it is too hot for guests to gather for any length of time and too dark for pictures. There are now many free applications available for phones that can give you exact times for sunrise and sunset many years in advance, and this knowledge can be very useful in the early stages of planning a wedding. If planning a ceremony when the sun is low in the sky, it is important to consider if it will be directly in the line of sight for the bride or groom. If this is likely, you may want to adjust the angle you stand at, so that the light is at a more comfortable position.

Outdoor venues also offer many different types of terrain, and these can present their own challenges. For ceremonies on soft, natural ground, such as sand or grass, you will need to choose footwear that is both practical and smart. Where there is uneven or soft terrain, elderly or infirm guests may have great difficulty reaching the ceremony site. For beach terrain, you may need to consider the tide, and how it will affect the exact position you want to perform the ceremony.

With both indoor and outdoor venues, you will need to understand the restrictions concerning the number of people a venue can comfortably accommodate. Tightly packing a large number into a small garden can be as discomforting for the participants as holding a ceremony in a large ballroom with just a handful of guests in attendance.

Ambient Noise

The noise from events taking place around a ceremony venue can have an enormous impact on the mood and success of the occasion. For city venues, the background sound from traffic and passersby can be surprisingly loud, and you may find you need to pause the ceremony briefly if a loud motorcycle or aircraft passes. On a beach, you will likely be competing with the sound of waves. I was not fully aware of how noisy an ocean can be until I performed my first beach wedding.

Where necessary, you may wish to stop and briefly make light of any intrusive noise, and in doing so put a nervous wedding party and guests at their ease. In rare cases, where an unexpected external noise is hugely disruptive, you may need to find an efficient way to manage it. I performed a recent ceremony outside a hotel, and quickly became aware that the maid service, going about their daily rounds, was chatting so loudly that it was disturbing the guests across an entire courtyard. Fortunately, the DJ was able to leave his post long enough to go and speak to them about the problem, and they were soon quieted. Perhaps the strangest example of this from my experience comes from a ceremony I performed next to a large pond. Shortly after the ceremony began, a number of toads began calling in very deep and rather humorous tones. Toads, of course, will not respond to polite requests for silence, so I stopped, and made a short improvised joke about nature expressing its loud approval of the wedding match. The intrusion acknowledged, we were all able to continue in greater comfort.

Public vs. Private

Many outdoor venues are located in public spaces, such as parks and on beaches. Most people, noticing that a wedding is taking place, will be very polite and respectful of the needs of the occasion. However, there may be occasions when passers-by become spectators. On very rare occasions a stranger may try to insert themselves into the proceedings. As a senior professional present, you may find the wedding party looking to you to take charge and manage the situation. In such circumstances, you should look to handle the situation as calmly, carefully, and quickly as possible. Your first concern, after the safety of those attending, is to minimize any disruption to the ceremony plans. You will almost always find park and law enforcement authorities very supportive of your case if called upon, especially if you have a permit for use of any public facility.

Layout

Although many established wedding venues are laid out in a simple way that fits the needs of ceremonies, this is less often the case with parks, houses, gardens, or beaches. You may have to adjust the procession and recession plans to allow for longer entrances and exits. You may also have to be more creative in how you prevent a bride and groom from seeing each other before the ceremony, if this is a tradition the couple has chosen to adopt.

Another frequent issue with adapted venues is sight lines. There may be barriers, such as walls, trees, or pillars, which prevent a view of the ceremony from certain vantage points. Quite often this can prevent musicians from being able to take their cues directly from watching entrances and exits, and they may become entirely reliant on your signals for when to start, change, or stop, a musical selection.

Rehearsal Availability

With popular or distant venues, the ceremony space may not be available for a rehearsal the day before the wedding. You may find you need to choose an alternate, improvised space, and use markers to stand in for any important landmarks, such as doors or seating layout. Where you encounter such a situation, try to view the location before the rehearsal, either from a visit, or pictures available online, and choose a surrogate location as close to it as possible in size and design.

Staffing

Many venues, especially those used regularly for ceremonies, will have dedicated staffing. They can be hugely helpful in helping you adapt a space for your needs, and are often happy to help with processional cues if asked. These individuals will have extensive experience of past ceremonies in that location, and their advice can be incredibly valuable in helping you effectively utilize the space. I always consider myself fortunate where there is an organizer or manager attached to the venue, as this makes the logistical part of ceremony organization much easier.

2.29 Special Arrangements

Multilanguage Ceremonies

Although this book is aimed primarily at countries where English is the dominant language, there will obviously be a need for modern ceremonies to be performed in other languages. Unless you are fluent in a particular language, I recommend that you not try to produce a ceremony alone, as errors in grammar and pronunciation will greatly distract from the meaning and focus of the occasion.

On some occasions, it may be useful to have the text of a ceremony offered in multiple languages simultaneously. This can happen, for instance, where a bride and groom are from different countries, and one of the families is located in a part of the world that is predominantly Non-English-speaking. If you are not fluent in both languages, the best solution is to have a translator who can repeat lines or segments in the second language, after you have spoken these in the first. There is often a family member whose knowledge of both languages is such that they can stand to one side and read the translated elements. They may even be able to produce the translation for you.

If your text is to be translated into a second language for the ceremony there are two important considerations. First, you should make the text of your primary language easier than if the only language used. This will allow for easy and efficient translation, as well as a better experience for those who only have limited fluency in both languages. Second, because lines are to be spoken twice, the structural content of the ceremony, should be made significantly shorter to allow for this repetition.

Virtual Guests

There are often occasions when important guests are unable to attend a ceremony. In modern times, it is now possible to broadcast a ceremony live, over the Internet, or to connect guests remotely using a service such as Skype.

If you have to set up a video connection, this should be done as discreetly as possible. If an amateur is to hold the camera or another device that is broadcasting, they should be given explicit instructions not to interfere with the view of professional photographers, or to disturb the ceremony in any other way.

If a computer is to be connected using a two-way service such as Skype, you should ensure that the speakers, although not the microphone, are silenced. This prevents any unexpected interruptions from the viewers, who may not have the same controlled conditions as at the venue. At the first ceremony I performed with guests viewing via Skype, we forgot to mute the speakers. As we moved into the vows, a lady in the remote audience began to cry. This was broadcast loudly around the room, and soon many others were crying too, as can often happen in a sort of domino effect during a wedding. We took a brief pause, to mute the sound on the computer, and that lesson is one I have taken great care to heed from that day forward.

2.30 What is a Wedding Rehearsal?

A wedding rehearsal is about 'Who, What Where, and When.'

Who has a job to do?

What is that job?

Where do they go to do it?

When do they do it?

A 'job' can be as simple as walking from point A to point B. In fact, during a wedding ceremony, those are the most common jobs of all. Everyone, from the bride and groom down to the youngest flower girl, needs to know what is expected of them, where they are expected to walk and stand, and exactly what their cue will be to proceed.

Deciding whether to hold a rehearsal can be a difficult choice. The is no doubt that everyone will begin the ceremony proper with greater confidence after a rehearsal has been held. Sometimes a couple may choose to hold their rehearsal without the presence of the Celebrant, but, if one is held, I strongly recommend you make the case for attending. When you do attend, you may often be asked to direct and orchestrate the rehearsal. It is therefore essential that you know what should be accomplished, and how it is best achieved. This section will cover the factors that help decide how important a rehearsal is for any particular ceremony, and how best to explain that to a couple. The following section details how to run a rehearsal to achieve maximum success in efficiently preparing the wedding party with the knowledge, techniques, and confidence they will need on the day.

Rehearsing a wedding is very similar to preparing a cast of actors to perform a piece of theater. Each cast member needs to know when and where to enter the stage, where to stand while they are on view, and what to do or say while they are in place. Directing the rehearsal is the Celebrant, the Event Planner, or the Venue Coordinator. Sometimes two or three of those professionals will run a rehearsal together, but it is usually more efficient if there is one instructor, a clear, knowledgeable guide, preparing the many performers for the live show. Much as with rehearsing a play, a wedding rehearsal is about making sure everything that has been planned on paper will work *in practice*, in the way we want and in the venue that has been chosen. It is common to have to make subtle adjustments to ceremony plans to compensate for the restrictions of the ceremony space.

2.31 Do You Need a Wedding Rehearsal?

Although a rehearsal always adds to the confidence of everyone involved in the wedding, there are times when a couple decides not to hold one. Here are the main factors that should affect their decision. How insistent you are that one is held will also be affected by the following:

Factor One: Number in the Wedding Party

The more people in the wedding party, the more important is the need for an organized rehearsal. If the ceremony includes only yourself, the couple, a best man, and a maid of honor, then you almost certainly don't need a formal rehearsal event. If there will be more than three each of the groomsmen or bridesmaids, or you are including parents, ring bearers, or flower girls, the value of rehearsal with all present increases considerably. As a guide, if the wedding party consists of the following numbers, this is what I advise:

Under five people: Unless the couple specifically requests it, a formal rehearsal should not be needed.

Between five and ten people: A rehearsal may be advisable, but the final decision will depend on the other factors listed below.

Between ten and fifteen people: A rehearsal is highly desirable. Not to hold one for a party of this size creates a serious risk of mistakes on the day.

Between fifteen and twenty-five people: A formal rehearsal is absolutely required for a party of this magnitude. Not to hold one will almost certainly lead to a noticeable degree of chaos and stress before, and during, the ceremony.

Over twenty-five people: A wedding party of this size is almost certainly too large. As tactfully as possible, you may want to advise the couple to trim this to a more manageable number.

Factor Two: The Complexity of the Procession

The more complex the choreography required for the entrances and exits of the wedding party, the more practice and instruction will be needed. For example, if a groomsman must escort a parent, and then double back to his starting position, or if a child must hand off the rings before being seated, walking these events through in practice will be crucial to preparing the participants.

Factor Three: The Complexity of the Ceremony

Many ceremonies involve individuals moving to different positions at particular points, perhaps to perform a reading or a Unity Ritual. Discovering exactly how this can work in practice, given the realities of the venue space, greatly ensures things will go as desired under the stresses of the formal occasion.

Factor Four: The Choice of Venue

Some venues, such as churches or banqueting halls, are designed specifically for the performing of ceremonies. Other locations can have a shape, size, or design that presents unexpected challenges. This is particularly true of weddings held in private homes or gardens. The best way to ensure your plans for managing the key players are possible, and practical, is to rehearse within the space where the ceremony will be performed, and then to make adjustments as you find these are needed.

Factor Five: The Availability of the Venue and Participants

Many venues will be booked for ceremonies and events other than your own. It may not be possible to find a time, on the day before the wedding is planned, to hold a full rehearsal in the same location. Where a rehearsal is necessary, you and your clients should consider alternative spaces. An open area in a park or garden, or even at the rear of a hotel, can be an adequate substitute for the venue itself. Map out the space, perhaps with chairs, or with small cones. Where this is the only possibility, it is worth beginning the rehearsal with a quick description of the space proper, and how it differs structurally from that you have accepted as your practice area.

For many weddings, participants may not arrive in the destination city until the night before the ceremony, or perhaps until the day itself. It may not, therefore, be possible to assemble all of the wedding party in place for a formal rehearsal the day before. If one or two individuals must be absent, you should still attempt to go ahead with the rehearsal. You should take notes, which can then be passed to those absent.

TIP: You may want to appoint a 'training buddy' for each person not able to attend. For example, where a groomsman cannot attend, pick another participant who will be taking a similar role, and appoint him that person's 'buddy'. His job will be to take notes and spend as long as needed, just before the ceremony, instructing his charge on the lessons he learned from rehearsing, before the ceremony begins. Also, you will want to have your own one-to-one with the missing player if possible, to answer any questions they may have.

Where fifty percent or more of a wedding party is unable to attend a wedding rehearsal, its usefulness becomes reduced to such an extent that it is probably not worth the time and expense. In such cases, you may want to arrive slightly earlier at the venue on the day of the wedding, and try to get a few minutes with the wedding party to go over the program in slightly greater detail than you normally would at that time.

Factor Six: The Experience of the Wedding Party

Though less important than other factors, an understanding of the experience level of those involved in the ceremony can tip the balance on your decision to hold a rehearsal. If the party consists only of adults, many of whom have been involved in ceremonies before this, rehearsal is less important than if the plans include children, or the participants lack in experience and confidence.

Factor Seven: The Extra Cost of the Rehearsal

As a professional, you will almost certainly charge an additional fee for attending the rehearsal. This is an entirely correct and proper practice, as it is a separate event, and is usually held on a different day to the ceremony itself. If attending a rehearsal, you are obviously unable to perform another ceremony at that time. You should be compensated accordingly.

It is undeniable that a wedding rehearsal can cause extra expense for the bride and groom, or for the parents paying the bills. Often, wedding budgets are very tightly managed. It is possible to hold a rehearsal without the presence of the Celebrant, but this is always less effective. Additionally, the couple may have to cover extra costs of transporting and housing the wedding party for that extra day.

You should work with the couple, explaining all these factors, to help them decide whether the cost of a rehearsal outweighs the cost of unexpected problems caused by unprepared participants on their wedding day.

The final decision to rehearse should always remain with the bride and groom. However, uncertainty on this decision is usually a sign that a rehearsal is needed. Every couple who decides not to hold one is, to some extent, taking a gamble on their wedding plans. A few, surprisingly carefree, couples may enjoy the notion of the unexpected and unplanned cropping up on their wedding day, but most will prefer security and peace of mind. Every experienced Celebrant knows that if you want to ensure everyone knows and understands his or her role in the ceremony, the only way to is to hold an organized rehearsal.

2.32 Running a Wedding Rehearsal

There is a tried and effective method for running a wedding rehearsal, one that you will find most Celebrants, Planners, and Coordinators quickly come to adopt. It is that approach I will outline in this section.

Most wedding rehearsals take the following pattern:

1. Gathering
2. Introductions, Explanations, and Rules
3. Establish Main Positions
4. Plan Recessional
5. Plan Pre-Ceremony Lineup
6. Plan Processional
7. Plan Important Ceremony Moments
8. Rehearse Recessional
9. Rehearse Lineup
10. Rehearse Processional
11. Rehearse Key Ceremony Moments
12. Rehearse Recessional
13. Repeat Steps 9-12 if required
14. Confirm Arrival Times for the Ceremony
15. Departure

1. Gathering

You should instruct the wedding party to begin gathering at the rehearsal site thirty minutes before the posted start time. This allows for any unexpected delays in traffic or parking. Some members of the wedding party may be unfamiliar with the area, and this allowance also gives them extra time to find the venue. When the party begins arriving, check for updates on the status of the group, as members may have called to inform of delays. If any member is absent ten minutes before the start time, have another wedding party member call them to confirm their status and expected arrival time. If some participants are going to be more than just a few minutes late it is acceptable to start without them, and then bring them up to speed when they arrive.

I make it my practice to arrive at least thirty minutes before the planned start time, or forty-five minutes if I am unfamiliar with the venue. This enables me to meet any staff members on the site and share the information and instructions we have been given. It also gives time to talk through the usual venue procedures and practices. If the venue has no staff, as is often the case with parks or beaches, this extra time allows you to walk the site, and plan out the best routes and timing for the ceremony.

Although the best processional and recessional routes, as well as places to stand, are almost always fairly obvious, it is wise to discuss this with the couple as soon as they arrive. Many couples have a vision for how the elements will play out in their chosen space, and understanding this will help you translate it into action. For example, their assumed ceremony layout may not be best placed from the viewpoint of guests, or their idea of the placement of a unity ritual table may block an important entry point.

If faced with any confusing situation, where the practicalities of the ceremony site conflict with any preplanned ideas, it is always best to look for the simplest solution. The more complicated any plan for a ceremony becomes, the more likely it is that there will be problems or mistakes on the day.

Once you feel the majority of the wedding party are present, call everyone to attention and begin the rehearsal process.

2. Introductions, Explanations, and Rules

It is best to start by gathering everyone in a circle and introducing yourself. Your job, at this time, is to set the ground rules, so the practice can take place as quickly and efficiently as possible.

Start by asking if anyone present does not have a role in the ceremony. There may be individuals who are simply a spouse, or friend, accompanying a participant. If so, thank them for coming, but politely ask them to find a comfortable place to wait, away from the area where you will be practicing. This is perfectly acceptable, and they should understand. Maintaining focus and order is difficult enough at any rehearsal, and non-participants can only serve as a distraction that will make the process harder and longer.

Once you have only the participants in place, reform the circle. Although many in a wedding party will know each other well, there will be members who are meeting for the first time. It is useful to go quickly around the circle, in whichever direction you prefer, and have each person identify themselves by name and their role in the wedding. If you keep this fun, it can also help to break the ice and set a warm, professional tone for what follows.

Once you have established identities, you should explain the rehearsal process stages as outlined here. Make it clear that anyone can ask a question at any time simply by raising their hand.

It is vital, at this time, to establish the rules. Rehearsals take patience, concentration, and consideration. The more attentions wander, and participants begin side conversations, the harder the process becomes. For this reason, I wear a whistle around my neck to all rehearsals. These can be purchased, for around five dollars, at any sporting goods store. I inform the party that, should they cease paying attention, or if inappropriate conversations break out, I will stop and blow the whistle. I then demonstrate this. Whistles are surprisingly loud and shrill, and it rarely takes more than two or three uses before the wedding party dreads the sound enough to cease chatting and begin to take things seriously.

In addition to the whistle, I also carry a clipboard with a copy of the ceremony attached. This enables me to take notes as we proceed, and has the bonus of further establishing authority.

You might also inform the wedding party that the quicker you get through the rehearsal, the sooner they can get to the rehearsal dinner and the bar. This also makes a good incentive to pay attention.

If you still have any missing party members, it is wise to appoint individuals to take notes on behalf of those absent, and who will be able to find the time, before the ceremony, to explain what took place and roughly what is expected. I often refer to these as 'rehearsal buddies'. For a missing bridesmaid, you may ask the maid of honor to take this role. For a missing groomsman, you might choose the best man. An excellent choice is someone who will be standing next to the missing party in the lineup, or during the ceremony itself. That gives them a natural position to explain what the individual missed at the rehearsal.

3. Establish Main Positions

With rules in place and questions answered, it is time to establish main positions. These are the locations each of the party will hold after the processional, and for the majority of the ceremony.

Begin by finding the spot where you will be standing. Next, place the bride and groom, followed by the groomsmen and bridesmaids. Follow this by allocating places for any flower girls or ring bearers (human or canine) who will remain standing for the ceremony. It should be noted that, for young children and animals, seating them is better to prevent both anxiety and fatigue.

For individuals who will be seated throughout the ceremony, such as parents, have them take these now, or have them stand in the approximate position where their chair will be placed on the day. Once you have established these seated locations, be sure the planner, coordinator, bride, or another appointed individual will be able to mark these seats as reserved at least an hour before the planned ceremony start time.

Where groomsmen and bridesmaids are stood on either side of the couple, encourage them to develop a symmetry, with each standing in a position that corresponds visually with that of his or her opposite number.

Once you have the groomsmen and bridesmaids correctly placed, it is worth giving them a short instruction on how to stand. They should face the guests but slightly angled toward the couple. For groomsmen, it is usual to have the left hand placed over the right wrist. (There is a theory that this displays the ring finger throughout the ceremony, and allows the guests to see which of these young men is still marriageable. However traditional this notion may be, it makes a lovely story to help the groomsmen remember which hand goes over which wrist.) For bridesmaids, they will usually be given small bouquets to hold, in which case these should be held level with the navel. If their hands are to be empty throughout the ceremony, they should adopt a stance similar to the groomsmen, with the left hand on the right wrist.

This is also a good time to say a few words about pockets. For participants such as groomsmen, whose wedding attire will have pockets, it is wise for them to empty these of everyday items before the ceremony. Bulk such as wallets, phones, and keys can create an unsightly bulge that ruin the line of tailored clothing, and looks unflattering in photographs. Similarly, if a best man will be carrying the rings in his pocket, it is wise to have him take them out of any bulky box they may be stored in. He should, of course, keep a firm control of those precious bands at all times.

When you are confident everyone is in the correct primary position, ensure you have everyone's attention, and have them take a few moments to mark the place they are located, and also the persons they are located next to. This should fix the location in their mind. However, you should also have each noted, so you can correct any errors that are made later in the practice.

4. Plan Recessional

The next stage is to choreograph the exiting of the bridal party. It is worth saying a few words to everyone about the final moments of the ceremony. Let them know what the pronouncement will be, and confirm the exact format of the pronouncement/kiss/presentation with the bride and groom. It is also useful to remind the couple to hold their kiss for at least six seconds, which should be enough time for the photographer to capture the moment.

After the kiss, and the words of presentation, if the couple has chosen for you to add those, the couple should hold hands, or link arms if preferred, and face their guests. This is the time for them to bask in the approval, cheering, and applause of those they love. You should instruct the couple to hold that moment for as long as they wish.

It is worth saying a few words to the wedding party about their job at this time, which is to act as cheerleaders and start the applause. Although it is natural to cheer at this point, some guests may need a form of 'social permission' as encouragement before they begin. The attendants, family, and friends should understand that it is their job to keep the climax of vocal celebration as high as possible, and make it last for as long as they can.

If the bride plans to enter with a bouquet, she will have passed this off, most likely to the maid/matron of honor, early in the ceremony. Now is the time she should take that back. Instruct her and the attendant holding the bouquet to do this. Of course, in the excitement of this moment, it is quite common for brides to forget this, and maids/matrons do better jobs of remembering. Be sure to cover this with them both each time you practice this part of the ceremony. However, if they forget this on the day, instruct the attendant not to worry, and just to carry the bouquet out herself. Under no circumstances should she chase after the bride if should she forget it, as that would be distracting and undignified.

You should establish the door, exit, or destination the parties will proceed to. A few factors will affect your decision, and some of these will only become known to you at this time. It is important to understand what plans the couple has for the time immediately after the ceremony. They may choose to proceed directly to photography, in which case they will usually have a gathering place in mind for this. It is rare for a photographer to attend a rehearsal, and so a final decision on the area to assemble for photographs may not be possible until shortly before the ceremony.

Alternatively, a couple may choose to take a few moments after the ceremony to cool down with a little private time. They may have a room set aside for this, and so will need to know how to proceed there after their formal exit from the ceremony space.

Once you know the final destination, it should be a simple matter to map out the recessional path. If you have a venue coordinator, or an event planner, working beside you, they will undoubtedly have valuable input on that decision.

Instruct the couple to take their time recessing. This is, after all, their moment of triumph! They should feel free to pause at a few points along their exit path, perhaps to allow for the photographer to take a shot before descending stairs, or turning a corner. As they do so, you should allow them the time they need, and also watch the photographer to ensure they have all they need, before you signal the rest of the party to exit.

Once the newlyweds have recessed a suitable distance, and their moment has been recorded sufficiently, it is time to bring together attendants to exit. Warn the attendants that, when they have watched the couple take their first few departing steps, they should return their attention to you, and prepare for the signals for their own exit. The signal you use should be a dignified one, such as a gentle motioning together with your hands, or a clear, short, nod of your head. Do not forget to keep smiling yourself, even while concentrating and directing the movements of others.

Signal the Best Man and the Maid/Matron of Honor to meet in front of the place just occupied by the bride and groom. They should turn, smile, link arms, and then slowly follow the route that the newlyweds have just taken. Again, you will watch to make sure that photographers can catch this exit sufficiently. You can then signal the second attendants to exit in the same manner. Although attendant children and animals are usually seated at this point, if they are stood among the bridesmaids and groomsmen, appoint a suitable adult to act as their escort, unless you have overwhelming confidence they will be able to manage the exit unaccompanied.

In this manner, you will work your way jointly along the lines of bridesmaids and groomsmen until all have exited.

At this point, if they have been chosen to be included in the recessional, you should signal the bride's parents to stand, ink arms, and follow after the attendants. They may need to be reminded at several points during the rehearsal to watch for your signal on the day before they leave their seats. Once they have exited, including any photographic moments needed, indicate the groom's parents to follow. You can then alternate, from each side, releasing any other family members, or friends, whom the couple wishes included in the formal exit.

For those present who are not formally recessing, explain what will happen at this point, and how the guests will be released. This is an excellent time to confirm and finalize plans for the guest's exit, in consultation with the planner or coordinator.

Once complete, this is a great time to take a pause for questions, and to congratulate everyone on how well they are already doing. If they need to be reminded to smile, or walk slowly, now is a good time to do this.

5. Plan Pre-Ceremony Lineup

You should now plan how the wedding party will line up outside the ceremony space, just before their entrance.

Importantly, there is a custom many couples still follow in which the bride and groom are not allowed to catch sight of each other before the ceremony. If this is being observed, you should allow for this in the way you line up the participants, and the way the cues are given during the processional.

Line everyone up in the order they will enter. If any member of the party has a dual role, such as the bride's father escorting his wife to her seat before doubling back to escort his daughter, they should be instructed to take the position for their first role. You should also decide, and make clear, the exact path of their return route.

It is hugely helpful, should they be available, for the planner or coordinator to be the one giving the cues, or 'shoulder taps', to each person or pair to begin their entrance. They will know what to watch for, whether it is the previous couple reaching an established point or a change in music.

Once you have everyone in line, in their first entrance order, say a few words about the pace and stance. You should encourage everyone to walk at a slow, dignified pace, in tempo with any music that is playing. If there are stairs to be traveled, these should be taken slowly, and with the greatest care. It is better that everyone take a few extra seconds to make their entrance than take a tumble because he or she felt the need to rush.

Additionally, individuals should be reminded to smile, and how to place their hands (left hand on right wrist, or object held at navel height).

6. Plan Processional

Ensure that everyone understands his or her signal to begin, their route, and their destination, and then begin the first run. Where music will be playing, especially where this will be used as a cue, you should signify starts, stops, and changes by calling these out, or perhaps with a short burst of your whistle.

A first run through will usually be quite slow, and you may need to take notes on minor adjustments, or small pieces of advice to give particular participants.

Walk everyone through their entrance, calling out musical changes and instructions if needed.

You should aim for everyone to finish at his or her main positions, as you decided previously.

An important point in your processional practice will be to clarify and rehearse what takes place at the point of presentation, or 'giving away,' should this occur.

Once everyone has reached their ceremony positions, at the point where the guests will be re-seated, congratulate the party on their progress so far, and go over any small notes you made through the run.

7. Plan Important Ceremony Moments

With everyone now in place, discuss the order things will happen during the ceremony proper.

If there are readings or blessings, instruct the readers where to come to stand, where to face, and what to do once they have finished their duties.

Discuss with the couple how their vows will be taken, and how they will receive any scripts to read from, should these be a part of the plan.

If an individual has been entrusted with the rings, instruct them as to what the cues will be to pass these when needed.

If there is to be a Unity Ritual, this is the time to consider how you will move to the required location, and to confirm how any tasks will be performed.

It may be that, as you go over these parts of the ceremony, you make a few minor adjustments to standing positions. This is perfectly acceptable, as the rehearsal is a process of bringing all the elements and processes together for the first time, and then adjusting for such unexpected practical factors.

Briefly, explain each part of the ceremony, up until the point where you reach the pronouncement. You will now have gone through every part of the ceremony, and returned to the point where you began!

8. Rehearse Recessional

You should now perform a second practice of the recessional. It is usual for some individuals to need gentle reminders about their cues to exit. Take notes as they run through, and go over any minor issues before the next phase of the rehearsal.

By this stage, you should notice everything beginning to fall into place. Hopefully, the wedding party will be starting to feel more confident and comfortable, but do keep encouraging them with praise and a positive tone.

Explain to the participants that you are now going to bring everything they have learned together, as it will be on the day.

9. Rehearse Lineup

Ask everybody to lineup, with as little prompting as possible. By now, they should have a good memory for where they stand, and whom they stand next to or behind. It is helpful to drop gentle notes of reminder about walking at a slow, dignified pace, remembering to smile, and for the groomsmen to hold that left hand over the right wrist. Check to see if anyone has any questions or concerns, and then cue your walk through.

Do not forget the need to rehearse yourself. You will likely be going in ahead of the wedding party, leaving them in the capable hands of a planner/coordinator. If unsupervised, be sure they are watching or listening attentively for their cues. As you walk your rehearsal route, visualize your pace on the day. This will be useful in mentally preparing as you travel to the venue. Focus in your poise, the rhythm of your steps, and don't forget to smile. If you have a book or another item you read from, hold this in front of you in a dignified way as you walk. Remind yourself to empty pockets of any bulky items before the ceremony. If you are a gentleman in pants/trousers, be sure to check you fly before you begin your processional walk.

10. Rehearse Processional

Rehearse the processional, trying not to prompt the participants unless required. It is nice to offer words of encouragement as each of the party reach their starting positions, with phrases such as 'beautifully done', and 'perfect, that's just right'. Building confidence, without letting them become complacent, is our goal at this point in the rehearsal.

11. Rehearse Key Ceremony Moments

At this point, you should have the activities of the ceremony itself nicely in place. If there are particular cues or movements, you should practice those again.

TIP: If the best man is to be holding both rings, and will be handing the bride's ring to the groom for the first exchange, you might offer him the following phrase, 'little ring first, big ring second', so that he can fix the right ring to choose for each section firmly in his mind. For same-sex marriages, of course, the rings may look almost identical. In this latter case, I have found the best practice is to keep the rings physically separate, either in small but noticeably different bags, or by having them held by different individuals before the exchange.

12. Rehearse Recessional

As you have the party in position, run through the recessional again. This time, use a minimum of prompting, but a maximum of encouragement. If the party has been paying attention, you should be pleased with how the process now seems to flow in a far more coordinated and dignified manner.

13. Repeat Steps 9 12 if required

By this point, you have been through the ceremony twice and tweaked your plan so that everything should work well in practice. The wedding party should be looking fairly confident, but, even in the second run through, may well have made a few small errors, and needed a few reminders along the way. It is wise to do a third run through, if time and participants are willing. This will truly help seal the actions in their mind until the following day.

A theatrical technique you might employ is a 'speed run-through'. This is where you have everybody line up and then walk through processional, ceremony, and recessional at double speed. Being made to do something fast helps fix it in the mind more firmly. It also has the bonus of injecting some more fun into the rehearsal, at a time when energy may be on the wane, especially among the youngsters.

At most rehearsals, three run-throughs should be sufficient to make everyone clear on what is expected of them. You will also find that this is the point where patience is running thin, and time is running short. However, for especially complicated ceremonies, or when a party is still making significant and troubling mistakes, you should carefully consider a fourth. By this point, you should aim to be prompting only as a last resort, to correct critical errors. However frustrated you may become, you should try to maintain an air of positive encouragement, and keep up a constructive and confident demeanor.

Once you have completed your final run-through, take any questions the party have. Remind them to smile, and that the wedding day is about enjoyment. Reassure them that all will be well.

14. Confirm Arrival Times for the Ceremony

The final, but hugely important, task is to confirm everyone's arrival time for the ceremony. This is very often a task handled by the wedding planner if one has been hired, but you should be prepared with advice if needed, and to confirm your own arrival time to them and the couple. I have found it good practice to plan to arrive around forty-five minutes before the anticipated ceremony start time.

15. Departure

Be sure to thank everyone for their participation, and wish them an enjoyable evening if they are going to a rehearsal dinner or party. If there are any last minute technical details, cover these with the event planner or coordinator. Ensure that everyone who may require it has your contact details, and encourage them to call if they have any questions, or if any unexpected problems occur.

However frustrating a rehearsal may have been, end of a positive note, and exit smiling, with confidence, and your head high. Never forget that you are a leader, and your example will have an enormous impact on the confidence and attitude of the wedding party.

A Note on Ushers

It is useful to have the ushers attend the rehearsal, if any have been appointed and are available. You may wish to mention this to the couple early in the planning process, as ushers are often left out of this part of the preparations (usually to keep down the numbers of those attending the rehearsal dinner). Later in the rehearsal, it is a good idea to call the ushers together for a special aside and ensure that they are familiar with the necessary, basic information they will need on the day. This can include the names of all the wedding party, the identities of the V.I.P. guests, and how they act as they are escorting guests to their seats. For a refresher on this, see the earlier section on the key participants in the ceremony. Ushers will also need to know what instructions need to be given to guests as they are leaving the ceremony, as to how the day is planned to continue. A good usher knows that their job is to keep the gears of the day turning for as long as they are needed, and that this is a serious and important responsibility. Always make a special point of thanking ushers particularly for their help on the day. This can be particularly useful if any of the feel slightly passed over in not receiving more 'prestigious' positions as bridesmaids or groomsmen.

If possible, have the couple hand you the license paperwork at the rehearsal. This will give them one less concern on the day, and you will know those important documents are safe. In some cases, you may also be able to collect the witness details and signatures at the rehearsal. Many Celebrants do this, and it is entirely legal, providing the paperwork is not filed before the wedding ceremony has taken place. An exception to this is if the couple desires a photographic record of the signing. In such cases, it is better to wait for the day and find a suitable moment, usually before the ceremony, where the witnesses and photographer are free. Signing rules and customs will vary from state to state, and country to country, and those should always, of course, take priority over convenience.

It should be noted that some Celebrants choose not to take charge of paperwork overnight between the rehearsal and the wedding, in case something should happen to them, and the couple therefore not have the paperwork for whoever would step in on the day. When I started out, I carefully considered this question. I felt that, on balance over a large enough sample of ceremonies, the likelihood was far higher for a couple to lose the paperwork than an unforeseen accident prevent my return. I still, therefore, take charge of the paperwork as early as possible. This is ultimately a matter for each Celebrant to decide; to weigh the responsibilities against the risk, and to act in the way that best protects the interests of both the couple and your own business. For reasons such as this, you may also consider investing in professional liability insurance.

TIP: For wedding rehearsals (not the ceremony, however tempted), purchase and wear a sports whistle. Many attendees will be eager to catch up on gossip, or engaged in the excitement of meeting new relations for the first time. This can make maintaining their focus a challenge. A whistle will allow you to get their attention without taxing your voice. Additionally, if worn around the neck on a brightly colored lanyard (cord), it can subtly help boost your authority by conjuring up childhood memories of gym class.

2.33 On the Day of the Wedding

The best way to ensure success on the day of the wedding is to understand the flow of the process. If you have a routine, perhaps even utilizing checklists, you will efficiently manage and complete the various tasks of the day. Preparation is the foundation of a successful wedding ceremony, indeed of any group celebration.

By the day of the wedding, you should have a prepared ceremony script, be fully aware of your timing and travel plans, and be very clear on all the duties you will be expected to perform.

What follows are sections addressing various aspects of the ceremony day itself, to prepare you for the right expectations and best practices.

2.33a Your Pre ceremony Routine

One of the secrets to a successful wedding day routine is to start before the day. Any task you can complete before the day of the ceremony will put you further at ease, and give you more time and flexibility in case anything unexpected occurs before, or during, your journey to the venue. I suggest you create a checklist of activities that can be accomplished at every stage of your preparations, and begin with anything you can address before the big day.

To help you begin, I have created a sample checklist.

Many tasks can be completed the day before the ceremony:

- Make post-rehearsal changes to your ceremony script.
- Prepare your ceremony book (see the next section).
- Iron and lay out your clothes.
- Pick up your dry cleaning.
- Shine your shoes.
- Fill the car gas tank.

- Pack your ceremony kit.
- Charge any electronics you plan to use.

Every item you complete will help give you a better night's sleep.

Before you go to bed on the evening before the ceremony, check exactly how long you will need to travel to arrive at the venue in good time. You can do this easily by putting your starting point and destination into a free service such as Google Maps, which also integrates with their calendar function. This will give you a very accurate travel time. If you use the service while driving it will also adjust for traffic conditions.

When you have your anticipated departure time, subtract 30 minutes. For example, if you calculate you need to leave at 1 PM, adjust this so you leave at 12:30 PM. The extra allowance gives you time for any unexpected delays on the route, and also for parking and getting into the venue at the other end. It is always better to arrive slightly earlier than needed, rather than the reverse. Even the feeling of being just a little behind schedule can unsettle your confidence.

If you have obligations to family members on the day of the wedding, be sure these are carried out in good time, and that everyone is aware of the importance of your schedule.

It is a good idea to keep your phone on you throughout the day of the ceremony, in case there are any questions or issues for which the wedding party or planners need to contact you. It is also a good idea to call a wedding planner on the morning of a ceremony, to check in and confirm there are no problems or changes. They will not mind you doing so, but will respect your thorough professionalism.

Before leaving for a ceremony, ensure that you have a light snack, and refreshing drink, so that your energy levels will remain high. Avoid spicy foods, or those likely to cause distinctive breath, as you will be in close proximity to others throughout the ceremony. For this reason, and several others, I like to carry a supply of refreshing mints in my Celebrant kit.

If you have a routine, and a handy checklist, you will leave for the ceremony with confidence.

My own greatest fear, just before I start my drive, is that I have forgotten my script. Don't worry if you feel the compulsion to check and recheck such items. It is better to take thirty seconds to stop and check your bag a third time, rather than spend your journey nursing a nagging doubt.

2.33b Your Wedding Day Book

You will need to prepare a copy of your ceremony to read from on the day. Some Celebrants, myself included, choose to read from a printed source. I have found this to be the simplest, and most reliable, method. Others prefer to read from an electronic device, such as a tablet or iPad.

If you select an electronic method for producing your ceremony book, you must ensure the device is suitably charged, has a surface that is easily readable in outdoor lighting, and is protected from the elements.

If using a printed source, you will need a tasteful, professional cover for your pages. Some Celebrants choose a high-quality ring binder. If you do so, it is a good idea to cover your pages with plastic pockets. This gives the paper protection against the elements, and adds extra weight, so they can be more easily controlled in a windy outdoor setting.

I currently use an art portfolio folder (Itoya Art Portfolios - ITYEV128), which is both stylish and lightweight. It has built-in clear internal plastic pockets, which are fitted for the standard 8' by 11' letter size printer paper. To maximize space, I place two sheets in each section, back to back.

A ceremony printed in a large font can run to a significant number of pages. For this reason, you should add page numbers to your print. This will ensure that you place the pages in the correct order, and know that none of the pages are missing. If you add an automatic header to the print, with the bride's name and ceremony date, you will be confident that all the pages are also for the correct event.

Whichever binder or object you use, the cover should ideally be black, or in a soft, muted tone.

When you create the text for your book, use a large font for excellent readability, such as Cambria, Helvetica, or Arial. I find sans-serif fonts make for an easier read. Lay out your text as it will be spoken, phrase by phrase, rather than in standard paragraph format. This structure will make your pauses sound more natural, and allow you to remove your eyes from the page for longer periods. An excellent skill to cultivate is scanning forward through a text, so you can look up and around at the guests and wedding party as much as possible, rather than spending the entire ceremony with your eyes on the page. You may also wish to underline, or italicize, words to which you will give particular emphasis.

If you are asked to produce reading cards for personalized vows, or for the readers, ensure these are on firm stock that will fit within your ceremony book with ease.

TIP: Many individuals have names that are difficult to pronounce, or which are pronounced very differently to how they are written on the page. Write each name out phonetically, as it should be vocalized. A notable example, used in the film 'Four Weddings and a Funeral' is that of the name St. John, which is pronounced 'Sinjin' in correct speech.

2.33c Visualization Techniques for Celebrants

As you journey to the venue to perform the ceremony, it is important that you create for yourself the correct mental state and attitude. I have found that a visualization routine has profoundly increased my confidence and performance level, and so decided to add this section to describe my technique.

Having the right external stimuli is important as we travel. Many of us listen to music, podcasts, or talk shows. For my ride to the venue, or, at least, the final hour if the drive is an exceptionally long one, I switch to music that is calming. For my tastes, that is spa or yoga music, perhaps with accompanying ocean or other natural sounds. The music that focuses you may be quite different, and I encourage you to experiment. However, I believe that instrumental tracks, rather than those with lyrics, are more suited for the focused thoughts we are trying to achieve in visualization.

With the right audio stimulus in place, start by putting irrelevant thoughts from your mind. Do not think about what you will make for supper, an argument you had with a family member, or an exciting new project you have begun. Focus your thoughts only on the ceremony.

If you held a rehearsal the day before, or if you have performed a previous ceremony at the same venue, you will be familiar with the layout, and should be able to visualize it easily. Imagine yourself arriving and walking inside, locating the appropriate parties to let them know you have arrived. See yourself smiling, and greeting them warmly.

Now visualize yourself dealing with any paperwork. See yourself filling out the license, which is often done as early as possible, and also receiving any payment you are still owed. That last part is important as it is crucial, but sometimes annoying, part of the process. Remind yourself that you are a professional who gives terrific value, and it is natural and correct that you be paid.

Next, visualize yourself just before you enter for the ceremony. In your mind, count the items you will carry in with you, such as your wedding book. If you are male, imagine checking your zipper. Now see yourself walking in, smiling, confident, and composed.

Play out the ceremony in your mind, block by block, until you are watching the couple walk back down the aisle together as newlyweds, your job completed successfully.

Repeat this visualization two or three times, perhaps imagining yourself from different angles. In all cases, see yourself doing a fantastic job.

What you have just performed is a technique used by many hugely successful athletes and actors across the world. You have just 'won the race before it has even begun'. By taking yourself through an exercise such as this, you are conditioning your mind to see it as entirely natural that you will do a successful job every step of the ceremony. This has two important consequences. The natural confidence allows your abilities to flower fully when you walk out into view. It will have become as natural to you as an everyday task or habit you do without concern. Additionally, because you are already mentally practiced and prepared, if anything unexpected does occur, you will find you automatically cope with it in a positive and productive manner. This is because your mind is expecting to reach the end of the ceremony with complete success.

Preparation is key to performing a great ceremony, and nowhere is this truer than in how we prepare our minds. If you make your pre-ceremony visualization as much a part of your preparation routine as putting on your shoes, you will notice that you quickly achieve a higher standard and confidence in your performance, and that you enjoy the occasion much more.

2.33d When you Arrive

I have always made it my practice to plan to arrive at a wedding venue between forty-five minutes to an hour before the scheduled ceremony start. Although some may feel this is a little excessive, it is always better to be early and on site rather than running late and yet to arrive. Driving is a strenuous activity and, among other things, you will need a few minutes between parking and performance to compose yourself. Additionally, it is important to remember that you are a leading central figure in the event, and on many occasions will be considered the person in charge. As such, you will be needed to help make decisions, or cope with problems or changes that arise. There are certain key activities that I recommend you add to your routine immediately after you arrive.

1. Locate your Primary Contact

Your primary contact at the ceremony will be the wedding planner, the location coordinator, or one (or both) of the couple, if no professional has been hired to administer the event. If there is no professional organizer, you will very frequently find that these duties fall, to a greater or lesser extent, on yourself.

It is vital, as soon as you arrive, to let the primary contact know you are on site. That will put their mind at ease, and they will also be needed for many of the other points listed below.

2. Obtain and Process Paperwork

Once you have officially 'checked in' with your primary contact, the next item of business is to gather and process the wedding license, if you did not already do so, and if this is not a cosmetic ceremony or vow renewal. The reason for beginning this process as soon as possible after you arrive is that, in some cases, paperwork and signatories may take a few minutes to locate. There will be a great deal going on at this point, such as dressing the bridal party, pre-ceremony photography, and general hubbub and excitement. If you do not feel your paperwork requests are being given suitable priority, do not be afraid to be insistent on this point. This is an essential part of the day, and one of your core duties as Officiant.

If possible, try to obtain the signatures before the ceremony. This is legal, unless local laws specifically stipulate otherwise, as the paperwork will not be filed until after the ceremony has taken place. Before you have anyone sign, alert the photographer. They, or the couple, may wish to capture the signing process as part of their record of the day.

Once you have the signatures in place, secure all the paperwork in a safe location. If you have sections you have still to complete, try to set aside time for this, but do not do so at the expense of the important action points below.

3. Settle Outstanding Payments

It is always better to settle outstanding payments before the ceremony, and preferably before the wedding day itself. For this reason, many Celebrants have a clause in their contract that requires full payment as much as seven days in advance (the sample contract later in this book contains such a clause). Many Celebrants find they are uncomfortable with this aspect of the business, but, as a professional, this is an important and natural part of the process. Additionally, having this matter dealt with allows you to focus entirely on the ceremony performance.

4. Walk the Ceremony Location

It is important to inspect the ceremony location as early as possible after you arrive on site. Although you may have been fortunate enough to work in the space for the rehearsal, in some cases this will be your first view of the site. Additionally, the setup and decoration process may have introduced unexpected factors for which you will have to compensate. Your experience and knowledge may enable you to see smaller issues that others have overlooked.

Stand in the position you will take during the ceremony. Ensure that you can see all the important locations and entry points. If you are expected to stand under an arbor, check that enough headroom has been allowed. If you are to be positioned on a beach, you may want to make a small x in the sand, at your ideal location, for reference as you enter at the start of the ceremony.

One important reason for walking the ceremony site as early as possible after you arrive on-site is that guests can sometimes arrive, and begin taking their seats, as soon as half an hour before the planned start time. When they do, your presence examining the ceremony space may not be possible, or appropriate.

5. Compare Notes with the Photographer and/or Videographer

Although the photographer will very likely be busy in the hour before the ceremony, it is important to try to obtain a moment with them or their assistant to swap notes. As a modern Celebrant, you probably do not place arbitrary restrictions on camera usage (particularly the use of flash) that some more traditional clerics do. Most photographers will know that, but it is still useful to make this clear.

If there are to be any unusual ceremony elements, such as a Unity Ritual, and especially something that might require a closer shot, it is useful to let them know. It is also helpful to let them know of any special arrangements, or instructions, for the processional or recessional, and to give them warning of which side you plan to move to during critical photographic moments, such as the kiss. Most photographers are impressively professional, and will be able to adapt quickly to whatever qualities the ceremony holds.

This is also your best opportunity to swap networking information with the photographer. Have a business card ready to offer them, and assure them that any photos they share from the ceremony will only be used with full photographic credit. Most photographers will be happy to share pictures from the event with you, but they will almost certainly need a follow-up reminder a few weeks after the ceremony. It is vital to get their contact information in return for yours.

On rare occasions, you may find a couple has entrusted an amateur, perhaps a family member or friend, with recording their day. I have been informed, on more than one occasion, that a photographer had not shot a wedding previously, and had been recruited based on the fact that he or she owned a camera. Such an individual may need a few minutes of instruction about what is due to take place, where they may want to stand for the processional and recessional, and what pictures a bride may be expecting to receive from the event (a standard shot list).

Where a videographer has been hired, they may well want to fit you with a microphone before the ceremony. Frequently this is a wireless lapel microphone (lavalier) that attaches onto your clothing and then feeds down to a small portable unit. They may want to fit this just a few minutes before the start of the ceremony, so they can set it recording and leave it. If so, arrange a time to reunite with them to get this done.

For extra information, see the previous section on wedding photography.

6. Compare Notes with the Sound and Music

If there are live musicians, they may already be seated and ready when you arrive. They may be preparing to begin playing their prelude selection, and so it is vital to confer with them as early as possible once you are both on site. It is rare for musicians or DJs to attend a rehearsal, so this will likely be the first chance you have had to meet and exchange notes.

It is important to confirm that they understand, and are comfortable with, the cues to start, stop, and change music during the ceremony, particularly at the climax, just before the triumphant recessional. In some cases, musicians will be looking to take their cues directly from your words, or a gesture you make to them at the appropriate time.

As with the photographer, take this opportunity to exchange professional information with the musical talent. Wedding vendors are often asked to recommend other types of professional they have worked with, and so networking is crucial to building your business.

Very often, the ceremony DJ is also tasked with providing the amplification for your voice. They may wish to take the earliest opportunity to fit you with a microphone. This is often a wireless lapel mic (lavalier) that feeds down through your clothing to a portable unit. With many units, you will be instructed to switch it to live just before the ceremony (to preserve battery life). The DJ will tell you how to do this, but for most units that means looking for a small green light.

Another reason for arriving early is to give you and the sound technician time for a test of the microphone volume before the guests arrive. If possible, stand in position and talk at the volume you will during the ceremony. If you are planning to read, you may wish to tilt your head down slightly for the test to give the most accurate simulation of your performance. A good indicator that you have the right volume is that you can just hear the amplification over your voice as you speak, but without it sounding too loud or having any echo. It is fun to pick a favorite quote, or snippet of wisdom to use as your test phrase for volume adjustments, rather than the dull and overused 'one, two, three' or 'how's this?'.

7. Hand Out Scripts to Readers

If there are readers planned for the ceremony, ensure they have their scripts, and are comfortable with their cues. I have long made it a practice to print and provide scripts for all readings, as well as personal statements of vows. In doing so I ensure that they are correct, in a large typeface, and on quality card stock that both looks beautiful, and can stand up to wind if the ceremony takes place outdoors. Many readers may be nervous, so an encouraging word from you can be a great help at this time, just as a congratulatory word after the ceremony can also be a kind reassurance.

8. Glance Through Your Script

Having dealt with all the other issues, it is important that you refocus your mind on your performance, and mentally prepare yourself. You may also wish to perform short vocal exercises to warm up your voice (see the section below), but please do so as discretely as possible to avoid alarming guests and wedding party. A couple of minutes before the line-up, glance through your ceremony script, and imagine the process in your mind. This also provides one last comforting check that all your pages are properly in place, or that your electronic reader is working correctly. Say the names of the couple over to yourself, and if possible to a member of the wedding party. This ensures you have them completely fixed in your mind, and that your pronunciation is entirely correct.

9. Final Wardrobe Changes

If you need to put on a robe, or add a stole (long ceremonial cloth) to your outfit, you should do so just before the ceremony. Take a few moments to check your attire in a mirror, and for male Celebrants verify that your fly is secure.

10. Silence your Cell Phone / Empty your Pockets

If you plan to carry your cell phone with you during the ceremony, make it a consistent habit to ensure it is switched to silent, or completely off, before you start the line-up. A best practice is to empty your pockets, and store items such as your keys and wallet in a secure location before you walk out into public view. This allows your clothing to fall correctly, and prevents any unsightly bulges from showing in photographs.

2.33e Vocal Warm up Exercises

Officiating a wedding is a vocal performance, much as in the dramatic arts. The voice is a muscle, and will function best if allowed to warm up before it is needed for any strenuous use. Many Celebrants find a brief vocal warm up useful in giving the voice the energy that will carry them through the ceremony.

It is important to remember that a wedding venue is often very public. If you intend on making any unusual sounds as part of your warm-up routine, you should do so discretely, and warn anyone around you in advance to avoid alarm.

Relax Your Breathing: Incorrect breathing most often causes tension and exhaustion in speaking. Start by standing still, and relaxing your upper body, section by section from the neck down. Breathe deeply, and ensure that your breathing comes from low in your abdomen. It can help to pace your hand just below your stomach, and to vocalize a soft hissing sound each time you exhale.

Release Your Jaw: If you tense your jaw and then release, you will be able to feel a tremendous difference. It helps to massage your cheeks between the palms of your hands lightly. You can then let your jaw hang loosely, and feel how much more malleable it has become. You will, of course, look utterly ridiculous while performing these exercises, so feel free to make them into a fun game, perhaps involving the junior members of the wedding party.

Lip Trilling: To trill is to produce any rapidly repeated sound. If you think of a bird call, you will be along the right lines. Place your lips together and then release your breath in a steady stream to create the trill, or a raspberry sound. First try it with an 'H' sounds. Then repeat on a 'B' sound. Hold the sound steady, and keep the air moving past the lips. Next try to repeat the b-trill gliding gently up and down the scales. Don't try to go too high, or too low, with your pitch.

Tongue Trilling: Position your tongue behind your upper teeth. Exhale, and trill your tongue with an 'R' sound. Hold the sound steady, and keep the breath continuous. Vary the pitch up and down the scale while trilling.

Vocal Scales: Start in a low pitch, and gently glide up the scale on a 'ME' sound. Increase the range gently each time you do the scales. Now reverse down the scale, from the top to the bottom, on an 'E' sound. You can also try this on the 'OOO' sound.

Siren Sounds: Pretend you are sucking in spaghetti with an inhalation. As you exhale, make the 'WOO' sound. It will be a buzz like sound. Hold the sound steady for two to three attempts. You can also combine this with scale exercises.

Humming: Breathe in, and then exhale while saying 'HUM.' Begin with a nasal sound, and slowly change from a high to a low pitch, as if you were sighing. Gently humming, while feeling the focus of the sound on the lips, is also an excellent way to cool down the voice after prolonged use.

2.33f Completing the Marriage License

For marriages that are not only 'cosmetic' (see that earlier section) or a renewal of vows, a core duty of the Celebrant is to ensure the license paperwork is completed correctly. When a license is issued, it will often be accompanied by an information sheet for new Officiants, which explains how to fill out and return the paperwork. You should make it your practice to read this, in case an issuing county has added, or changed, any of their guidelines. The exact requirements for completion will vary from region to region, but there are many usual or common factors, which I discuss below.

Witnesses

Most locations will require that you have two witnesses sign the marriage license around the time of the ceremony. As the signatures are not dated, it is possible to obtain these at a rehearsal the day before, providing those individuals will be present for the main event. The usual requirements for a witness are that (a) they are present for the wedding, (b) they are over eighteen years of age, and (c) that they can use a pen. Of course, the couple cannot self-witness, and as the solemnizer, you cannot also witness the marriage in this capacity.

Although it is often considered traditional that the best man and maid/matron of honor act as the witnesses, many couples also choose parents, perhaps both mothers, to act in this regard. This is both legal and acceptable.

As previously mentioned, it can be more efficient to obtain the witness signatures before the ceremony, rather than waiting till after. During that period, the signature parties often have more availability, as they are not busy with photography or celebrating. If you wish to do his, you should confirm it as acceptable with the couple, and ensure the photographer has a chance to capture the moment, if this is desired.

Officiant Title

If requested, you should write your title as it appears on your certificate of ordination. Most often the term 'Minister' is the one the clerical officer filing will be expecting, so if something unusual is used, they may, on rare occasions, ask for clarification.

Your Affiliation

If asked to include this information, you should write the full title of your body of ordination.

Your Denomination

If you are acting under a particular denomination, either as specified by your ordaining organization, or because the ceremony was explicitly performed under that denomination banner, you should write that in. If 'non-denominational', write in that it is such. On rare occasions, a clerk may question a lack of denomination. If that is unacceptable, for whatever reason, write the full name of your ordaining organization.

Ceremony Type: Civil or Religious?

If you are acting in any capacity through ordination, your ceremony is classed as religious, and you should complete the paperwork as such. A civil ceremony is only such if you are acting in the capacity as a qualified government officer, such as a notary or a judge.

The Souvenir Certificate

Many regions will provide a separate souvenir certificate for you to complete, and hand to the couple as a keepsake. You may wish to create your own design, and offer this as part of your package. If completing a keepsake certificate, you should write all names out in full in your best handwriting, and spell any dates, rather than using numbers. For example, use 'twelfth' rather than '12th'.

Once you have completed the license, ensure it is returned in accordance with the instructions given by the appropriate governing body. Instructions on this are almost always included in the license packet issued to the couple. In some areas, where multiple copies are required to be completed, you may be instructed to return a copy to the couple. You should do so before you leave the venue. If it is not convenient to hand them paperwork at that time, find a responsible party to take care of that document until they can be passed to the newlyweds.

It is important to remember that the license copies are legal documents, and should be kept safe at all times. Before you return them to the appropriate government body, you may wish to take copies for safe keeping, and for your records.

2.33g Dealing with a Crisis

A wedding is a highly charged, emotional situation. As an experienced professional, it is inevitable that members of any wedding party, as well as other vendors, will look to you in a time of difficulty.

A wedding 'crisis' often occurs because of a logistical failure. Wine may not have been delivered. Flowers may not be as promised. The amplification system may fail. The wrong color glitter may have been used on the tablecloths. Bizarre as it seems, the last example once caused tears and a half hour delay at a wedding I performed. In situations such as these, the best option is almost always to stay out of the way, and to let the appropriate professional provide the resolution. It is important to understand that, in your professional capacity, you have been hired to perform a particular task. As long as you are successfully fulfilling your remit, you have no professional concern with other matters. It is natural to want to 'step in', and be of aid in times of adversity. However, it is crucial to take the time to understand when this is helpful, and when it is not. A wedding works much like a machine, in that many parts work together to create a successful outcome. If you step outside your professional role in an attempt to solve a problem, you may easily make a situation much worse. Always take a careful and considered pause between any event and your response to it.

When a problem occurs, you should begin by listening to those involved. When emotions are high, the literal meaning of the words does not always convey the full significance of the situation. You should seek to understand the underlying need of each party. Anger and frustration at a small technical issue may be representative of a different, deeper concern. If you listen carefully, and try hard to understand this before you offer any response, the solution you find will be vastly more effective. In the glitter problem above, the color itself was not the correct issue, but was being used as a focus to express a deeper worry of the bride, that the record of her day would not look beautiful, and that she felt the day was slipping from her control.

It is a characteristic of most weddings that any size of problem can seem like a major international crisis. In fact, almost all problems encountered on any wedding day will have a simple solution. You, or the other professionals, will likely have encountered the same problem at a previous event, and be able to offer a tried and trusted solution quickly.

You may encounter scenes of familial breakdown. Emotions between family members are often at a high point during a wedding. It is important always to remain impartial, and to remember two key points:

1. The day is first about the couple, their wishes, and their bond.

2. Your job is to ensure the ceremony goes ahead as planned, but not to heal family feuds.

If you passed through a formal ordination process, you should have shown that you have good judgment, and a good understanding of positive human values and principles. If you use these as your guide, you will find the best outcome, and you will be acting in the professional manner expected by the organizations your represent.

2.33h What to do if you Mess Up

On rare occasions, errors and mistakes will occur. Fortunately, the vast number will be slight, and of that portion, a considerable number will also go unnoticed by the majority of those attending. The chance for error rapidly decreases if your preparations are full and clear, not only in your ceremony script but also in your mental and psychological routine for the day. The importance of preparation cannot be understated, and this is why it is always true that weddings for which a rehearsal has been held go more smoothly, and with greater confidence, than those where a couple takes the risk of not holding one.

Many small errors can be easily prevented. Mistakes such as misspeaking, or mispronouncing, a name can be avoided by cultivating a habit of double checking factual information every step of the process. If you are sufficiently rested, and have planned your time so that you are not forced to rush any part of the process, you will also see a massive reduction in simple errors.

There are several fears that plague even the most attentive and prepared Celebrant. These include, in addition to saying the wrong name, misplacing the script, arriving late to the venue, forgetting a cue, or dropping an important item, such as a ring. These again can be prevented almost entirely, by active and sensible preparation.

However, there is always the chance that a serious problem will occur. Although in most cases, such as a technical failure, these will be the responsibility of others, what should you do if the fault is your own?

The first, and most important, response to any mistake or error is to be considered and proactive, rather than just blindly reacting. Between any event and your response to it, there is an opportunity to consider your actions and their consequences. Always take that opportunity, and act out of reason and consideration rather than out of knee-jerk emotion. Here are the things to consider when you are thinking how best to recover from a mistake.

First, any response to an error on your part must not compound or increase the problem for those involved. Most problems do have a positive and constructive solution though this is often not the first response that springs to mind. Seek to understand what harm, if any, has been caused by an error, and ensure that any action you take, or words you speak, from that point do not magnify the problem.

Second, consider the needs of the other party before your own. The best and most positive solutions to any problem almost always involve understanding, and empathizing with, the needs of the other parties involved. Consider how your error may have affected the bride or groom, and what needs they have for any solution you may offer. For example, if your vehicle fails on route to a venue, understand that the couple's first need is to complete their established plans. You may then rightly choose to find another way to continue to the venue, perhaps by taxi, and complete your promised role in the day before trying to address any repair to your car. If a mistake is during the ceremony, the need that the couple has may well be that their ceremony be carried out with dignity and sophistication. A shorter apology at the time, followed up at greater length once the ceremony has concluded, may then be the best solution. If you honestly and sincerely put the needs of others ahead of your own in any situation where you have erred, you will always find yourself steered towards the correct course of action.

Third, it is important that you take ownership and responsibility for any mistakes you have made. This is perhaps the most important factor in recovering from any error, however accidental, and even one where the cause was not entirely your own. Accepting responsibility, clearly, and without reserve, demonstrates a maturity and professionalism that will always impress even the most disgruntled client. You will also find that, once you have taken ownership of an issue, you are highly motivated to find a positive outcome, rather than one that merely serves as damage limitation for yourself.

Fourth, it is important to offer a sincere and unreserved apology for any error or mistake on your part, even if the error was accidental and unintentional. The hallmarks of an effective apology are simple. Your apology should be unqualified and unreserved. It should be sincere, and stated simply. It should explicitly address the problem that was created, show that you understand and value the needs of the other party, and offer a constructive solution to either right the error, or make sufficient restitution. Lastly, an apology should show how you intend to learn from the situation, and act to prevent any recurrence of the problem.

For a catastrophic error, financial restitution may be in order. This is one excellent reason for considering a modest investment in business insurance, which I discuss later in the book. If there is any possibility at all of legal action, you should immediately consult a lawyer without any further contact with the other parties involved.

In almost all cases, from the smallest slip to the gravest mistake, if you are unsure how best to right a situation, seek to understand the needs of the other party. Doing this is often merely a matter of offering a sincere apology, and asking humbly how you might make amends.

Please do not be alarmed by this section of the book. Although mistakes do happen, almost all you experience will be minor, and quickly righted. In many cases, a simple and sincere apology will be more than sufficient. Each error should be treated as a chance to learn, and improve your working process. For experienced Celebrants, small errors are a timely reminder that we should never allow our years of practice to cause us to become complacent, or feel ourselves beyond simple mistakes.

If you act as a prepared professional, your career as a Celebrant will be one of vastly more successes and triumphs than of problems and regret. Be sure to celebrate your successes, but never be afraid to acknowledge, and learn from, any small failings.

2.33i Intoxication and Weddings

In section one, I placed sobriety high on my list of recommended behavior guidelines, second only to treating others with respect at all times. I firmly believe that all professional Celebrants should abstain from consuming any intoxicating substance, in even the smallest amounts, while they are acting in a professional capacity. In my opinion, this extends to all the time spent at a venue, or with clients, not just the ceremony itself.

Weddings are intoxicating events in themselves. The mix of emotions, stresses, interpersonal tensions, and high expectations, creates in those attending an abnormal state of mind, and feelings that too often suppresses rational thought and behavior. The effect of alcohol on such a mental state is only ever to amplify its worst qualities. However, you will often find that those involved in a wedding begin consuming alcohol far earlier in the day than is normal or sensible, and the key parties, the bride and groom, will often skip meals while doing so.

Additionally, you may find that the wedding rehearsal is often treated as an informal preliminary, or get-together, by those attending. Although this is understandable and forgivable, it can make the role of the marriage professionals much harder.

As the Celebrant, you are in an elevated position of authority and respect throughout the occasion. As such, part of your role is to seek to maintain control, ensure that high spirits of any kind do not impede what must be achieved, and do not lessen the enjoyment of those involved.

One way of doing this is to add a clause to your contract stipulating that you have the right to refuse to solemnize a marriage, at your discretion and without penalty to yourself, if you believe either party to be intoxicated to the extent that it is visibly impairing the judgment or behavior. The sample contract later in this book includes such a clause.

There are some areas of the country where specific laws and statutes are in place to address the issue of solemnizing a marriage while either party is intoxicated. One example is in Minnesota, and I have reproduced the statute below. Every marriage Celebrant should make it a professional priority to become familiar with the laws pertaining to wedlock in every region they intend to practice. If you have questions regarding the laws in your location, your ordination body should be able to provide guidance. There are also many online forums where such issues are discussed, and I have included links to these resources later in this book.

Minnesota Statute 518.02 Voidable marriages.

A marriage shall be declared a nullity under the following circumstances:

(a) A party lacked capacity to consent to the marriage at the time the marriage was solemnized, either because of mental incapacity or infirmity and the other party at the time the marriage was solemnized did not know of the incapacity; or because of the influence of alcohol, drugs, or other incapacitating substances; or because consent of either was obtained by force or fraud and there was no subsequent voluntary cohabitation of the parties;

2.33j Knowing When to Leave a Wedding

The ceremony is over, the paperwork has been completed, and all payments have been gratefully received. What then becomes the role of the Celebrant? In short, it is time to say goodbye, and to depart. Although you may find you are asked to stay for the reception and party, there are some excellent reasons to decline such offers.

Although your official duties are complete, if you are acting in a professional manner you should still consider yourself 'on-duty.' It is important to remember that your behavior reflects on your business, and also on the other members of your profession and ordination body. Your behavior is under constant scrutiny, and a slip while celebrating could ruin your reputation, not to mention your chances for an excellent testimonial. The safest course is an early, dignified exit.

If you do choose to stay, you will likely find you are among strangers. The marriage celebration is one based on family and community bonds, and an Officiant who is an outsider can be left feeling a little alone on such occasions.

The best argument for leaving is that you are a professional who has just finished an excellent piece of work, and you have earned the right to go home.

My routine often involves a quick post-ceremony picture with the bride and groom, something many couples and professional photographers will expect and request. I then ensure that the newlyweds have no more questions, for example about paperwork and the legal process. I then often hug them both a final time, bid the rest of the wedding party farewell, collect my things, and head for home.

If you do this, and know you have performed an inspiring and professional ceremony, you will find a spring in your step that you truly deserve. It is at these moments especially that Celebrants know why this is a terrific profession to be a part of.

If you have it with you on the day, double check before you leave that you have all paperwork and materials you should be taking with you.

2.33k Networking

Establishing contacts and relationships with other wedding professionals is crucial to growing your reputation and business as a Wedding Celebrant. Create business cards, something that can be done cheaply online at a site such as Vistaprint.com, and carry them with you at all times. At a convenient moment before the ceremony, exchange cards with the photographer, DJ, event planner, and any other professionals you encounter. The more you establish word-of-mouth recommendations, the less time and money you will have to spend on advertising and promotion.

TIP: Many people are now choosing to scan business cards they receive into applications such as Evernote. This saves on storage space, and allows for easier reference. To ensure your own cards scan easily and effectively, have a high contrast between font color and background color. Use a plain background, or one with a slight gradient, and choose fonts that are clear and readable (sans-serif fonts scan well). Although software capabilities are improving all the time, most will still have problems reading, for example, an ornate yellow text on a white background.

Where possible, following the ceremony, establish an online connection with your preferred vendors, either through mutual website links, which are very beneficial for your search engine placement, or by endorsing their work on a professional listing site such as WeddingWire (weddingwire.com).

It is a useful practice to keep a vendor list, perhaps in an address book or stored online, as you will almost certainly find you are asked by couples to recommend other professionals. In the course of performing ceremonies, you will have the chance to assess the abilities, and the professionalism, of the vendors you encounter. If you decide an individual is worth endorsing, you might add them to your list, perhaps with notes about their style or the regions they cover. It can also be useful to keep a second, much smaller, list of those you would rather not recommend. Although almost all wedding professionals you meet will be a true pleasure to work with, there may be one or two whose work, or attitude, you would rather not be associated with. Be careful whom you recommend, as a poor outcome from an endorsement could reflect badly on yourself.

2.34 After the Wedding Ceremony

At this point you are on your way home, or perhaps onto your next ceremony of the day. Congratulations! You are a success, and have played a vital, central role in a day those attending will remember for many years to come. Take a moment, in fact, take two, but realize that there are likely still a few important tasks to complete before the day is done.

First, although it is mandated only in a few regions, such as Hawaii, it is important for a Celebrant to keep records. Not only is this useful in recalling important information about past ceremonies, but it also helps you record your progress over time.

Start by photocopying each part of a completed license. Although multi-part licenses may look as though the pages are simply copies, there may be subtle differences in each section, and so it is important to retain a full and exact copy of all the official documents you plan to return. If you do not have access to a photocopier, you can take a digital scan using a smartphone application such as Evernote (evernote.com), and ensure this electronic file is uploaded to a secure backup location.

For those planning to perform more than one ceremony, I recommend purchasing a quality record book from a stationers. On each line, record the date, couple's names, and location of the ceremony. Do this immediately following every wedding you perform. It will be truly satisfying for you to watch as each page fills, and when referencing your past work in creating new ceremonies, this will become a useful index.

With every page of the completed license successfully copied, you should seal the documents carefully in their envelope, usually provided inside the packet by the issuing office, and fix a stamp before placing in the mailbox. You should get into the habit of completing this task thoroughly, immediately after the ceremony, before you settle down to relax for the evening. Doing so is not only the safest course, but will set your mind at ease that the documents are safely on their way from your charge.

If you feel, as you almost certainly will, that the couple might be happy to give you a testimonial, you should consider contacting them by e-mail to request this. My experience has shown that such e-mails are most effective if sent about two weeks after the event. What follows is an example text based on a review request email I have used successfully on many occasions:

Dear [Bride] and [Groom],

This is just a short note to thank you again for making me a part of your big day. I also wanted to let you know that the paperwork was completed and returned immediately after the wedding, though I also took copies as an extra safety precaution.

If you have a free moment over the next few days, I would be hugely grateful for a review or testimonial from one or both of you. These are extremely important to my business, as they are often my introduction to a new couple, and lets them know if I might be a good fit for their wedding day.

If you would like to leave a review you can do so by clicking the following link:

[Insert link here]

Thank you so much again, and don't hesitate to contact me at any time in the future if I can be of help in any way.

Wishing you both many wonderful years of smiles and happiness to come,

[Your name and details]

2.35 Pricing your Wedding Services

I hope that you now have a much fuller vision of the time and tasks involved in your role, from the first contact with the couple to the final time you close their file after you return from the ceremony. Your time and your skills are valuable, and it is both important and fair that you receive proper compensation for offering them.

Many non-Celebrants, and even some other wedding professionals, have a limited understanding of our role in the day, and because of this, they tend to devalue our efforts. It is important, both for your business and your sense of professional worth, that you believe in your value.

When you start to practice professionally, there are two key tasks that will help you set your prices. First, you should perform a competitor analysis for your region. Visit the websites of other Celebrants, and take note of any prices they have posted. Do not be afraid to ask other Celebrants what they charge. Many ordination bodies, such as the Society of Celebrations, will also be happy to offer you their current information and analysis on prices in your area. It is important that you maintain parity with your peers to a large degree. Although you may be tempted to offer bargain rates to undercut your competitors, in doing so you will be narrowing or eliminating your profits, as well as devaluing the Celebrant profession as a whole. If couples find you are available for a fraction of the usual price, they will have reduced respect for your role, and may have doubts about your skills, experience, and professionalism.

Second, you should examine your costs in producing and attending a ceremony, and ensure that all these are covered as an absolute minimum. You should never operate your Celebrant business at a net loss. To do so is not only pointless, but will have a very damaging impact on your own self-esteem and situation in life. You may wish to write down your anticipated expenses, or perhaps create a spreadsheet using a program such as Open Office (openoffice.org) to map out your costs and income.

Laura Cannon, of the International Association of Professional Wedding Officiants (iapwo.org), recently conducted an analysis of Officiant pricing across the United States. She found that, for any region, the average price of a Wedding

Celebrant falls at about 35% of the price for the top professional DJs in that location. You may wish to consider that figure when deciding what prices you will charge for your services.

Part Three
Funerals and Memorials

3.1 Introducing Modern Memorials

A modern memorial is a celebration of the life and legacy of an individual. They should be a positive event, personalized in ways that ensure every aspect reflects the personality of the deceased, and their wishes, and those of their closest family and friends.

It is an unavoidable fact that many traditional funerals and memorials are often hugely impersonal, or worse at odds with the facts and style that characterized the life of the deceased. Many religiously focused services are highly formulaic, with texts and readings of a highly generalized nature, or which refer only to scripture or supernatural concepts. This depersonalizing, and often dehumanizing, of the ceremony frequently leaves them an unfulfilling, unpleasant experience for those who attend.

There is a growing percentage of the population that does not hold supernatural beliefs, and so is unaffiliated with any church. Many of these individuals have no wish for a memorial that focuses on concepts such as 'passing on', or 'moving on' to some notion of an afterlife. Indeed, such ideas may be seen as offensive, in that they diminish the value of life that has been led. Terms such as 'going to a better place', 'reward', or the hurtful expression 'home-going', imply that the life that we have assembled to recognize was in some way inferior, or a 'practice' for another life utterly separate. While those of deeply held faith may find such ideas comforting, for many others they are unrealistic, distressing, and, in the worst cases, can increase the difficulty of the grieving process. In a modern end-of-life ceremony, death is seen as part of a natural process, and referenced as a factor or observable life.

A modern memorial should be a positive event. It should focus on the very best in the life of the deceased, and on the moments of their greatest success, love, and laughter. Too often, traditional ceremonies emphasize a life of pain, tears, and sorrow. This is done to promote the notion of an afterlife, usually the primary sales pitch of a church or faith, as something superior and desirable. It can be clearly observed, and is now an accepted psychological fact, that treating death as a chance to celebrate life is far healthier during the grieving process. Treating death as a natural occurrence, and personalizing the associated community events, allows friends and family to return to normal life more quickly, with far less psychological trauma.

Modern end-of-life ceremonies, therefore, have two major goals. The first is to provide a cathartic experience for the deceased's loved ones. The second is to provide a suitable, and personal, tribute to the life that was lived. In this regard, a personalized, life-centered, ceremony succeeds far more than traditional formulas. These then are the primary factors a modern humanistic Celebrant must keep foremost in mind when preparing, and performing, a memorial or funeral.

The Difference between Funeral and Memorial

It is worth clarifying the difference between the two terms used at the end of the last paragraph. A *funeral*, by definition, implies the presence of the deceased, either as a corpse or in the form of ashes contained within an urn. A *memorial* takes place without such a physical presence, and often after the deceased has been interred. As a modern Celebrant, particular when serving the non-religious community, you will almost certainly be asked to oversee many more memorials than funerals or interments. For Humanists, and others without supernatural faith, the body itself is often considered just a natural form, and of no sacred or spiritual value once life has ended.

3.2 The Role of the End of Life Celebrant

In your function as a modern end-of-life Celebrant, practicing humanistic, non-traditional, and non-religious ceremonies, you will find the skills required and utilized are very similar to those necessary for the performance of other ceremonies, such as weddings. Skills such as public speaking, working with your clients and other professionals, working in highly emotional situations, and creating and structuring a ceremony are still the core attributes of this role.

However, when comparing the role in the ceremony itself, the part played in memorials is often less of a performer and more of a facilitator and coordinator. Compared to a wedding, you will find you are the one speaking for a vastly smaller fraction of the ceremony time, and that for the majority of the proceedings, other individuals are the focus of attention. You will likely find that the average length of a memorial is longer than that of a wedding ceremony, running at perhaps twice to three times that length.

Your main tasks before a modern memorial service can be summarized as follows:

- Provide Practical Planning Information
- Act as a Center of Emotional Stability
- Reduce Concerns About the Event
- Identify the Needs of the Client and Family
- Interpret the Wishes of the Client
- Offer Possible Solutions
- Create a Plan for the Event

Your main tasks during a modern memorial service can be summarized as follows:

- Create and Maintain the Ceremony Structure
- Establish the Tone
- Provide a Context
- Introductions and Thanks
- Control Timing
- Provide an Emotional Anchor

There are a number of scenarios that can take place at the end of life:

An individual may choose to be cremated immediately following death, and this is followed some time later by a memorial service. This is a very popular option in the United States.

A body may be bequeathed, or donated, to medical science. This would usually take place immediately after death, and then be followed at a later date by a memorial service.

A body may be cremated, and then the ashes retained to be present at the celebration event, followed by a private committal ceremony, scattering the ashes on either land or water.

A funeral may take place within a day or two of death, at which time the body is present in a casket. Relatives and friends may have a period of opportunity to view the deceased before the funeral. After the funeral ceremony, the body will be taken to its final place of disposition, either for burial or cremation. A burial committal ceremony may take place immediately following a funeral. Ashes may be interred or scattered within the grounds of a crematorium immediately after cremation.

You may wish to familiarize yourself with the processes of burial and cremation. Most funeral homes and crematories are happy to answer questions, and give tours of their facilities.

3.3 Defining 'In Need' and 'Preplanning'

There are two similar, but distinct, types of planning process associated with creating and 'end of life' ceremony, occasion, or celebration. When the individual whose life is to be celebrated has already passed away, that circumstance is referred to as 'in need'. Where a person chooses to engage in preparatory work for their own memorial, this is called 'preplanning'. Preplanning can occur at any point in life, not necessarily when death is imminent.

An 'In need' situation occurs after someone has died, or occasionally in the days immediately before this event, where a terminal individual is unable to assist in their planning. As a Celebrant, you will find yourself working with a family, or their representative, to create a ceremony. The service venue may already be booked, perhaps through a Funeral Home or other appropriate location, and you may find yourself working with Funeral Directors to coordinate the practical arrangements for the day. If you are planning to make your services available on a regular basis to clients in this situation, your lifestyle should allow you to keep flexible hours, and make appointments at short notice.

In a 'preplanning' situation, you are helping an individual to consider, and then specify precisely, their wishes for their memorial. For many individuals, it is important that they are assured any ceremony of remembrance will correctly reflect their values and spiritual outlook. For individuals who are Humanist or Non-religious, it can be crucial to know that their memorial will not be overtaken, or 'hijacked' by a default religious tone. Many such individuals may have experienced ceremonies that misrepresented a loved one in such a way, and are therefore acutely aware of the dissatisfaction this causes, and that having a misrepresentative ceremony can be genuinely harmful to the grieving process of relatives and friends. Unlike In-need, Preplanning appointments often happen over a longer period, and with far less urgency. If you choose to do so, this may be a service you offer to particular groups who have strong special concerns about the way their memorial takes place. Such groups might include Freethought and Humanist Societies, Environmental Groups, and other organizations whose members bond over spiritual or philosophical issues.

3.4 The In Need Process

Where a family reaches out to a modern Celebrant at the time of a relative's passing, it is often an indicator that they are looking for a more secular and humanistic memorial ceremony. Where the individual, or family group, had been devoutly religious throughout their life, it is far more likely that the relatives would have reached out through the official, traditional avenues provided by an established church of which the deceased was a member.

Although you will be dealing with clients experiencing some very painful and negative emotions, the family and friends will almost certainly be looking to accentuate the positive, and to celebrate their loved one's memory and legacy. You should be prepared, during your questioning and information gathering process, always to enquire about and accentuate the positive aspects of the deceased's life. You will want to learn about their family bonds, personal successes and triumphs, passions in life, and the most told stories and tales that others have often shared about that person. Almost all individuals have one or two popular anecdotes that have evolved into beloved family lore over the years.

With a humanistic ceremony, it is often important that it does not distort memories of the deceased into unrealistic ideals, or that the remembrances become generic and impersonal in nature. One of your roles, as the organizer and leader of such a ceremony, is to ensure that everything possible is done to maintain such marvelous personal color. Humanists accept that no one leads a life without trials or setbacks. It is possible, and often desirable, for those personal troubles to give color and depth to the experience and message of life, and ultimately to give greater dimension to the triumphs that were achieved despite them. Such anecdotes and references can make for some of the most cathartic and heartwarming parts of a modern memorial ceremony.

In preparing for this type of event, you are not trying to condense a life into a service only you will be performing. Rather, your role will be closer to that of a facilitator, helping those close to the deceased find how they can best contribute to, and take part in, the ceremony. You should always keep in mind that, on the day, your role will primarily be to preside over the ceremony, rather than to perform it. As you gather your information, look for the individuals best suited to actively participate in the different sections of the event.

Throughout your preparations, you should give consistent thought to controlling the flow and length of the occasion. When considering flow, keep in mind a broad timeline of the life of the deceased. Ideally, recollections from earlier times in their life, perhaps remembered by school or college friends, should come before stories of the departed's later life. Those closest to the deceased at the time of their passing should be given the opportunity to close the period of recollections. An ideal length for a modern memorial service will be no less than twenty minutes, but no longer than an hour.

3.4a The Initial Contact

When you are first contacted by family, friends, or a representative of the deceased, it is important first to discover the time and place of the ceremony. You should immediately check your calendar to ensure you are available. Your next step should then be to arrange a time for the consulting interview. This should take place as soon as convenient, and in a suitable location.

Several factors will affect the choice of venue in which you plan to meet with bereaved friends and family members. Unlike the discussion of wedding plans, a public location such as a restaurant or cafe is almost never appropriate for the planning of a funeral or memorial. You should seek to hold your discussion somewhere private, and where interruptions can be avoided. It is also beneficial if the meeting takes place somewhere the bereaved feel naturally comfortable. For this reason, many consulting interviews are held in the home of the deceased, or one of their closest family or friend.

Once you have established your availability, for both the ceremony and the consultation interview, it is important to collect some basic facts about the deceased: name, age at the time of passing, gender, and date and place of death. More personal details are best-gained face to face, but where these are offered during the first contact, you should make careful notes to be used later on.

Included with this book is a sample memorial questionnaire to aid you in remembering to collect all the required information.

3.4b Pricing

Discussions of pricing and payments are never comfortable in circumstances surrounding a bereavement. However, as a professional it is important to ensure that your costs, financial and otherwise, are met. If this subject is approached with sincere tact and respect, clients will understand that you are acting with dignified professionalism.

The base amount you choose will depend on various factors: geographic location, your estimations of your costs, the amount you are comfortable charging, and whether you elect to offer any special discounts for particular groups, such as veterans.

It is important that you conduct local research into what prices other Celebrants are charging for comparable services. The average pricing in the U.S. varies considerably by location, but most often falls in a band between $200 to $500 for creating and performing a ceremony.

As with every other kind of service you choose to provide, you may need to adjust your fee to allow for travel expenses. In 2016, the I.R.S. stipulated business rate for travel is $0.54 per mile of your journey. The rates are adjusted each year, at the start of January, and you can find the latest information by visiting this web address:

https://www.irs.gov/Tax-Professionals/Standard-Mileage-Rates

When calculating your travel addition, do not forget to total your miles for a round trip. You should be compensated for both legs of the journey.

For further information see Section 5.10.

3.4c Contracts

When providing 'In Need' end-of-life services, there is often a very short period between the booking and the ceremony. For this reason, you may choose not to ask for a deposit. However, a contract is always important when conducting any business as a professional. Having your terms laid out clearly on paper can also be reassuring to the family of the deceased, as money factors are often a great cause of concern at times of bereavement. Any contract should cover what is expected on both sides, and should state the core information about your particular involvement in the ceremony, such as your date and time of arrival and departure, what you will be expected to wear, any items (such as amplification equipment) that you will be expected to bring, and when your final payment must be received, as well as who is responsible for paying it, and what form the payment should take. Again, although discussion of financial matters can feel uncomfortable in situations of bereavement, by setting this out clearly on paper, you are avoiding any doubts, and acting in a clear, honest manner that demonstrates your professional integrity.

Both the senior representative of your clients and yourself should sign and date the contract. Later in this book, I have created sample contracts for you to use as a guide. However, I recommend that you seek professional legal advice when creating any contract for your business that you wish to be confident will be fully binding in, and meet the requirements of, your particular region.

3.4d The Consulting Interview

Your primary tasks at the consulting interview are first to listen, and then to advise. If you have only previously been involved in planning wedding ceremonies, much of the discussion may be more free form, and loosely structured, than that you are used to. The family will likely be keen for you to know as much as possible about the life and achievements of the departed, as well as the 'great tales' of their living years that have most often been lovingly recounted at family gatherings. It is polite form to allow them to do his in their own style and time, gathering the salient points where these emerge. This retelling is an important part of the grieving process, as much as your primer on the deceased. You should take as many notes as possible. Although I have provided a sample questionnaire later in this book, a pen and pad will be handy for taking down the relevant points in a more natural manner. You will able to review and collate your notes after the interview has concluded.

As you listen to the remembrances of the family, look for themes and highlights that you may gently allude to in your opening remarks during the ceremony. It is crucial, however, that your opening words do not reveal any 'spoilers' regarding the stories, or other references, speakers are likely to share during their remarks on the day. Always remember that your primary role is as a *facilitator* for the commemoration and grieving of others.

If the narrative of the family goes on too long, or begins to repeat, use your questions to draw things back into a more useful format. The more practical your questions become at this point, the more progress you will make in resolving decisions about the form and content of the ceremony.

Be sure to establish the correct pronunciation of the name of the deceased, and, just as importantly, how those closest knew them. Discover if they had a nickname, or any affectionate monikers that may have been used, especially by younger generations. Establish the ages at which they passed the most important milestones in their life, such as graduation, marriage, parenthood, military service, and retirement. Make careful note of all the roles they were most known for, both professionally and personally, such as a spouse, parent, grandparent, son, daughter, job title, military rank, and any other position they may have held in the community.

Where a family has chosen a secular ceremony, they may still have questions relating to spirituality in a broader sense, and about your own spiritual or religious outlook. In almost all cases, such questions are asked simply to reassure themselves that you are in a position to fully understand, appreciate, and respect the outlook of the deceased and their family.

Friends and relatives may often have questions about Humanist and Secular approaches to grieving and the non-religious understanding of death. It is useful to make yourself aware of these, so you can answer such questions in a confident and reassuring manner.

By the end of the interview, you should have enough information to confidently put together a draft order of ceremony. You will have gathered the names, roles, and contact information for any proposed speakers or performers. If further information must be collected, agree upon a single individual who will provide this information, and then communicate it to you by phone, or email, within 24 hours.

After the interview, you may wish to connect with the venue to discuss any technical or logistical requirements. It should not be your job to act as a booking intermediary between the site and the family, unless there are very good reasons for doing so, and you understand the issues involved. However emotionally connected you become, and that is to be encouraged, you are the ceremony professional contracted to create that part of the day. To step outside that role can often create more problems than it solves. For any matters outside the ceremony, seek only to advise where you are able. There are certain practical matters a family must handle for themselves, and doing so is an essential part of the grieving process.

Before you leave the consulting interview, confirm the time you will next talk or meet with your primary contact. As you approach the date of the ceremony, you should ensure you available as far as practically possible to answer any follow-up questions or concerns the family may have.

3.5 Preplanning with the Living

Many feel it is important to plan for the final celebration of one's life, even though this may well be a party one is particularly unable to attend. This is especially true for those who hold clear, and strongly held spiritual philosophies, and who are anxious that these may not be fully respected and represented at a default, traditional ceremony. When many citizens die, the short planning period available, combined with community assumptions and generalizations, can often lead to a default funeral or memorial service. In the United States, this would very often be Christian. When this disconnection occurs, it can become apparent to the mourners all too late that the ceremony misrepresents the deceased, and that the default prayers, platitudes, and supernatural references have no resonance with the life they are supposed to be commemorating. At best this can be an uncomfortable experience, but worse it can often be insulting, distressing, and damaging to the grieving process.

There is often a discomfort, particularly in western countries, with preparing one's memorial. There are still many, mostly unnecessary, taboos surrounding the process of death, and social reaction to it. There is also the often stated truism that 'memorials are for the living, rather than for the dead.' There is, however, no doubt that a ceremony that truly reflects the deceased, which carries the essence of their voice, can have far greater benefit to the grieving process of those attending than one which only speaks from the viewpoint of the mourners.

When preplanning, you are helping an individual to consider, and then explicitly specify, their wishes for their memorial. The elements of the ceremony that you will discuss with them will be almost identical to those you would cover during an in-need interview. The obvious addition, however, is the discussion of any personal message, perhaps written, recorded, or filmed, that an individual may wish played to those attending their final farewell.

The experience of preplanning can often be a surprisingly pleasant one. It gives that individual an uncommon opportunity to remember and revisit their life and loves. They can then pause to consider how to best commemorate these aspects of their life. This process can also bring comfort to those loved ones who would otherwise have to make such difficult emotional decisions when the time arrives. Some may choose to go through this alone, while others may wish to do so with their family present. However approached, the many questions that arise during the process have created an increased need for professional, modern memorial preplanning.

With the continuing rise in the numbers of individuals defining themselves as non-religious, there is a growing demand for secular memorial ceremonies that reflect that position. One way for any person to ensure that their memorial matches their wishes is to spend a short time planning for when that time comes. If you are associated with your local Humanist or Freethought community, you may want to offer this service to them, and perhaps even suggest yourself as a guest speaker.

Before offering this service within your community, you should carefully consider your own attitudes to preplanning, and the psychological effect this process will have on you. This is certainly not a role in which every Celebrant will feel comfortable. Remember that just because you have chosen to take on the position of Celebrant, you are not obliged in any way to offer every possible form of service or ceremony, and I would strongly advise everyone in the profession to only take on the types of bookings and projects that bring you positive emotional fulfillment.

During this preplanning process, you will be almost exclusively focused on the content of the ceremony, and may only touch briefly on the wider practical issues surrounding death. Funeral Homes usually offer preplanning services that address those logistical and legal aspects of the process. Where a funeral home has already been chosen, you should be ready to contact them, and introduce yourself as the appointed Celebrant for an individual. You will find most Funeral Directors very friendly and accommodating.

3.5a The Initial Contact

Although some rare individuals prefer to plan years in advance, most preplanning for a memorial will take place close to the anticipated end of life. Many requests for these services may come via local groups whose members have a particular concern that their wishes will be respected immediately following their death. You may have left literature with a local Freethought group, and find that an individual, perhaps diagnosed with a life-threatening medical condition, decides it is time to put these plans in order.

When you are contacted, your two immediate tasks will be to make that person aware of your terms of service, and then to arrange a mutually convenient time for the consulting interview. You should ensure that you collect full contact information for the person and also establish clearly who will be present and partake in the planning process.

As with an 'in need' consultation, you will seek to hold your discussion somewhere private, where interruptions can be avoided. It is also beneficial if it takes place somewhere the planners feel naturally comfortable. For this reason, many consulting interviews take place in the client's home, or that of their closest family member or friend.

3.5b Pricing

The amount you charge for preparing a memorial service plan is very much a matter for your discretion. In cases where the passing is imminent, you may wish to waive payment of the planning portion of the fee until the service takes place. This is only a viable choice, however, where the immediate family are actively and positively involved in the planning process, and where you have a contract establishing this arrangement. In cases where you are planning with an individual alone, or a friend who has no legal involvement with that person's estate, you should collect any expected fees upon completion of your ceremony plan.

It is vital to establish, clearly and positively, very early on in the planning process exactly what payments will be made, when they will be made, who will be responsible for them, and what payment methods will be used. Understandably, many Celebrants will be uncomfortable raising such matters, but clients will respect your honesty, integrity, and plain speaking for doing so. An individual who has chosen to pre-plan their memorial service will usually be someone pragmatic in nature, and will, therefore, respect that attitude in others.

For preplanning as a stand-alone service, you may wish to quote a price and receive payment at the consulting interview. Alternatively, you may choose to invoice the client and receive payment when you deliver the final draft of the ceremony plan. For obvious reasons, this is not a service one would offer credit terms for, and you should avoid any situation that may leave you chasing final payments after you have delivered on your contracted tasks. For every type of ceremony process you will perform as a Celebrant, payment before, or at the time of, service is always the best policy.

If you are involved in a particular group, such as your local Humanist Association, you may decide to offer your preplanning services as a donation, or at a significantly reduced rate, particularly if the group is willing to promote your services in their literature or online.

You should decide whether, in all cases or each case based on the particular needs, you should charge a stand-alone fee for preplanning, or have it included in a package, along with your reimbursement for eventually performing the ceremony. A typical fee for a stand-alone service might be between $70 to $100 in the United States.

However you choose to arrange payment, it is vital that you not operate this service under a net loss as a standard procedure. Do not forget that your time, skill, and materials deserve compensation. If your operation is not, *at the very minimum*, self-sustaining, you will quickly become disheartened, or be forced to close your practice. By short-changing yourself in such a way, you will only be serving to eventually deprive your local community of a valuable and much needed human resource.

3.5c Contracts

If the preplanning is sufficiently close to the likely time of death as to form part of a combination with arranging the ceremony, you may wish to provide a contract to the client, or their representatives, that covers all stages of planning and performance. You should then decide if you take separate payments for each section of the process, or a balance to cover the entirety. My recommendation is that you keep your contracts for preplanning distinct from any you produce for the ceremony. By keeping the two separate, you lessen the chance for any confusion, and also allow for any unexpected changes in the arrangements. For instance, if your preplanning contract also included a ceremony date, but the client went into sudden remission or recovery, this would cause you to rework the entire situation. If your contracts for each stage had been separate, you could complete your planning in a tidy fashion, and inform the clients cheerfully that you are glad you do not yet have to contract for the final part of the process. Keeping contracts simple, and every process transparent, will always make for happier Celebrants and clients.

The contracts you produce should contain all the core information about both parties, and lay out exactly what is expected, as well as the date it is anticipated. Again, individuals who seek memorial preplanning are most likely pragmatic in nature, and will, therefore, respect a careful approach.

Later in this book, I have created sample contracts for you to use as a guide. However, I recommend that you seek professional legal advice when creating any contract for your business that you wish to be confident will be fully binding in, and meet the requirements of, your particular jurisdiction. For more information on contracts, deposits, and receiving payments, please see section 5.10 later in this book.

3.5d The Consulting Interview

The consulting interview for planning the details of the memorial service may take place at the client's home, a nursing home, a rehabilitation center, hospice, or hospital. The ideal location will be a place that guarantees privacy, and interruptions can be prevented. You may wish to be alone with the client, or they may want to include a family member or close friend. On occasion, several family members may want to be present. You should be aware that larger groups will lengthen the time needed for the interview, and may result in significantly higher emotional tension during the process. However, where a family group is especially close and harmonious in nature, a planning 'get-together' can be a rewarding experience, providing the conversation remains structured and on-topic.

You should allocate a minimum of an hour for discussion, but be prepared to spend more time if needed. This is a fluid process that cannot, and should not, be rushed. The planning process is often a delicate one, involving extended time reminiscing, and viewing family albums.

Your goal, during the interview, is to arrive at a set of wishes that can be clearly communicated to those who will have the final task of executing them. Such intentions should be clear enough that they will make immediate sense to friends, family members, and other end-of-life professionals not intimately familiar with the dynamics of that particular family group. Although you should allow for unstructured reminiscences, wherever possible try to guide the conversation back onto the key tasks set out in your questionnaire. You will want to talk about the structure of the ceremony and the options for each stage. During this process, you should try to take as many notes as possible. You may wish to augment your questionnaire fields with copious free notes, so I advise you to take an extra pad of paper with you for the interview. Your final aim is to leave the meeting with enough information to allow you to write a complete ceremony plan that will condense the outline onto a single page of information; that is then augmented by accompanying pages of details, footnotes, and useful associated information, such as the contact information for all participants.

3.5e Completing the Process

Once you have gathered the required information, you should write up your notes into a 'memorial plan' draft. This should include full details of the client's wishes concerning anticipated speakers, readings, music, ceremonial additions, and all other aspects of the occasion. The client should review and approve this document. You should be prepared to produce a second draft with revisions, if this is requested after they have reviewed the first version, and they have given further thought to the details you discussed at the first consultation.

You may wish to enclose the physical copy of the plan in a nice binder. You should also ensure that your details are clear on each page of every draft, and that all pages are numbered (with a total page number next to them, for example, 'Page 7 of 9'). Those measures prevent any critical information becoming lost when the document is reviewed or changes hands.

Once the ceremony plan is approved, you must make sure that all the relevant people know the information exists, and where it is stored. It goes without saying that you should retain a copy, both in physical form and as an off-site, electronic backup. You should discuss this issue with the client during the process, and be prepared to produce several copies of the final draft, so that they may be stored in several safe locations.

Storing the ceremony plan alongside the will is usually not ideal for any document needed in the earliest planning stages following a death. This is because a will is not often accessed and read immediately, and in some cases may not be produced until after a funeral has taken place, or is well into the final planning stages. Storing the ceremony plan in a safe deposit box, rented by the client, is also not recommended, as these are often sealed upon death, and the contents may not then be accessible for a considerable period. A good place to store the wishes for a ceremony is alongside other immediately required papers, such as the client's birth certificate and passport.

It is important that everyone mentioned as a participant in the final version of the plan is made aware of this fact, and that the plan's existence, and location, is also communicated to every major party in the planning process. Ideally, such communication with participants should come from the client, or a close friend or family member acting on their behalf. Even the most positive plans for a memorial are delicate, emotional issues, and best communicated by a familiar voice.

Once the development process is complete, arrange a time to check in again with the client. In the case of a shorter expectancy of need, this may be in a few days, but for those only making contingency plans for all eventualities, a check-in period of six months might be sufficient. Mark this check-in date on your calendar and be sure to maintain all your notes alongside the ceremony plan within your filing system. For more on creating your Celebrant filing system, see section 5.8 later in this book.

3.6 Core Elements of a Memorial

One of the great advantages of a modern memorial ceremony is its power of flexibility, in both form and style. There are, however, core elements that are often expected, and that define the occasion as a memorial. Although tradition works best as a guide, and not as a set of rules, some traditional customs add not only great flavor and color to a memorial but also have actual benefits to the grieving process for those who attend. What follows are the main sections you may expect to include in many ceremonies you perform, but feel free to adapt, add, or remove any ideas or parts, as you and your clients find appropriate.

3.6a Opening Words

As with a wedding ceremony, two key roles of the presiding Celebrant are to welcome those attending, and to explain the nature of what is about to take place. Although you may wish to say a few words of your own about the deceased, and this is appropriate if you knew them personally, it is crucial that you do not give away any 'spoilers' regarding the anecdotes, and references, others are likely to offer during their contribution to the ceremony. Always remember that, when officiating a memorial, your primary role is as the facilitator for the commemorations and grieving of others. I am going to share with you a few brief words that I have used to set the tone of a secular memorial service.

Sample Memorial Opening Words

'Ladies and gentlemen, friends and family of [Deceased], welcome and thank you all for attending today to celebrate the life, journey, and achievements of someone who made such a lasting impact on those who knew him/her. In a few moments you will hear memories, stories, and recollections some of you have prepared for today. As you listen and bring to mind your memories of [Deceased], do not be afraid to smile and laugh. The best moments in life, the ones we should always cherish, are the ones that gave us happiness, a joy that still echoes within us. Our time today is short; far too short to do justice to any life. Therefore, if you come forward to speak and share with us today, please keep your comments to just a few minutes. With some stories that is harder than with others, as some do deserve the fullest telling. So, I encourage everyone today to share from the heart. I will be seated to the side, and if you see me rise, that will let you know it will soon be time for another person to share their thoughts and memories. If you had not planned to speak today but find you wish to do so, we will try our best to put a little time aside for you towards the end. If you have a written message, please bring that forward in a few moments.

I will keep my words brief. In my role, one I feel very fortunate to have, joining others to celebrate life, legacy, and the meaning we give to each other's lives, I have found two things to be always true. The first is that a life lived can be compared to a painting. With each action, interaction, adventure, triumph, or sacrifice we add new brush strokes, and colors, to the canvas of our lives. As with any painting, we cannot appreciate the meaning completely until the picture is complete, and the last brush stroke has left the campus. It is then that we can see the full picture of life's work, and feel its effect upon us. These are feelings and images that stay with us all our lives, often for many years after the painter has left the room.

I am also reminded each time I join a group of people, as I am here today, that each life is like a stone thrown into a pond. It sends out ripples that touch first those closest, but which continue to spread and reach so many others, changing so many lives in unexpected ways, long after the stone has disappeared beneath the surface of the waters.

I, therefore, ask you today, as you sit and share memories of [Deceased], that you consider this completed picture of life, and how it affects you. Think also of the image that you are now painting, and will one day leave to stand alongside that of

[Deceased]. When your last brush stroke has left the campus, how will the picture of your life touch the hearts of others.

Think also today of those ripples that spread from [Deceased]'s life, and the times they touched your own. Consider, and commemorate, the moments when this person made a difference in your life. As you do so, think of the ripples your own life spreads across your family your friends, your community, across the whole world. It is my hope that those we send out will always raise up the lives of others, for each time one life is increased all lives are raised. Now, let us move to our first speaker for today.'

3.6b Personal Statements and Recollections

At the core of a modern, humanistic memorial ceremony are the statements, recollections, comments, and stories given and told by family and friends of the departed. These come in two general forms: the pre-arranged eulogy, or address, and the spontaneous comments or recollections offered on the day.

Great care should be taken, when planning your lineup of memorial speakers, to allocate time in a manner that suits your arrangements for other activities, as well as any limiting factors particular to the location, such as the end of the venue booking period. Keep in mind that a good length for a memorial service is between thirty minutes to an hour, and there may be other activities, such as a meal or mingling over drinks, which must have time allocated for their completion.

For each speaker, a balance should be made between allowing them the opportunity and latitude to give full expression to their thoughts and feelings, and avoiding overrunning. Some speakers will inevitably take longer than expected to deliver their recollections, while others may be highly organized and surprisingly brief.

It is useful, before the speakers begin, to explain the time limitations in a careful and sensitive manner, and to arrange a subtle signal for any who go on a little longer than planned. Explain that such controls must be implemented to give everyone a fair time. If said with genuine care and consideration, everyone will understand the need for brevity as a consideration to all. A signal I have employed in the past is to sit off to the side during each speaker's turn at the microphone. If they begin to overrun their allotted time window, I stand up. This is usually enough of a sign for all but the most over-enthusiastic speakers. If standing is ineffective at drawing a conclusion, I step forward to a position slightly behind and to the side of the speaker. I have found this is always sufficient as a reminder of the time limitations we share.

A Message from the Departed

On some occasions, particularly where a Memorial was preplanned, the deceased may have left a message, or short piece of writing, to be communicated during the ceremony. On rare occasions, they may even have left instructions for an audio or video message to be played. Where this is the case, special care should be taken to prepare those attending for this moment, as this can be an overwhelmingly emotional experience, particularly for those closest to the departed, and especially if the death has only very recently taken place. In choosing where to put such a message within the ceremony structure, it is useful to examine what the deceased was communicating. If the message is one of welcome to loved ones, it is sensible to place this early in the proceedings. If the message is one of heartfelt farewell, it may make more sense to place this nearer the end. In all cases, the placement of such an addition should only be made after careful consultation with those closest to the deceased.

3.6c Preplanned Recollections

Where a ceremony was preplanned, the deceased may have expressed strong wishes as to those they would like to speak on the day. Where this is the case, such friends or family members should have been given this request sufficiently in advance of the ceremony to prepare their words. However, many may still leave such preparation until the latest possible time, and you should be prepared, even in the final stages of planning, to offer such individuals advice or guidance on what they may choose to include. It is also true that, when faced with the actual moment of standing and sharing their thoughts and memories, some may then decide that this is too emotionally painful. It is useful to suggest, to all speakers who feel they may be in this position on the day, that they prepare a few words in writing, that you will then be able to read on their behalf.

It is incredibly difficult for any spouse to give a eulogy for someone who was so close. In many cases, you may be asked to read a message on behalf of the husband, or wife, of the deceased. Such an addition should come at the very end of all other recollections and activities. Giving this type of reading is perhaps the most difficult and emotional task you will have to perform in any memorial service. The words will often be very profound and heartfelt, and the author may well be sat in front of you, being comforted by those closest. Take as much time as you can to practice such an address, speak the words slowly, and with natural dignity. When you complete the statement, leave a few seconds pause to allow the importance of the words to be fully considered by those listening.

With 'In Need' ceremonies, you will have less time to prepare those who will be speaking, and the list of those offering their recollections may change up until the last moment. Family and friends will be able to suggest those best able and suited to speak. Where a ceremony is created at very short notice, the spontaneous recollections may make up a greater part of the service.

You should leave a portion of the time available to read written messages from those unable to attend. Very often, you will perform this task, but occasionally a family member, or close friend, may wish to do so.

The time allocated for each speaker will vary according to the time available for the ceremony as a whole and the number of speakers who wish to participate. A good length for a speech is often between two to seven minutes. Any longer than this should be discouraged, unless the immediate family requests an extended address by a particular individual. A consistent aspect of your role will be to manage time, and ensure that the program timeline is maintained as closely as possible.

3.6d Spontaneous Statements

During any memorial ceremony, there may be friends or family members who decide, at the last moment, that they wish to say a few words about the deceased. It is useful to allocate a short segment of time to allow for this, but only if other plans make this possible. A proper place for such an addition is often after the main body of preplanned speakers have given their statements, but before those of the closest family members, and any message or address from the spouse. For those time prevents offering a spoken address, do make available a book of remembrances or condolences, so they may have the opportunity to share in some other form. In a few cases, spontaneous statements may require a little extra moderation and time control. Where it is necessary to manage speakers in this way, always do so with kindness and respect.

3.6e Music

Music can be crucial in setting the tone, and feel, of a ceremony. Many of the best tunes are secular, rather than religious, as these often provided the soundtrack to the life of the deceased. Songs that have the most impact at a memorial are often those that were favorites of the deceased, or those whose lyrics and style reflect the life, loves, and achievements of that person. When preplanning, you will often find that this is the one element many individuals have already considered at some point in their lives.

Music to accompany a funeral or memorial can be purely instrumental, or with accompanying lyrics. It may be a live performance, if logistics and budget allow, or music may be prerecorded. Almost all funeral homes, and many rented venues, such as restaurants, have the ability to play prerecorded music. At a minimum, you should consider a short selection of music that can be played as guests enter, and then another selection to accompany their departing the ceremony location.

Where there is a member of the family, or a close friend, with musical abilities, it can be a highly personal and meaningful gesture to offer them the chance to play during the ceremony.

TIP: As politely as possible, you should assess the level of skill of every amateur musician who is suggested as a performer at the ceremony. It is a sad, but undeniable, fact that an unaccomplished musician may provide uncomfortable moments, or unwanted amusement, for which a ceremony may be primarily remembered later by those who attended. In avoiding such situations, you should always act with tact and discretion. However, the final decision should almost always be that of the immediate family.

If it is felt appropriate, you may choose to include a song sung by all those in attendance. Any such group song should very strongly resonate with the life, and legacy, of the deceased, and, ideally, be one that is familiar to the majority of those present.

Songs that include lyrics should be chosen with great care to reflect the sensitivities of those attending. This is particularly true concerning spiritual content. For a nonreligious ceremony the inclusion of songs that reference the afterlife, or any concepts of heavenly reward, are obviously hugely inappropriate. Where any song is suggested, you should try to obtain a copy of the lyrics, and read these through to safely ensure their complete suitability. An unfortunate choice of phrase, overlooked when making musical selections, can have a profound, and damaging, effect upon the entire ceremony.

Some Possible Musical Choices for a Modern Memorial

'Always Look on the Bright Side of Life' by Monty Python
'Arms' by Christina Perri
'Breathe' by Pearl Jam
'Come Away With Me' by Norah Jones
'Dancing In The Sky' Dani & Lizzi
'Don't fear the reaper' by Blue Oyster Cult
'Everything I Own' by Bread
'Far Side Banks of Jordan' by Cox Family
'Fare Thee Well Love' The Rankins
'Fields of Gold' by Eva Cassidy
'Fix You' a cover by Young at Heart
'Go Rest High on The Mountain' by Vince Gill
'Good Riddance' by Green Day
'Harbour Lights' by The Platters
'He Ain't Heavy, He's my Brother' The Hollies
'Highway to Hell' by AC/DC
'Keg On My Coffin' by The Push Stars
'One More Morning' by Steve Winwood
'One Red Rose' by Reapers Riddle

'Pristina' by Faith No More

'Prop Me Up Beside The Jukebox (If I Die)' by Joe Diffie

'Remember When' by Alan Jackson

'Roll Me Up And Smoke Me When I Die' by Willie Nelson

'Satisfied Mind' by Jeff Buckley

'Ships of Heaven' from Blackhawk

'Shooting Star' by Bob Dylan

'Softly as I Leave You A Portrait of my love' by Matt Munroe

'Somewhere Over the Rainbow' by Israel Kamakawiwo'Ole

'The Colors of My Life' by Howard Keel

'The Parting Glass' Traditional Irish song by The Wailin Jennys

'The Wonder of You' by Elvis

'There you'll Be' By Faith Hill

'These are the Days of our Lives' by Queen

'To Live is to Die' by Metallica

'What A Difference You've Made In My Life' by Ronnie Millsap

'Wish You Were Here' by Pink Floyd

'You Can Close Your Eyes' by James Taylor

'You Can't Always Get What You Want' by The Rolling Stones

'Your Long Journey' by Alison Krauss & Robert Plant

'Let Her Go' by Passenger

3.6f Readings

Many people choose to include readings in a memorial service. The Celebrant may perform these, but it is preferable that they are given by a friend or family member. Where a memorial is preplanned, readings may have been selected by the deceased, and these may reflect favorite literary choices.

The best readings, those that are most helpful to the grieving process, have a positive theme or message. Great care should also be taken that the content of texts reflects the spiritual outlook and sensibilities desired in the ceremony.

Where there has been conflict over the religious or spiritual nature of a memorial, readings are one area where a party with firmly held opinions may try to assert their viewpoint. You should be mindful of such situations, and use tact to ensure that all additions meet with the approval of all of the immediate family, and constitute a positive addition, rather than a possible object of contention.

A reading may be a piece of either prose or poetry. In some cases, it may be appropriate to read the lyrics of the deceased's favorite song.

For each chosen reading, you should prepare a printed copy, using a large and easy to read font. However, on some occasions, friends and family members who will be reading may choose to bring their own copy. You should introduce each reader with a line such as, 'I now ask [reader name] to come forward and read to us from [title] by [author].'

Where a program has been created for the ceremony, it can be useful to provide the text of a poem, or the lyrics to a song, that is used.

Where a service is prepared at short notice, or for a preplanning client who has no particular preference, you may be asked to suggest readings. Below are some excellent contemporary texts that would make a positive addition to a memorial ceremony.

Readers will usually require a podium on which to place their notes. It is also useful to have water available.

Some Suggested Secular Memorial Readings

Below is a list of fifty readings that that can work well, if used appropriately, with the opening lines to give you a flavor of the style. On order to save space, the full texts are not reproduced here, but are available online. No list of memorial readings will ever be definitive. I encourage you, and the clients you are working with, to be creative, and to pick passages that reflect the style, personality, and story of the deceased. Never be afraid to inject a little humor into this part of the ceremony. Smiles are always welcome guests when we are remembering a wonderful life.

1. 'A Death Has Occurred' by Paul Irion
'A death as occurred and everything is changed.
We are painfully aware that life can never be the same again,
That yesterday is over,
That relationships once rich have ended…'

2. 'A Life That Matters' by Unknown

'Ready or not, some day it will all come to an end.

There will be no more sunrises, no minutes, hours, days.

All the things you collected, whether treasured or forgotten,

will pass to someone else.

Your wealth, fame and temporal power will shrivel to irrelevance...'

3. 'Afterglow' by Helen Lowrie Marshall

'I'd like the memory of me

To be a happy one.

I'd like to leave an afterglow

Of smiles when day is done...'

4. 'Alzheimer's' by Dick Underwood

'You didn't die just recently,

You died some time ago.

Although your body stayed a while,

And didn't really know...'

(For full version see: http://www.funeral-poems.net/funeral-poem/alzheimers)

5. 'Courage' - To Kill a Mockingbird by Harper Lee

'I wanted you to see what real courage is, instead of getting the idea that courage is a man with a gun in his hand. It's when you know you're licked before you begin but you begin anyway and you see it through no matter what. You rarely win, but sometimes you do.'

6. 'Dirge Without Music' by Edna St. Vincent Millay

'I am not resigned to the shutting away of loving hearts in the hard ground.

So it is, and so it will be, for so it has been, time out of mind:

Into the darkness they go, the wise and the lovely. Crowned

With lilies and with laurel they go; but I am not resigned...'

7. 'Do Not Go Gentle Into That Good Night' by Dylan Thomas
'Do not go gentle into that good night,
Old age should burn and rave at close of day;
Rage, rage against the dying of the light…'

8. 'Do not Stand at my Grave and Weep' by Mary Elizabeth Frye
'Do not stand at my grave and weep
I am not there. I do not sleep.
I am a thousand winds that blow.
I am the diamond glints on snow…'

9. 'Dry Your Tears' by David Harkins
'You can shed tears that she is gone or you can smile because she has lived.
You can close your eyes and pray that she'll come back or you can open your eyes and see all she's left,
Your heart can be empty because you can't see her or you can be full of the love you shared…'

10. 'Epitaph on a Friend' by Robert Burns
'An honest man here lies at rest,
The friend of man, the friend of truth,
The friend of age, and guide of youth:
Few hearts like his, with virtue warm'd,
Few heads with knowledge so inform'd;
If there's another world, he lives in bliss;
If there is none, he made the best of this.'

11. 'Funeral Blues' by W. H. Auden
'Stop all the clocks, cut off the telephone,
Prevent the dog from barking with a juicy bone,
Silence the pianos and with muffled drum
Bring out the coffin, let the mourners come…'

12. 'Gone Fishing' by Dalmar Pepper
'I've finished life's chores assigned to me,

So put me on a boat headed out to sea.
Please send along my fishing pole
For I've been invited to the fishin' hole…'

13. 'Goodbye My Friend' by Anonymous
'Though we never know
Where life will take us,
I know it's just a ride
On the wheel…'

14. 'Grandad' by Dick Underwood
'Grandad, you were just a lad,
So many years ago.
You had your loves and had your dreams,
You watched us come and go…'

15. 'Grandmother' by Unknown
'A Grandmother is one of life's best gifts,
Someone to treasure all life through,
She's caring and loving,
Thoughtful and true…'

16. 'Happy the Man' by John Dryden
'Happy the man, and happy he alone,
He who can call today his own:
He who, secure within, can say,
Tomorrow do thy worst, for I have lived today.
Be fair or foul or rain or shine,
The joys I have possessed, in spite of fate, are mine.
Not Heaven itself upon the past has power,
But what has been, has been, and I have had my hour.'

17. 'His Old Bones Creaked' by Jamie Samms
'His old bones creaked and his pace was slow
But his smile was blindingly bright

His mind was sharp, and his voice was kind
His manner was a true delight…'

18. 'How Do We Know' by Marjorie Pizer
'How do we know who is to go,
Who is to leave this world
Suddenly, unexpectedly or in long pain?
There is no saying who will be with us tomorrow…'

19. 'If' by Rudyard Kipling
'If you can keep your head when all about you
    Are losing theirs and blaming it on you,
If you can trust yourself when all men doubt you,
    But make allowance for their doubting too…'

20. 'In the Presence of Death' by Rodney Murphy
'In the presence of death we stand awkward, and ill at ease;
For death is a well-known stranger whom we recognize, but do not wish to know…'

21. 'In the Presence of Death' by Seneca
'In the presence of death, we must continue to sing the song of life.
We must be able to accept death and go from its presence better able to bear our burdens and to lighten the load of others.
Out of our sorrows should come understanding…'

22. 'Life Must Go On' from A Navaho Prayer
'Grieve for me, for I would grieve for you.
Then brush away the sorrow and the tears
Life is not over, but begins anew,
With courage you must greet the coming years…'

23. 'Memories' by Earl Grollman
'Memories - tender, loving, bittersweet they can never be taken from you,
Nothing can detract from the joy and the beauty you and your loved one

shared...'

24. 'No Man is an Island' by John Dunne
'No man is an island,
Entire of itself,
Every man is a piece of the continent,
A part of the main...'

25. 'Not, How Did He Die, But How Did He Live?' By Anonymous
'Not - How did he die? But - How did he live?
Not - What did he gain? But - What did he give?
These are the things that measure the worth
Of a man as a man, regardless of birth...'

26. 'O Beautiful End' by Rabindranath Tagore
'Peace, my heart, let the time for the parting be sweet.
Let it not be a death but completeness.
Let love melt into memory and pain into songs.
Let the flight through the sky end in the folding of the wings over the nest...'

27. 'One at Rest' by Unknown
'Think of me as one at rest,
for me you should not weep
I have no pain no troubled thoughts
for I am just asleep...'

28. 'Remember' by Christina Rossetti
'Remember me when I am gone away,
Gone far away into the silent land;
When you can no more hold me by the hand,
Nor I half turn to go yet turning stay...'

29. 'Remember Me' by David Harkins
'Do not shed tears when I have gone but smile instead because I have lived.
Do not shut your eyes and pray to God that I'll come back but open your eyes

and see all that I have left behind…'

30. 'Something Beautiful Remains' by Martha Vashti Pearson
'The tide recedes, but leaves behind
Bright seashells on the sand.
The sun goes down but gentle warmth
Still lingers on the land…'.'

31. 'Success' by Bessie Anderson Stanley
'He has achieved success
who has lived well,
laughed often, and loved much…'

32. 'The Clock of Life' by Robert H. Smith
'The clock of life is wound but once,
And no man has the power
To tell just when the hands will stop
At late or early hour…'

33. 'The Comfort and Sweetness of Peace' by Helen Steiner Rice
'After the clouds, the sunshine,
after the winter, the spring,
after the shower, the rainbow,
for life is a changeable thing…'

34. 'The Dash' by Linda Ellis
'I read of a man who stood to speak
at the funeral of a friend.
He referred to the dates on the tombstone
from the beginning…to the end…'

(For the full text please visit: http://www.linda-ellis.com/the-dash-the-dash-poem-by-linda-ellis-.html)

35. 'The Day You Left' by Unknown

'With tears we saw you suffer,
As we watched you fade away,
Our hearts were almost broken,
As you fought so hard to stay.
We knew you had to leave us,
But you never went alone,
For part of us went with you
The day you left your home'

36. 'The Glory of Life is Love' by Unknown

'The Glory of Life is not that it endures forever, but that, for a time, it includes so much that is beautiful.

It is a tree to those that grasp it, and happy are all who retain it…'

37. 'The Last Hero (Discworld 27)' by Terry Pratchett

"Ah. well, life goes on,' people say when someone dies. But from the point of view of the person who has just died, it doesn't. It's the universe that goes on. Just as the deceased was getting the hang of everything it's all whisked away, by illness or accident or, in one case, a cucumber. Why this has to be is one of the imponderables of life, in the face of which people either start to pray … or become really, really angry.'

38. 'The Road Not Taken' by Robert Frost

'Two roads diverged in a yellow wood,
And sorry I could not travel both
And be one traveler, long I stood
And looked down one as far as I could
To where it bent in the undergrowth…'

39. 'The Unknown Shore' by Elizabeth Clark Hardy

'Sometime at eve when the tide is low,
I shall slip my moorings and sail away,
With no response to a friendly hail,
In the silent hush of the twilight pale,
When the night stoops down to embrace the day

And the voices call in the water's flow…'

40. 'There Is No Death' by J. L. McCreery
'There is no death! The stars go down
To rise upon some other shore,
And bright in heaven's jeweled crown
They shine forevermore…'

41. 'Those we Love Remain with Us' by Unknown
'Those we love remain with us for love itself lives on, and cherished memories never fade because a loved one's gone. Those we love can never be more that a thought apart. For as long there is a memory, they'll live on in our hearts.'

42. 'To Be by a Lake' by David Spall
'To be by a lake, with rod and line, Any time of day, suits me just fine, To see the silent mist, of a day just begun, Or watch the rays of light, from the setting sun…'

43. 'To Laugh Often and Much' by Ralph Waldo Emerson
'To laugh often and much;
to win the respect of the intelligent people
and the affection of children;
to earn the appreciation of honest critics
and endure the betrayal of false friends…'

44. 'Warning' by Jenny Joseph
'When I am an old woman I shall wear purple
With a red hat which doesn't go, and doesn't suit me.
And I shall spend my pension on brandy and summer gloves
And satin sandals, and say we've no money for butter…'

45. 'We Look Back' by Clare Jones
'As we look back over time
We find ourselves wondering
Did we remember to thank you enough

For all you have done for us?
For all the times you were by our sides…'

46. 'We Remember Him' by From The Yizkor Service - Adapted
'When we are weary and in need of strength,
When we are lost and sick at heart,
We remember him.
When we have a joy we crave to share…'

47. 'When Tomorrow Starts Without Me' by David M. Romano
'If tomorrow starts without me, and I'm not there to see,
If the sun should rise and find your eyes all filled with tears for me;
I wish so much you wouldn't cry the way you did today,
while thinking of the many things we didn't get to say.
I know how much you care for me, and how much I care for you,
and each time that you think of me I know you'll miss me too…'

48. 'With These Hands' by Pam Ayres
'With these hands so soft and clean,
On which I stroke the Vaseline,
I soothe the fever, cool the heat,
Lift verrucas out of feet,
Slap the plasters on the knees,
Dig the garden, prune the trees…'

49. 'Woodland Burial' by Pam Ayres
'Don't lay me in some gloomy churchyard shaded by a wall
Where the dust of ancient bones has spread a dryness over all,
Lay me in some leafy loam where, sheltered from the cold
Little seeds investigate and tender leaves unfold…'

50. 'Young & Old' by Charles Kingsley
'When all the world is young, lad,
And all the trees are green;
And every goose a swan, lad,

And every lass a queen…'

3.6g A Moment of Silence

Many families choose to add a moment of silence during a Memorial. In faith based ceremonies, this would be a time for personal prayer. It is important to note that requesting prayer, or leading prayer, can be highly inappropriate in a ceremony for a deceased person who was not religious, or where a notable portion of those attending do not subscribe to a particular faith. At a modern memorial, it is very often wiser to offer those attending a moment of consideration, or contemplation, to use as they desire. This allows those of faith a chance to express this in prayer, and the nonreligious individuals present a moment to consider the life of the deceased, their memories, emotions, and what the legacy of that person means for their own lives. After announcing, and explaining the purpose of, this moment of silent contemplation, you should clearly signal its beginning, allow an appropriate and comfortable time to pass, and then clearly indicate its ending. A short but effective length is somewhere between fifteen and twenty seconds.

3.7 Ceremonial Additions

One of the great advantages of modern, humanistic ceremonies, is that strict rules and traditions do not constrain them. The ways in which we celebrate a life and legacy, and express our grief, are limited only by our imagination. Here are a few possible additions that can be made to a modern memorial ceremony:

A photo collage, tastefully placed to be viewed by those arriving for the ceremony.

A tasteful, symbolic, **life-size figure**, perhaps made of wood, wicker, or bamboo. This could be clothed or decorated with objects owned by, or highly significant to the life of, the deceased.

A slideshow, if sufficient time is available to prepare, and this is practical in the chosen venue.

Memorial stones. Each guest selects the stone as they arrive and writes upon it a brief memory or message. They then place this in a basket that is then presented to the next of kin.

Memory notes. Instead of putting notes of condolence in a box, you may choose to have these attached to a tree or structure, perhaps by ribbons or clips. This then makes all available for the guests to read, and these can be collected by the family following the ceremony.

Candy bars. If the deceased had a sweet tooth, you might wish to offer candy bars for guests to enjoy as they share their memories. Of course, many other types of favor may be appropriate to the life and memory of an individual. You should, of course, check with the venue before offering any consumables.

Seeds, or cuttings from plants, may be a lovely commemorative gift to offer attendees.

You may choose to make a recording of the ceremony, by audio or video, for those unable to attend. Alternatively, if the facilities are available, you may choose to stream the service on the Internet.

If part of the ceremony takes place outdoors, and local laws allow, you may consider a lantern release.

3.8 Committal Ceremonies

Committal ceremonies, where the physical body of the deceased is delivered to its ultimate destination, may form part of the funeral, or may be a separate event. It is not uncommon for a memorial service to be held entirely separate to, for example, a private scattering of the ashes. Many funerals begin with a formal ceremony in one venue followed by a separate committal in a second location. Many attendees at the former may decide not to attend the latter, and committal services are often intimate in nature.

Depending on the nature of the committal, you may be asked to attend and say a few words. These are best when brief, and you should allow those grieving as much time as possible to experience the process in uninterrupted dignity.

3.9 On the Day

On the day of the ceremony, you should ensure that you arrive in good time. Most funeral homes have a private room for clergy to prepare. For other types of venue, you may need to dress, and perform any other kind of preparation, before you arrive. As most modern Celebrants choose only a formal suit or gown, these can easily be worn during travel.

You should check with the coordinator, or director, the day before the ceremony, to ensure you have completely accurate information on the timeline for events immediately before and after. It is wise to arrive at least half an hour before the anticipated start time. In some cases, you may need as much as an hour to prepare the family, or ensure the venue has met all technical and logistical requirements. You may need some time to greet guests as they arrive. You should factor the possibility of poor traffic into all your travel plans.

When you arrive, check in immediately with the event coordinator, funeral director, or location manager. Ensure that all physical and technical requirements and provisions have been made. As with other types of ceremony, you should arrange to have the balance of any fee outstanding paid before you begin.

At a funeral home, it is normal for those closest to the deceased to gather in the 'family room', or 'family area', before their entry into the main ceremony space. You will meet with them at this time, along with the location director if needed, to formally introduce yourself to those you have not met, and to privately express your personal condolences. You should take the time to explain the order of events to those who were not involved in the planning process. You should be prepared to answer any questions they may have about the ceremony.

When all parties are ready for the ceremony to begin, you will lead the entry of the family into the ceremony space. You will take your position at the front, and the family will take their positions on reserved seating that you will have ensured has been kept clear. You will then signal for any music to lower, and begin your words of introduction.

At the end of the ceremony, it is appropriate for you to give instructions to the guests on the plans immediately following, even if those are also detailed in the ceremony program. If there is a scheduled follow-up event, you should instruct guests on who is invited to attend, and where they may find destination details. It is useful to ask the coordinator, or the funeral director, if they have any special instructions they would like you to give on their behalf. The immediate family may also have reasonable requests to be passed on regarding how the remainder of the day will be conducted.

Above is a description of the regular set of circumstances. However, many modern, humanist end-of-life celebrations may vary in the format and procedures that are used. These may be much more relaxed in nature. This freedom of creativity and expression is one of the great strengths of modern ceremonies.

Part Four
Other Celebrations

4.1 Introducing Modern New Life Ceremonies

In addition to weddings and memorials, there are a number of other ceremonies a modern Celebrant may be asked to perform. Any milestone in the life of an individual, couple, family, group, or community can be a cause for an organized celebration.

For anyone who treasures and values life, it is hugely appropriate that we celebrate the birth of a new individual, and all the potential and promise they hold.

There is an extremely important distinction to be made between religious new life traditions and modern, secular ones. In many religions, a new life is seen as one born into sin, or requiring a symbolic marking, cleansing, or approval of an established church. For many faiths, such ceremonial acts are perceived as validating, and accepting, that new life. Humanistic and nonreligious viewpoints differ significantly from those church traditions. They hold that each new life starts free of guilt, and untainted by concepts such as sin. They believe a new life needs no validation, and requires no formal marking or acceptance to be welcomed into a community. You will not, therefore, find humanistic new life ceremonies containing elements of baptism, circumcision, or pledges of holding to a particular faith doctrine.

In many cases, a modern new life celebration will be highly informal. The ceremonial element may act as a center, or focus, for a more party-like celebration held throughout the day.

The most important first step is to listen carefully to what the new parents envision for their celebration, and then to guide them in shaping this into something structured, meaningful, and wholly positive.

Although the structure of a modern new life ceremony is highly fluid, many common elements are both expected and useful. I detail some of these below.

4.2 Core Elements of a New Life Ceremony

Once the participants have gathered, it is useful to say a few words of instruction. As the nature of many new life celebrations is quite informal, it is useful, on occasion, to remind participants that their attention and respectful behavior is important to the new parents. You may wish to ask attendees to turn off their cell phones, ensure they have taken all necessary bathroom breaks, and, for occasions that warrant it, that all glasses have been topped up.

In an informal setting such as a home, you may want to arrange the guests circled, or grouped, around the parents and the newborn. Parents should not have to remain standing for the entire event, and it can be nice to have them seated comfortably in places of honor. You may choose to have them flanked on either side by other prominent participants in the ceremony.

4.2a The Welcoming

It is usual for the ceremony to begin with words of welcome, spoken by the Celebrant. These explain to everyone why they have gathered together, and give an outline of what is about to take place. It is also useful, especially for those new to the idea of this kind of ceremony, to say a few words about its meaning. These words should be brief, simple, and from the heart. Below is an example of some words of welcome to open a new life event.

Example New Life Welcome

Friends and family of [Mother] and [Father], thank you so much for joining us today as we welcome a new life into our world, and into our lives. Each person who comes into the world brings with them new hope, new promise, and new potential. This is a beginning, but also a continuing of a journey we all share. This is a human journey, and a human story. On the day of his/her birth, a new book was opened, and we have come together here to pledge that we will stand beside this new child, as they grow to become a boy/girl, and then a man/woman. We will support them, and guide them, as they write this story. We will applaud their victories, and be ready always to reach out our hand when they stumble. As new life gives its promise of the future, so you will hear promises today from [Father] and [Mother], as well as others. Today, they announce to the world their willingness to take on these brave new roles of parent, mentor, support, friend, and teacher. They do so without condition, and always with love. Let this serve as a gentle and happy reminder to all of us that we are bonded together as a family of humanity, and when we remember that bond, and act with love, we make our world a better place. Let us strive to make their world a place of beauty and wonder, that we watch over, and which one day this child will inherit. As you listen to the words spoken today, think about the promises of your life that you have made to each other, and to yourselves, and let this day remind you that the future is always one of opportunity, potential, and an incredible story you awake to begin writing each day.

4.2b Announcing the Name

Formally announcing the name is an important part of a new life ceremony. Although everyone present will almost certainly already know the name, this is an opportunity to explain why it was chosen, and its significance to the parents and family. Usually, a great deal of thought goes into selecting a name. Middle names can also have an important family, or symbolic, significance. It is often best for the parents to explain the choice directly, rather than through the words of the Celebrant.

Be sure to let those present know how the parents wish their child to be addressed. Many names have several shortened variations, and choosing which they prefer was probably an important part of the selection process. In some cases, the parents may have decided to use the middle name in everyday conversation.

Once the explanations have been given, You may want to end this section with words such as, '*and now let us formally welcome for the first time, [Babies full name].*'

4.2c Parents' Promises

Parents promises to their new child can be similar in structure to the wedding vows a couple makes to each other. They may take the form of a short statement, lines offered by the Celebrant that are repeated, or the answers to questions about their willingness to accept particular obligations over the coming years. Promises can be made separately, by each parent in turn, or they can be affirmed together, with each parent speaking alternately.

The style of the promises can be either formal or informal. The best guide to choosing both style and format is to find that which will let the parents express their pledges clearly and simply, and comfortably conveys honest and sincere emotions and feelings. Many parents may have difficulty knowing how to begin in constructing their promises. You may advise them to set aside time, and sit together and discuss the values that are important to them both, and that they feel it is most important to convey to their new child. They may ask themselves how they plan to care for their new son or daughter, what values and character strengths they intend to encourage, how they will help the child to learn, and how they will protect and support them as they grow and mature. While many of these points are serious, there is no harm in injecting a little fun into these promise statements. This can give them a genuine feeling of warmth and sincerity. Each parent may also wish to include promises to the other, that they will work together to support and nurture the child, and strive to build a secure, safe, and loving family environment together.

4.2d Guide Parents' Promises

Humanist and nonreligious parents may be uncomfortable with the notion of 'godparents'. They may, however, still wish other adults to pledge and accept the roles of caretaker, or mentor, to the newborn. In such cases, these individuals are usually referred to as guide parents or guardians. The promises such individuals make when accepting these duties are made directly to the parents and child, and witnessed by others present, rather than given as oaths to any supernatural entity. The statements of promise given by guide parents are often shorter, and simpler, than those made by the parents, and may just involve giving an affirmative answer to a prearranged set of questions.

4.2e The Closing

When closing the ceremony, the Celebrant should take the time to express the hopes of all present for the future of the newborn. These closing words often end with a signal for a toast, and the beginning of further celebration.

4.3 Possible Additions to a New Life Ceremony

There are many wonderful additions you can use to personalize a new life ceremony. These include:

- Joining together in song
- A best wishes book
- Releasing sky lanterns
- Creating handprint art
- Planting a tree
- Filling and sealing a time capsule
- Starting a college fund
- Naming a star

4.4 Pricing a New Life Ceremony

It is up to you to decide on your standard fee for preparing and performing a new life ceremony. Amounts charged in the United States vary widely, but appear to fall between $150 and $400. When calculating what you should charge, it is important that you be properly compensated for your time, expertise, and any materials you use. If you are not compensated in a way that allows you to, at the minimum, cover your costs in a reasonable way, your ongoing role as a Celebrant will not be sustainable, and you will not feel satisfied that the wonderful services you provide have been sufficiently valued, and respected, by your clients. As with any emotional occasion, it is tempting to offer services as a gift, or gratis, but this is not the attitude of a professional, and in doing so the work of the Celebrant community as a whole can be devalued. Where you incur travel expenses, it is important that these also be compensated for at an acceptable rate. See other sections on pricing and costs later in this book.

4.5 Invocations

An invocation is a formal, ceremonial statement given by an individual at the start of a special occasion or gathering. Its intention is to call to mind, and focus on, the meaning and spirit of that event. A good invocation should capture the themes of the event, and give those attending relevant concepts to consider throughout its duration, and beyond. An invocation is usually quite short in length. It is best between 100 to 200 words. It may include a quotation, if this is useful in illuminating the speaker's intentions. An invocation should always be both positive and constructive in tone.

4.5a Defining a Modern Invocation

Traditional, faith-based invocations often focus solely on an address, or pleading, to a supernatural entity appropriate to a particular religion. In contrast, a modern, nonreligious, or humanist invocation is intended to express, and evoke, aspects of man and nature. The appeal is to the best qualities, and aspirations, of which humanity can be proud, and those that are most relevant to the specific occasion at which the invocation is performed. Such qualities often include empathy, kindness, courage, love, loyalty, service, and charity. In calling these qualities forth, a modern invocation is not asking for deference or supplication, and, therefore, should not ask for kneeling or the bowing of heads. In fact, it is quite common for the Celebrant to ask those addressed to raise their heads, and for eyes to focus symbolically on the high ideals of humanity.

4.5b Gathering Information for the Invocation

When approached to give an invocation, a Celebrant should try to gather as much information as possible, first about the date, time, and location of the request, and then about the intentions, and expectations, of the organizers. In addition to the style of address they require, the organizers will undoubtedly have some key points, or issues, which they will wish you to mention. It is crucial to understand the themes of the event that you are being asked to open. For some occasions, the organizers may make contributions, or supply all or part of the text for your invocation. Do not be afraid to offer comments or suggestions, if you feel these are needed and helpful. You should also feel able to question any content that you feel conflicts with the spirit of your invocation, or which you feel uncomfortable speaking at the event.

4.5c What an Invocation is Not

An invocation is not, under any circumstances, to be used to make criticism of any religious, or political, position. An invocation is also not meant as an opportunity to proselytize. At all times, your words must be positive, constructive, encouraging, and respectful. You will often find yourself addressing a gathering that contains individuals with many different viewpoints, particularly regarding faith and spirituality. You should consider yourself as acting as an ambassador for all those who share your point of view, and treat the occasion with the integrity required by such a position. When given the honored role of performing an invocation, your goal should be to invoke human values to which all reasonable people should be able to relate and subscribe.

4.5d Pricing an Invocation

Many Celebrants choose not to charge for giving an invocation, as these are considered a rare honor, and often performed for charitable, or public, institutions. They can also be an excellent source of publicity. However, there is no harm in accepting an honorarium, or a free dinner, if the organizers offer them.

When you perform an invocation, try to capture your performance on video. You can then post this on your blog, or via social media, as an example of your work in the community, and your abilities as a Celebrant.

4.5e Example Invocations

1. Invocation for a City Council Meeting

As you, our Council, gather here to make judgments affecting the people of [Place}, know that all those you represent today hope you will lift your heads, and set your eyes on the highest purpose, and that you will always do so with openness of mind, and of heart.

Let our first duty always be to the community we share, to the examples we set, to the decisions we make, and in all things to the legacies we leave for every man, woman, and child who gives us their trust.

All the people look to their leaders in the hope that they will represent our greatest, most courageous, most noble values and intentions. This is the task, and the demand, embodied in the mandate of all public office.

The actions taken in this council chamber must enthusiastically welcome the judgment of history.

Let us take pride in ensuring that it is said of us that we set a bright, and clear, example of human goodness and bravery, that we stood as a courageous shield for the people, and environment, of our [Place] home.

Let us leave today, and every day, knowing that we have done right, and left our world the better for our brief term of responsibility.

Let us strive together for a growing success.

Let it be one shared by all.

Let our decisions always be guided, and tempered, by love, and care, reason, and compassion.

On behalf of the people, I thank all here for their service to our great city.

2. Invocation for a Veterans Event

Today we choose to remember, acknowledge, and celebrate, with the most sincere pride and gratitude, the service, and sacrifice of our brothers and sisters, sons and daughters, mothers and fathers, our friends, and fellow Americans who we do not know, working and fighting today, and in all the generations past.

For those here who have given service, and continue to do so each day, we gather to offer thanks.

You are the courageous and unwavering shield of our nation, and the honest sword, lifted in wisdom, that defends the human joy of American freedom.

On the day of July of each year when we celebrate liberty, and turn to the flag, we must remember we raise it in pride, on ALL days, to represent the very best of humanity, that it flies only because of the courage, and dedication, of brave Americans.

It is our constant duty to remember, and give the greatest consideration, to these values today, tomorrow, and throughout our lives.

Without a dedication to duty, there can be no freedom.

It should be our pledge, a noble one, to pass this knowledge, these highest and most wonderful of human values and ideals to all future generations, to tell those that come after us about the great American journey, and the best in the American people that we recognize today, embodied in the tradition of service that means we will always and assuredly be free, and an example for all the peoples of the world.

For all this we celebrate today. Thank you.

4.6 Modern Blessings

Blessings are still popular in many parts of the world. However, there is no need for any blessing to follow a traditional, or faith-based, model. Humanist blessings can make tremendously positive additions to both family and community events. In creating a humanist, or nonreligious, blessing, the Celebrant is not seeking the approval of, or giving thanks to, any supernatural entity. Rather, they are asking for all present to consider the importance of the event to their lives, their history, and their community. They are also asking others to contemplate, and express, their gratitude to those individuals who continue to contribute their time, energy, and resources for the sake of others. Put simply, a nonreligious blessing is asking others to appreciate the human efforts involved in a particular occasion. A blessing is often much like an invocation, though less formal. Always positive, the blessing very often ends with a toast or a cheer.

4.6a Festive Blessings

Many wonderful festive occasions throughout the year can be celebrated with a modern, nonreligious blessing. In fact, many festivals are celebrated with greater meaning when viewed in the context of the very real human values underlying them. These values include family, friendship, and gratitude for the cycles of life we find in the natural world.

4.6b Dinner Blessings

A modern dinner blessing is much like an invocation, though usually far less formal. This type of blessing relates specifically to the food placed before the group, and expresses gratitude towards those individuals who have prepared the meal. The object is to praise those accomplishments as an example of the contribution to our common humanity, and express the hope that these will continue to be an inspiration to others long into the future.

4.7 Dedications

When work on any project is complete, or a crucial stage in its development has been reached, such as with the launching of a boat, or the setting of the cornerstone of a building, there is a long tradition of saying a few words to mark this occasion. For a secular Celebrant, the words offered are not to thank a deity for this progress or achievement, but rather to praise, and acknowledge, the human individuals responsible for these accomplishments. You may also wish to offer the hope that the memory of these achievements will continue to inspire others to excel in their endeavors long into the future.

4.8 Pet Ceremonies

A ceremony for a beloved pet can easily be as emotional an occasion as that for a friend or relation. They may, however, be held in a far less formal manner. The most common form of ceremony organized for a pet is a short funeral or memorial. However, lighthearted dog weddings, and celebration events for the birth of a litter of puppies, are now occasionally held. Much as with other ceremonial roles, you may be asked to give opening and closing remarks. To do so effectively, it is useful to gather some facts from the pet owners to use in your text. Your job, when not speaking, is often to act as a facilitator for others in expressing their feelings, perhaps grief at the loss of a pet, and to give the formal signal for any planned burial or scattering of ashes.

Part Five
Building a
Celebrant Business

5.1 Introduction to the Celebrant Business

If you find you enjoy creating and performing ceremonies, and feel you have high abilities and enthusiasm, you may decide to turn your Celebrant practice into a business. As with any business venture, you will need to undertake significant planning and preparation, and to put in the work necessary to make your enterprise a success. The role of a modern professional Celebrant is about far more than just a paycheck, and is certainly not an easy way to get rich quick, or a path to millionaire status. Although you will, and should, receive financial compensation for the work you do, just as significant will be the rewards of personal fulfillment that you find, and those begin at your first ceremony. In taking this role, you are helping individuals and families to celebrate unique moments and landmarks in their lives. You are helping others to enjoy, and savor, the deepest human values. The role of a Celebrant is more than a job. You will be acting as a guide, leader, and ambassador for all the values you hold most important.

In this section, I will address the practical aspects of working as a Celebrant on a regular basis. If you wish to create a viable, and sustainable, Celebrant practice, it is crucial that you treat it as a business enterprise, with all the seriousness and attention that requires. Even if you only plan to perform a few ceremonies each year, the instructions in this section are still necessary to ensure that you reach, and maintain, an appropriate level of standards and practices. If you approach your Celebrant work with careful planning and organization, you will find the process of ceremony becomes even more rewarding, and that you better serve those people who place their trust in you to guide them during some of the most significant moments of their lives.

In the United States, it is very easy to begin practicing as a Celebrant. For that reason, many approach the role without sufficient preparation, planning, forethought, or care. Many important ceremonies have suffered in the past because the Celebrant did not understand, or respect, correct professional practices. If you study the information in this section you will be not only protecting your clients, but also in a position to build your Celebrant practice into one which will be both financially and personally rewarding. As with all business, your success is directly linked to the amount of work you put in. If you follow this guide, and commit to developing all the aspects of your Celebrant life, you will find success. The market for modern professional Celebrants is still high and growing everywhere. If you choose to build your business the right way, both clients and success are waiting for you.

5.2 Your State's Celebrant Requirements

If you plan to perform legal wedding ceremonies, formally known as the solemnizing of marriages, as part of your Celebrant duties, you must fulfill the legal requirements laid down by the government authorities in each location you wish to practice. As part of this book, you will find a list of those requirements sorted by state for the US, and also for Australia, Canada, and the different regions of the United Kingdom. You should familiarize yourself with the appropriate sections, and stay alert for any changes to these regulations. Your chosen body of ordination, or licensing, should be able to answer any questions you have regarding the laws in your location. Your local courthouse, or government office, should also be able to clarify the meaning of any local laws or statutes.

In the United States, and most Western countries, there are no specific legal licensing requirements to perform ceremonies other than the marriage. You may safely celebrate a new life, or memorial service, at any time.

5.3 Becoming Ordained or Licensed

Ordination, or licensing, is a crucial step towards performing legal wedding ceremonies. In the United States, there are some organizations willing, and able, to ordain Humanist, non-religious, and non-denominational Celebrants. It is possible to get an online ordination that becomes effective almost immediately. However, it is important to realize that some states in the US have significant concerns about such a fast track process. For this reason, you should examine the appropriate local statutes carefully before choosing your body of ordination, and making your application. If you plan to work in a professional capacity, and perform legal marriage ceremonies regularly, and in multiple locations, I strongly recommend that you apply for ordination through an organization that has a thorough evaluation process, and offers membership status.

One of the factors many states consider in assessing the validity of ordination is whether you are in 'good standing' with your body of ordination. By this, they are asking if you have been ordained indefinitely, as is the case with fast track, online ordinations, or whether you must re-apply, at some specified interval, to renew your status. Their belief is that organizations that require periodical reassessment are taking a more serious approach, and giving more oversight, to those they ordain. Such groups are seen as likely to produce Celebrants that meet higher professional standards. Do not be afraid to send a list of questions to any body of ordination you are considering. They should be happy to clarify their requirements, and application process, and the rights and duties that will be conferred if you are accepted.

The Society of Celebrations (societyofcelebrations.org) is an organization established to train, and ordain, professional Humanist, nonreligious, and non-denominational Celebrants. Submitting an application is free, but if accepted the annual membership fee is currently $75.

The Humanist Society (humanist-society.org) is another organization that gives ordination to Humanist Celebrants. Currently, they charge a $40 application fee, and $100 per year annual membership. There is also a requirement for membership of the American Humanist Association. Other bodies of ordination are listed in the resources section, later in this book.

5.4 State Registration

In addition to ordination, a number of US states require that you register with the local government authority before you may legally perform wedding ceremonies. In most cases, a single registration with one County ensures you are registered for an indefinite period across an entire state. In some rare cases, you may need to register in each County. In almost all cases, the additional registration process is an inexpensive formality.

Australia, the United Kingdom, and Canada all have specific, and differing, rules regarding registration.

Details of state registration, and other legal requirements for Celebrants, are given by region later in this book.

List of States where Registration Rules Apply [See Appendix A]

Arkansas	New Hampshire
District Of Columbia	New York
Hawaii	Ohio
Louisiana	Oklahoma
Massachusetts	Vermont
Minnesota	Virginia
Mississippi	West Virginia
Nevada	

5.5 Know the Marriage Laws

The next step to solemnizing marriages is to understand the legal processes, and formalities, that must be completed by the couple and yourself, concerning the marriage license. The marriage application process, and the price charged by the local authority, varies considerably from location to location. There is also a great deal of variation in the process of completing, and returning, the documents. This is a vital part of your role as a marriage Celebrant, and couples will expect you to be able to answer any questions they have about all stages of the licensing process. Additionally, failure to complete the paperwork correctly, or to return it within the specified time frame, can lead to possible fines and criminal charges. As with your ordination requirements, the local government office will be happy to answer any questions you have regarding the process, as should be your body of ordination. To guide you, this book contains details of the laws and procedures by state, as they stand at the time of publication. It is important that you stay alert for any changes in local regulations that may affect you, or the couples you serve.

5.6 Tax and Small Business Law

When starting a new business of any kind, even one that will consist only of yourself, it is important to ensure you are in full compliance with all local business laws and tax regulations. In almost all cases, it is a good idea to register your business locally. Many cities require that you register a 'doing business as', or DBA, or they may require that you purchase a business license in a particular category. These are usually easily obtained, and inexpensive, but must be renewed annually in some regions.

It may be beneficial to register yourself with the state as a corporation, or as a limited liability business. Doing so often has significant tax advantages, as well as providing some additional legal protection.

I strongly recommended you spend an hour with a good local accountant, discussing the tax and licensing laws appropriate for your business. Where your only income comes from practicing Celebrant duties, you may be entitled to some special tax incentives. When searching for a good accountant, or another business professional, the best place to start is to ask your friends, and family, if they have any recommendations. Just as with your own business, the very best guide to the quality of service you can expect comes from personal testimonials.

It is important to keep your earnings, and other business finances, separate from your personal accounts. You should open a bank account that you then use solely for these purposes. This will make preparing, and reporting, your taxes much easier. Many banks require proof that you have registered your business before they will open such an account.

Before you begin charging for services, you should enquire as to whether you need to apply sales tax. In some locations, this tax is not applicable to services, defined as situations where expertise is provided rather than goods. Where sales tax, or a similar levy, is required of service professionals, be sure of the current percentage rate you are required to charge your clients, and the frequency with which you must report your earnings. An accountant will very quickly be able to guide you in this regard, but you should be wary that tax rates can frequently change, and are sometimes adjusted as much as twice a year.

5.7 Recording Sales, Expenses, and Earnings

If you are receiving money for services, and spending on items such as gasoline and dry cleaning, you must keep records of these, both for yourself and, most especially, for tax reporting. If the number of transactions is small, you may be able to keep track using a spreadsheet program, such as Microsoft Excel, or an equivalent program, such as Apache OpenOffice. However, once your business begins to grow, and you have significantly more records to keep, you should look to using a dedicated bookkeeping software, such as Intuit QuickBooks. It is surprisingly easy to get started, using the company set up 'wizards' contained in these programs. Most local community colleges also offer inexpensive courses, from beginner to advanced levels, to teach you to use these software packages. Additionally, a good bookkeeping program will have the ability to export your data in a way that smoothly interfaces with the software used by any professional accountants you may hire, as well as personal tax software.

If you plan to travel to perform ceremonies, or to attend meetings with clients or other professionals, it is important to keep records of these expenses. Small, inexpensive mileage books are available at most stationary stores, and can be kept to hand, along with a pen, in your vehicle for a whole year to record every journey you take.

Another excellent habit to cultivate is to keep receipts from every purchase, however small. You may wish to keep a little box near the entrance of your home, to quickly store these each time you return. For electronic receipts you receive via email, create a separate folder within the software to save these for later use.

When clients are making payments, they should be given a receipt in return. Small, inexpensive receipt books can be purchased at many stores, and can easily be carried in your bag or briefcase.

You should keep records of the payments each client makes alongside their other information, and regularly check which anticipated payments are coming due, so that you may remind the customer if needed.

Before you begin to spend any significant amount of money establishing your Celebrant business, you should set an annual budget to help you best control, and understand, how you use your money. Accounting software often includes budgeting functions, and instructions can also be found online, or from your accountant.

I highly recommend seeking out, and joining, one or several of the excellent online communities created for professional Celebrants. Most will be able to offer you good advice from their experience, and answer any questions you have, or show you where to go to find the information you seek. Some of these communities are listed later in this book, alongside other useful online resources.

5.8 Your Filing System

If you plan to perform ceremonies for more than one client, you will need a system to keep different information separate and organized. For each ceremony booking, you should create a file, clearly marked with the name, date, and time relevant to that client. In the front of the file, you should have a sheet that clearly summarizes all the important information about that booking. In my work, I have combined the information sheet with the client contract, and an example of this format is included later in this book.

You should make it a habit to keep all materials related to each ceremony project, including any notes made from telephone calls or face-to-face meetings, photocopies of checks received, printouts of important email communications, even thank you cards you may receive from clients.

Following a wedding, whether legally required by your location or not, you should create a photocopy of the completed documents before they are returned to the relevant government offices.

In my work, I keep a small caddy of hanging files next to my desk. I have created a set of thirteen hanging file sections. Each section is identified at the top with a plastic tag. The first twelve are labeled with the months of the year, and the thirteenth is marked 'next year'. I keep the current month at the front, as these are the ceremonies on which I am most frequently working. Behind this, the following months are arranged sequentially, with my file for anything more distant placed at the back. At the end of each month, I move the front pocket to put it behind the other months, but before the next year's section. In this way, I keep a rolling annual feed of the work ahead quickly to hand. I then add to it anything from the next year's section relevant to that month. Each ceremony has a manila folder, with a tab at the top rear, and easily slots into these pockets. I have found the system to be easy and efficient, but you may wish to create your own. The important thing is to have a system that allows you to quickly find any information you need.

5.9 Liability Insurance

Accidents do happen. We also live in an extremely litigious culture. Even with the best intentions, and greatest care, occasionally unfortunate incidents do occur. Although it is rare for a Celebrant to be the focus of an incident that insights a lawsuit or claim for damages, if something were to happen, and the judgment went against you, you could find yourself faced with a bill that might cripple your business and home life. For this reason, every company should invest in some form of basic liability insurance. A reasonable policy should only cost you a couple of hundred dollars, or the local equivalent, per year. At the time of writing, the author has not found an insurance company that offers a policy made specifically for Celebrants, at least here in the United States. You may, therefore, need to look for the kinds of policies used to cover entertainers and performers, as a comparable role used for these purposes. You should start by approaching your current insurance provider, the one you use for your home or vehicle, and asking if they provide such a policy, or have a preferred vendor they can recommend. You should also request quotes from other reputable insurance companies based in your region. Do not be afraid to approach other local Celebrants in your network, or online, to ask about their experiences in working with insurance companies. For further advice on legal matters, I recommend visiting weddingindustrylaw.com.

5.10 Services, Payments, and Pricing

If you are planning to serve as a ceremony professional in any way, and for any length of time, it is critical that, at the barest minimum, you ensure you break even on the ceremonies you contract to perform. Under no circumstances should your business model plan for you to make a loss. If you deliberately choose to perform ceremonies without adequate financial compensation, the best that will happen is that you will soon go out of business as a Celebrant. More likely, the financial hit will affect your family relationships, your morale, and your personal well-being. You will also be devaluing the work of Celebrants across the wider community, and in doing so contributing to a lower standard of ceremony for everyone. As a Celebrant, what you do takes work, skill, experience, energy, and resources. Never devalue these things in yourself. Always remember that what you create deserves to be acknowledged and properly compensated. Just because you are not creating, or selling, a tangible item, such as a dress or cake, does not make your contribution any less valuable.

One important aspect of your pricing will be how you choose to charge for travel to ceremony locations. Travel is expensive, and if you do not charge for this, or factor it into your overall pricing structure, your business will soon find itself in trouble financially. In the United States, the Internal Revenue Service publishes an annual rate per mile which they feel acceptable, and which you will use for tax deduction purposes. This new figure is published at the beginning of each January, and you can find the current information available at this web address:

https://www.irs.gov/Tax-Professionals/Standard-Mileage-Rates

5.10a Choosing your Services

As a Celebrant, among the first things you must do is decide which services you will offer. At no time are you obliged to perform every type of ceremony that is requested, or that other Celebrants may provide. You may decide you only wish to perform wedding ceremonies, or that you only want to officiate at memorial services. That is perfectly acceptable, but will have a significant impact on the way you market yourself, and other important aspects of your career, such as the name of your business.

In addition to choosing the types of ceremony you plan to perform, you should also give careful thought to the locations that you wish to serve. While some Celebrants are willing to travel far, and even stay overnight to perform a ceremony if requested, others will not want the strain of a long-distance commute. You may also decide that you only work some months of the year, or perhaps only offer your services at weekends. Almost all Celebrants begin by working alongside another job, building their practice to the point where they can work full-time. If this is true for you, you should consider how the Celebrant services you offer will fit into other responsibilities in your daily life. These are questions you should answer very early on when planning your Celebrant business.

5.10b Setting Prices

One of the most common questions new Celebrants face is how to establish prices for the services they provide. Prices for ceremonies vary widely by location and by the type of service that you perform.

You should begin by examining the rates charged by other Celebrants in your area. Although this will give you a broad indication, it is important to note that some Celebrants will be offering types of service for those working with minimal needs, and within tight budgets. Other Celebrants will be focusing on areas of the markets where people are seeking more in-depth, and personalized, services that take greater preparation. You should carefully consider these factors when doing your comparison study.

It is crucial that the prices you charge adequately cover your costs and expenses, as well as providing you reasonable compensation for your time, skills, and experience. Many Celebrants, especially those just starting out, set their prices far too low to sustain a viable business. New Celebrants often feel that they must begin by operating at a loss, as a way of compensating, or apologizing, for their lack of experience. This is a mistake. If you undercharge, you will not be able to sustain your business, as you will be operating at a loss. Additionally, on a personal level, you will feel unappreciated, and insufficiently valued, and this will have a hugely negative impact on your enthusiasm for your work.

In addition to researching other Celebrants, you should make a list of your costs, including a reasonable hourly rate for your time, and ensure that the prices you charge exceed the total of these by a significant percentage, for example, 50%. This is your profit margin, a phrase that should be viewed positively, as this is the portion of your income that allows you to continue, and grow, in your Celebrant business. That margin is the fuel that will give your business health, as well as allowing you to develop, and improve, the services you provide.

Laura Cannon, president of the International Association of Professional Wedding Officiants (IAPWO.org), an organization I highly recommend membership of, recently gave a presentation in which she offered another formula that may help us calculate our pricing. She undertook an analysis of wedding Celebrant pricing across the United States and compared it to similar pricing levels used by the top wedding DJs in the same locations. She found that, on average, a reasonable price for wedding ceremonies in any location was often around 35% of the price offered for a similar event by the top DJs in that area. This may be another indicator you wish to consider.

For services other than wedding ceremonies, you should again use a process of researching the prices your colleagues charge for services similar to those you plan to provide in your location.

5.10c Taking Deposits and Payments

You should offer several ways to receive payments, to make the booking process as easy as possible for your clients. In addition to accepting cash and checks, it is now easy for any small business to take credit card payments via the Internet, or through a small device that attaches to your smartphone. Such services include PayPal (paypal.com) and Square (squareup.com). Your bank may also offer a service, perhaps using technology such as provided by authorize.net, which can integrate payment gateways directly into your website. Most electronic payment services ask a small subscription fee, as well as taking a small percentage of each payment. You should take the time to compare the prices, and business terms of the different services available in your location. Once again, do not be afraid to reach out to the Celebrant network, locally and online, to discover what others have found to work well in practice.

When you accept a booking, it is a wise practice to take a deposit on the payments for your services, usually of between 30% to 50% of the final amount. This deposit gives you insurance against any cancelation of the booking, especially where you have to turn down work because that place on your calendar is already taken. Any deposit should be nonrefundable, and this should be stated clearly in your business contract. You should ensure that any outstanding balance is received before the ceremony begins. It is never good business practice for a Celebrant to have to chase couples, or their families, for money after the day of the event.

5.10d Your Business Contract

If you are working with clients on a professional basis, it is always wise to set out your agreement in the form of a contract. This document should clearly stipulate what is expected by both parties. Later in this volume, I have provided a template contract. However, when creating, or adopting, the contract you will use in your own business, it is a wise practice to have a local lawyer look over your terms and conditions, to ensure they conform to the correct statutes, and best practices, for your location. There are also some excellent resources available online. If you have questions regarding aspects of your contract, I recommend visiting the website weddingindustrylaw.com, run by top wedding business lawyer, Rob Schenk.

5.11 Choosing a Business Name

Choosing the name you will use for your business is a big step, but it can also be an important turning point in establishing your Celebrant practice. If you are working alone, you may only want to use your given name, and you will then become your own brand. However, you may have an excellent, catchy business name in mind, and adopting such a name may be more appropriate, if you plan to involve other Celebrants in your company, or you do not wish your name to be the primary focus of your brand. Here are some important factors to consider when deciding on the name by which your business will be known:

Should you use the name of a town or state in your company name?

Many Celebrants choose to focus on providing services to a particular location. If this is true for your practice, you may wish to include the name of that area in the name of your business. Not only does this emphasize that you are a local vendor, something many clients will find appealing, but it can also boost your ranking in online search results specific to that location. The downside of having a location specific business name is that it may work against you if you decide to expand your coverage beyond this region. Additionally, you may not rank so highly in online searches that utilize alternative place names for your area, such as a county name instead of that of the city.

Is your business name memorable and appealing to the ear?

The best company names are easy to pronounce, easy to remember, and easy to read on a business card. If your given name is long, hard to pronounce, or has an unusual spelling, then you should consider an alternative business name to use in its place. Consider how easy it will be to communicate each name you are considering over the phone, within your Internet domain name, or as an email address. Try out your ideas among friends and family. Evaluate which choice they find easiest to understand, spell, and remember. You should also take care that any business name you choose has no unexpected, unfortunate alternative meanings or associations. That being said, some of the best business names introduce a dash of creative humor. Resist the temptation to use puns. If you are a local vendor, consider something local clients will find appealing, but which can also boost your ranking in online search results specific to that location.

Should your name be descriptive?

If your business provides a particular service, you might consider including that as part of your company name. Some examples might be: John Smith Officiant, Anytown Wedding Celebrant, Ceremonies by John, etc. As with using locations within the name of your business, you should take a long view, and consider whether your business may ever wish to expand beyond such specific services. Your goal should be to strike a balance between having a name that communicates what you provide, and making this applicable to the broadest range of client inquiries. For example, it may be unwise to include the word wedding in your business name if you also plan also to offer yourself as a memorial Celebrant.

Is the DBA available?

Many locations require you to file a 'doing business as', or DBA, and pay a small fee for that registration. Additionally, if you decide to incorporate your business, it is important that no one else has already registered a company under the same name. Begin by checking with your local government office, or a search of their website, for the legal registration requirements in your location. You can find more information by the IRS (irs.gov), and the Small Business Association (sba.gov).

Is a friendly and memorable domain name available?

In the 21st century, your business name goes hand in hand with your Internet domain name. This is the address at which your website will live, and which will show up in a client's Internet browser. Examples of business names that have been directly mapped onto a domain name include CNN.com, BBC.com, Nike.com, and barnesandnoble.com. When choosing a domain name, it is important to consider how easy it will be to remember, type, and spell. Spelling is especially important, and you should watch for words, or names, that contain silent or double letters.

Your domain name must be available to register. Domains are never owned outright forever, after one single payment, but are registered for a block of years at a time. If you are the registrant, you are always the first to have the option to renew your registration, but if you do not do so, others will be given the opportunity to take control of your domain, once your time expires. It is vital, to keep the access details for your domain safe, and to receive email alerts whenever it is approaching the time for renewal.

To see if the domain you have in mind is available, visit your chosen registrar. I register my domain names through GoDaddy.com. Type the name into the search bar, and you will quickly be told of its availability. If unavailable, you may be given options to purchase from the current owner, or the registrar may suggest slight variations on the name that are still available.

In choosing your type of domain, you will almost certainly be seeking the .com suffix. This is the standard for business, and in offering Celebrant services for payment you do constitute a commercial enterprise. .org names are usually taken only by nonprofit organizations. In recent years, many other types of domain name have become available, but you should be careful to choose a domain that is clear, simple, and that will in no way confuse any reader or listener.

5.12 Your Individual Style or 'Hook'

It is important for any business to stand out in the crowd, to show what unique qualities it has that separate it from its competitors, and make it readily identifiable to the right sort of client. As a Celebrant, your individual qualities and personality will guide you in how you color your personal brand. If you are known for your terrific sense of humor, or for an elegant sense of style, these qualities can provide a superb focus that makes you stand out. You may decide to define yourself as a specialist in certain types of ceremony, such as beach weddings. You may also choose to describe yourself as providing expert services for a particular group, such as the LGBTQ community.

When beginning your Celebrant business, imagine your ideal client. Make a list of the qualities they will have, and the type of ceremony you would find most enjoyable to create and perform. When you have these factors clearly in mind, let these be your guide in defining how you promote yourself, and to whom you market. If you are too general in your marketing, you may attract clients who are not, in actuality, seeking the sort of service you provide. This can make your business life difficult and less enjoyable. The qualities of your ideal client should guide many aspects of your business development, including the look of your website, the range of your pricing, and the locations you focus on for marketing.

Why not talk with friends and family, and ask them about the qualities they see that make you special, and which they think will be appealing to the sorts of clients you hope to attract.

5.13 Online Marketing

If you plan on business success, your online marketing should be the primary focus of your sales activities. With each passing year, the Internet becomes the first place individuals, couples, and families turn to when seeking professionals. Your online presence, in the form of your website, and your social media activities, defines your brand. However, although this area of business is both essential and unavoidable, you need not spend large amounts of money, and hundreds of working hours to build an effective online presence. The secret to success in building your online platform is in planning, research, and preparation. Before making any decision, or spending any money on your website or online marketing activities, take the time to investigate and understand the options available, and the realistic results that you should expect.

What follows is a brief introduction. As you read, make a list of questions that you have. State these in their simplest form. Many of the answers can be found with a simple Google search. For others, do not be afraid to approach friends or other Celebrants. If you post a question in one of the online groups, or forums, dedicated to Celebrants, or wedding professionals in general, you will be surprised how quickly you receive many useful, informative, and detailed responses. For this topic of website building, and Internet marketing in general, there are dedicated groups that are particularly focused on ceremony professionals. I have included some of these in the list of online resources that you can find later in this book. Here then, are a few outlines of the areas you should consider when establishing your Celebrant business online.

5.13a Creating a Website

For any business, ceremony related or not, a website is now essential. It is your storefront, your first point of contact, the showcase for pictures, videos of you in action, and reviews of your work by satisfied former clients. Although it is the foundation stone of your business marketing, it need not be expensive to create, maintain, and develop over time.

Types of Web Site Available

Broadly speaking, there are three types of website construction that you might consider. Each has its advantages and disadvantages. Do not let cost be the only factor in deciding which design route you take, as this is an area where cutting corners, and taking bargain options early on, can lead to increased costs and expenses a little further down the road.

The first type of website you might consider is one created on a builder platform using a template. These can be constructed very simply and quickly for a minimal monthly cost. When you register your domain name (see the section, a few pages back, on selecting your business name), your registrar may give you the option to create an easy template site on their servers for an additional monthly payment. Alternatively, there are services such as Weebly or Wix, that offer this sort of service separately. The advantages of taking this route are that it is cheap, has a very short and easy learning curve, and you can have your website online within a matter of hours. However, and you knew there would be a catch, there are drawbacks to this method. The website you create will be very limited in scope, and you will have only a few design templates to choose from. The number of pages your website can have will be limited, as will the types of content you can place on each page. Additionally, optimizing your website to rank well on search engines can be difficult, as you have little control over anything but the most basic elements. Perhaps the greatest disadvantage of this method is that the website you create cannot be moved or expanded beyond that platform. Most businesses find they very quickly outgrow the needs of their first small site, and are then shocked to discover that they need to begin the design process again if they wish to have a more extensive website that meets their needs. For this reason, if you are in any way serious about building your Celebrant business, I recommend against going this route.

The second type of website you may choose would be to pay for a hosting account, with one of the many companies that offer these, and have them install a 'content management system' such as WordPress. This type of hosting account should cost no more than around $100 per year, and WordPress itself is free software. However, and yes, this method has its drawbacks too, the initial WordPress installation is very plain, and must always be expanded using a 'theme', which adds additional design and function elements, or by paying a good web designer to customize WordPress to meet your business needs, and desired visual style. Excellent quality themes can be purchased for under $100, but will require that you spend some time configuring them with your personal information and specifications. If you use a good quality web design company to configure your installation and ensure you are well-optimized for search engines, you should expect to pay around $1500. Of course, the more extensive and detailed the work on your website becomes the more you will need to spend, particularly if you need logo design work, or pay to have other content created. The greatest strength of WordPress is that, once your website is established, you can add and manage your own content. For this reason, if you choose this design method, I highly recommend investing in a couple of hours of training in using your new website. This will not only save you on the costs of continually hiring professionals for many aspects of your site but will also give you much greater confidence, and understanding, of this incredibly important area of your business.

The third option, if you wish to place your site entirely in the hands of professionals, or want to be able to specify very particular, extensive, and detailed functions for your site, is to have it custom coded and designed from the ground up by a web design company. Although this route is the most expensive of the three I mention here, it does give you the full ability to specify the form and function of every single element of your website, down to the last detail. Perhaps the greatest advantage is that, if you are highly averse to the technological side of business, you can pay to leave this in the hands of others, and leave yourself free to concentrate entirely on creating, and performing, ceremonies for your clients. For an entirely custom designed website, you should expect to pay at around $3000, but the possibilities, as well as the price, are limited only by your budget and imagination.

Content your Web Site Should Contain

What are the essential elements that any business website must have? To understand the answer to this question you first have to understand the concept of a 'call to action.' By this, I mean that it is first important to know what you expect each visitor to do, from the moment they arrive at your website to the moment they leave. If your primary goal is to generate leads in the form of telephone calls, you need to have your phone number available immediately to anyone who arrives on your homepage, to place it at the foot of every page on your site, and to have a contact page that is very easy to locate. If you wish your clients to email you, or fill out and submit an information form, these must be immediately available to every visitor, and designed for maximum ease-of-use.

For most Celebrants, their personality and style are the key selling points of their business. It is vital that you offer information about yourself, your experience, your methodology, the types of ceremony you specialize in, and your approach to ceremonies in general. Potential clients will want to sense, in the shortest time possible, whether you are a good fit for the celebration they are planning.

Testimonials and reviews are hugely important to couples and families planning a ceremony. Visitors will be looking to read what others have said about their experiences of working with you. For this reason, it is hugely important to gather reviews from past clients where possible, and place these in a dedicated area of the website, easy for any visitor to find.

The Internet is an incredibly visual medium. For this reason, pictures and video are critical to giving prospective clients an immediate feeling as to whether you are right for the style of ceremony they are planning. It is important to network with photographers you meet at the ceremonies you perform, and to obtain copies of the pictures to use in a gallery. The same is true of wedding videos, which can easily be uploaded to a service like YouTube, and then embedded in a dedicated page on your website.

Whether to include your pricing on your website is a subject often debated among all wedding professionals. Some feel that this information is best conveyed personally, once a prospective client makes contact while others believe it is best to be upfront about prices, and thus avoid disappointments, or wasted conversations with unrealistic bargain hunters.

It is wise to include your terms of business on your website, as this gives high transparency about the way you work, as well as helping to avoid confusion.

Many Celebrants choose to include helpful information, and resources, for their clients on their website. Such information may include local wedding license regulations, recommended vendors of other types, and guides to help couples in creating their vows, or understanding the different parts of ceremonies. You may also wish to include lists of music, or readings, which you have seen work well. All the items mentioned in this paragraph are referred to as 'value content', and are important in providing a terrific experience for anyone visiting your website. Increasingly, this type of information is also critical to achieving high ranking on search engines, such as Google.

Understanding Keywords

You may have the most beautiful website in the world, but, if it is hidden from view, no one will pay it a visit. It is vital that your site appears in the different types of searches clients may make online. The primary method by which searches are made, and by which search engines know which results to show, is in the use of 'keywords.' These are words or combinations of words that define the content on your pages. Words such as Celebrant, Officiant, wedding, ceremony, or memorial are obviously important, but used alone these words hold little meaning when typed into a search engine. For this reason, keywords primarily refers to *combinations* of words.

Short combinations of two words are known as a 'head term.' Examples include: wedding Officiant, professional Celebrant, and marriage vows. These are the starting point for creating the list of words you want to focus on in the text of your website and the titles of your web pages.

'Long tail keywords' are combinations of three or more words, and used for a more defined search. These are usually created by taking your head term, and adding other words that specify information, for example, 'Humanist wedding

Officiant'. You may add a geographic location, for example, 'New York funeral Celebrant', or specify a transaction, or action, the searcher wishes to complete, such as 'write marriage vows.'

A full discussion of keywords, and optimization, is beyond the scope of this book, but I have included suggested resources later on. It is important, however, that you begin to consider the relevant keywords for your business *before* you create any online content.

Registering Your Business Locally   Local Listings

Unless you have an extremely unusual client base, you will be marketing yourself as a local business, either to your City, County, or across portions of the state, or region. As such, it is important that search engines associate you geographically with those locations. Not only should you be including geographical terms within your keyword list, and using these prominently across your site, but you should ensure that you have verified local listings with all the main search directories. This is easy enough to check with a visit to the website moz.com, which has a free listing checker (https://moz.com/local/search). Where this service finds omissions, or problems, it will point you in the direction of a solution. Creating, correcting, and verifying a complete set of listings across all directories can be a time-consuming process. However, there are paid solutions that can take on the job, if your budget allows. Prices range from between around $80-$500 per year, depending on how extensive a range of listings you wish to complete.

Tracking Your Web Site Performance   Analytics

Not only is your website the most powerful first contact portal for your business, but you need to ensure you are targeting the right people in the most efficient way. The production, and reporting, of website traffic statistics, is referred to as 'analytics'. You should ensure that your site is connected to the free Google Analytics service, and then take the time to understand how to interpret the data provided, at least at a high level. You should be able to see which keywords are working for your site, and be able to make planned changes, to focus your content, over a number of weeks or months, toward those combinations that are performing well. In the resources section of this book, I recommend reading and services that you can use to research further this topic, or find professionals who can assist you.

5.13b Email Addresses

The email address that you use on your website, business card, and all other material says a great deal about the professional level of your business. You should not be using free, generic email addresses, such as @Gmail.com, @yahoo.com, or @aol.com. To do so is a clear, immediate indicator to your clients, and other professionals, that you do not take your business image seriously. Your email address should include your business domain name, in place of the generic element (for example, name@awesomecelebrantbusiness.com). You can easily set up a domain name to work with, or forward your email to, your existing service. If the technical instructions are beyond your capacities, your email provider, or your web hosting company, will be able to assist you. Such a service should cost you no more than a few dollars each month.

5.13c Social Media

In addition to your website, it is important to have a profile, and presence, on social media. Ceremonies, especially weddings, have an enormous social focus, and to neglect this area will be to overlook an important source of clients. Also, many wonderful professional communities exist on social media, and these can help you network to solve many problems, answer questions, or address issues you may encounter with your business. As with your website, you should not attempt to conquer all social media at once, but rather focus on one area, and slowly develop your profile and reputation. As with search engine optimization, a full analysis of social media strategies requires more than the scope of this volume. However, in this section, I cover the most important social media applications you should be using, as a Celebrant, and outline the minimum you should do to establish yourself in each. For further reading and resources, see those sections later in the book.

Before turning to each social network, I offer a slight word of warning. Without sufficient self-control, social media can rapidly overtake your life, and consume valuable parts of your day that are best used in other ways. This is referred to as social media 'time suck', which is an unpleasant, but accurate, description of what can happen if you do not plan and focus your activities carefully. You may wish to set aside a strict 30 minute period each day to work with social media, and then close out from these applications completely.

Facebook

The most important social network for professional Celebrants is undoubtedly Facebook. To begin, you will need to establish a personal profile. However, you should not use your profile as your point of contact with clients. Rather, you should create a 'page' for your business. This is free to do, and Facebook provides very clear instructions on how to do this quickly. Your business page should contain your contact details, a link to your website, your photograph, brief biographical information, and a summary of the services you provide. You should upload as many professional-standard photos, and videos, to your business page as you have available. You should also post regular updates to your page, perhaps to showcase ceremonies you have performed, or to provide useful information to your clients. You will then encourage other Facebook users to 'like' your page, and former clients to post reviews, if they have time to do so.

Pinterest

Pinterest is the next social platform on which you should create an account. You begin by creating a personal account, which you should then convert to a business account, as it is free to do so. You should fully complete your profile, using your company name, and primary location, in your profile name, and ensuring you link back to your website. The object of Pinterest is to create virtual notice boards on to which you 'pin' links to pictures and websites that you like, and wish to share. You can create as many boards as you like, one for each theme or subject. You should create boards based on your primary keywords. Within each board, do not just post material from your website, but rather steadily, and regularly, add quality, attractive material you encounter from your Internet browsing. You can also 're-pin' material from other Pinterest user's boards to your own. The important thing is to provide content that will be useful, and attractive, to the ideal client you have profiled as the target for all your marketing.

Instagram

Instagram is another highly visual social platform. After signing up, and creating your profile, which should link back to your main website, you should regularly post picture updates relevant to your client base. This may include photos from ceremonies you have performed, locations you have discovered, or anything useful, or interesting, that relates to your business. You should begin to follow other profiles, and 'like' posts you particularly admire. As with other social media, you can also share posts you believe will be of interest. Instagram is most useful when installed as an application on a smartphone with a camera, as you can capture, and post, images immediately, documenting significant and memorable moments of your professional life as they happen. If you are using Instagram, or any social network for business purposes, you should avoid posts that are too personal, irrelevant, controversial, or inappropriate.

LinkedIn

The last social platform I will cover here is LinkedIn. This is primarily a network to connect with other professionals, but it is important in establishing your profile as a business. In addition to your personal profile, you should create a listing for your business. You should ensure that all the information about your company, including your business name, telephone number, address, and website are the same across all platforms and online listings.

5.13d Professional Wedding Website Advertising

Almost from the time you announce the launch of your business online, you will start receiving marketing phone calls from wedding professional listing networks, such as WeddingWire.com, theknot.com, Mywedding.com, and others. These sites offer free listings, but will push hard for you to take out a paid plan, for featured placement, with which you will appear higher in search results for people who visit their website. There is a great deal of ongoing debate among wedding professionals about the effectiveness of such paid listings, particularly as the prices are often increasing, and subscriptions for a single geographical location can cost around $1000 per year, which is a very significant portion of any marketing budget. Among Celebrants, and other types of wedding vendor, you will find strong advocates for, and against, each platform. Results appear to vary wildly based on geographic location. Unfortunately, a broad analysis of how effective each platform is in driving leads that convert to sales is extremely difficult. My current advice on this is not to rush into any decision, or contract, with any sales representative, but rather to discuss with other professionals their experiences, and which networks they have found have worked for them in your area. Additionally, it is not just selecting the right network, but how you use that platform, and shape your profile to target the right sort of client for your practice. If you decide to try a paid professional listing, begin only in your primary geographic location, to test the effectiveness of this marketing spending. Additionally, the sales representatives are often keen to make sales, even if they must offer discounts to induce these. Never take the first price quoted. Always hold out for the best deal they have, which is often the third or fourth price they offer. Lastly, you should never devote your entire marketing budget to a single platform, in case that platform fails. Spread your budget as widely as possible, but your business website should *always* be where you put your first efforts, your greatest care, and the largest investment of time and money.

5.13e Blogging

Blogging is the best way to add regular content to your website, that will appeal to both your clients, and raise your perceived value with search engines.

While most of the pages on your site will be relatively static, rarely changing from month-to-month, and contain information that does not relate to any particular date, blog posts are a different form of content.

Posting to a blog can be much like making an online diary entry, in that many posts will relate to a specific event, or a point in time for your life or business. You may wish to record your thoughts, or post photographs, from a successful ceremony you have just performed, or you may want to comment on a trend you have noticed this season. However, some posts are 'evergreen', in that the content remains fresh, and relevant, despite the passing of time. One example of this might be a post you write on a particular type of unity ritual, or how one can successfully incorporate their pet into a ceremony without overwhelming chaos.

Blog posts are often short, but most effective when they have text length of at least 300 words and are focused on a specific keyword. Where a post contains mostly photographs, you should add commentary.

If your website was created in WordPress, adding a blog is straightforward. In fact, WordPress was originally developed as a blogging platform. If yours is a template site, adding a blog may be more difficult. In that case, the only solution you may have is to create your blog in a separate location, such as on blogger.com, which is a blogging network you can join for free.

The second important reason for blogging is to be able to post guest posts, or articles on other professional websites. You may be contacted, and asked to do this, but more usually you would approach other sites with an idea, or perhaps the text already written, and they choose whether or not your material is a good fit for their platform. In most cases, you will not be paid for this writing, but it is an excellent way to bring visitors to your own website, as your author profile should provide a link to your homepage. Having this also raises your perceived value in the eyes of search engines. If you are a keen writer, regular blog posts are a terrific way to build your online reputation and exposure.

A word of caution if you are planning to create a blog for your website. Only do so if you intend to post consistently, and regularly. While a regular blog, kept fresh and up-to-date, can add enormous value to your website, a blog that is left to stagnate, to which you post very rarely, and where the latest post is over a few months old, can look dreadful. A neglected blog implies a neglected business and a lack of enthusiasm for your subject. It is quite sufficient, however, to post only once or twice a month, providing this happens at regular intervals.

Blogging can, and should, be fun. It can also be an excellent way to practice your writing skills on a regular basis.

5.14 Offline Marketing

Despite the fact that most of the contacts for your business will likely come from online sources, marketing in the real world is still a hugely important part of business promotion strategy. In-person connections, and printed materials, still have a tremendous value. What follows are important real-world ways you can build, and promote, your business.

5.14a Networking

Building personal relationships with other professionals in your industry is vital to your business. Although growing a network of trust and reciprocation, where others will begin to recommend your services, can take time, there are some basic strategies that you can use to fuel this growth, and increase the momentum.

The simplest strategy is to exchange contact details with every professional you meet, especially those you encounter at ceremonies you perform. Never attend any event without a stack of your business cards to hand, and always take the time to greet every other person working the event, and exchange your card for theirs. If they are impressed by your work, they will then have these details to hand, to recommend to others who seeking an excellent Celebrant in your area.

Always treat other professionals with the greatest respect, even when you find yourself silently disagreeing with decisions, or choices, you see them making. Your reputation among your colleagues is just as important as your reputation among your clients, perhaps more so. Ensure that you are friendly and helpful at all times, even when the situation is difficult. Be the person they will be excited to see when you next meet, as no community of local wedding professionals is so large that your paths may not cross again, and you will certainly be interacting with many of the same people. Your reputation is your most valuable business assets, and it is built through active, and successful, interaction with your peers, clients, and colleagues.

TIP: Keep a small stack of thank you cards on your desk, along with a book of stamps. When another professional has been helpful, friendly, and a pleasure to meet, take a few moments to write a brief thank you note, and send it across. Do this within 48 hours of returning from that event. The effect of a personal thank you, delivered in such a charming way, cannot be overstated. You will have created a lasting, positive memory in the mind of a colleague, and will have taken a step towards gaining a reputation as an individual willing to take that extra step. In the wedding business, such a reputation is pure gold.

5.14b Professional Events and Gatherings

Organized gatherings are an excellent way to meet both clients and colleagues. Most cities, and regions, hold regular events aimed at couples planning their wedding day. These are often organized by local professional organizations, or by media companies who specialize in the wedding industry. For a fee, you may set up a table, hand out literature, give away items or prizes, and mingle with couples for a few hours. Such events do require a fair amount of preparation and energy. As Celebrants, we often have few physical items to display, as we are the product. It is, therefore, vital to carry an ample supply of business cards. You may also wish to create flyers, and other instructional materials, or offer free gifts such as pens and notepads branded with your logo, and the contact information for your business. Where you encounter a couple with whom you would fit well, be sure to have your pen and paper ready to take down the details, so you can follow up very shortly after the event by phone or email. Ask other wedding professionals you encounter, as well as other Celebrants in your area, about events they have attended, or that they know any planned for the near future.

On a national level, there are several large conferences held each year for wedding industry professionals, and these can be a tremendous way to network, and to learn from the very best about what works in the business. Examples include the annual event held by Wedding MBA in Las Vegas, and the annual WeddingWire convention. Such conferences are often held during the week, so that they do not clash with weekend events, as this is still the day on which most weddings are held. National conventions usually have a website, and a strong social media presence, so look for them online.

5.14c Printed Materials

The first printed items that you should look to obtain are your business cards. Do not opt for the cheapest options, as a thin and ugly business card will do more harm than good. Fortunately, good-quality cards, with excellent designs, can be obtained at a very reasonable price from online services such as vistaprint.com.

It is important that your business card be clear, and easy to read. Resist the temptation to use fonts that are overly ornate, or colors that blend in with the background. Not only do such things place a strain on the human eye, but many people now use software to scan business cards into a database. Complicated designs interfere with the scanning process. If your business card has a dark background, ensure your text is white, or very lightly colored. If your card is light, and sure the lettering is dark.

There are certain items every business card should contain:

- Your personal name
- Your business name
- Your telephone number
- Your email address
- Your website address
- Your job title
- A logo

It is useful to leave the reverse side of your business cards blank. Not only does this save on printing costs, but it also provides a handy space to write extra information, if needed.

Give your business cards to everyone you meet, keep a stack in your car, in your purse or wallet, and on your desk. Include one in all the correspondence you send by mail for your business, including the thank you notes you send to clients and colleagues. Many organizations, such dry cleaners, allow local small businesses to display stacks of their cards. Always take an opportunity to do this, where you see one available. Be proud of your business cards, and hope the whole world sees them.

Proofread your business card very well before you give final authorization for printing. Do not proof alone. Show your design to friends, and family members, as, in addition to input on how the design is working, they will often find simple errors that it is very easy for the designer (yourself) to overlook. Unlike your website, mistakes made on printed materials are tough to correct. If you do make an error, it is better to discard an entire batch then try to correct with pen or whiteout.

Another printed item you may consider for your business is a threefold flyer, which can be given to event planners, and venues, to explain your services and style, and for them to pass on to interested clients. As with business cards, these are now very easily created online, where you will find many beautiful templates that can be quickly customized with your information. When producing flyers, and other printed material, be sure that the style, and coloring, matches all other documents, such as your business cards, and your website. This will maintain an easy reference point, showing that all these items belong to your Celebrant brand.

Most importantly, you must include your full contact information on *every single item* of printed material that you produce.

5.14d Mailings

When starting out in your Celebrant business, you may wish to send out a physical mail shot to introduce, and advertise, your services. This is most effective when sent to planners and venues, and it should not be necessary for you to send your packets of printed materials to all the other types of vendor, such as photographers and florists. A search of any professional advertising sites, such as WeddingWire.com, will quickly give you a list of the contacts you need.

Although a physical mailing is more expensive than sending a simple email, it will have a much greater impact on receipt, and will provide the recipient with materials that they can keep handy. You should include a brief, and friendly, cover letter, your threefold flyer if you have produced one, and two or three copies of your business card. Do not be afraid to reuse, or adapt, previously written text from other marketing materials, such as your website. The reverse is also true. Writing an introductory letter can be a great way to create content that can then be used on your website homepage. Although a mail shot can be an effective marketing tool, building your website, and creating your business cards, should always be given the highest priority.

5.15 Building your Professional Kit

As you begin your Celebrant practice, you will start to collect the physical items you will need on a regular basis. Make a budget, and plan your purchases carefully. It is wise to compare vendors, and pricing, on every item, as well as watching for regular sales on items such as shirts, or business cards. As with other aspects of your Celebrant business, ask your friends, family, and especially your Celebrant network to recommend reliable, and reasonably priced, vendors.

What follows are suggestions based on my experience, and you can find links to these items, from recommended vendors, as well as the most up-to-date list, on my website. If you have a suggestion for an item that may be useful for Celebrant work, and which I have not mentioned here, please do let me know, so that I can include it on the latest Internet list, as well as in any future editions of this book. Many talented Celebrants contributed ideas and suggestions to this edition, and I have offered a very sincere thank you in the acknowledgments at the beginning of this book. You can contact me, and view the latest lists and suggestions, at the website hanhills.com.

5.15a Clothing

Although there is no official, traditional, or required attire for modern Celebrants, you will need an adequate supply of smart, clean, formal wear. If there is a possibility that you may perform several ceremonies in a single week, you need to ensure you have enough sets of clothing to cover the times when your other outfits are being washed or dry-cleaned. It is also worth owning different footwear for the various environments in which a ceremony may take place. Appropriate footwear for a beach, or a park, will be quite different to that suitable for a ballroom, or funeral home.

In some cases, you may choose, or have been requested, that you wear a robe and/or stole. Formal robes, such as those used by judges and traditional clerics, can be hugely expensive. A much better option is to purchase a graduation gown, which can usually be obtained for as little as $20. Stoles, the long ceremonial cloths draped over the shoulders of the Celebrant, can be purchased in almost any color, blank or with designs such as the happy humanist, from small artisanal vendors on websites such as Etsy.com.

5.15b Tools of the Trade

There are many useful items that you might consider including in your Celebrant toolkit. In addition to a professional-quality book or binder, this list may include:

- Notebook
- Receipt book
- Tissues
- Pens (X3)
- Electronic card reader (for taking payments on your phone)
- Business cards
- A copy of your ordination certificate, in a plastic cover for protection
- A copy of your letter of good standing, covered for protection
- Blank questionnaire forms
- Blank contracts
- Breath mints

5.15c Useful Apps and Software

Unless you are extremely technologically averse, you will use software to help you carry out your Celebrant business. Over the years, I have tried out various systems and products and am currently fond of the Google suite of applications, which includes a calendar, maps, and email, as well as document production and storage systems. These have two excellent advantages. First, they exist online, which means the same information can be accessed from multiple devices, and if my computer fails, no information I have stored on Google is lost. The second advantage is that all these systems integrate with each other. If I place a booking on the calendar, for example, I can add a location that is linked directly through to the maps application. I can have it send me email notifications, and (my favorite feature) I can upload the text of the ceremony to the calendar listing, so that even if I forget the script on the day, all I need is my phone to rescue the situation. The Google suite is free, although a personalized email and larger document storage space are available in a premium version, for around $5 per month.

Calendar

Google calendar is a terrific and simple to use application. Each event listing can be used to store a great deal of information, including the ceremony itself. One advantage of this online solution is that calendars can be shared with colleagues, friends, and family. This helps avoid booking issues, and clashes between business and personal life.

A popular off-line solution is Microsoft Outlook, which also integrates email and calendar functions.

Apple computers have a suite of applications as standard, which includes a calendar program.

Notes, Planning, and Memos

For organizing notes and to-do lists, Evernote (evernote.com) is a terrific application. You can create entries from text, voice, photos, web pages, and even scan business cards directly into an information database (if the card has been designed in a clear and readable way). The application is free, but there is a paid version that allows extra functionality.

Writing

MS Word is still a very popular choice for producing documents, such as ceremonies and letters. However, an excellent free alternative, with most of the same features, can be found in the Open Office Suite (OpenOffice.org).

Accounting

Although it is possible to keep your financial records on a spreadsheet, such as Microsoft Excel or the Calc program found free with open office, you may quickly find you outgrow this method. Intuit QuickBooks is a very attractive solution for small business accounting, and integrates with most other systems, which can be useful if you plan to have someone else prepare your taxes.

5.16 Working with Clients

When working with clients, it is important always to be a polite, punctual, and prepared, even if the customer is not. Before each meeting, you should have a plan of what you will discuss, and a rough estimate of how long the meeting will take. Preparation will save you a tremendous amount of time, as well as ensuring that you do not accidentally miss any important discussion points.

5.16a Your Service Questionnaires

When taking your first inquiry from any clients, and then during your initial interview and subsequent meetings, it is helpful to have a copy of the important questions regarding the ceremony and related topics. Included with this book are examples of both inquiry and interview forms for weddings and memorials.

You may also wish to create a list of standard questions that you can send to a client, for them to complete before your meeting.

5.16b Meeting Locations

The choice of meeting location can be crucial. Although you may sometimes be asked to meet at the client's home, and this may be preferable for memorial planning, a restaurant is also a common choice. When choosing a venue, make sure the ambient noise will be low, that you will have sufficient privacy, and that the table space available will be enough for you to take notes comfortably. You should also check the opening hours of any commercial establishment you choose to use. Do not automatically assume that a client will cover the cost of your coffee or the tasty muffin that you consume during your meeting, although many clients will offer to do so, as an additional small thank you for your time and assistance.

5.17 Sales Techniques for Celebrants

Although you are often performing a valuable social and community service, it is important to realize that in offering time, and expertise, for any reward you are acting as a business, and should follow best business practices. To do so does not mean to act without empathy, or with selfish or dubious motivations. Rather, by following best business practices, you are ensuring high standards of experience and satisfaction, for both the client and yourself. If you hold yourself to high standards, and consider yourself a professional, you will find a far greater level of success and reward. If you treat your work with respect, you will earn the respect of others. What follows are not tips on how to manipulate a client, but rather practices that help everyone to succeed, and achieve the results they desire with the fullest satisfaction.

1. Always Respond Quickly

It is vital to respond quickly to all customer inquiries and requests. Studies have shown that the professionals with the fastest response times to telephone calls, and emails, are by far the most likely to secure bookings, and to receive excellent reviews following the completion of the contract.

For phone calls, you should enable an answer phone service, and test to make sure it is working correctly. Most current answering services will notify you when receiving a message, and it is important to stay alert for such notifications. Many clients, however, may prefer not to use an automated answering system. It is, therefore, a good idea to return all telephone calls one has missed, if this is done within a few hours of the call.

You should try to check your email a couple of times a day at minimum, and ensure that you respond to all communications within 24 hours. If you need longer to prepare a full response, send a short note informing the client that you are doing so. If a customer has sent documents, it is polite to confirm receipt, even if no immediate response is needed.

2. Honesty and Integrity

In all your dealings with clients and other professionals, you will find that honesty is always the best choice. Excuses, or any massaging of the truth, will almost always be noted, and regarded as deceitful and unimpressive. Even when you have made an error or omission, it is best to be frank, and open, about having done so, and to offer a full, sincere, and unreserved apology. You need to show the clients that you have understood a mistake, realized its importance, and have learned from the error in a way that will make it highly unlikely for you to repeat it.

3. The Power of Empathic Listening

When listening to what a client is telling you, try to place yourself in their position. By this, you are not attempting to understand what *you* would do, or desire, in this situation, but rather to understand their viewpoint, and frame of reference. Issues that may seem minor to you may have a huge importance your clients, or be indicators of significant underlying problems that have not been stated directly. By seeking to understand not just the words you are hearing, but also the motivation and subtext behind them, you will be able to offer that client effective and efficient solutions that will go to the heart of their needs. Although staying focused can take patience, and practice, it is important to keep your attention present at all times during a conversation, and not to become distracted, as you may end up missing a small, but significant, piece of information that can move the discussion forward in a useful way.

4. Identify your Client's Needs

Your first goal, when interacting with a customer, is to determine their needs.

These go deeper than the mere literal sense of needing a ceremony, or being in a location at a particular time. Many things you discuss in planning a celebration may seem straightforward, but often serve less obvious needs held by an individual. An example might be in the case of a bride who insists on wearing a veil for an outdoor ceremony, even though this is slightly impractical in high winds. Her mother may have worn the veil, and doing so herself is a way either consciously, or unconsciously, of honoring an important person in her life. Alternatively, such an object may have been deeply associated with concepts of prestige since early childhood, and this may be an important need for her to fulfill as part of the wedding ceremony. Only by fully understanding the needs each request, or discussion point, serves can you achieve the results needed.

5. Offer Solutions

Once you have identified your clients needs, the most important thing to do is offer solutions, rather than attempt to realign those needs, or explain why a solution is unnecessary, or impossible. In approaching any problem, be open to embracing alternative ideas and solutions. There may be a third alternative, in addition to the first ones considered by the client and yourself, which may work better for everyone concerned. It is far more important to find the best solution to a problem, rather than to be the one to take credit for that solution.

6. Positivity

You will find the best solutions are arrived at, and the highest level of client satisfaction obtained, if you act, and speak, in all you do with a spirit of positivity. Once you have identified your customers needs and considered possible solutions and responses, always frame these using positive terms, words, and examples. By establishing a habit, and mindset, where things are accomplished rather than compromised, even problems can be seen in a positive and useful light. You will encounter many clients who are highly nervous and apprehensive, and a positive attitude can be critical to putting them at the ease, and making them believe that solutions are achievable. Positivity over small parts of the planning process can have an enormous cumulative effect on the entire experience, and can turn the tide completely, from the perception of failure to the belief in a happy success.

7. Build a Rapport

From your first contact with the client, it is important to focus on the aspects you have in common, and the areas of life you find most important. In actively seeking common areas of enthusiasm, you will immediately find a greater empathy with the client, a larger understanding of their needs, and solutions that work for all concerned will far more readily present themselves. Ceremonies that mark the significant milestones in life are often highly emotional affairs, and an understanding that we are working alongside someone who shares our values, and outlook, is hugely beneficial. Although you may find your life, and experience, to be very different from that of a client, you still have in common the fundamental human needs. You should also seek, and remain alert for, smaller aspects of life you share, from a mutual love of a television show, or food, to something more general, such as a passion for animals. When you have discovered these common attributes, it is helpful to phrase your solutions, and examples, around these concepts. In doing so, you will more readily maintain interest and ease of understanding.

8. Focus on Their Success First

You will find the greatest success in your Celebrant life if your attitude is always to place the success of the clients before that of yourself. When we reach out to others in a genuine spirit of care, and selflessness, to address their needs and problems, they are naturally inclined to reciprocate with care for our happiness and well-being. In taking that extra step, or devoting additional time, though it is not necessary, or rewarding, for ourselves, we are setting an example, and demonstrating that we genuinely value the client and their needs. The job of the Celebrant, particularly, is not one that is taken on solely for personal reward, and the events that will give you the most satisfaction are the ones where you made the choice to excel, and were rewarded by the happiness of others. In giving of ourselves without calculating personal benefits, we are contributing to greater humanity for everyone, today and for future generations. These concepts are important in the ceremonies you perform, and if you practice them in daily life, this will be conveyed to sincerely when you create, and offer, your celebration event.

9. Follow Up with your Promises

If we make a commitment to our clients, however small, it is important always to see this through. Because of this, be careful not to overpromise on items you will then find tough to deliver. If preparing the ceremony, or writing up meeting notes, is going to take some extra time, it is far better to be honest about this, rather than offering excuses for missing deadlines, or falling through on other promises you have made. Clients will respect that you have other activities in your life apart from their ceremony, but they will appreciate it far more when you always act as you had stated and agreed. Nothing is guaranteed to produce a glowing client testimonial more than the Celebrants ultimately coming through on every statement or promise they made.

10. Be Open about Pricing

It is far better to be open about your pricing from the first. To camouflage this issue, or defer it, implies that you are somehow ashamed of the price you charge, which itself implies that you may not be 100% convinced that it is the real value of your work. If you believe that you offer excellent value for what you charge, be open about those prices, and the clients who also see the value in your work will be happy to find you. Customers who do not value your work highly are not the clients you should be working with, or that will give you any satisfaction. When clients try to haggle over money, you should often take this as a warning sign of what the rest of the working experience will entail. You will find many clients readily accept your fee as a necessary part of the process, and are also glad to get that topic out of the way, so they can concentrate on the more exciting, and emotionally rewarding, parts of the ceremony creation process.

11. Educate your Clients

Many clients will have little understanding of what your job entails, or the process of creating and performing a ceremony. It is, therefore, important to quickly, and positively, educate your clients as to the value you will bring to their event. This is best accomplished when you understand the values that are most important to your customers. Many couples are worried that their wedding will be chaotic, or boring. If you can quickly explain how you will add security, or humor, this will demonstrate why you are an excellent choice for such an important occasion. Word your explanations within a framework of understanding and enthusiasm. Avoid excessive use of technical terms, unless you can quickly explain those terms in an entertaining and informative way. If you take an active role in demonstrating your value, rather than just expecting others to see this, the working experience will be far more pleasurable, and the financial and emotional rewards will also come more readily.

12. Don't Negotiate Against Yourself

Do not offer discounted rates, or lavish bonuses, in your urgency to close a sale. Some Celebrants are so eager to secure a booking that they take a moment of silence, or hesitation, they hear in the client, and use it to work against themselves. Instead of trying to find ways to sweeten the deal for a customer, your time is better served by educating them as to the value you bring to the ceremony. Have confidence in the value you have already placed on your service and expertise. In moments of doubt, remind yourself that what you offer comes at an excellent price. You are not trying to sell yourself, but rather communicate how you can help an individual, couple, or family create a ceremony that they will remember fondly for years to come. If they hear this confidence in your voice, which can only come from belief in yourself, they will far better perceive that you are worth the modest fee you ask as compensation for your services.

13. Listen for the Close

As you discuss a potential booking with a client, listen for their readiness to take the actions necessary to make a deposit, and secure the date. This may occur a lot earlier in the conversation than you expect, and that decision may have already been taken in the mind of the client before they even picked up the phone. This is a primary reason or making it easy to accept deposit payments in many different forms. It is also entirely reasonable for you to remind a potential client, in a gentle and positive way, that demand for your services does require you to offer each date, or time, to the person who is first willing to put down the deposit payment. You should not hold the date and reject other bookings, without having this security. It is easy to become enthusiastic early on in a conversation, talking about the various aspects of ceremonies, and forget the formality of booking. Until the booking is confirmed, and the deposit has been placed, listen attentively for the opportunity to do those things. There will be plenty of opportunities to discuss exciting ceremonial additions once that formality has been completed.

5.18 Continuing Growth

The skills of the Celebrant are so many, deep, and varied that an individual can practice for decades, and still find new things to learn. It is important that your work as a Celebrant does not become stagnant, and that you embrace new opportunities, and fresh challenges. If you do so, you will find greater success and rewards, and excellent possibilities and potential that you had not previously considered will suddenly become visible, and attainable. If you are choosing the role of the Celebrant, most likely you view this more as a vocation, rather than just as a job. This can be one of the most exciting, and rewarding, roles you will play in life, and if you embrace it in the spirits of always exploring your mastery of the craft, you will become both respected, and in high demand.

5.18a Building your Skills

At the beginning of this book, there was a short questionnaire that addressed the skills necessary to the role of the Celebrant. No Celebrant has ever existed who has been so perfect on every scale that they could not further grow, and expand their knowledge, experience, and repertoire.

It is useful to be continually reading books, articles, and blog posts about the craft of celebrancy, and the business of being a ceremony professional. There are also many excellent podcasts, and video chats, now available, which add to their episode list regularly. If you wish to hone your performance skills, you may like to sign up for a course in public speaking, or join a local theatrical group. Many local clubs are always seeking guest speakers, and this can be an excellent way to practice that skill. There are also groups specifically devoted to enjoying the public speaking skills of others, and offering constructive feedback on their work.

Increasingly, you do not even have to leave your home to further your education. New online academies and courses are appearing every year. Many of them are excellent, and very reasonably priced. I will be starting to offer several courses, which you can find details of on my website (hanhills.com). In the resources section of this book, I have also listed a few locations where you may go to see further skill building opportunities.

5.18b The Celebrant Community

The Celebrant community is a fun and lively one. I very strongly encourage you to seek out other Celebrants in your location and arrange a time for coffee. You will find that you both gain considerably from the experience. Not only that, but by building your local Celebrant network, you will be able to offer alternative practitioners to clients when you are unable to perform the ceremony.

The online Celebrant community has grown remarkably in the last few years, and is a terrific place to post questions, and receive answers, from the most knowledgeable and experienced practitioners around the world. In the resources section of this book, I have included links to groups, and forums, you may like to visit or join.

If you get the opportunity, I highly recommend attending one of the professional conferences that are held around the country, or in other countries, throughout various times of the year. Many of these are aimed at all types of wedding professional, but increasingly there are events created primarily for

Celebrants and Officiants. Notices of these are often posted in the online groups I have listed in the resources section. Attendance fees are not usually expensive, and the process can be hugely inspirational for your Celebrant work. You will find you return home brimming over with new ideas, and enthusiasm for the following season.

There are several professional organizations for Celebrants and Officiants, to which membership can be highly advantageous in gaining opportunities to learn from the experience of others, as well as making terrific new friends. If you have not already done so, I highly recommend you pay a visit is to the website for the International Association of Professional Wedding Officiants (iapwo.org). The founder, Laura Cannon, is one of the groundbreaking visionaries of our profession, and she, and other members of the Association, are leading our wonderful profession into a new era of practices, and achievements. I know they would love for you to join them on their journey.

5.18c Mentors and Mentoring

When you are just beginning as a Celebrant, you will have many questions, and probably find there are times of high anxiety, especially before performing your first ceremony. It can be useful, at this time, to have a mentor, or professional colleague, to turn to with your questions, to act as a sounding board for your ideas, and even accompany you to your first events. Do not be afraid to reach out to other Celebrants who seem approachable, which I would hope is most of us, and ask if they would mind sharing the benefit of their experience on a one-to-one basis. Many will be honored, and privileged, to do so; myself included.

If you are reading this as an experienced Celebrant, with concerns and hopes that the standards of our profession will remain high, I encourage you to offer yourself as a mentor for the talented newcomers to the Celebrant life. It may be that, in doing so, you will find, as I have, that your energy and enthusiasm receives a boost as a result, and that you come to view your work with a fresh perspective. It is in the noble tradition of the greatest professions that the master practitioners pass on their knowledge to the generations that follow. This is one of the most significant ways that you can ensure your legacy lives on for many years after the ink is dry on your last wedding license.

5.18d Avoiding Burnout

When I was creating this edition of the book, a psychologist friend of mine suggested that I write a few words about avoiding burnout. If you have read everything this far, you will know how complex, and extensive, the work of a ceremony professional can be. When your practice begins to take off, it is tempting to agree to as many bookings as possible, and fill your free time with ceremonies. It is important, however, that you adopt a pragmatic view of the number of services you can perform throughout any season, and still maintain a fresh, professional standard of which you will be truly proud. Particularly at the end of a long season, every Celebrant finds they have to work harder to maintain the energy that they found easily at the start of the professional year. This is entirely natural and understandable, considering the amounts of dedication, care, and emotional investment that a good Celebrant gives to their work. Always give yourself pause to recover, whether this means something as small as a long enough break between ceremonies on any one day, or scheduling a single week in the summer to take away from your work, spent with the people you love. Why not give yourself a holiday, as a reward you can look forward to at the end of whatever month is the busiest in your part of the world. For most Celebrants, their career is one that will last years, even decades. This is a long road; beautiful though the scenery may be. On any journey, a traveler needs to take time for rest, and renewal of energies. Never let your Celebrant work overwhelm you to the point where you tire so much that you cease to find it enjoyable. Even a short pause can renew your spirits to where you remember once again why this is the profession you chose.

5.18e Celebrating your Achievements

As you travel on your Celebrant journey, be sure to celebrate the triumphs along the way. Be proud of the work you do, the things you achieve, the ceremonies you create, and the positive way you change the lives of those you meet. Place your ordination certificates, or other official licenses and awards, in nice frames on your office wall. Invest in a high-quality record book, in which you record the names, dates, and locations of each ceremony you perform. Create a section for each year, and from time to time look back through the entries. Remind yourself of all the wonderful things you have accomplished in your community. You may also like to celebrate particular milestones along your journey. A successful first ceremony is always a cause for celebration, but why not also raise a glass at your tenth, your fiftieth, and your hundredth performance. Share your accomplishments with your family and friends, and especially with the Celebrant community, who will truly appreciate what you have achieved. They will likely want to know the secret of your success. Share your stories, and do it proudly. You will have earned the right.

5.19 The Next Level – The Celebrant Team

After they have been working for a few years, and developed their practice, many Celebrants find that they now have more opportunities for work than can be accepted, or taken on by one person. In such a situation it can be a terrific idea to involve other Celebrants in your business, even if only in a small way.

At this point, you have established an excellent reputation, invested a lot in successful marketing, and are working to produce inquiries. It is only fair, if you pass on these opportunities directly to another Celebrant, you ask them for a small referral fee as a professional courtesy for doing so. When you reach this point, you may wish to approach other Celebrants within your network, especially those new to the business, and see if this is a professional relationship with which they would be comfortable. It is reasonable to ask for a referral fee of between 10% to 15% of the amount earned on the booking.

You may decide to engage in an arrangement with one or more Celebrants, whereby you take on a greater role in managing their business. Where this is the case, you may arrange to take between 30% to 50% of the booking fee for your role as manager, and marketer. You will then find that your company has become a multi-Celebrant organization. There are Celebrants now, across the world, who have already created such a business, and in the space of a few years have gone from their first ceremony to a six-figure income. It is entirely possible. If you have the enthusiasm for this profession, and work steadily, and intelligently, to build your skills and reputation, there is no reason you too cannot achieve this level of success. You can receive life-changing rewards that you never dreamed of in those first moments when it was suggested that you would make a wonderful choice to perform a ceremony. That is exactly how it was for me. I have written this book because I believe it is possible for you too. Because life should be a celebration.

5.20 New Celebrant Business Checklist

Verify your State's Ordination Requirements.
Become Ordained.
Register with your State, or Local Jurisdiction, if Needed.
Learn your State Marriage Laws and License Process.
Confirm your Local Tax and Small Business Laws.
Create a System to Record your Sales, Earnings, and Expenses.
Decide on the Services you will Offer.
Decide on the Prices you will Charge.
Decide on your Payment and Deposit Policies.
Create a Contract for Services.
Decide on your Company or Professional Name.
Register your Name if Required Locally.
Decide on your Advertising Budget.
Register your Professional Internet Domain Name.
Ensure you have the Clothing you will Need.
Create a Website.
Create a Facebook Page.
Create a LinkedIn Profile.
Create a Profile on WeddingWire.
Have Business Cards Printed.
Put Together your Celebrant Case or Kit.
Create your Questionnaires and Enquiry Sheets.
Set Up a Client Filing System.
Create an Introduction Letter for Venues and Vendors.
Create a Flyer for Clients.
Continue to Learn More about Ceremonies.

Appendix A
Wedding Laws by U.S. State

Alabama Wedding Officiant Regulations

Statute: Alabama Code - Section 30-1-7: Persons Authorized To Solemnize Marriages

(a) Generally. Marriages may be solemnized by any licensed minister of the gospel in regular communion with the Christian church or society of which the minister is a member; by an active or retired judge of the Supreme Court, Court of Criminal Appeals, Court of Civil Appeals, any circuit court, or any district court within this state; by a judge of any federal court; or by an active or retired judge of probate.

(b) Pastor of religious society; clerk of society to maintain register of marriages; register, etc., deemed presumptive evidence of fact. Marriage may also be solemnized by the pastor of any religious society according to the rules ordained or custom established by such society. The clerk or keeper of the minutes of each society shall keep a register and enter therein a particular account of all marriages solemnized by the society, which register, or a sworn copy thereof, is presumptive evidence of the fact.

(c) Quakers, Mennonites, or other religious societies. The people called Mennonites, Quakers, or any other Christian society having similar rules or regulations, may solemnize marriage according to their forms by consent of the parties, published and declared before the congregation assembled for public worship.

What You Need to Know

An Officiant must be over 18 years of age to perform a legal marriage.

In the state of Alabama you are not required to register with the government before performing a marriage ceremony. However, you should be prepared to produce proof of ordination by a recognized body, in the event that this is ever requested. If you have any questions regarding the legality of your ordination in this state you should contact your local government office, or your ordination body itself.

What Couples Need To Know

Where do couples apply for a license? The County Clerk's Office.

What are the age requirements? The legal age to marry in Alabama (age of majority) is 18. Individuals ages 16 and 17 can marry in Alabama with parental consent. Both parents or legal guardians must appear with the teenager to obtain the marriage license, and provide valid identification and written consent. If the parents are divorced and one parent has full custody, he or she must bring the legal proof of divorce and full custody. If a parent has died, the teenager should provide the death certificate. Legal guardians must provide a certified copy of their court-appointed guardianship.

According to the Alabama Code Section 30 1-4, individuals under the age of 16 may not marry.

How much does a license cost? (Can vary by county) $43.35+ for marriage license only. $63+ for license, ceremony and a certified copy. Cash or credit card requirement varies depending on County. Some locales charge $2 for using a credit card. For individuals under 18 the state also requires a $200 bond to be executed, payable to the State of Alabama.

What documents are needed? You will need a valid Driver's License or Birth Certificate if you are over 18. All applicants must also provide a Social Security number.

If either of you are under 18, you will need a certified copy of your birth certificate. Both parents must be present with identification, or if you have a legal guardian they must be present with a court order and identification. If one or both parents are deceased, proper evidence of such must be provided.

Are there residency requirements? You do not have to be a resident of Alabama. However, some counties may require non-residents to wait three days before being able to have a wedding ceremony performed by a county marriage official.

Is there a waiting period? There is no waiting period in Alabama except after being divorced. Then there is a 60 day waiting period after your divorce is final.

Nonresidents who want to be married by a county official may have to wait three days. Please contact the county offices to verify whether or not you will have a waiting period.

How long is a license valid? An Alabama marriage license is valid for 30 days.

Where is a license valid for use? The license can only be used within the State of Alabama.

What if someone has been married previously? If you were divorced within the last 6 months of your wedding date, you will need to show a copy of your Divorce Decree. According to Section 30-2-10 of the Alabama Code, there is a 60 day restriction on getting married after a divorce.

Are there any required tests? No blood or medical tests are required.

Are proxy marriages allowed? No.

Can cousins marry? Yes.

Are common law marriages recognized? Yes. A valid common law marriage exists in Alabama when there is a capacity to enter into a marriage, present agreement or consent t be husband and wife, public recognition of the existence of the marriage, and consummation.

How to Handle the Marriage License

Read and follow the instructions which come with the license on how to fill out your section, and ensure all other sections have been fully and correctly completed.

The person performing the marriage must endorse and return the license to the clerk within 30 days after the marriage ceremony. Failure to do so is a misdemeanor.

The Celebrant is not required to keep records of marriages.

Alaska Wedding Officiant Regulations

Statute AS 25.05.261. Who May Solemnize.

(a) Marriages may be solemnized

(1) by a minister, priest, or rabbi of any church or congregation in the state, or by a commissioned officer of the Salvation Army, or by the principal officer or elder of recognized churches or congregations that traditionally do not have regular ministers, priests, or rabbis, anywhere within the state;

(2) by a marriage commissioner or judicial officer of the state anywhere within the jurisdiction of the commissioner or officer; or

(3) before or in any religious organization or congregation according to the established ritual or form commonly practiced in the organization or congregation.

(b) This section may not be construed to waive the requirements for obtaining a marriage license.

What You Need to Know

An Officiant must be over 18 years of age to perform a legal marriage.

In the state of Alaska you are not required to register with the government before performing a marriage ceremony. However, you should be prepared to produce proof of ordination by a recognized body, in the event that this is ever requested. If you have any questions regarding the legality of your ordination in this state you should contact your local government office, or your ordination body itself.

What Couples Need To Know

Where do couples apply for a license? Vital Statistics Office or Alaska Court

What are the age requirements? Both parties must be at least 18 years of age for a marriage license to be issued without consent from parents or legal guardians. Exception: an applicant who is under the age of 18, a member of the U.S. armed forces, and on active duty.

If either person is at least 16 years of age and under 18 years of age, they must have written consent from their legal parents. A birth certificate must be issued within 30 days of the date of the marriage license and must be submitted with the marriage application.

If either person is 14 or 15 years of age, a court order allowing the person to be married is required before the marriage license can be issued.

How much does a license cost? The license fee is $60.00.

What documents are needed? The Groom and Bride must present a government-issued photo ID showing their name, sex, and date of birth before a marriage license can be issued.

Are there residency requirements? There are no residency requirements.

Is there a waiting period? There is a 3 business day waiting period that begins once a mailed or faxed application is received by the issuing office. This means you must wait at least three full business days after the application is submitted before you can pick up the license and the marriage ceremony can be performed.

How long is a license valid? The license is valid for 3 months from the date of issuance. The marriage must be performed before the three-month expiration or the license will no longer be valid. Refunds and extensions cannot be granted.

Where is a license valid for use? The license is valid only for marriages performed in Alaska or in Alaska State waters.

What if someone has been married previously? All divorces must be final and filed with the courts in the state granted. If either party has been married previously, the beginning and ending dates of all previous marriages must be listed on the application. Submitting a copy of a divorce decree is only required if the divorce or dissolution occurred less than 60 days prior to applying for the marriage license.

Are there any required tests? No blood test or physical exam is required.

Are proxy marriages allowed? Proxy marriages are not permitted in Alaska. The two parties must be present before two witnesses and the Officiant for the ceremony to be performed.

Can cousins marry? Yes.

Are common law marriages recognized? No.

How to Handle the Marriage License

Read and follow the instructions which come with the license on how to fill out your section, and ensure all other sections have been fully and correctly completed.

The person performing the marriage must complete two short-form certificates, and, after that person and the two witnesses have signed them, give one to each of the parties to the marriage. The original marriage certificate shall be filed as required by AS 18.50 (Vital Statistics Act) and regulations adopted under it. It must be done within 7 days.

The Celebrant is not required to keep records of marriages.

Arizona Wedding Officiant Regulations

Statute 25-124. Persons authorized to perform marriage ceremony; definition

A. The following are authorized to solemnize marriages between persons who are authorized to marry:

1. Duly licensed or ordained clergymen.

2. Judges of courts of record.

3. Municipal court judges.

4. Justices of the peace.

5. Justices of the United States supreme court.

6. Judges of courts of appeals, district courts and courts that are created by an act of Congress if the judges are entitled to hold office during good behavior.

7. Bankruptcy court and tax court judges.

8. United States magistrate judges.

9. Judges of the Arizona court of military appeals.

B. For the purposes of this section, 'licensed or ordained clergymen' includes ministers, elders or other persons who by the customs, rules and regulations of a religious society or sect are authorized or permitted to solemnize marriages or to officiate at marriage ceremonies.

What You Need to Know

An Officiant must be over 18 years of age to perform a legal marriage.

In the state of Arizona you are not required to register with the government before performing a marriage ceremony. However, you should be prepared to produce proof of ordination by a recognized body, in the event that this is ever requested. If you have any questions regarding the legality of your ordination in this state you should contact your local government office, or your ordination body itself.

What Couples Need To Know

Where do couples apply for a license? A Marriage License Office

What are the age requirements? If you are 16 or 17 years old, you must have the notarized consent of your parents or legal guardian. If you are under 16, you must have the notarized consent of your parents or legal guardian as well as a court order.

How much does a license cost? $76.00 Cash or money order.

What documents are needed? Drivers license or identification card or other ID showing current address and date of birth. Bringing a certified copy of your birth certificate is recommended because some counties require it if you are younger than 30.

If you are 16 or 17 years old, you must have the notarized consent of your parents or legal guardian. If you are under 16, you must have the notarized consent of your parents or legal guardian as well as a court order.

Are there residency requirements? You do not have to be a resident of Arizona.

Is there a waiting period? There is no waiting period.

How long is a license valid? The license is valid for 1 year.

Where is a license valid for use? The license can only be used within the State of Arizona.

What if someone has been married previously? Copies of the divorce decree are not required.

Are there any required tests? No tests are required.

Are proxy marriages allowed? No.

Can cousins marry? Yes, first cousins may marry if both are sixty-five years of age or older. If one or both first cousins are under sixty-five years of age, they can marry if they show proof to a superior court judge that one of them is unable to reproduce.

Are common law marriages recognized? No.

How to Handle the Marriage License

Read and follow the instructions which come with the license on how to fill out your section, and ensure all other sections have been fully and correctly completed.

The person solemnizing the rites of matrimony shall endorse the act of solemnization on the license and shall return the license to the clerk within thirty days after the solemnization.

The Celebrant is not required to keep records of marriages.

Arkansas Wedding Officiant Regulations

Statute 9-11-213. Persons who may solemnize marriages.

(a) For the purpose of being registered and perpetuating the evidence thereof, marriage shall be solemnized only by the following persons:

(1) The Governor;

(2) Any former justice of the Supreme Court;

(3) Any judges of the courts of record within this state, including any former judge of a court of record who served at least four (4) years or more;

(4) Any justice of the peace, including any former justice of the peace who served at least two (2) terms since the passage of Arkansas Constitution, Amendment 55;

(5) Any regularly ordained minister or priest of any religious sect or denomination;

(6) The mayor of any city or town;

(7) Any official appointed for that purpose by the quorum court of the county where the marriage is to be solemnized; or

(8) Any elected district court judge and any former municipal or district court judge who served at least four (4) years.

(b) (1) Marriages solemnized through the traditional rite of the Religious Society of Friends, more commonly known as Quakers, are recognized as valid to all intents and purposes the same as marriages otherwise contracted and solemnized in accordance with law.

(2) The functions, duties, and liabilities of a party solemnizing marriage, as set forth in the marriage laws of this state, in the case of marriages solemnized through the traditional marriage rite of the Religious Society of Friends shall be incumbent upon the clerk of the congregation or, in his or her absence, his or her duly designated alternate.

What You Need to Know

In the state of Arkansas all Celebrants wishing to perform a legal marriage ceremony must be over 18 years of age. Celebrants are not required to be resident in the state.

All Celebrants wishing to perform a legal solemnization in Arkansas must register with a County Clerk's office prior to performing the ceremony. The registration may be with any county, and is afterward valid in all counties across the state. The application process varies slightly between counties. However, all counties require documents from the Celebrant's body of ordination. In most cases this will be:

Your Ordination Certificate

A Letter of Good Standing with your body of ordination

Your ordination body will be able to provide these documents, and should also be able to answer any questions you have about the registration process in your chosen location. However, I advise you to contact the local County Clerk first with any enquiries, as they are certain to have access to the most up to date information.

What Couples Need To Know

Where do couples apply for a license? County Clerk's Office.

What are the age requirements? Males and Females over 18 may apply for a marriage license on their own. Males age 17 or females ages 16 or 17 may be married with parental consent.

How much does a license cost? Approximately $58+ (determined by county). Cash only. No checks accepted. No refunds.

What documents are needed? Males and females 21 or under must present a state-certified copy of their birth certificates or an active Military Identification Card or valid passport.

Males and females 21 or older may present a valid driver's license showing their correct name and date of birth or any documents listed above.

If your name has changed through a divorce and your driver's license does not reflect this change, you will need to bring a certified copy of your divorce decree.

Are there residency requirements? No.

Is there a waiting period? The license may be used immediately.

How long is a license valid? Marriage licenses are valid for 60 days. License must be returned, used or unused, within 60 days for recording or a $100 bond will be executed against all applicants for license.

Where is a license valid for use? The license may be used anywhere in the state of Arkansas, but must be returned to the County Clerk's Office where you first applied.

What if someone has been married previously? If your name has changed through a divorce and your driver's license does not reflect this change, you will need to bring a certified copy of your divorce decree. There is no waiting period required on Arkansas after a divorce is final.

Are there any required tests? No.

Are proxy marriages allowed? No.

Can cousins marry? No.

Are common law marriages recognized? No.

How to Handle the Marriage License

Read and follow the instructions which come with the license on how to fill out your section, and ensure all other sections have been fully and correctly completed.

No witnesses are required in Arkansas.

The marriage license must be completed by the Celebrant, and returned to the county clerk within 60 days from the date the license was issued.

The Celebrant is not required to keep records of marriages.

California Wedding Officiant Regulations

Statute FAMILY.CODE SECTION 400-402

400. Although marriage is a personal relation arising out of a civil, and not a religious, contract, a marriage may be solemnized by any of the following who is 18 years of age or older:

(a) A priest, minister, rabbi, or authorized person of any religious denomination. A person authorized by this subdivision shall not be required to solemnize a marriage that is contrary to the tenets of his or her faith. Any refusal to solemnize a marriage under this subdivision, either by an individual or by a religious denomination, shall not affect the tax-exempt status of any entity.

(b) A judge or retired judge, commissioner of civil marriages or retired commissioner of civil marriages, commissioner or retired commissioner, or assistant commissioner of a court of record in this state.

(c) A judge or magistrate who has resigned from office.

(d) Any of the following judges or magistrates of the United

States:

(1) A justice or retired justice of the United States Supreme Court.

(2) A judge or retired judge of a court of appeals, a district court, or a court created by an act of Congress the judges of which are entitled to hold office during good behavior.

(3) A judge or retired judge of a bankruptcy court or a tax court.

(4) A United States magistrate or retired magistrate.

(e) A legislator or constitutional officer of this state or a Member of Congress who represents a district within this state, while that person holds office.

400.1. In addition to the persons specified in Section 400, marriage may also be solemnized by a county supervisor, the city clerk of a charter city or serving in accordance with subdivision (b) of Section 36501 of the Government Code, or a mayor of a city elected in accordance with Article 3 (commencing with Section 34900) of Chapter 4 of Part 1 of Division 2 of Title 4 of the Government Code, while that person holds office. The county supervisor, the city clerk, or mayor shall obtain and review from the county clerk all available instructions for marriage solemnization before the county supervisor, the city clerk, or mayor first solemnizes a marriage.

401. (a) For each county, the county clerk is designated as a commissioner of civil marriages.

(b) The commissioner of civil marriages may appoint deputy commissioners of civil marriages who may solemnize marriages under the direction of the commissioner of civil marriages and shall perform other duties directed by the commissioner.

402. In addition to the persons permitted to solemnize marriages under Section 400, a county may license officials of a nonprofit religious institution, whose articles of incorporation are registered with the Secretary of State, to solemnize the marriages of persons who are affiliated with or are members of the religious institution. The licensee shall possess the degree of doctor of philosophy and must perform religious services or rites for the institution on a regular basis. The marriages shall be performed without fee to the

parties.

What You Need to Know

An Officiant must be over 18 years of age to perform a legal marriage.

In the state of California you are not required to register with the government before performing a marriage ceremony. However, you should be prepared to produce proof of ordination by a recognized body, in the event that this is ever requested. If you have any questions regarding the legality of your ordination in this state you should contact your local government office, or your ordination body itself.

What Couples Need To Know

Where do couples apply for a license? The County Clerk's Office.

What are the age requirements? California is one of just a few states lacking a minimum age for marriage. However, minors (under the age of 18) must obtain both parental consent and a court order before they may legally tie the knot. Although couples seldom get married before they reach the age of majority, it is made available primarily to allow pregnant minors to marry.

How much does a license cost? The fee for a marriage license in California varies from county to county. It will cost you between $35.00+ and $100.00+ to get married in California. Some California counties will only accept cash. Please call ahead to verify whether or not you need cash.

What documents are needed? Both parties must appear in person and bring valid picture identification to the County Clerk's Office. Valid picture identification is one that contains a photograph, date of birth, and an issue and expiration date, such as a state issued identification card, drivers license, passport, military identification, etc. Some counties may also require a copy of your birth certificate.

Are there residency requirements? You do not need to be a California resident to marry in California.

Is there a waiting period? No.

How long is a license valid? Marriage licenses are valid for 90 days from the date of issuance. If you do not get married within 90 days, you must purchase a new license.

Where is a license valid for use? The license is valid anywhere in California

What if someone has been married previously? If you have been married before, you will need to know the specific date your last marriage ended, and how it ended (death, Dissolution, Divorce or Nullity). Some counties may require a copy of the final judgment if your previous marriage ended by dissolution or nullity.

Are there any required tests? No tests required.

Are proxy marriages allowed? No.

Can cousins marry? Yes.

Are common law marriages recognized? No.

How to Handle the Marriage License

Read and follow the instructions which come with the license on how to fill out your section, and ensure all other sections have been fully and correctly completed.

Ministers must complete the marriage license and return it to the county clerk within 4 days after the marriage.

The Celebrant is not required to keep records of marriages.

Colorado Wedding Officiant Regulations

Statute 14-2-109. Solemnization and registration.

(1) A marriage may be solemnized by a judge of a court, by a court magistrate, by a retired judge of a court, by a public official whose powers include solemnization of marriages, by the parties to the marriage, or in accordance with any mode of solemnization recognized by any religious denomination or Indian nation or tribe. Either the person solemnizing the marriage or, if no individual acting alone solemnized the marriage, a party to the marriage shall complete the marriage certificate form and forward it to the county clerk and recorder within sixty three days after the solemnization. Any person who fails to forward the marriage certificate to the county clerk and recorder as required by this section shall be required to pay a late fee in an amount of not less than twenty dollars. An additional five-dollar late fee may be assessed for each additional day of failure to comply with the forwarding requirements of this subsection (1) up to a maximum of fifty dollars. For purposes of determining whether a late fee shall be assessed pursuant to this subsection (1), the date of forwarding shall be deemed to be the date of postmark.

(2) If a party to a marriage is unable to be present at the solemnization, such party may authorize in writing a third person to act as such party's proxy. If the person solemnizing the marriage is satisfied that the absent party is unable to be present and has consented to the marriage, such person may solemnize the marriage by proxy. If such person is not satisfied, the parties may petition the district court for an order permitting the marriage to be solemnized by proxy.

(3) Upon receipt of the marriage certificate, the county clerk and recorder shall register the marriage.

What You Need to Know

An Officiant must be over 18 years of age to perform a legal marriage.

In the state of Colorado you are not required to register with the government before performing a marriage ceremony. However, you should be prepared to produce proof of ordination by a recognized body, in the event that this is ever requested. If you have any questions regarding the legality of your ordination in this state you should contact your local government office, or your ordination body itself.

What Couples Need To Know

Where do couples apply for a license? County Clerk's Office.

What are the age requirements? If you are 16 or 17, in Colorado you will need consent of both parents (or parent having legal custody), or guardian, or seek judicial approval. If you are under 16, a Judicial Court Order along with parental consent is necessary.

How much does a license cost? Marriage license is $30. Cash only. No Credit Cards or Checks accepted.

What documents are needed? In Colorado, you will need to bring government issued ID such as your driver's license, visa, passport, state or military ID. Bring your social security cards.

Are there residency requirements? No.

Is there a waiting period? No.

How long is a license valid? License is valid for 30 days.

Where is a license valid for use? License is valid in Colorado.

What if someone has been married previously? Divorced persons must provide the approximate date of divorce and a location where the decree was issued. If the divorce occurred within 90 days of the request for a marriage license, a copy of the decree must also be present.

Are there any required tests? No.

Are proxy marriages allowed? Marriage by proxy is allowed in Colorado only if either the groom or bride cannot appear due to illness, is out of the state of Colorado, or incarcerated.

In these cases, the bride or groom can obtain an absentee application. It must be notarized. Identification for the absent party must be provided by the other soon to be spouse when applying for the license

Can cousins marry? Yes.

Are common law marriages recognized? Yes

How to Handle the Marriage License

Read and follow the instructions which come with the license on how to fill out your section, and ensure all other sections have been fully and correctly completed.

Ministers must send a marriage certificate to the county clerk.

The Celebrant is not required to keep records of marriages.

Connecticut Wedding Officiant Regulations

Statute Sec. 46b-22. (Formerly Sec. 46-3). Who may join persons in marriage. Penalty for unauthorized performance.

(a) Persons authorized to solemnize marriages in this state include (1) all judges and retired judges, either elected or appointed, including federal judges and judges of other states who may legally join persons in marriage in their jurisdictions, (2) family support magistrates, state referees and justices of the peace who are appointed in Connecticut, and (3) all ordained or licensed members of the clergy, belonging to this state or any other state, as long as they continue in the work of the ministry. All marriages solemnized according to the forms and usages of any religious denomination in this state, including marriages witnessed by a duly constituted Spiritual Assembly of the Baha'is, are valid. All marriages attempted to be celebrated by any other person are void.

(b) No public official legally authorized to issue marriage licenses may join persons in marriage under authority of a license issued by himself, or his assistant or deputy; nor may any such assistant or deputy join persons in marriage under authority of a license issued by such public official.

(c) Any person violating any provision of this section shall be fined not more than fifty dollars.

(1949 Rev., S. 7306; 1951, S. 3001d; 1967, P.A. 129, S. 1; P.A. 78-230, S. 4, 54; P.A. 79-37, S. 1, 2; P.A. 87-316, S. 3; June Sp. Sess. P.A. 01-4, S. 27, 58; P.A. 06-196, S. 276; P.A. 07-79, S. 5.)

History: 1967 act specified validity of marriages witnessed by Spiritual Assembly of the Baha'is; P.A. 78-230 divided section into Subsecs., deleted reference to county and reordered and rephrased provisions in Subsec. (a) and substituted 'may' for 'shall' in

Subsec. (b); P.A. 79-37 authorized retired judges and state referees to perform marriages; Sec. 46-3 transferred to Sec. 46b-22 in 1979; P.A. 87-316 applied provisions to family support magistrates; June Sp. Sess. P.A. 01-4 amended Subsec. (a) by adding provision re federal judges and judges of other states who may legally join persons in marriage in their jurisdictions, effective July 1, 2001; P.A. 06-196 made a technical change in Subsec. (a), effective June 7, 2006; P.A. 07-79 amended Subsec. (a) to add Subdiv. designators (1) to (3), revise provisions re persons authorized to solemnize marriages within the state and make technical changes.

Annotations to former section 46-3: Minister who solemnizes marriage must be 'settled in the work of the ministry'. 2 R. 382. Ordained deacon performing usual duties of minister held to be authorized. 4 C. 134. A clergyman in performing marriage ceremony is a public officer and his acts in that capacity prima facie evidence of his character. Id., 219. Proof of celebration of marriage raises a presumption of its validity. 85 C. 186; 93 C. 47. In absence of proof of authority of justice of peace, marriage void. 129 C. 432. Our law does not recognize common law marriages. Id. Marriage, deficient for want of due solemnization, voidable. 163 C. 588.

Annotation to present section: Former section General Statutes (Rev. 1949) S. 7302 cited. 182 C. 344.

What You Need to Know

An Officiant must be over 18 years of age to perform a legal marriage.

In the state of Connecticut you are not required to register with the government before performing a marriage ceremony. However, you should be prepared to produce proof of ordination by a recognized body, in the event that this is ever requested. If you have any questions regarding the legality of your ordination in this state you should contact your local government office, or your ordination body itself.

What Couples Need To Know

Where do couples apply for a license? The Town Clerk's Office. Although you do not have to be a resident of Connecticut, you do need to apply in either the town where one of you lives, or in the town where you plan on getting married.

If it is difficult for you both to appear at the same time at the Clerk's office to apply for your marriage license, you can appear individually.

What are the age requirements? If under 18 years of age, parental consent is needed. If under 16 years of age, the written consent of the judge of probate for the district where the minor resides must be obtained.

How much does a license cost? The fee is $30. Most locales won't accept credit cards or out-of-state checks. Cash is best.

What documents are needed? Connecticut law requires that you present photo ID such as a driver's license or a passport. You also need to know the following:

1. Your social security numbers.
2. Your mother's maiden name.
3. Your parent's birthplaces.
4. Date and location of your wedding.
5. Name and contact info of your wedding Officiant.

Are there residency requirements? Although you do not have to be a resident of Connecticut, you do need to apply in either the town where one of you lives, or in the town where you plan on getting married.

Is there a waiting period? No. Some towns may require you to pick the license up the next day.

How long is a license valid? A marriage license in Connecticut is valid for 65 days.

Where is a license valid for use? A marriage license in Connecticut is only valid in Connecticut.

What if someone has been married previously? You will need to show your divorce decree, or have information regarding date, county and state of death of previous spouse. If your name has changed, you need to bring a certified copy of your divorce decree.

Are there any required tests? No.

Are proxy marriages allowed? No.

Can cousins marry? Yes.

Are common law marriages recognized? No.

How to Handle the Marriage License

Read and follow the instructions which come with the license on how to fill out your section, and ensure all other sections have been fully and correctly completed.

Marriage license must be completed by the minister and returned to the city or town clerk.

The Celebrant is not required to keep records of marriages.

Delaware Wedding Officiant Regulations

Statute § 106 Solemnization of marriages; production of license; penalty; registration of persons authorized to solemnize marriages.

(a) A clergyperson or minister of any religion, current and former Judges of this State's Supreme Court, Superior Court, Family Court, Court of Chancery, Court of Common Pleas, Justice of the Peace Court, federal Judges, federal Magistrates, clerks of the peace of various counties and current and former judges from other jurisdictions with written authorization by the clerk of the peace from the county in Delaware where the ceremony is to be performed may solemnize marriages between persons who may lawfully enter into the matrimonial relation. The Clerk of the Peace in each county for good cause being shown may:

(1) Allow by written permit within that Clerk's respective county, any duly sworn member of another state's judiciary, to solemnize marriages in the State between persons who may lawfully enter into the matrimonial relation.

(2) Allow by written permit within that Clerk's respective county, the Clerk of the Peace from another county within the State to solemnize marriages in the State between persons who may lawfully enter into the matrimonial relation.

Within the limits of any incorporated municipality, the Mayor thereof may solemnize marriages between persons who may lawfully enter into matrimonial relation. Marriages shall be solemnized in the presence of at least 2 reputable witnesses who shall sign the certificate of marriage as prescribed by this chapter. Marriages may also be solemnized or contracted according to the forms and usages of any religious society. No marriage shall be solemnized or contracted without the production of a license issued pursuant to this chapter.

(b) For purposes of this section, the words 'resident of this State' shall include the son or daughter of a person who has been domiciled within the State for 1 year or more, notwithstanding the actual place of residence of the son or daughter immediately prior to the date of the marriage.

(c) In the case of absence or disability of the duly elected Clerk of the Peace, the chief deputy or, if there is no chief deputy, a deputy employed in the office of the Clerk of the Peace, shall be authorized to solemnize marriages.

(d) Whoever, not being authorized by this section, solemnizes a marriage, shall be fined $100, and in default of the payment of such fine shall be imprisoned not more than 30 days, and such marriage shall be void, unless it is in other respects lawful and is consummated with the full belief of either of the parties in its validity.

(e) Other than as provided in this subsection, nothing in this section shall be construed to require any person (including any clergyperson or minister of any religion) authorized to solemnize a marriage to solemnize any marriage, and no such authorized person who fails or refuses for any reason to solemnize a marriage shall be subject to any fine or other penalty for such failure or refusal. Notwithstanding the preceding sentence, a clerk of the peace who issues a marriage license, or a deputy thereof, shall be required to perform a solemnization of such marriage if requested by the applicants for such license.

What You Need to Know

An Officiant must be over 18 years of age to perform a legal marriage.

In the state of Delaware you are not required to register with the government before performing a marriage ceremony. However, you should be prepared to produce proof of ordination by a recognized body, in the event that this is ever requested. If you have any questions regarding the legality of your ordination in this state you should contact your local government office, or your ordination body itself.

What Couples Need To Know

Where do couples apply for a license? Clerk of the Peace

What are the age requirements? You must be at least 18 years of age to marry without authorization. Minors must petition Family Court for authorization to marry.

How much does a license cost? $50.00 if either applicant is a Delaware resident. $100.00 if neither applicant is a Delaware resident.

What documents are needed? The couple must apply together in person.

A valid state ID or Driver's License issued by the DMV, Passport, U.S. Visa I.D. Card, Federal Driver's License, Military I.D. or Government Consulate I.D. is required to apply for a marriage license.

To verify the authenticity of an applicant's identification, the office of the Clerk of the Peace may also require additional documentation such as birth certificate or social security card.

Special authorization is required if either party is on probation or parole.

Are there residency requirements? No.

Is there a waiting period? Persons intending to be married in Delaware shall obtain a marriage license at least 24 hours prior to the time of the ceremony. This applies to residents as well as non-residents.

How long is a license valid? Marriage licenses are valid for 30 days.

Where is a license valid for use? Marriage licenses are only valid in Delaware.

What if someone has been married previously? If individuals have previously been married, an original or certified copy of the Divorce Decree, Annulment, or Death Certificate is required.

Are there any required tests? No.

Are proxy marriages allowed? No.

Can cousins marry? No.

Are common law marriages recognized? No.

Note: Neither Bride nor Groom may be married under the influence of alcohol.

How to Handle the Marriage License

Read and follow the instructions which come with the license on how to fill out your section, and ensure all other sections have been fully and correctly completed.

Ministers do not need to be licensed to perform marriages but they must report their name and address to the local registrar in the district in which they live. Ministers must keep a copy of the marriage license for at least one year. Also, the minister must, within 4 days, complete and return forms required by the State Board of Health to the Clerk of the Peace.

District of Columbia Wedding Officiant Regulations

Statute § 46–406. Persons authorized to celebrate marriages.

(a) For the purposes of this section, the term:

(1) 'Civil Celebrant' means a person of a secular or non-religious organization who performs marriage ceremonies.

(2) 'Religious' includes or pertains to a belief in a theological doctrine, a belief in and worship of a divine ruling power, a recognition of a supernatural power controlling man's destiny, or a devotion to some principle, strict fidelity or faithfulness, conscientiousness, pious affection, or attachment.

(3) 'Society' means a voluntary association of individuals for religious purposes.

(4) 'Temporary Officiant' means a person authorized by the Clerk of the Superior Court of the District of Columbia ('Court') to solemnize a specific marriage. The person's authority to solemnize that marriage shall expire upon the filing of the marriage license, pursuant to § 46-412.

(b) For the purpose of preserving the evidence of marriages in the District of Columbia, a marriage authorized under this chapter may be solemnized by the following persons at least 18 years of age at the time of the marriage:

(1) A judge or retired judge of any court of record;

(2) The Clerk of the Court or such deputy clerks of the Court as may, in writing, be designated by the Clerk and approved by the Chief Judge of the Court;

(3) A minister, priest, rabbi, or authorized person of any religious denomination or

society;

(4) For any religious society which does not by its own custom require the intervention of a minister for the celebration of marriages, a marriage may be solemnized in the manner prescribed and practiced in that religious society, with the license issued to, and returns to be made by, a person appointed by the religious society for that purpose;

(5) A civil Celebrant;

(6) A temporary Officiant;

(7) Members of the Council;

(8) The Mayor of the District of Columbia; or

(9) The parties to the marriage.

(b-1) All persons authorized by subsection (b) of this section to solemnize marriages shall comply with the requirements of § 46-412.

(b-2) The Court shall charge a reasonable registration fee for authorization to solemnize marriages; provided, that the registration fee for a temporary Officiant shall not exceed $25.

(c) No priest, imam, rabbi, minister, or other official of any religious society who is authorized to solemnize or celebrate marriages shall be required to solemnize or celebrate any marriage.

(d) Each religious society has exclusive control over its own theological doctrine, teachings, and beliefs regarding who may marry within that particular religious society's faith.

(e) (1) Notwithstanding any other provision of law, a religious society, or a nonprofit organization that is operated, supervised, or controlled by or in conjunction with a religious society, shall not be required to provide services, accommodations, facilities, or goods for a purpose related to the solemnization or celebration of a marriage, or the promotion of marriage through religious programs, counseling, courses, or retreats, that is in violation of the religious society's beliefs.

(2) A refusal to provide services, accommodations, facilities, or goods in accordance with this subsection shall not create any civil claim or cause of action, or result in a District action to penalize or withhold benefits from the religious society or nonprofit organization that is operated, supervised, or controlled by or in conjunction with a religious society.

What You Need to Know

All Celebrants wishing to perform a legal marriage ceremony in District of Columbia must be over 18 years of age and are required to register with the DC Marriage Bureau prior to performing the ceremony.

There are two types of application available to Marriage Celebrants in District of Columbia:

The Standard Officiant Application

You will need to download and complete the application form from the Bureau web site:

http://www.dccourts.gov/internet/documents/Officiant-Application.pdf

You will need to have the form notarized, and you should not sign and date the document until you are in the presence of the notary.

The Temporary Officiant Application (limited to a single ceremony).

For further information on temporary applications, please visit:

http://www.dccourts.gov/internet/legal/aud_family/marriage.jsf

The application fee is $35 at the time of writing ($25 for temporary applications), but you are encouraged to contact the Marriage Bureau prior to application, as they will have access to the most up to date information.

They can be contacted at:

District of Columbia Marriage Bureau

Moultrie Courthouse

500 Indiana Ave NW

Washington, DC 20001

Tel: (202) 879-4840

Hours: 8:30AM - 5:00PM Mon - Fri

What Couples Need To Know

Where do couples apply for a license?

Moultrie Courthouse

500 Indiana Avenue, N.W.

Room 4485

Washington, DC 20001

(202) 879 4840

8:30 AM – 5:00 PM M-F

What are the age requirements? If 16 or 17 years of age consent of the parent or guardian is required. Proof of age for the applicants must be shown at the time of application and may be demonstrated by drivers licenses, birth certificates, passports, or similar official documents.

How much does a license cost? $45 (Cash or Money Order).

Note: $35 portion of the fee may be waived for couples who are registered in the District as domestic partners. These couples should bring their proof of registration and

$10 license fee.

What documents are needed?

- A completed application form.
- Proof of age.

Note: You must include the name of the Officiant performing the wedding ceremony on your application. Your Officiant must be authorized by the Court and registered by the Marriage Bureau to legally perform ceremonies in the District of Columbia.

Are there residency requirements? No.

Is there a waiting period? 3 full business days must pass between the day of application and the day that the license can be issued. In addition, there may be a processing delay. Confirm your day of pickup when you apply.

How long is a license valid? No expiration date.

Where is a license valid for use? The District of Columbia.

What if someone has been married previously? If you were previously married, the date of your divorce or the date of your spouse's death must be provided. Bring a certified copy of the divorce decree or death certificate. If necessary, a copy of your divorce records or spouse's death certificate can be ordered from your local vital records office and mailed to you.

Are there any required tests? Yes, the couple is required to take a blood test for syphilis prior to receiving a license. The bride is also required to take a blood test for venereal disease. The blood test must be analyzed by a state certified laboratory and recorded on a state form. This form can be obtained from the physician, clinic, or the Office of the Town Clerk. Test results become invalid after 30 days.

Are proxy marriages allowed? No.

Can cousins marry? Yes, cousin marriages (first, second, etc) are allowed to take place.

Are common law marriages recognized? Yes.

How to Handle the Marriage License

Read and follow the instructions which come with the license on how to fill out your section, and ensure all other sections have been fully and correctly completed.

Marriage licenses are addressed to the minister who will perform the ceremony. The minister must complete a marriage certificate for the bride and for the groom and return another certificate to the clerk of the District of Columbia Court of General Sessions within 10 days after the marriage.

The Celebrant is not required to keep records of marriages.

Florida Wedding Officiant Regulations

Statute 741.07   Persons authorized to solemnize matrimony.

(1)   All regularly ordained ministers of the gospel or elders in communion with some church, or other ordained clergy, and all judicial officers, including retired judicial officers, clerks of the circuit courts, and notaries public of this state may solemnize the rights of matrimonial contract, under the regulations prescribed by law. Nothing in this section shall make invalid a marriage which was solemnized by any member of the clergy, or as otherwise provided by law prior to July 1, 1978.

(2)   Any marriage which may be had and solemnized among the people called 'Quakers,' or 'Friends,' in the manner and form used or practiced in their societies, according to their rites and ceremonies, shall be good and valid in law; and wherever the words 'minister' and 'elder' are used in this chapter, they shall be held to include all of the persons connected with the Society of Friends, or Quakers, who perform or have charge of the marriage ceremony according to their rites and ceremonies.

What You Need to Know

An Officiant must be over 18 years of age to perform a legal marriage.

In the state of Florida you are not required to register with the government before performing a marriage ceremony. However, you should be prepared to produce proof of ordination by a recognized body, in the event that this is ever requested. If you have any questions regarding the legality of your ordination in this state you should contact your local government office, or your ordination body itself.

What Couples Need To Know

Where do couples apply for a license? County Clerk's Office

What are the age requirements? If an individual is under 18 years of age, but older than 16 years of age, a marriage license can be obtained with parental consent. If a parent has sole custody or the other parent is dead, the permission of one parent is sufficient if proof of custody is supplied. If a person is under the age of 16, the marriage license has to be issued by a county judge, with or without parental permission. If a minor's parents are both deceased and there is not an appointed guardian, he / she may apply for a marriage license and produce death certificates for both parents. A minor who has previously married may apply for a license. A minor who swears that they have a child or are expecting a baby, can apply for a license if the pregnancy has been verified by a written statement from a licensed physician. A county court judge may at his / her discretion issue or not issue a license for them to marry.

How much does a license cost? $93.50. Marriage license fees can be reduced by up to $32.50 if you complete a licensed Florida pre-marital course. Many locales do accept credit cards now, but be sure to check with the local county recorder or clerk to make sure. Here credit cards are accepted an extra charge may be required.

What documents are needed? Florida requires that you have a picture ID such as a driver's license and your Social Security card or a valid passport or I-94 card. You may be asked for a certified copy of your birth certificate. You will need a copy of your birth certificate if under 18 years of age.

Are there residency requirements? No.

Is there a waiting period? There is no waiting period for Florida residents who have completed a state sanctioned marriage preparation course within the last 12 months. There is a three-day waiting period for Florida residents who have not taken the course. Court Clerks are allowed to waive the three-day waiting period in the event of a 'hardship' case.

How long is a license valid? License is valid for 60 days.

Where is a license valid for use? Anywhere in Florida.

What if someone has been married previously? If you have been previously married, the date of your divorce or date of your spouse's death must be supplied. If the divorce or spouse's death occurred within the past 30 days, a certified copy of the divorce decree or death certificate is required.

Are there any required tests? No.

Are proxy marriages allowed? No.

Can cousins marry? Yes.

Are common law marriages recognized? No.

Note: Effective January 1999 Florida couples have to consider the consequences of divorce before they can get married. Prospective brides and grooms are now required to read a small booklet which describes situations such as how a court would divide their assets and information about child support payments. The good side of all this is that licenses are available at a reduced price if a couple attends a four-hour course to improve communication, financial and parenting skills before marriage.

How to Handle the Marriage License

Read and follow the instructions which come with the license on how to fill out your section, and ensure all other sections have been fully and correctly completed.

Ministers must complete a certificate of marriage on the marriage license and return it to the office from which it was issued.

The Celebrant is not required to keep records of marriages.

Georgia Wedding Officiant Regulations

Statute 19-3-30.

(c) The license shall be directed to the Governor or any former Governor of this state, any judge, including judges of state and federal courts of record in this state, city recorder, magistrate, minister, or other person of any religious society or sect authorized by the rules of such society to perform the marriage ceremony; such license shall authorize the marriage of the persons therein named and require the Governor or any former Governor of this state, judge, city recorder, magistrate, minister, or other authorized person to return the license to the judge of the probate court with the certificate thereon as to the fact and date of marriage within 30 days after the date of the marriage. The license with the return thereon shall be recorded by the judge in a book kept by such judge for that purpose.

What You Need to Know

An Officiant must be over 18 years of age to perform a legal marriage.

In the state of Georgia you are not required to register with the government before performing a marriage ceremony. However, you should be prepared to produce proof of ordination by a recognized body, in the event that this is ever requested. If you have any questions regarding the legality of your ordination in this state you should contact your local government office, or your ordination body itself.

What Couples Need To Know

Where do couples apply for a license? The County Probate Court.

What are the age requirements? You must be at least 16 years of age in order to obtain a license in Georgia. If you are 16 or 17 years of age, both parents and legal guardians must give their consent in person unless his / her rights have been terminated by an Order of a court (in which case the order must be presented).

How much does a license cost? It costs approximately $65.00 + to get married in Georgia. Most counties will only accept cash. The amount of the marriage license fee will be decreased by showing proof of receiving premarital counseling.

Note on Premarital Education: Under Georgia Law, a man and woman who present to the court at the time of making application a certificate of completion of a qualifying premarital education program shall not be assessed a full marriage license fee. The premarital education shall include at least six hours of instruction involving marital issues, which may include but not be limited to conflict management, communication skills, financial responsibilities, child and parenting responsibilities, and extended family roles. The premarital education shall be completed within 12 months prior to the application for a marriage license and the couple shall undergo the premarital education together. The premarital education shall be performed by:

(1) A professional counselor, social worker, or marriage and family therapist who is licensed pursuant to Chapter 10A of Title 43;

(2) A psychiatrist who is licensed as a physician pursuant to Chapter 34 of Title 43;

(3) A psychologist who is licensed pursuant to Chapter 39 of Title 43; or

(4) An active member of the clergy when in the course of his or her service as clergy or his or her designee, including retired clergy, provided that a designee is trained and skilled in premarital education.

Cobb County offers a free Marital Workshop called Focus On Forever. It is a skill-based non-religious workshop designed to address issues concerning communication and listening skills, anger management, and financial planning. Contact the Cobb County Superior Court for more information.

By state law, counties in Georgia now charge more for a marriage license if you do not show certification of a premarital education program.

What documents are needed? Two valid forms of ID such as driver's license, birth certificate, U.S. passport, Armed Forces ID card, or Resident Alien ID card. Applicants will also be asked to fill out a brief form.

Note: The applicants must designate on the application the legal surname that will be used after the marriage. An applicant may choose his or her given surname or his or her surname as changed by order of the superior court, the surname from a previous marriage, the spouse's surname, or a combination of the spouse's surname and the applicant's given or changed surname from a previous marriage.

Are there residency requirements? No.

Note: If one of the parties is a resident of Georgia, the license can be issued in any county.

If neither party is a resident of Georgia, the license must be issued in the county in which the marriage ceremony is to be performed.

Is there a waiting period? No.

How long is a license valid? Your marriage license will never expire once it's been issued. However, some counties prefer the license to be used within six months.

Where is a license valid for use? A Georgia marriage license is valid state wide.

What if someone has been married previously? If divorced, however long ago, you will need to show a copy of your divorce decree. You can obtain a copy of your final divorce decree from the Superior Court in the county in which you filed for divorce.

Are there any required tests? No.

Are proxy marriages allowed? No.

Can cousins marry? Yes. First cousins may marry.

Are common law marriages recognized? If before 1987 your common law marriage is recognized with documentation. Otherwise, common law marriage is not recognized.

How to Handle the Marriage License

Read and follow the instructions which come with the license on how to fill out your section, and ensure all other sections have been fully and correctly completed.

Ministers must complete a certificate of marriage and return it within 30 days after the marriage.

The Celebrant is not required to keep records of marriages.

Hawaii Wedding Officiant Regulations

Statute §572-12 By whom solemnized.

A license to solemnize marriages may be issued to, and the marriage rite may be performed and solemnized by any minister, priest, or officer of any religious denomination or society who has been ordained or is authorized to solemnize marriages according to the usages of such denomination or society, or any religious society not having clergy but providing solemnization in accordance with the rules and customs of that society, or any justice or judge or magistrate, active or retired, of a state or federal court in the State, upon presentation to such person or society of a license to marry, as prescribed by this chapter. Such person or society may receive the price stipulated by the parties or the gratification tendered.

What You Need to Know

All Celebrants wishing to perform a legal marriage ceremony in Hawaii must be over 8 years of age, and register with the Hawaii Department of Health prior to the wedding. Celebrants are not required to be resident in Hawaii.

In Hawaii, you can apply in person or online. If applying online, the Hawaii Department of Health requires that you do so during the period from 2 months to 2 weeks before the date of the ceremony. At the time of writing the application fee is $10.

You can find the online application available here:

https://emrs.ehawaii.gov/emrs/public/registration.html

You can contact the Hawaii Department of Health at:

1250 Punchbowl St. Room 101

Honolulu, Hawaii 96813

Tel: (808) 586-4540

Hours: Mon - Fri 8:00AM - 4:00 PM

What Couples Need To Know

Where do couples apply for a license? Marriage License Office.

What are the age requirements? You must be at least 18 years of age or older to marry without parental consent. A birth certificate may be necessary to show proof of age.

If either partner is under 18, parental consent forms must be signed. You will need a certified copy of your birth certificate. If you are under 16 you cannot marry without a court order. In the case of pregnancy parental consent is still required or consent of the judge of family court.

How much does a license cost? $65.($5 of which is processing fee) Cash only. For this they get one certificate mailed. Each extra is $10.

What documents are needed? Two valid forms of ID such as a driver's license, birth certificate, U.S. passport, Armed Forces ID card, or Resident Alien ID card. Applicants will also be asked to fill out a Marriage License Application Form.

Both the bride and groom must prepare an official application and file the application in person with the marriage license agent. The application will not be accepted if sent by either postal mail or e-mail.

Note: The Hawaii Visitors and Convention Bureau at (808) 924-0266 maintains a list of persons licensed to perform weddings in Hawaii.

Are there residency requirements? No.

Is there a waiting period? No.

How long is a license valid? 30 days.

Where is a license valid for use? Only within Hawaii.

What if someone has been married previously? If previously married, the date of divorce or date of spouse's death must be provided.

Are there any required tests? No.

Are proxy marriages allowed? No.

Can cousins marry? Cousins may marry. However, the blood relationship between the prospective bride and groom cannot be closer than first cousins.

Are common law marriages recognized? No.

How to Handle the Marriage License

Read and follow the instructions which come with the license on how to fill out your section, and ensure all other sections have been fully and correctly completed.

Ministers must report all marriages they perform to the department of health.

Ministers must keep a record of all marriages they perform. In practice, this means you should record all ceremonies in a record book, and keep copies of the documents stored securely.

Idaho Wedding Officiant Regulations

Statute 32-303. By whom solemnized.

Marriage may be solemnized by any of the following Idaho officials: a current or retired justice of the supreme court, a current or retired court of appeals judge, a current or retired district judge, the current or a former governor, the current lieutenant governor, a current or retired magistrate of the district court, a current mayor or by any of the following: a current federal judge, a current tribal judge of an Idaho Indian tribe or other tribal official approved by an official act of an Idaho Indian tribe or priest or minister of the gospel of any denomination. To be a retired justice of the supreme court, court of appeals judge, district judge or magistrate judge of the district court, for the purpose of solemnizing marriages, a person shall have served in one (1) of those offices and shall be receiving a retirement benefit from either the judges retirement system or the public employee retirement system for service in the Idaho judiciary.

What You Need to Know

An Officiant must be over 18 years of age to perform a legal marriage.

In the state of Idaho you are not required to register with the government before performing a marriage ceremony. However, you should be prepared to produce proof of ordination by a recognized body, in the event that this is ever requested. If you have any questions regarding the legality of your ordination in this state you should contact your local government office, or your ordination body itself.

What Couples Need To Know

Where do couples apply for a license? The County Clerk or Recorder. These offices, some of which are referred to as the 'marriage license bureau,' are usually located in the county probate court or circuit court.

What are the age requirements? Both parties age 18 or older – no consent requirements.

Between 16 and 17 – Applicants must present one of the following:

Original Birth Certificate or Certified Copy

Current Driver's License

Passport

Under 16 years – Applicants must present a Court Order

How much does a license cost? $30. Cash Only.

What documents are needed? Valid Driver's License and Birth Certificate.

Are there residency requirements? No.

Is there a waiting period? No.

How long is a license valid? There is no expiration on the license. It remains good as long as the same two parties listed use it.

Where is a license valid for use? Only in Idaho.

What if someone has been married previously? If previously married, the date of divorce or date of spouse's death must be provided.

Are there any required tests? No blood tests. Idaho Code 32-412A requires both parties to read and sign a premarital AIDS educational pamphlet.

Are proxy marriages allowed? No.

Can cousins marry? No.

Are common law marriages recognized? Yes.

How to Handle the Marriage License

Read and follow the instructions which come with the license on how to fill out your section, and ensure all other sections have been fully and correctly completed.

Ministers must give a marriage certificate to the bride and to the groom. Also, the minister must complete the license and marriage certificate and return it to the recorder who issued it within 30 days after the marriage.

The Celebrant is not required to keep records of marriages.

Illinois Wedding Officiant Regulations

Statute Sec. 209. Solemnization and Registration.

(a) A marriage may be solemnized by a judge of a court of record, by a retired judge of a court of record, unless the retired judge was removed from office by the Judicial Inquiry Board, except that a retired judge shall not receive any compensation from the State, a county or any unit of local government in return for the solemnization of a marriage and there shall be no effect upon any pension benefits conferred by the Judges Retirement System of Illinois, by a judge of the Court of Claims, by a county clerk in counties having 2,000,000 or more inhabitants, by a public official whose powers include solemnization of marriages, or in accordance with the prescriptions of any religious denomination, Indian Nation or Tribe or Native Group, provided that when such prescriptions require an Officiant, the Officiant be in good standing with his or her religious denomination, Indian Nation or Tribe or Native Group. Either the person solemnizing the marriage, or, if no individual acting alone solemnized the marriage, both parties to the marriage, shall complete the marriage certificate form and forward it to the county clerk within 10 days after such marriage is solemnized.

(a-5) Nothing in this Act shall be construed to require any religious denomination or Indian Nation or Tribe or Native Group, or any minister, clergy, or Officiant acting as a representative of a religious denomination or Indian Nation or Tribe or Native Group, to solemnize any marriage. Instead, any religious denomination or Indian Nation or Tribe or Native Group, or any minister, clergy, or Officiant acting as a representative of a religious denomination or Indian Nation or Tribe or Native Group is free to choose which marriages it will solemnize. Notwithstanding any other law to the contrary, a refusal by a religious denomination or Indian Nation or Tribe or Native Group, or any minister, clergy, or Officiant acting as a representative of a religious denomination or Indian Nation or Tribe or Native Group to solemnize any marriage under this Act shall not create or be the basis for any civil, administrative, or criminal penalty, claim, or cause of action.

(a-10) No church, mosque, synagogue, temple, nondenominational ministry, interdenominational or ecumenical organization, mission organization, or other organization whose principal purpose is the study, practice, or advancement of religion is required to provide religious facilities for the solemnization ceremony or celebration associated with the solemnization ceremony of a marriage if the solemnization ceremony or celebration associated with the solemnization ceremony is in violation of its religious beliefs. An entity identified in this subsection (a-10) shall be immune from any civil, administrative, criminal penalty, claim, or cause of action based on its refusal to provide religious facilities for the solemnization ceremony or celebration associated with the solemnization ceremony of a marriage if the solemnization ceremony or celebration associated with the solemnization ceremony is in violation of its religious beliefs. As used in this subsection (a-10), 'religious facilities' means sanctuaries, parish halls, fellowship halls, and similar facilities. 'Religious facilities' does not include facilities such as businesses, health care facilities, educational facilities, or social service agencies.

(b) The solemnization of the marriage is not invalidated: (1) by the fact that the person solemnizing the marriage was not legally qualified to solemnize it, if a reasonable person would believe the person solemnizing the marriage to be so qualified; or (2) by the fact that the marriage was inadvertently solemnized in a county in Illinois other than the county where the license was issued and filed.

(c) Any marriage that meets the requirements of this Section shall be presumed valid.

What You Need to Know

An Officiant must be over 18 years of age to perform a legal marriage.

In the state of Illinois you are not required to register with the government before performing a marriage ceremony. However, you should be prepared to produce proof of ordination by a recognized body, in the event that this is ever requested. If you have any questions regarding the legality of your ordination in this state you should contact your local government office, or your ordination body itself.

What Couples Need To Know

Where do couples apply for a license? County Clerk Office

What are the age requirements? People older than 18 years of age who are not blood relatives may marry without parental consent.

Applicants between the ages of 16 and 17 may obtain a marriage license by presenting the following information:

- Sworn consent from each parent, each legal guardian or a judge – in person – before the county clerk at the time of the application. Those giving consent must provide proper identification, including a: valid driver's license; valid state identification card; valid Illinois Department of Public Aid card; valid passport. (If the legal guardian is giving consent, a certified copy of the guardianship papers must be provided.)

How much does a license cost? $30 (though some counties mat charge $60. The cost of receiving a marriage license varies from county to county and some Illinois counties will only accept cash.

What documents are needed? Any of the following documents will be accepted:

· Valid U.S. Driver's License

· Valid U.S. state identification card

· Valid U.S. passport, Valid U.S. military identification card,

· Valid Illinois Department of Public Aid card (the I.D. and the medical card).

If you do not have any of the above forms of identification, then you MUST present TWO (2) of the following pieces of identification:

· A certified copy of a birth certificate.

· A valid U.S. resident alien card.

· U.S. naturalization papers.

· A valid foreign passport.

· All consulate identification cards. Affidavits are not acceptable.

· A baptismal record (the date of birth of the applicant must appear on this record).

· A life insurance policy, which has been in effect for one (1) year (the applicant's date of birth must appear on the document).

· A certified copy of their birth certificate.

· A second piece of identification showing date of birth.

· At least one parent of any applicant under the age of 18 must be present.

Are there residency requirements? No. However, non-residents cannot obtain a marriage license if said marriage would be void in their state.

Is there a waiting period? No.

How long is a license valid? 60 Days.

Where is a license valid for use? License is valid only in the county in which it was issued.

What if someone has been married previously? If either applicant is divorced, they must provide final divorce papers signed by the judge. If you were previously married, the date of your divorce or the date of your spouse's death must be provided. If the divorce or spouse's death had taken place within the last 6 months, bring a certified copy of the divorce decree or death certificate. If necessary, a copy of your divorce records or spouse's death certificate can be ordered from your local vital records office and mailed to you.

Are there any required tests? No.

Are proxy marriages allowed? No

Can cousins marry? First cousins older than the age of 50 may marry.

Are common law marriages recognized? No.

How to Handle the Marriage License

Read and follow the instructions which come with the license on how to fill out your section, and ensure all other sections have been fully and correctly completed.

Either the person solemnizing the marriage, or, if no individual acting alone solemnized the marriage, both parties to the marriage, shall complete the marriage certificate form and forward it to the county clerk within 10 days after such marriage is solemnized.

The Celebrant is not required to keep records of marriages.

Indiana Wedding Officiant Regulations

Statute IC 31-11-6-1 Persons authorized to solemnize marriages

Sec. 1. Marriages may be solemnized by any of the following:
(1) A member of the clergy of a religious organization (even if the cleric does not perform religious functions for an individual congregation), such as a minister of the gospel, a priest, a bishop, an archbishop, or a rabbi.
(2) A judge.
(3) A mayor, within the mayor's county.
(4) A clerk or a clerk-treasurer of a city or town, within a county in which the city or town is located.
(5) A clerk of the circuit court.
(6) The Friends Church, in accordance with the rules of the Friends Church.
(7) The German Baptists, in accordance with the rules of their society.
(8) The Bahai faith, in accordance with the rules of the Bahai faith.
(9) The Church of Jesus Christ of Latter Day Saints, in accordance with the rules of the Church of Jesus Christ of Latter Day Saints.
(10) An imam of a masjid (mosque), in accordance with the rules of the religion of Islam.

What You Need to Know

An Officiant must be over 18 years of age to perform a legal marriage.
In the state of Indiana you are not required to register with the government before

performing a marriage ceremony. However, you should be prepared to produce proof of ordination by a recognized body, in the event that this is ever requested. If you have any questions regarding the legality of your ordination in this state you should contact your local government office, or your ordination body itself.

What Couples Need To Know

Where do couples apply for a license? The County Clerk's Office where one of the couple resides, or for non-residents in the county where the marriage will be solemnized.

What are the age requirements? If both applicants are 18 or over a license can be issued without consent.

If one or both applicants are 17, parents or legal guardians must be present to provide consent.

If one or both applicants are younger than 17 they must have a court order granting permission for the marriage license.

How much does a license cost? Indiana's marriage license application fee is $18 if one or both parties are Indiana residents and $60.00 for out-of-state residents.

Some offices also charge an additional document fee of $2.00. Each copy of the Certified Marriage License (required for name change at BMV, SSN, etc.) is also $2.00.

Most counties require these fees to be paid in cash.

What documents are needed? You will need any one of the following forms of identification to prove your identity and date of birth:

Current, valid driver's license or state issued ID card.

Passport

Birth Certificate

You will also be required to provide your Social Security Number, although your Social Security Card may not be required.

The Clerk's Office will collect some family information from you that will be reported to the Indiana State Library for the purposes of genealogical research. You will need to provide the following for both parents:

Full Name

Last known address

Birthplace (state or foreign country)

Are there residency requirements? No.

Is there a waiting period? No.

How long is a license valid? 60 Days.

Where is a license valid for use? Only in the State of Indiana.

What if someone has been married previously? You will need to know how the marriages ended (death, divorce, annulment) and the month and year the marriages ended. A few counties require a copy of the divorce decree if divorced within the last two years.

Are there any required tests? No.

Are proxy marriages allowed? No.

Can cousins marry? Applicants cannot marry if they are more closely related than second cousins (though there is an exception if you are first cousins and both are at least 65 years of age).

Are common law marriages recognized? No.

How to Handle the Marriage License

Read and follow the instructions which come with the license on how to fill out your section, and ensure all other sections have been fully and correctly completed.

Ministers must return the marriage license and a certificate of marriage to the clerk of the circuit court within 3 months after the marriage.

The Celebrant is not required to keep records of marriages.

Iowa Wedding Officiant Regulations

Statute 595.10 WHO MAY SOLEMNIZE.

Marriages may be solemnized by:

1. A judge of the supreme court, court of appeals, or district court, including a district associate judge, associate juvenile judge, or a judicial magistrate, and including a senior judge as defined in section 602.9202, subsection 3.

2. A person ordained or designated as a leader of the person's religious faith.

What You Need to Know

An Officiant must be over 18 years of age to perform a legal marriage.

In the state of Iowa you are not required to register with the government before performing a marriage ceremony. However, you should be prepared to produce proof of ordination by a recognized body, in the event that this is ever requested. If you have any questions regarding the legality of your ordination in this state you should contact your local government office, or your ordination body itself.

What Couples Need To Know

Where do couples apply for a license? County Clerk's Office

What are the age requirements? Applicants 16 or 17 years of age need to have parental consent.

How much does a license cost? The marriage license fee is roughly $35.00 dollars, although fees may vary from county to county. Accepted forms of payment are cash.

What documents are needed? Picture identification is required. You also need to provide Social Security information.

Note: You need to have one witness (over 18 years of age) with you when you apply for the license.

Are there residency requirements? No.

Is there a waiting period? Yes. There is a waiting period of 3 business days.

How long is a license valid? 6 months.

Where is a license valid for use? In the state of Iowa.

What if someone has been married previously? If previously married, the date of divorce or date of spouse's death must be provided.

Are there any required tests? No.

Are proxy marriages allowed? No. However, if one of you can't be present at the Recorder's Office to apply for the license, the absent party can sign the Iowa marriage license application before a Notary Public.

Can cousins marry? No.

Are common law marriages recognized? Yes.

How to Handle the Marriage License

Read and follow the instructions which come with the license on how to fill out your section, and ensure all other sections have been fully and correctly completed.

The minister must report the marriage to the clerk of the district court within 15 days after the marriage.

The Celebrant is not required to keep records of marriages.

Kansas Wedding Officiant Regulations

Statute 23-2504. Solemnizing marriage; persons authorized to officiate.

(a) Marriage may be validly solemnized and contracted in this state, after a license has been issued for the marriage, in the following manner: By the mutual declarations of the two parties to be joined in marriage, made before an authorized officiating person and in the presence of at least two competent witnesses over 18 years of age, other than the officiating person, that they take each other as husband and wife.

(b) The following are authorized to be officiating persons:

(1) Any currently ordained clergyman or religious authority of any religious denomination or society;

(2) any licentiate of a denominational body or an appointee of any bishop serving as the regular clergyman of any church of the denomination to which the licentiate or appointee belongs, if not restrained from so doing by the discipline of that church or denomination;

(3) any judge or justice of a court of record;

(4) any municipal judge of a city of this state; and

(5) any retired judge or justice of a court of record.

(c) The two parties themselves, by mutual declarations that they take each other as husband and wife, in accordance with the customs, rules and regulations of any religious society, denomination or sect to which either of the parties belong, may be married without an authorized officiating person.

What You Need to Know

An Officiant must be over 18 years of age to perform a legal marriage.

In the state of Kansas you are not required to register with the government before performing a marriage ceremony. However, you should be prepared to produce proof of ordination by a recognized body, in the event that this is ever requested. If you have any questions regarding the legality of your ordination in this state you should contact your local government office, or your ordination body itself.

What Couples Need To Know

Where do couples apply for a license? Clerk of the District Court.

What are the age requirements? Any applicant who is under 18 must have either:

Notarized, written consent of all then living parents and legal guardians OR

Notarized, written consent of one parent or legal guardian and consent of a district court judge.

How much does a license cost? $85.50. Cash is required in most counties. Money orders are accepted in some counties and should be payable to 'Clerk of the District

Court'. The money is non-refundable.

What documents are needed?

A certified Birth Certificate.

Full name (First, Middle and Last)

Residence (City, county and state)

Birthplace (State or foreign country)

Date of Birth

Race

Highest level of education completed

Both applicants fathers' full name (First, Middle and Last)

Both applicants mothers' full name (First, Middle and Maiden)

All birthplaces (State or foreign country)

Name and address of person performing ceremony, if known.

Are there residency requirements? No.

Is there a waiting period? There is a 3 day waiting period, after the application is made, before you may pick up the license.

How long is a license valid? 6 months.

Where is a license valid for use? In the State of Kansas.

What if someone has been married previously? If previously married, how last marriage ended and when. Number of this marriage.

Are there any required tests? No.

Are proxy marriages allowed? No.

Can cousins marry? No.

Are common law marriages recognized? Yes.

How to Handle the Marriage License

Read and follow the instructions which come with the license on how to fill out your section, and ensure all other sections have been fully and correctly completed.

The Minister must return the marriage license and a certificate of marriage to the probate judge who issued the marriage license within 10 days after the marriage.

The Celebrant is not required to keep records of marriages.

Kentucky Wedding Officiant Regulations

Statute 402.050 Who may solemnize marriage -- Persons present.

(1) Marriage shall be solemnized only by:

(a) Ministers of the gospel or priests of any denomination in regular communion with any religious society;

(b) Justices and judges of the Court of Justice, retired justices and judges of the Court of Justice except those removed for cause or convicted of a felony, county judges/executive, and such justices of the peace and fiscal court commissioners as the Governor or the county judge/executive authorizes; or

(c) A religious society that has no officiating minister or priest and whose usage is to solemnize marriage at the usual place of worship and by consent given in the presence of the society, if either party belongs to the society.

(2) At least two (2) persons, in addition to the parties and the person solemnizing the marriage, shall be present at every marriage.

What You Need to Know

An Officiant must be over 18 years of age to perform a legal marriage.

In the state of Kentucky you are not required to register with the government before performing a marriage ceremony. However, you should be prepared to produce proof of ordination by a recognized body, in the event that this is ever requested. If you have any questions regarding the legality of your ordination in this state you should contact your local government office, or your ordination body itself.

What Couples Need To Know

Where do couples apply for a license? The County Clerk

What are the age requirements? You must be at least 18 years of age or older to marry without parental consent. A birth certificate may be necessary to show proof of age.

If either partner is under 18, parental consent forms must be signed. You will need a certified copy of your birth certificate. If you are under 16 you cannot marry without a court order. A minor who is pregnant does not need parental consent as long as the pregnancy is verified in a written statement by a licensed physician. Minors cannot marry if parents or guardians are not residents of the state.

How much does a license cost? $35.50 - $37.00. Fees vary from county to county. Cash, certified check, cashier's check, or money order only.

What documents are needed? Acceptable forms of ID in accordance with the statute and recorders manual include: Drivers License, current picture ID, Social Security

Card, birth certificate, or passport.

Are there residency requirements? No.

Is there a waiting period? No.

How long is a license valid? 30 Days.

Where is a license valid for use? In the State of Kentucky.

What if someone has been married previously? If previously married, the date of divorce or date of spouse's death must be provided.

Are there any required tests? No.

Are proxy marriages allowed? No.

Can cousins marry? No.

Are common law marriages recognized? No.

How to Handle the Marriage License

Read and follow the instructions which come with the license on how to fill out your section, and ensure all other sections have been fully and correctly completed.

Ministers must return the marriage license and marriage certificate to the county clerk within three months following the marriage.

The Celebrant is not required to keep records of marriages.

Louisiana Wedding Officiant Regulations

Statute RS 9:202 — Authority to perform marriage ceremony

A marriage ceremony may be performed by:

(1) A priest, minister, rabbi, clerk of the Religious Society of Friends, or any clergyman of any religious sect, who is authorized by the authorities of his religion to perform marriages, and who is registered to perform marriages;

(2) A state judge or justice of the peace.

What You Need to Know

Celebrants wishing to conduct a legal marriage ceremony in Louisiana must be over 18 years of age, and must register with the clerk of the district court of the parish or with the registrar of vital records by providing 'an affidavit stating his or her lawful name, denomination, and address'.

The affidavit is available online here:

http://new.dhh.louisiana.gov/assets/oph/Center-RS/vitalrec/leers/Marriage/M3-MarriageOfficiantAffidavit.pdf

You will need to have the document notarized before you submit. Do not sign the form until you are in the presence of the notary. Along with your application, you will need to provide:

A photocopy of your ID or Driver's License

A photocopy of your ordination certificate

Return your completed form by mail to Clerk of Court in the parish where you intend to perform the majority of your marriages. For Orleans Parish, for example, you would return the form to:

Center for Records and Statistics

ATTN: Marriage Office P.O. Box 60630

New Orleans, LA 70160

What Couples Need To Know

Where do couples apply for a license? Parish Clerk of Court

What are the age requirements? Applicants under 18 years of age must also bring: Both parents to sign consent forms. Both parents must bring their drivers license.

If one parent has full custody, that parent must come in to sign consent forms with his/her driver's license and custody papers showing full custody. Joint custody requires both parent's consent.

How much does a license cost? $25 - $32. The cost varies from parish to parish and some will only accept cash.

What documents are needed?

A certified copy of each party's birth certificate or birth card. If either party was born out-of-country, a translated notarized birth certificate along with a valid state ID card or driver's license must be presented.

Each party must have proof of their social security number.

If either party was born outside the United States their must present a valid passport or naturalization certificate or residency card.

Plus: Address for bride and groom and whether such is within city limits, father's and mother's full name plus maiden name and the state in which each was born, and the highest grade of education completed by the bride and groom.

Are there residency requirements? No.

Is there a waiting period? 72 hours between issuance of the license and the ceremony. The waiting period can be waived by a district judge or justice of the peace in the parish where the license was issued.

How long is a license valid? 30 days.

Where is a license valid for use? Any parish in Louisiana.

What if someone has been married previously? If either party is divorced, he/she must present a certified copy of the final divorce decree.

If either party is widowed, he/she must present a certified copy of a death certificate.

Are there any required tests? No.

Are proxy marriages allowed? No.

Can cousins marry? No.

Are common law marriages recognized? No.

How to Handle the Marriage License

Read and follow the instructions which come with the license on how to fill out your section, and ensure all other sections have been fully and correctly completed.

After performing a marriage, the Celebrant must complete a marriage certificate and return it to the clerk of the district court.

The Celebrant is not required to keep records of marriages.

Maine Wedding Officiant Regulations

Statute Title 19-A Part 2 Chapter 23 Subchapter 1 §655. Authorization; penalties

1. Persons authorized to solemnize marriages.   The following may solemnize marriages in this State:

A. If a resident of this State:

(1) A justice or judge;

(2) A lawyer admitted to the Maine Bar; or

(4) A notary public under Title 4, chapter 19;

B. Whether a resident or nonresident of this State and whether or not a citizen of the United States:

(1) An ordained minister of the gospel;

(2) A cleric engaged in the service of the religious body to which the cleric belongs; or

(3) A person licensed to preach by an association of ministers, religious seminary or ecclesiastical body; and

C. A nonresident of the State who has a temporary registration certificate issued by the Office of Data, Research and Vital Statistics pursuant to subsection 1-A.

1-A. Temporary registration certificate. The Office of Data, Research and Vital Statistics may issue a temporary registration certificate to solemnize a marriage ceremony to an individual who is a resident of another state and who is authorized under the laws of that state to solemnize marriages.

A. An individual seeking a temporary registration certificate under this subsection must submit to the Office of Data, Research and Vital Statistics:

(1) A copy of a valid commission or other indicia of authority to perform marriage ceremonies in the individual's state of residence as proof of existence of the authority;

(2) A copy of the other state's statute that grants the individual authority to solemnize marriages in that state;

(3) The names and residences of the 2 parties whose marriage the individual proposes to solemnize and the expected date of the marriage ceremony; and

(4) A $100 registration fee.

B. Upon finding that the individual has satisfied the requirements of paragraph A, the Office of Data, Research and Vital Statistics shall issue to the individual a temporary registration certificate authorizing the individual to solemnize the marriage of the parties whose names were provided pursuant to paragraph A, subparagraph (3). The Office of Data, Research and Vital Statistics may decline to issue a temporary registration certificate if complaints filed against the individual for actions in this State have been substantiated or for other good cause, even if the state in which the individual is authorized to solemnize marriages has not taken disciplinary action.

C. A temporary registration certificate does not authorize the individual to solemnize any marriage other than the marriage of the parties provided pursuant to paragraph A, subparagraph (3).

D. A temporary registration certificate under this subsection expires upon the individual's signing the marriage license or 90 days after issuance, whichever occurs first.

E. The Office of Data, Research and Vital Statistics shall keep a permanent record of all temporary registration certificates issued under this subsection. The records must contain the name and residence of each individual to whom a temporary registration certificate is issued.

2. Enforcement. The State Registrar of Vital Statistics shall enforce this section as far as it comes within the state registrar's power and shall notify the district attorney of the county in which the penalty should be enforced of the facts that have come to the state registrar's knowledge. Upon receipt of this notice, the district attorney shall prosecute the person who violated this section.

3. Religious exemption. This chapter does not require any member of the clergy to perform or any church, religious denomination or other religious institution to host any

marriage in violation of the religious beliefs of that member of the clergy, church, religious denomination or other religious institution. The refusal to perform or host a marriage under this subsection cannot be the basis for a lawsuit or liability and does not affect the tax-exempt status of the church, religious denomination or other religious institution.

What You Need to Know

An Officiant must be over 18 years of age to perform a legal marriage.

In the state of Maine you are not required to register with the government before performing a marriage ceremony. However, you should be prepared to produce proof of ordination by a recognized body, in the event that this is ever requested. If you have any questions regarding the legality of your ordination in this state you should contact your local government office, or your ordination body itself.

What Couples Need To Know

Where do couples apply for a license? Town Clerk / Town Office

If both of you are residents of the state of Maine, you must both apply in the town where the Maine resident holds residency. If you are residents of different Maine towns, you both may apply in one town or the other – you do not need to apply separately in each town.

If one is from out of state, then both of you should apply in the town where one holds residency.

If neither of you is resident in Maine, then you may apply in any Maine town Office. It need not be the same town where you plan to be married.

What are the age requirements? Applicants must be over 18 years old. Written parental consent is required for an applicant under 18. Written parental consent and written consent of a judge are required for an applicant under 16.

How much does a license cost? $40

What documents are needed? Photo ID and a driver's license.

Are there residency requirements? No.

Is there a waiting period? No.

How long is a license valid? 90 Days.

Where is a license valid for use? The State of Maine.

What if someone has been married previously? If this is not the first marriage for one of you, bring a certified copy (raised seal) of the divorce from or death certificate of the last spouse.

Are there any required tests? No.

Are proxy marriages allowed? No.

Can cousins marry? No. First cousins must have pre-marital counseling.

Are common law marriages recognized? No.

How to Handle the Marriage License

Read and follow the instructions which come with the license on how to fill out your section, and ensure all other sections have been fully and correctly completed.

After the marriage, the minister must file a copy of the record of marriage with the town clerk where the license was issued. The license must be returned within seven days.

The Celebrant is not required to keep records of marriages.

Maryland Wedding Officiant Regulations

Statute §2–406. (2)

A marriage ceremony may be performed in this State by:

(i)   any official of a religious order or body authorized by the rules and customs of that order or body to perform a marriage ceremony;

(ii)   any clerk;

(iii)   any deputy clerk designated by the county administrative judge of the circuit court for the county; or

(iv)   a judge.

What You Need to Know

An Officiant must be over 18 years of age to perform a legal marriage.

In the state of Maryland you are not required to register with the government before performing a marriage ceremony. However, you should be prepared to produce proof of ordination by a recognized body, in the event that this is ever requested. If you have any questions regarding the legality of your ordination in this state you should contact your local government office, or your ordination body itself.

What Couples Need To Know

Where do couples apply for a license? The local Clerk of the Court

What are the age requirements? If under 18 parental consent is required. If between 16 and 18 years of age, one of your parents or a guardian must be with you and provide written consent.

If under 16 years of age, you will need both the written consent of your custodial parent or guardian and the written approval of a judge of the Orphans' Court Division of the Court of Common Pleas.

If you are under 18, pregnant or have a child, and show certificate from a licensed physician stating you are pregnant or have had a child, the parental consent requirement may be waived.

How much does a license cost? Between $35 and $85. The charge varies from city to county.

If you have completed a state recognized pre-marital preparation course, you may receive a discount on the license fee.

What documents are needed? Photo ID and Social Security number. A birth certificate may be necessary to prove your age. However, a non-resident form may be applied for by non-US residents. This form must be certified by the equivalent official in your country of residence.

Are there residency requirements? No.

Is there a waiting period? There is a waiting period of 48 hours in Maryland to get married. You receive the license on application but it does not become valid for 48 hours.

How long is a license valid? 6 Months

Where is a license valid for use? You must be married in the county where you purchased your license.

What if someone has been married previously? Maryland requires you have information regarding date, county and state of death of your previous spouse.

Are there any required tests? No.

Are proxy marriages allowed? No.

Can cousins marry? Yes. First cousins may marry.

Are common law marriages recognized? No.

How to Handle the Marriage License

Read and follow the instructions which come with the license on how to fill out your section, and ensure all other sections have been fully and correctly completed.

The Minister must complete the marriage license and marriage certificate and give one certificate to the couple. The official certification must be returned to the clerk of the court offices within five days after the marriage.

The Celebrant is not required to keep records of marriages.

Massachusetts Wedding Officiant Regulations

Statute Part II, Title III, Chapter 207, Section 38

A marriage may be solemnized in any place within the commonwealth by the following persons who are residents of the commonwealth: a duly ordained minister of the gospel in good and regular standing with his church or denomination, including an ordained deacon in The United Methodist Church or in the Roman Catholic Church; a commissioned cantor or duly ordained rabbi of the Jewish faith; by a justice of the peace if he is also clerk or assistant clerk of a city or town, or a registrar or assistant registrar, or a clerk or assistant clerk of a court or a clerk or assistant clerk of the senate or house of representatives, by a justice of the peace if he has been designated as provided in the following section and has received a certificate of designation and has qualified thereunder; an authorized representative of a Spiritual Assembly of the Baha'is in accordance with the usage of their community; a priest or minister of the Buddhist religion; a minister in fellowship with the Unitarian Universalist Association and ordained by a local church; a leader of an Ethical Culture Society which is duly established in the commonwealth and recognized by the American Ethical Union and who is duly appointed and in good and regular standing with the American Ethical Union; the Imam of the Orthodox Islamic religion; and, it may be solemnized in a regular or special meeting for worship conducted by or under the oversight of a Friends or Quaker Monthly Meeting in accordance with the usage of their Society; and, it may be solemnized by a duly ordained nonresident minister of the gospel if he is a pastor of a church or denomination duly established in the commonwealth and who is in good and regular standing as a minister of such church or denomination, including an ordained deacon in The United Methodist Church or in the Roman Catholic Church; and, it may be solemnized according to the usage of any other church or religious organization which shall have complied with the provisions of the second paragraph of this section.

Churches and other religious organizations shall file in the office of the state secretary information relating to persons recognized or licensed as aforesaid, and relating to usages of such organizations, in such form and at such times as the secretary may require.

http://www.sec.state.ma.us/pre/premar/masmarriage.htm

Section 39 Justice or Non-resident clergymen

The governor may in his discretion designate a justice of the peace in each town and such further number, not exceeding one for every five thousand inhabitants of a city or town, as he considers expedient, to solemnize marriages, and may for a cause at any time revoke such designation. The state secretary, upon payment of twenty-five dollars to him by a justice of the peace so designated, who is also a clerk or an assistant clerk of a city or town or upon the payment of fifty dollars by any other such justice, shall issue to him a certificate of such designation.

The state secretary may authorize, subject to such conditions as he may determine, the solemnization of any specified marriage anywhere within the commonwealth by the following nonresidents: a minister of the gospel in good and regular standing with his church or denomination; a commissioned cantor or duly ordained rabbi of the Jewish faith; an authorized representative of a Spiritual Assembly of the Baha'is in accordance with the usage of their community; the Imam of the Orthodox Islamic religion; a duly ordained priest or minister of the Buddhist religion; a minister in fellowship with the Unitarian Universalist Association and ordained by a local church; a leader of an Ethical Culture Society which is recognized by the American Ethical Union and who is duly appointed and in good and regular standing with the American Ethical Union; a justice of a court or a justice of the peace authorized to solemnize a marriage by virtue of their office within their state of residence; and, it may be solemnized in a regular or special meeting for worship conducted by or under the oversight of a Friends or Quaker Monthly Meeting in accordance with the usage of their Society. A nonresident may solemnize a marriage according to the usage of any church or religious organization which shall have complied with the provisions of the second paragraph of section 38. A certificate of such authorization shall be issued by the state secretary and shall be attached to the certificate issued under section twenty-eight and filed with the appropriate city or town clerk. If one of the nonresidents enumerated above solemnizes a specified marriage anywhere within the commonwealth without having obtained a certificate under this section, the state secretary, upon application of such person, may issue a certificate validating such person's acts. The certificate of validation shall be filed with the certificate issued under section twenty-eight of chapter two hundred and seven.

http://www.sec.state.ma.us/pre/premar/marnon.htm

One Day Marriage Designation

In addition to the foregoing, the governor may designate any other person to solemnize a particular marriage on a particular date and in a particular city or town, and may for cause at any time revoke such designation. The state secretary, upon the payment to him of *twenty-five dollars* by said other person, shall issue to said person a certificate of such designation. Such certificate shall expire upon completion of such solemnization.

http://www.mass.gov/governor/constituent-services/one-day-marriage/one-day-marriage-designation-new-application.html

What You Need to Know

For Celebrants Resident in Massachusetts

Section 38 of Chapter 207 of the Massachusetts General Laws states in relevant part that a marriage may be solemnized according to the usage of any church or religious organization which has filed information relating to persons recognized or licensed as aforesaid and in relation to usage of such organizations in such form and at such times as the Secretary of the Commonwealth may require. Pursuant to this statute, a representative of the church must file the following with the Commissions Section of the Public Records Division:

A copy of his/her ordination papers. If ordination is not applicable, a license similar certificate issued by the religious organization will be accepted.

A letter of good standing from the leader of the religious organization on church letterhead.

Clergy must be a Massachusetts resident.

As of January 1, 2004, all churches and religious organizations must file ANNUALLY information relating to persons recognized or licensed by that entity and information relating to the 'usages' of that organization.

Upon receipt of the above information, this office will consider the individual duly recorded to perform marriage ceremonies within the Commonwealth of Massachusetts.

Information must be mailed to the following address:

Secretary of the Commonwealth

Commissions Section

One Ashburton Place, Room 1719

Boston, Massachusetts 02108

If you have any further questions, please contact the Commissions Section at 617-727-2836.

For Celebrants Not Resident in Massachusetts

Pursuant to the provisions of M.G.L. Chapter 207, Section 39 states in part that,

The state secretary may authorize, subject to the approval of the Governor, the solemnization of any specified marriage anywhere in the Commonwealth by the following nonresident clergy members: a minister of the gospel, a commissioned cantor or duly ordained rabbi, authorized representative of a Spiritual Assembly of the Baha'is, the Imam of the Orthodox Islamic religion, a duly ordained priest or minister of the Buddhist Religion, a minister in fellowship with the Unitarian Universalist Association, a leader of an Ethical Cultural Union, a justice of the court or a justice of the peace, … in a regular and special meeting … of a Friends or Quaker monthly meeting.

A nonresident clergy member may also solemnize a marriage according to the usage of any church or religious organization which shall have complied with the provisions of the second paragraph of section 38. (C. § 38 …Churches and other religious organizations shall file in the office of the state secretary information relating to persons recognized or licensed as aforesaid, and relating to usages of such organizations, in such form and at such times as the secretary may require.) A certificate of such authorization shall be issued by the state secretary and shall be attached to the certificate issued under section twenty-eight and filed with the appropriate city or town clerk.

Please complete the application and return it to this office promptly. The application may be mailed or sent by facsimile transmission to 617-727-5914. Upon receipt of a completed application, a Certificate of Solemnization will be mailed to the Nonresident Clergy member shown on the application. The Clergy member is responsible for filing said Certificate with the appropriate town or city clerk pursuant to G.L. ch. 207.

(Source: Secretary of the Commonwealth of the State of Massachusetts)

You can download the Non-resident application from the following location:
http://www.sec.state.ma.us/pre/prepdf/nonresclergyapp.pdf

The Special One Day Marriage Designation

Massachusetts has provided a special designation to allow a single ceremony application. You can download the application from the following location:
http://www.mass.gov/governor/docs/constituent-services/one-day-marriage-

instructions.pdf

The Governor of Massachusetts has provided the following information with regard to this special application:

Please download the application posted above before going through these instructions. The following instructions should help you complete the application for your one day marriage designation. Please refer to the most frequently asked questions section if you have questions about this process.

1. Reason for Designation: A personal explanation for why you have been selected to solemnize the wedding ceremony of Party A and Party B
Example: 'Party A is my former roommate, I recognize their relationship with Party B and I am honored to take part in their wedding ceremony.'
2. Applicant Information: Full name, direct email, street address and telephone number of applicant who wishes to officiate the marriage
3. Party A and Party B: Full legal names before wedding ceremony occurs. Full contact information. Names will appear on the certificate as written here
4. City/Town of Wedding: Please state which of the 351 Cities or Towns in Massachusetts the wedding will take place
5. Date of Proposed Marriage: Please state the exact calendar date the wedding ceremony is set to take place in said City or Town within the borders of the Commonwealth of Massachusetts

Note: We cannot accept applications submitted more than 3 months in advance of the ceremony.

A complete application will have the following materials submitted to the Governor's Office:

Application Form
Letter of Reference. The letter must be written on behalf of the individual applying to officiate the wedding attesting to the applicant's high standard of character. Cannot be written or signed by the applicant, Party A or Party B. The letter must be signed by its author. Note: judges, appointed and elected officials do not require letters of recommendation
$25 Processing Fee. The fee must be in the form of check or money order only made out to 'The Commonwealth of Massachusetts'. The Governor's Office will not accept

cash, debit or credit cards.

Please mail all completed application materials to:
Office of Governor Charlie Baker
Room 271M
Attn: One-Day Marriage Designation
State House
Boston, MA 02133

Note: Applicant will receive an email from the governor's office notifying them of their acceptance. Applicant will also receive a hard-copy of the certificate of solemnization to perform the wedding ceremony approximately four weeks prior to the wedding date. Once the applicant receives the email from our office they can solemnize the ceremony. It is not necessary to have the certificate on hand

Additional Information

1. We require that applications be submitted with adequate time for processing, which could be anywhere between 4-6 weeks, especially during spring/summer months. i.e. an application received on June 22nd for a wedding on July 4th will NOT be processed in time.
Please do not submit applications more than three months in advance of the wedding date
2. Following the wedding, the Certificate of Solemnization must be submitted, along with the completed marriage license, to the city or town hall at which the couple applied for the license.
3. Statute requires the Governor to specify the specific date of the wedding and the city or town in which it will be held. Therefore, you will need to submit a new application if either of those details changes along with a $5 processing fee (check/money order only).

(Source: http://www.mass.gov/governor/constituent-services/one-day-marriage/one-day-marriage-designation-new-application.html)

What Couples Need To Know

Where do couples apply for a license? City or Town Clerk
What are the age requirements? Parental consent is needed if under 18 years of age. If you are between 16-18 years of age, one of your parents or guardian must be with you

and provide written consent.

If you are under 16 years of age, you will need both the written consent of your custodial parent or guardian and the written approval of a judge of the Orphans' Court Division of the Court of Common Pleas.

If you are under 18, pregnant or have had a child, and show a certificate from a licensed physician stating you are pregnant or have had a child, the parental consent requirement may be waived.

How much does a license cost? The fee for filing the Intention of Marriage varies from town to town. The state statute stipulates a fee of $4 for the license but it allows cities and towns by a vote of their city councils, boards of selectmen or town meeting, or by a change in the by-laws, to set their own fee.

What documents are needed? Picture ID such as driver's license. You should know your Social security numbers.

Are there residency requirements? No.

Is there a waiting period? 3 days. Sundays and holidays are included in the three days, but the day the application is made is not. For example, if you apply on Friday, your license will be issued on or after Monday. Check with your town clerk to determine whether you must pick it up in person, or if it can be mailed.

How long is a license valid? 60 Days.

Where is a license valid for use? Within the Commonwealth of Massachusetts.

What if someone has been married previously? You are not required to present a divorce certificate when filing intentions to marry. However, it is extremely important that an individual who has been divorced be certain that his/her divorce is absolute. If you are uncertain as to the absolute date of your divorce, you should contact the court where the divorce was granted. In Massachusetts, a divorce does not become absolute until 90 days after the divorce nisi has been granted, regardless of the grounds for divorce.

Are there any required tests? No.

Are proxy marriages allowed? No.

Can cousins marry? Yes.

Are common law marriages recognized? No.

How to Handle the Marriage License

Read and follow the instructions which come with the license on how to fill out your section, and ensure all other sections have been fully and correctly completed.

Ministers must return a certificate of the marriage to the town clerk or registrar who issued the marriage license and to the town clerk of the town where the marriage was performed.

Ministers must keep records of all marriages they perform. In practice, this requires you to keep a record book containing details of each ceremony, as well as copies of all documents you have completed and returned.

Michigan Wedding Officiant Regulations

Statute 551.7 Persons authorized to solemnize marriage; records; return of licenses and certificates; disposition of fees charged by mayor or county clerk.

Sec. 7.

(1) Marriages may be solemnized by any of the following:

(a) A judge of the district court, anywhere in this state.

(b) A district court magistrate, anywhere in this state.

(c) A municipal judge, in the city in which the judge is serving or in a township over which a municipal court has jurisdiction under section 9928 of the revised judicature act of 1961, 1961 PA 236, MCL 600.9928.

(d) A judge of probate, anywhere in this state.

(e) A judge of a federal court.

(f) A mayor of a city, anywhere in a county in which that city is located.

(g) A county clerk in the county in which the clerk serves, or in another county with the written authorization of the clerk of the other county.

(h) For a county having more than 1,500,000 inhabitants, an employee of the county clerk's office designated by the county clerk, in the county in which the clerk serves.

(i) A minister of the gospel or cleric or religious practitioner, anywhere in this state, if the minister or cleric or religious practitioner is ordained or authorized to solemnize marriages according to the usages of the denomination.

(j) A minister of the gospel or cleric or religious practitioner, anywhere in this state, if the minister or cleric or religious practitioner is not a resident of this state but is authorized to solemnize marriages under the laws of the state in which the minister or cleric or religious practitioner resides.

(2) A person authorized by this act to solemnize a marriage shall keep proper records and return licenses and certificates as required by section 4 of 1887 PA 128, MCL 551.104.

(3) If a mayor of a city solemnizes a marriage, the mayor shall charge and collect a fee to be determined by the council of that city, which shall be paid to the city treasurer and deposited in the general fund of the city at the end of the month.

(4) If the county clerk or, in a county having more than 1,500,000 inhabitants, an employee of the clerk's office designated by the county clerk solemnizes a marriage, the county clerk shall charge and collect a fee to be determined by the commissioners of the county in which the clerk serves. The fee shall be paid to the treasurer for the county in which the clerk serves and deposited in the general fund of that county at the end of the month.

What You Need to Know

An Officiant must be over 18 years of age to perform a legal marriage.

In the state of Michigan you are not required to register with the government before performing a marriage ceremony. However, you should be prepared to produce proof of ordination by a recognized body, in the event that this is ever requested. If you have any questions regarding the legality of your ordination in this state you should contact your local government office, or your ordination body itself.

What Couples Need To Know

Where do couples apply for a license? County Register of Deeds.

Residents need to apply for their marriage license in the county in which one of them lives. Non-residents need to apply for their marriage license in the county where they plan on getting married.

Even though you apply for your marriage license in the county you live in you can get married any place in the state.

What are the age requirements? If you are 16 or 17 years old, you can get married with parental consent. Your parents must appear with their own identification and if a custodial parent, proof of their custody. If you are 15 or younger, you will need both parental consent and the approval of the probate court.

How much does a license cost? $20 if you are a resident of Michigan. $30 for non-residents. Some counties may charge more. Bring cash. Most counties do not accept checks.

What documents are needed? Picture ID such as Drivers License. You can also use Military ID. You must also have a certified copy of your birth certificates.

You will need to know your parents addresses, and your mothers' maiden names. Foreign birth certificates need to be translated into English, and be notarized.

Are there residency requirements? No.

Is there a waiting period? There is a mandatory 3 day waiting period before your license is issued to you. In most states, the waiting period does not include Saturdays,

Sundays or federal holidays. In some instances, the day the application is filed is not included within the waiting period timeline.

How long is a license valid? 33 Days.

Where is a license valid for use? Anywhere in the State of Michigan.

What if someone has been married previously? You need to know the date (mm/dd/yy) and how the last marriage ended. If it was within the last 6 months, you will need to bring proof of the divorce that can be left with the Clerk.

Are there any required tests? No.

Are proxy marriages allowed? No. However, only one of you need to be present and have all required documentation when applying for a marriage license. You will need to show a photocopy of the front and back of your partner's driver's license.

Can cousins marry? No.

Are common law marriages recognized? No.

How to Handle the Marriage License

Read and follow the instructions which come with the license on how to fill out your section, and ensure all other sections have been fully and correctly completed.

Ministers must complete a marriage certificate and give one to the couple. Another marriage certificate must be returned to the county clerk who issued the license within 10 days after the marriage.

The Celebrant is not required to keep records of marriages.

Minnesota Wedding Officiant Regulations

Statute 517.04 PERSONS AUTHORIZED TO PERFORM CIVIL MARRIAGES.

Civil marriages may be solemnized throughout the state by an individual who has attained the age of 21 years and is a judge of a court of record, a retired judge of a court of record, a court administrator, a retired court administrator with the approval of the chief judge of the judicial district, a former court commissioner who is employed by the court system or is acting pursuant to an order of the chief judge of the commissioner's judicial district, the residential school superintendent of the Minnesota State Academy for the Deaf and the Minnesota State Academy for the Blind, a licensed or ordained minister of any religious denomination, or by any mode recognized in section 517.18. For purposes of this section, a court of record includes the Office of Administrative Hearings under section 14.48.

What You Need to Know

Unlike most states of the U.S., Minnesota stipulates that you must be at least 21 years of age to legally solemnize a marriage within state borders.

Every Celebrant wishing to perform a legal wedding ceremony within the state of Minnesota must register at any one county office before the date of the first ceremony. You will need to apply at the local Vital Records office.

Each Celebrant will be asked to fill out a Certificate of Filing, and then have this notarized.

You will need to provide a copy of your Certificate of Ordination. If your certificate is unavailable, one of the following may be substituted:

A letter from the main church body (such as the Archdiocese or Synod) with the signature of one official, OR

A letter from the church, which must:

Be on church letterhead (if not, the officials' signatures must be notarized)

State that the church authorizes you to solemnize marriages

Be signed by three other officials of the church

The form will ask you to stipulate the expiration date of your ordination license, or that it has none. Do not sign and date your form until you are in the presence of the notary.

There will be a small filing fee, which varies by county but is usually between $5-$10.

You will also be required to show a government issued photo ID at the time of filing.

In many counties, you can apply by mail, enclosing the documents listed above along with your completed and notarized certificate of filing.

Below is a link to an example of the registration form for Hennepin County. Whichever county you choose, the form should be broadly similar to this. Remember, you can register in any county in order to be eligible to perform ceremonies throughout the state.

http://www.hennepin.us/~/media/hennepinus/residents/licenses-certificates-permits/documents/ministerial-certificate.pdf

What Couples Need To Know

Where do couples apply for a license? The County Recorder.

What are the age requirements? Applicants must be 18 years of age to obtain a license without parental consent.

If either partner is under 18, parental consent forms must be signed. You will need a certified copy of your birth certificate. If you are under 16 you cannot marry without a court order.

How much does a license cost? The marriage license fee is $40.00 for parties who have completed at least 12 hours of premarital education (see requirements below). The fee for the license is $115.00 if you have not met the premarital education requirements.

Reduced Fee Requirements: In order to qualify for the reduced fee, the parties must submit a signed and dated statement from the person who provided the premarital education confirming that it was received. The premarital education must be provided by a licensed or ordained minister or the minister's designee, a person authorized to solemnize marriages under Minnesota Statutes, section 517.18, or a person authorized to practice marriage and family therapy under Minnesota Statutes, section 148B.33. The education must include the use of premarital inventory and the teaching of communication and conflict management skills.

The statement from the person who provided the premarital education must have the following wording on their business letterhead stationery, signed and notarized or under church seal or follow the format found in Minnesota Statutes, section 517.08 subd 1b:

I, (name of educator), confirm that (full legal name of both parties) received at least 12 hours of premarital education that included the use of a premarital inventory and the teaching of communication and conflict management skills. I am a licensed or ordained minister, a person authorized to solemnize marriages under Minnesota Statutes, section 517.18, or a person authorized to practice marriage and family therapy under Minnesota Statutes, section 148B.33.

The names of the parties in the educator's statement must be identical to the legal names of the parties as they appear in the marriage license application. This document must be clear and legible and on 8 1/2 X 11 paper.

What documents are needed? A valid photo ID and proof of your Social Security number. You may also need to bring a copy of your birth certificate. You must provide after-marriage names and addresses.

Are there residency requirements? No.

Is there a waiting period? 5 days between applying for and receiving your license.

How long is a license valid? 6 Months.

Where is a license valid for use? The State of Minnesota.

What if someone has been married previously? If previously married and now divorced, you must bring the divorce decree with you.

Are there any required tests? No.

Are proxy marriages allowed? No.

Can cousins marry? No.

Are common law marriages recognized? No. However, the state does recognize common law marriages that are valid in other states.

How to Handle the Marriage License

Read and follow the instructions which come with the license on how to fill out your section, and ensure all other sections have been fully and correctly completed.

Ministers must give a marriage certificate to the bride and groom and also file a certificate with the clerk of the district court in the county which issued the marriage license.

The Celebrant is not required to keep records of marriages.

Mississippi Wedding Officiant Regulations

Statute § 93-1-17. By whom marriages may be solemnized

Any minister of the gospel ordained according to the rules of his church or society, in good standing; any Rabbi or other spiritual leader of any other religious body authorized under the rules of such religious body to solemnize rites of matrimony and being in good standing; any judge of the Supreme Court, Court of Appeals, circuit court, chancery court or county court may solemnize the rites of matrimony between any persons anywhere within this state who shall produce a license granted as herein directed. Justice court judges and members of the boards of supervisors may likewise solemnize the rites of matrimony within their respective counties. Any marriages performed by a mayor of a municipality prior to March 14, 1994 are valid provided such marriages satisfy the requirements of Section 93-1-18.

§ 93-1-19. Marriage may be solemnized according to religious customs

It shall be lawful for a pastor of any religious society in this state to join together in marriage such persons of the society to whom a marriage license has been issued, according to the rules and customs established by the society. The clerk or keeper of the minutes, proceedings, or other books of the religious society wherein such marriage shall be had and solemnized, shall make a true and faithful register of all marriages solemnized in the society, in a book kept by him for that purpose, and return a certificate of the same to the clerk of the circuit court of the county, to be by him recorded, under the penalty prescribed in Section 93-1-21.

What You Need to Know

An Officiant must be over 18 years of age to perform a legal marriage.

In the state of Mississippi you are not required to register with the government before performing a marriage ceremony. However, you should be prepared to produce proof of ordination by a recognized body, in the event that this is ever requested. If you have any questions regarding the legality of your ordination in this state you should contact your local government office, or your ordination body itself.

What Couples Need To Know

Where do couples apply for a license? Circuit Clerk's Office

What are the age requirements? In the event that the female applicant shall be under the age of 21 years of age, and s a resident of the State of Mississippi, the application of marriage shall be made to the Circuit Clerk of the county of residence of the parent or legal guardian of such female applicant.

If either applicant is under 21 years of age, parental consent is needed. If the parent does not accompany the applicant to the office when applying, the Clerk shall send notice of filing the application via certified mail to the parents or legal guardian.

Marriage licenses cannot be issued unless the MALE applicant is at least 17 years of age, and the female applicant is at least 15 years of age.

How much does a license cost? The marriage license fee is $21+ in cash.

What documents are needed? You will need:

Full names and addresses of both parties.

Names and addresses of the parents of both parties applying (maiden name of Mother)

Age, Date of Birth, and State of Birth (or Foreign County)

Proof of Age (Driver's License, Birth Certificate, School Record, etc.)

Highest Grade Completed in School

Are there residency requirements? No.

Is there a waiting period? No.

How long is a license valid? 90 Days.

Where is a license valid for use? The State of Mississippi.

What if someone has been married previously? You will need to show:

The number of previous marriages.

How the last marriage ended.

Date last marriage ended. Bring proof of divorce, if was within the last six months.

Are there any required tests? No.
Are proxy marriages allowed? No.
Can cousins marry? No.
Are common law marriages recognized? No.

How to Handle the Marriage License

Read and follow the instructions which come with the license on how to fill out your section, and ensure all other sections have been fully and correctly completed.

Ministers must send a certificate of marriage to the clerk who issued the marriage license within three months after the marriage.

The Celebrant is not required to keep records of marriages.

Missouri Wedding Officiant Regulations

Statute 451.110. Marriages solemnized by whom.

Every person solemnizing marriages under this chapter shall issue and deliver to the parties to such marriage a certificate thereof, which shall be furnished in blank by the officer who issues such license, setting forth the names and residence of the parties and the date of such marriage, and the county from which the license was issued and the date of same; and such certificates shall be prima facie evidence of the facts therein stated in all courts of this state.

451.115. Marriages illegally solemnized--penalty.

Every person who shall solemnize any marriage, having knowledge of any fact which renders such marriage unlawful or criminal in either of the parties under any law of this state, or, having knowledge or reasonable cause to believe that either of the parties shall be under the age of legal consent, or is prohibited by section 451.020 from entering into such marriage, or where to his knowledge, any other legal impediment exists to such marriage, and every person not authorized by law to solemnize marriages who shall falsely represent that he is so authorized, and who, by any pretended marriage ceremony which he may perform, shall deceive any innocent person or persons into the belief that they have been legally married, shall, on conviction, be adjudged guilty of a class C misdemeanor.

451.120. Penalty for solemnizing marriage without license, or failing to keep a record thereof.

Any person who shall solemnize any marriage wherein the parties have not obtained a license, as provided by this chapter, or shall fail to keep a record of the solemnization of any marriage, shall be deemed guilty of a misdemeanor, and upon conviction shall be fined not exceeding five hundred dollars, and in addition shall be subject to a civil action by the parent, conservator or other person having care or custody of the person so married, to whom services are due wherein the recovery shall not exceed the sum of five hundred dollars; and any recorder who shall issue a license contrary to the provisions of this chapter shall be subject to a like punishment.

What You Need to Know

An Officiant must be over 18 years of age to perform a legal marriage.

In the state of Missouri you are not required to register with the government before performing a marriage ceremony. However, you should be prepared to produce proof of ordination by a recognized body, in the event that this is ever requested. If you have any questions regarding the legality of your ordination in this state you should contact your local government office, or your ordination body itself.

What Couples Need To Know

Where do couples apply for a license? The Recorder of Deeds

What are the age requirements? A person under the age of 18 cannot marry without the consent of the custodial parent or guardian.

A person under age 15 cannot marry without approval of a judge in the county where the marriage license is sought. The statute states that the judge should grant approval only upon a showing of 'good cause' and that unusual conditions make the marriage 'advisable'. Persons lacking mental capacity to consent to marriage cannot marry without court approval.

How much does a license cost? $58+

What documents are needed? Picture ID such as Drivers License, and Social Security Card.

Are there residency requirements? No.

Is there a waiting period? No.

How long is a license valid? 30 Days. Confirm this for you specific location, as a few counties may have an expiry of 15 days.

Where is a license valid for use? The State of Missouri.

What if someone has been married previously? If you were previously married, the date of your divorce or the date of your spouse's death must be provided. Applicants must wait at least 30 days after the divorce has been finalized before applying for a marriage license. If necessary, a copy of your divorce records or spouse's death certificate can be ordered from your local vital records office and mailed to you.

Are there any required tests? No.

Are proxy marriages allowed? Yes.

Can cousins marry? No.

Are common law marriages recognized? No.

How to Handle the Marriage License

Read and follow the instructions which come with the license on how to fill out your section, and ensure all other sections have been fully and correctly completed.

They must give the couple a marriage certificate and must complete the marriage license and return it to the recorder of deeds within 90 days after the marriage license was issued.

Ministers must keep a record of all marriages they perform.

Montana Wedding Officiant Regulations

Statute 40-1-301. Solemnization and registration.

(1) A marriage may be solemnized by a judge of a court of record, by a public official whose powers include solemnization of marriages, by a mayor, city judge, or justice of the peace, by a tribal judge, or in accordance with any mode of solemnization recognized by any religious denomination, Indian nation or tribe, or native group. Either the person solemnizing the marriage or, if no individual acting alone solemnized the marriage, a party to the marriage shall complete the marriage certificate form and forward it to the clerk of the district court.

(2) If a party to a marriage is unable to be present at the solemnization, the party may authorize in writing a third person to act as proxy. If the person solemnizing the marriage is satisfied that the absent party is unable to be present and has consented to the marriage, the person may solemnize the marriage by proxy. If the person solemnizing the marriage is not satisfied, the parties may petition the district court for an order permitting the marriage to be solemnized by proxy.

(3) The solemnization of the marriage is not invalidated by the fact that the person solemnizing the marriage was not legally qualified to solemnize it if either party to the marriage believed that person to be qualified.

(4) One party to a proxy marriage must be a member of the armed forces of the United States on federal active duty or a resident of Montana at the time of application for a license and certificate pursuant to 40-1-202. One party or a legal representative shall appear before the clerk of court and pay the marriage license fee. For the purposes of this subsection, residency must be determined in accordance with 1-1-215.

What You Need to Know

An Officiant must be over 18 years of age to perform a legal marriage.

In the state of Montana you are not required to register with the government before performing a marriage ceremony. However, you should be prepared to produce proof of ordination by a recognized body, in the event that this is ever requested. If you have any questions regarding the legality of your ordination in this state you should contact your local government office, or your ordination body itself.

What Couples Need To Know

Where do couples apply for a license? Clerk of the District Court.

If both parties are non-residents of Montana, obtain the license application from the Clerk in the county in which the ceremony will be performed. If one party is a non-resident, his/her part can be sworn to or affirmed in the county and state in which he/she resides.

What are the age requirements? If you are 16 or 17 years old, you must have the consent of both parents unless only one parent has legal custody of you. Proof of age must be in the form of a certified copy of your birth certificate. Both of you, as a couple, will also have to attend at least two counseling sessions that are at least 10 days apart. This has to be done with a designated counselor who will then have to provide a letter that states the names of the couple, their ages, the dates of the counseling sessions, and what the counselor thinks about their possible marriage. Then judicial consent signed by a district court judge must be given for the Clerk of court's office to issue a marriage license. No one 15 years of age or younger may marry in Montana.

How much does a license cost? $53. Cash Only.

What documents are needed? Certified copies of birth certificates, blood test waiver (form available in the Clerk's office) and certified copies of divorce decrees. If your birth certificate is from a foreign country, the Clerk's office will need a certified copy of the certificate. It must then be translated to English, by a person authorized to do so, and their signature must be notarized.

Are there residency requirements? No.

Is there a waiting period? No waiting period unless under the age of 18.

How long is a license valid? 30 Days.

Where is a license valid for use? The State of Montana

What if someone has been married previously? A certified copy of the divorce decree is required.

Are there any required tests? As of October 1, 2007, a rubella blood test is no longer required for a bride between the ages of 18 and 50. The parties may sign an Informed Consent/Waiver of Requirement of Blood Test form. This form is available at the Clerk of District Court's Office or online at the MT Dept. of Public Health & Human Services website. If you obtain the form from a source other than the Clerk of District Court, please bring the form with you when applying for your marriage license. If the bride is over the age of 50, no waiver is required.

Those persons desiring to consummate a marriage by written declaration without solemnization must secure the premarital blood test waiver (available in the Clerk's office) for the female prior to executing the declaration (40-1-311 through 313 & 40-1-323).

Are proxy marriages allowed? Yes.

Can cousins marry? No.

Are common law marriages recognized? Yes.

How to Handle the Marriage License

Read and follow the instructions which come with the license on how to fill out your section, and ensure all other sections have been fully and correctly completed.

Ministers must complete and return a marriage certificate to the clerk of the district court within 30 days after the marriage. Also the minister must provide marriage certificates to the bride and groom upon request.

The Celebrant is not required to keep records of marriages.

Nebraska Wedding Officiant Regulations

Statute 42-108. Marriage ceremony; who may perform; return; contents.

Every judge, retired judge, clerk magistrate, or retired clerk magistrate, and every preacher of the gospel authorized by the usages of the church to which he or she belongs to solemnize marriages, may perform the marriage ceremony in this state. Every such person performing the marriage ceremony shall make a return of his or her proceedings in the premises, showing the names and residences of at least two witnesses who were present at such marriage. The return shall be made to the county clerk who issued the license within fifteen days after such marriage has been performed. The county clerk shall record the return or cause it to be recorded in the same book where the marriage license is recorded.

What You Need to Know

An Officiant must be over 18 years of age to perform a legal marriage.

In the state of Nebraska you are not required to register with the government before performing a marriage ceremony. However, you should be prepared to produce proof of ordination by a recognized body, in the event that this is ever requested. If you have any questions regarding the legality of your ordination in this state you should contact your local government office, or your ordination body itself.

What Couples Need To Know

Where do couples apply for a license? County Clerk/Comptroller's Office.

What are the age requirements? Any person who is at least 19 years old may apply for a marriage license without consent.

Any minor who is 17 or 18 years old may apply for a marriage license with a parental or legal guardian consent. The consent form must be notarized.

If either applicant is under 17 years of age, a license cannot be issued in the State of Nebraska.

How much does a license cost? $15.00

What documents are needed?

Proof of Identity / Age: Valid driver's license, passport or birth certificate. If a birth certificate is used it must be a certified copy.

Social Security numbers of both bride and groom are requested on the marriage license application.

Applicants must supply the names of their parents (including mother's maiden name), and their parents' birthplaces (city and state or foreign country).

Are there residency requirements? No.

Is there a waiting period? No.

How long is a license valid? 1 Year.

Where is a license valid for use? The State of Nebraska.

What if someone has been married previously? If either applicant has been married previously, the date the previous marriage ended will be requested (court date or date of death). A copy of the divorce decree or death certificate is not required.

Are there any required tests? No.

Are proxy marriages allowed? No.

Can cousins marry? No.

Are common law marriages recognized? No.

How to Handle the Marriage License

Read and follow the instructions which come with the license on how to fill out your section, and ensure all other sections have been fully and correctly completed.

Ministers must report marriages they perform to the county judge who issued the marriage license within 15 days after the marriage. Also the minister must provide marriage certificates to the bride and groom upon request.

The Celebrant is not required to keep records of marriages.

Nevada Wedding Officiant Regulations

Statute NRS 122.062

Licensed, ordained or appointed ministers, other church or religious officials authorized to solemnize a marriage, notaries public and chaplains of Armed Forces to obtain certificates from county clerk; temporary replacements; solemnization by minister or other authorized person who resides in another state or who is retired.

1. Any licensed, ordained or appointed minister or other church or religious official authorized to solemnize a marriage in good standing within his or her church or religious organization, or either of them, incorporated, organized or established in this State, or a notary public appointed by the Secretary of State pursuant to chapter 240 of NRS and in good standing with the Secretary of State, may join together as husband and wife persons who present a marriage license obtained from any county clerk of the State, if the minister, other church or religious official authorized to solemnize a marriage or notary public first obtains a certificate of permission to perform marriages as provided in NRS 122.062 to 122.073, inclusive. The fact that a minister or other church or religious official authorized to solemnize a marriage is retired does not disqualify him or her from obtaining a certificate of permission to perform marriages if, before retirement, the

minister or other church or religious official authorized to solemnize a marriage had active charge of a church or religious organization for a period of at least 3 years.

2.   A temporary replacement for a licensed, ordained or appointed minister or other church or religious official authorized to solemnize a marriage certified pursuant to NRS 122.062 to 122.073, inclusive, may solemnize marriages pursuant to subsection 1 for a period not to exceed 90 days, if the requirements of this subsection are satisfied. The minister or other church or religious official authorized to solemnize a marriage whom he or she temporarily replaces shall provide him or her with a written authorization which states the period during which it is effective, and the temporary replacement shall obtain from the county clerk in the county in which he or she is a temporary replacement a written authorization to solemnize marriage and submit to the county clerk an application fee of $25.

3.   Any chaplain who is assigned to duty in this State by the Armed Forces of the United States may solemnize marriages if the chaplain obtains a certificate of permission to perform marriages from the county clerk of the county in which his or her duty station is located. The county clerk shall issue such a certificate to a chaplain upon proof of his or her military status as a chaplain and of his or her assignment.

4.   A licensed, ordained or appointed minister, other church or religious official authorized to solemnize a marriage, active or retired, or a notary public may submit to the county clerk in the county in which a marriage is to be performed an application to perform a specific marriage in the county. The application must:

    (a) Include the full names and addresses of the persons to be married;
    (b) Include the date and location of the marriage ceremony;
    (c) Include the information and documents required pursuant to subsection 1 of NRS 122.064; and
    (d) Be accompanied by an application fee of $25.

5.   A county clerk may grant authorization to perform a specific marriage to a person who submitted an application pursuant to subsection 4 if the county clerk is satisfied that the minister or other church or religious official authorized to solemnize a marriage, whether he or she is active or retired, is in good standing with his or her church or religious organization or, in the case of a notary public, if the notary public is in good standing with the Secretary of State. The authorization must be in writing and need not be filed with any other public officer. A separate authorization is required for each

marriage performed. A person may not obtain more than five authorizations to perform a specific marriage pursuant to this section in any calendar year and must acknowledge that he or she is subject to the jurisdiction of the county clerk with respect to the provisions of this chapter governing the conduct of ministers, other church or religious officials authorized to solemnize a marriage or notaries public to the same extent as if he or she had obtained a certificate of permission to perform marriages.

NRS 122.006

'Other church or religious official authorized to solemnize a marriage' defined. 'Other church or religious official authorized to solemnize a marriage' means a person of any church or religious organization, other than a minister, who has been authorized to solemnize a marriage according to the usages of that church or religious organization.

NRS 122.066 Database of ministers or other persons authorized to solemnize a marriage; maintenance of database by Secretary of State; entry of certain information into database by county clerk; approval of application for certificate; validity of certificate; revocati

1. The Secretary of State shall establish and maintain a statewide database of ministers or other persons authorized to solemnize a marriage. The database must:
(a) Serve as the official list of ministers or other persons authorized to solemnize a marriage approved in this State;
(b) Provide for a single method of storing and managing the official list;
(c) Be a uniform, centralized and interactive database;
(d) Be electronically secure and accessible to each county clerk in this State;
(e) Contain the name, mailing address and other pertinent information of each minister or other person authorized to solemnize a marriage as prescribed by the Secretary of State; and
(f) Include a unique identifier assigned by the Secretary of State to each minister or other person authorized to solemnize a marriage.

2. If the county clerk approves an application for a certificate of permission to perform marriages, the county clerk shall:

(a) Enter all information contained in the application into the electronic statewide database of ministers or other persons authorized to solemnize a marriage maintained by the Secretary of State not later than 10 days after the certificate of permission to perform marriages is approved by the county clerk; and

(b) Provide to the Secretary of State all information related to the minister or other person authorized to solemnize a marriage pursuant to paragraph (e) of subsection 1.

3. Upon approval of an application pursuant to subsection 2, the minister or other person authorized to solemnize a marriage:

(a) Shall comply with the laws of this State governing the solemnization of marriage and conduct of ministers or other persons authorized to solemnize a marriage;

(b) Is subject to further review or investigation by the county clerk to ensure that he or she continues to meet the statutory requirements for a person authorized to solemnize a marriage; and

(c) Shall provide the county clerk with any changes to his or her status or information, including, without limitation, the address or telephone number of the church or religious organization or any other information pertaining to certification.

4. A certificate of permission is valid until the county clerk has received an affidavit of revocation of authority to solemnize marriages pursuant to NRS 122.0665.

5. An affidavit of revocation of authority to solemnize marriages that is received pursuant to subsection 4 must be sent to the county clerk within 5 days after the minister or other person authorized to solemnize a marriage ceased to be a member of the church or religious organization in good standing or ceased to be a minister or other person authorized to solemnize a marriage for the church or religious organization.

6. If the county clerk in the county where the certificate of permission was issued has reason to believe that the minister or other person authorized to solemnize a marriage is no longer in good standing within his or her church or religious organization, or that he or she is no longer a minister or other person authorized to solemnize a marriage, or that such church or religious organization no longer exists, the county clerk may require satisfactory proof of the good standing of the minister or other person authorized to solemnize a marriage. If such proof is not presented within 15 days, the county clerk shall revoke the certificate of permission by amending the electronic record of the minister or other person authorized to solemnize a marriage in the statewide database pursuant to subsection 1.

7. If any minister or other person authorized to solemnize a marriage to whom a

certificate of permission has been issued severs ties with his or her church or religious organization or moves from the county in which his or her certificate was issued, the certificate shall expire immediately upon such severance or move, and the church or religious organization shall, within 5 days after the severance or move, file an affidavit of revocation of authority to solemnize marriages pursuant to NRS 122.0665. If the minister or other person authorized to solemnize a marriage voluntarily advises the county clerk of the county in which his or her certificate was issued of his or her severance with his or her church or religious organization, or that he or she has moved from the county, the certificate shall expire immediately upon such severance or move without any notification to the county clerk by the church or religious organization.

8. The Secretary of State may adopt regulations concerning the creation and administration of the statewide database. This section does not prohibit the Secretary of State from making the database publicly accessible for the purpose of viewing ministers or other persons who are authorized to solemnize a marriage in this State.

What You Need to Know

Every Celebrant wishing to perform a legal marriage ceremony in the state of Nevada must register with the local county. All the information you need is listed in the statutes above in this section.

Processing time for applications can take 2-3 weeks depending upon the type of application submitted and the results of the background check.

The application fee is $25 (cash only).

Background checks are required for the following types of applications and require payment of a $45 fee to the third-party vendor conducting the background check:

1) Notary Publics (permanent only)
2) Religious Officials (permanent only)
3) Religious Officials (retired status)
4) Religious Officials (temporary replacements)

Faxed documents will not be accepted. Original documents are required.

To avoid any delays in processing, check to ensure that the documents are signed by the appropriate party and notarized.

Las Vegas is located in Clark County. Here is a link to their information section for Marriage Celebrants:

http://www.clarkcountynv.gov/depts/clerk/services/pages/ministerlicenses.aspx

The Secretary of State maintains a list of marriage Officiants in the state of Nevada who have been licensed and approved, or who have been temporarily licensed, by the state's county clerks:

http://www.nvsos.gov/MinisterPublicApp/SearchHome.aspx

Washoe County has a useful FAQ section for Marriage Celebrants:
https://www.washoecounty.us/clerks/faq/index.php

What Couples Need To Know

Where do couples apply for a license? County Clerk or Recorder.

What are the age requirements? If you are 16 or 17 years old, you must have one parent or legal guardian present. A notarized written permission is also acceptable. It must be written in English and needs to state the name, birth date, age of the minor child, along with the relationship of the person giving consent. The notary must note that the parent or guardian personally appeared before or was subscribed and sworn to.

If you are under 16, marriage can be authorized only by court order when the request has been filed by either parent or legal guardian.

How much does a license cost? $35 - $65 depending on county.

What documents are needed? Valid picture identification. Acceptable identification includes valid Driver's license, valid Identification Card from DMV, valid Passport, Resident Alien card, Military ID, or Certified or original Birth Certificate.

If a foreign birth certificate, it must be translated into English and notarized.

You also need to know you Social Security number.

Are there residency requirements? No.

Is there a waiting period? No.

How long is a license valid? 1 Year.

Where is a license valid for use? The State of Nevada.

What if someone has been married previously? If you were previously married, your divorce must be final. You need to know the date of your divorce and the location where you were divorced.

Are there any required tests? No.

Are proxy marriages allowed? No.

Can cousins marry? Not nearer of kin than second cousins or cousins of half blood.

Are common law marriages recognized? No.

How to Handle the Marriage License

Read and follow the instructions which come with the license on how to fill out your section, and ensure all other sections have been fully and correctly completed.

Ministers must report marriages they perform to the county judge who issued the marriage license within 15 days after the marriage. Also the minister must provide marriage certificates to the bride and groom upon request.

The Celebrant is not required to keep records of marriages.

New Hampshire Wedding Officiant Regulations

Statute 457:31 Solemnization of Marriage.

A marriage may be solemnized in the following manner:

I. In a civil ceremony by a justice of the peace as commissioned by the state, by a state supreme court justice, superior court judge, or circuit court judge, and by judges of the United States appointed pursuant to Article III of the United States Constitution, by bankruptcy judges appointed pursuant to Article I of the United States Constitution, or by United States magistrate judges appointed pursuant to federal law; or

II. In a religious ceremony by any minister of the gospel in the state who has been ordained according to the usage of his or her denomination, resides in the state, and is in regular standing with the denomination; by any member of the clergy who is not ordained but is engaged in the service of the religious body to which he or she belongs, and who resides in the state, after being licensed therefore by the secretary of state; or within his or her parish, by any minister residing out of the state, but having a pastoral charge wholly or partly in this state.

What You Need to Know

Only ministers who are not New Hampshire residents are required to register with the New Hampshire Town Clerk's office. The application fee is $25 and the minister must be at least 18 years of age.

For ordained or unordained ministers residing outside the state:

The secretary of state may issue a special license to an ordained minister or unordained minister who resides outside of New Hampshire to perform a single marriage in New Hampshire. An application, available through the Secretary of State's Office (or the above link) is required, along with the statutory fee of $25.00. A special license will be issued to perform one marriage only. This special license is required to be filed with the regular marriage license which the couple obtained from the town or city clerk.

For unordained ministers residing in the state:

The secretary of state may issue a license to an unordained clergy who is a resident of New Hampshire and who is a member of and engaged in the service of a religious body which is chartered by the state if he or she presents a certification from that body that he or she is in its service, together with an application and the statutory fee of $5.00. The license issued by the secretary of state shall authorize the clergy to solemnize marriages in New Hampshire as long as he/she retains a good standing in his/her religious body.

For an individual who resides outside of New Hampshire, who is authorized or licensed by law in their state of residence to perform marriages:

The secretary of state may issue a special license to an individual residing out of state who is authorized or licensed by law to perform marriages in such individual's state of residence, authorizing him or her in a special case to marry a couple within the state. The secretary of state may require the submission of a copy of a valid commission or other indicia of authority to marry in the individual's state of residence as proof of existence of that authority. The names and residences of the couple proposed to be married in such special case shall be stated in the license, and no power shall be conferred to marry any other parties than those named therein. The fee for such license shall be $25.00.

The application to perform marriages in New Hampshire is now available online here:

http://sos.nh.gov/WorkArea/DownloadAsset.aspx?id=8589950435

For more information you may contact the Secretary of State's Office at 603-271-3242 or contact the Bureau of Vital Records at 603-271-4651.

What Couples Need To Know

Where do couples apply for a license? City or Town Clerk

What are the age requirements? Applicants 18 and over can marry without parental consent.

Non-residents under the age of 18 may not marry in New Hampshire.

No female below the age of 13 or male below the age of 14 may be married in New Hampshire under any conditions.

Female applicants between the ages of 13 and 17 and male applicants between the ages of 14 and 17 can only be married with a waiver and permission from their parent or legal guardian.

How much does a license cost? $45. Be prepared to pay cash or check. Marriage certificates cost $15.

What documents are needed? Valid picture identification (with Date of Birth). Acceptable forms of identification include:

Valid driver's license or identification card from Department of Motor Vehicles.

Valid Passport

Valid Military card

Original or certified birth certificate (Foreign birth certificates must be translated into English and notarized).

Applicants should be prepared to furnish their social security number.

Are there residency requirements? No.

Is there a waiting period? No.

How long is a license valid? 90 Days.

Where is a license valid for use? The State of New Hampshire.

What if someone has been married previously? A certified copy of a death certificate of a former spouse, if applicant is widowed; a certified copy of a final divorce decree, if the applicant is divorced; a certified copy of an annulment decree, if the applicant's previous marriage was annulled. Note: This must be a certified copy of the decree. If your decree has an official seal and the judges signature this may be taken in lieu of a certified decree.

Are there any required tests? No.

Are proxy marriages allowed? No.

Can cousins marry? No.

Are common law marriages recognized? No.

How to Handle the Marriage License

Read and follow the instructions which come with the license on how to fill out your section, and ensure all other sections have been fully and correctly completed.

Ministers must send a copy of the marriage license to the town clerk within six days.

The Celebrant is not required to keep records of marriages.

New Jersey Wedding Officiant Regulations

Statute 37:1-13. Authorization to solemnize marriages and civil unions.

Each judge of the United States Court of Appeals for the Third Circuit, each judge of a federal district court, United States magistrate, judge of a municipal court, judge of the Superior Court, judge of a tax court, retired judge of the Superior Court or Tax Court, or judge of the Superior Court or Tax Court, the former County Court, the former County Juvenile and Domestic Relations Court, or the former County District Court who has resigned in good standing, surrogate of any county, county clerk and any mayor or the deputy mayor when authorized by the mayor, or chairman of any township committee or village president of this State, and every minister of every religion, are hereby authorized to solemnize marriages or civil unions between such persons as may lawfully enter into the matrimonial relation or civil union; and every religious society, institution or organization in this State may join together in marriage or civil union such persons according to the rules and customs of the society, institution or organization.

What You Need to Know

An Officiant must be over 18 years of age to perform a legal marriage.

In the state of New Jersey you are not required to register with the government before performing a marriage ceremony. However, you should be prepared to produce proof of ordination by a recognized body, in the event that this is ever requested. If you have any questions regarding the legality of your ordination in this state you should contact your local government office, or your ordination body itself.

What Couples Need To Know

Where do couples apply for a license? Local Registrar.

The marriage license application is to be made in the New Jersey municipality in which either party resides and the license is valid throughout the State of New Jersey.

If neither applicant is a New Jersey resident, submit the application in the municipality where the marriage ceremony will be performed. Such license is only valid in the issuing municipality.

What are the age requirements? If you are under 18 years of age, you will need both parents to give consent in front of two witnesses in order for you to receive a marriage license. Those under 16 need judicial approval. In the case of pregnancy or the birth of a child, special provisions may apply.

How much does a license cost? $28. Cash only in some locales.

What documents are needed? Picture ID such as Drivers License, and certified copies of birth certificates, or naturalization certificates, or valid passports or alien cards. US citizens also need to know their Social Security numbers.

Are there residency requirements? No.

Is there a waiting period? There is a mandatory 3 day waiting period before your license is issued to you. In most states, the waiting period does not include Saturdays,

Sundays or federal holidays. In some instances, the day the application is filed is not included within the waiting period timeline.

How long is a license valid? 30 Days.

Where is a license valid for use? The State of New Jersey.

If neither applicant is a New Jersey resident, submit the application in the municipality where the marriage ceremony will be performed. Such license is only valid in the issuing municipality.

What if someone has been married previously? If you were previously married, the date of your divorce or the date of your spouse's death must be provided. Bring a certified copy of the divorce decree or death certificate. If necessary, a copy of your divorce records or spouse's death certificate can be ordered from your local vital records office and mailed to you.

Are there any required tests? No.

Are proxy marriages allowed? No.

Can cousins marry? Yes.

Are common law marriages recognized? No.

How to Handle the Marriage License

Read and follow the instructions which come with the license on how to fill out your section, and ensure all other sections have been fully and correctly completed.

The individual performing the ceremony should file the license with the registrar in the municipality where the marriage took place within 5 days of the wedding.

The Celebrant is not required to keep records of marriages.

New Mexico Wedding Officiant Regulations

Statute 40-1-2. Marriages solemnized; ordained clergy or civil magistrates may solemnize.

A. The civil contract of marriage is entered into when solemnized as provided in Chapter 40, Article 1 NMSA 1978. As used in Chapter 40, Article 1 NMSA 1978, 'solemnize' means to join in marriage before witnesses by means of a ceremony.

B. A person who is an ordained member of the clergy or who is an authorized representative
of a federally recognized Indian nation, tribe or pueblo may solemnize the contract of marriage without regard to sect or rites and customs the person may practice.

C. Active or retired judges, justices and magistrates of any of the courts established by the constitution of New Mexico, United States constitution, laws of the state or laws of the United States are civil magistrates having authority to solemnize contracts of marriage. Civil magistrates solemnizing contracts of marriage shall charge no fee therefor.

What You Need to Know

An Officiant must be over 18 years of age to perform a legal marriage.

In the state of New Mexico you are not required to register with the government before performing a marriage ceremony. However, you should be prepared to produce proof of ordination by a recognized body, in the event that this is ever requested. If you have any questions regarding the legality of your ordination in this state you should contact your local government office, or your ordination body itself.

What Couples Need To Know

Where do couples apply for a license? County Clerk's Office.

What are the age requirements? If the applicant is 16 or 17, parental consent is required.

If the applicant is 15 years of age a court order is required.

How much does a license cost? $25+. Cash only.

What documents are needed?

A legal picture ID, or birth certificate.

Proof of Social Security number.

Couples living in foreign countries need a passport.

Are there residency requirements? No.

Is there a waiting period? No.

How long is a license valid? 1 Year.

Where is a license valid for use? The State of New Mexico.

What if someone has been married previously? If previously married, the date of divorce or date of spouse's death must be supplied.

Are there any required tests? No.

Are proxy marriages allowed? No.

Can cousins marry? Yes.

Are common law marriages recognized? No.

How to Handle the Marriage License

Read and follow the instructions which come with the license on how to fill out your section, and ensure all other sections have been fully and correctly completed.

Ministers must provide the county clerk with a marriage certificate within 90 days after the marriage.

The Celebrant is not required to keep records of marriages.

New York Wedding Officiant Regulations

Statute § 11. By whom a marriage must be solemnized.

No marriage shall be valid unless solemnized by either:

1. A clergyman or minister of any religion, or by the senior leader, or any of the other leaders, of The Society for Ethical Culture in the city of New York, having its principal office in the borough of Manhattan, or by the leader of The Brooklyn Society for Ethical Culture, having its principal office in the borough of Brooklyn of the city of New York, or of the Westchester Ethical Society, having its principal office in Westchester county, or of the Ethical Culture Society of Long Island, having its principal office in Nassau county, or of the Riverdale-Yonkers Ethical Society having its principal office in Bronx county, or by the leader of any other Ethical Culture Society affiliated with the American Ethical Union; provided that no clergyman or minister as defined in section two of the religious corporations law, or Society for Ethical Culture leader shall be required to solemnize any marriage when acting in his or her capacity under this subdivision. 1-a. A refusal by a clergyman or minister as defined in section two of the religious corporations law, or Society for Ethical Culture leader to solemnize any marriage under this subdivision shall not create a civil claim or cause of action or result in any state or local government action to penalize, withhold benefits or discriminate against such clergyman or minister.

2. The current or a former governor, a mayor of a village, a county executive of a county, or a mayor, recorder, city magistrate, police justice or police magistrate of a city, a former mayor or the city clerk of a city of the first class of over one million inhabitants or any of his or her deputies or not more than four regular clerks, designated by him or her for such purpose as provided in section eleven-a of this article, except that in cities which contain more than one hundred thousand and less than one million inhabitants, a marriage shall be solemnized by the mayor, or police justice, and by no other officer of such city, except as provided in subdivisions one and three of this section.

3. A judge of the federal circuit court of appeals for the second circuit, a judge of a federal district court for the northern, southern, eastern or western district of New York, a judge of the United States court of international trade, a federal administrative law judge presiding in this state, a justice or judge of a court of the unified court system, a housing judge of the civil court of the city of New York, a retired justice or judge of the unified court system or a retired housing judge of the civil court of the city of New York certified pursuant to paragraph (k) of subdivision two of section two hundred twelve of the judiciary law, the clerk of the appellate division of the supreme court in each judicial department, a retired city clerk who served for more than ten years in such capacity in a city having a population of one million or more or a county clerk of a county wholly within cities having a population of one million or more; or, 3-a. A judge or peacemaker judge of any Indian tribal court, a chief, a headman, or any member of any tribal council or other governing body of any nation, tribe or band of Indians in this state duly designated by such body for the purpose of officiating at marriages, or any other persons duly designated by such body, in keeping with the culture and traditions of any such nation, tribe or band of Indians in this state, to officiate at marriages.

4. A written contract of marriage signed by both parties and at least two witnesses, all of whom shall subscribe the same within this state, stating the place of residence of each of the parties and witnesses and the date and place of marriage, and acknowledged before a judge of a court of record of this state by the parties and witnesses in the manner required for the acknowledgment of a conveyance of real estate to entitle the same to be recorded.

5. Notwithstanding any other provision of this article, where either or both of the parties is under the age of eighteen years a marriage shall be solemnized only by those authorized in subdivision one of this section or by (1) the mayor of a city or village, or county executive of a county, or by (2) a judge of the federal circuit court of appeals for the second circuit, a judge of a federal district court for the northern, southern, eastern or western district of New York, a judge of the United States court of international trade, or a justice or a judge of a court of the unified court system, or by (3) a housing judge of the civil court of the city of New York, or by (4) a former mayor or the clerk of a city of the first class of over one million inhabitants or any of his or her deputies designated by him or her for such purposes as provided in section eleven-a of this chapter.

6. Notwithstanding any other provisions of this article to the contrary no marriage shall be solemnized by a public officer specified in this section, other than a judge of a federal district court for the northern, southern, eastern or western district of New York, a judge of the United States court of international trade, a federal administrative law judge presiding in this state, a judge or justice of the unified court system of this state, a housing judge of the civil court of the city of New York, or a retired judge or justice of

the unified court system or a retired housing judge of the civil court certified pursuant to paragraph (k) of subdivision two of section two hundred twelve of the judiciary law, nor by any of the persons specified in subdivision three-a of this section, outside the territorial jurisdiction in which he or she was elected, appointed or duly designated. Such a public officer, however, elected or appointed within the city of New York may solemnize a marriage anywhere within such city.

7. The term 'clergyman' or 'minister' when used in this article, shall include those defined in section two of the religious corporations law. The word 'magistrate', when so used, includes any person referred to in the second or third subdivision.

§ 11-b. Registration of persons performing marriage ceremonies in the city of New York.

Every person authorized by law to perform the marriage ceremony, before performing any such ceremonies in the city of New York, shall register his or her name and address in the office of the city clerk of the city of New York. Every such person, before performing any marriage ceremonies subsequent to a change in his or her address, shall likewise register such change of address. Such city clerk is hereby empowered to cancel the registration of any person so registered upon satisfactory proof that the registration was fraudulent, or upon satisfactory proof that such person is no longer entitled to perform such ceremony.

What You Need to Know

In all New York of New York state you must be over 18 years of age to solemnize a marriage.

Registration requirements in New York state vary depending on the particular policies of the County, City, or Town in which the marriage takes place. All Celebrants planning to perform a legal marriage ceremony within New York City; defined as Bronx, Brooklyn, Manhattan, Queens, and Staten Island, are required to register with the City Clerk prior to the ceremony. Outside these areas, you should contact the local Clerk's office as soon as possible to ascertain the particular requirements for the location of the planned ceremony.

To register as a Marriage Officiant in New York City, you can either mail in your application to the address below, or begin your application online by visiting:
https://www1.nyc.gov/cityclerkformsonline/
You will need to provide the following documents:
Your Ordination Certificate

A Letter of Good Standing (addressed to the New York City Clerk)
A Completed New York City Marriage Officiant Registration Form
Valid ID

Your ordination body should be able to provide these documents upon request, and they will also be able to answer any questions you have about the registration requirements for your particular location.

For more detailed information regarding eligibility and the application process, I encourage you to visit:

http://www.cityclerk.nyc.gov/html/marriage/Officiant_reg.shtml

The Manhattan City Clerk's Office:

Hours: 8:30 am to 3:45 pm, Monday through Friday

141 Worth Street

New York, NY 10013

What Couples Need To Know

Where do couples apply for a license? The Town or City Clerk.

What are the age requirements? If either you or your prospective spouse is under the age of 16 years, you are required to have written parental consent to obtain a Marriage License.

You will need a government issued photo ID.

Be prepared to show proof of your date of birth. You may show one of the following forms of identification to prove your age:

- Original or certified copy of birth certificate
- Baptismal record
- Passport
- Driver license
- Naturalization record
- Court records

Both of your parents must be present to consent and have proper identification at the time of application for the Marriage License and at the Marriage Ceremony if the ceremony is performed in our offices.

If one parent is deceased, the surviving parent must appear and a death certificate for the deceased parent must be produced.

If both parents are deceased, the legal guardian must appear instead and show proof of legal guardianship.

If either prospective spouse is under the age of sixteen years, in addition to parental consent, the written approval of a Judge of the Supreme Court or Family Court is needed.

A person under the age of fourteen years cannot be married.

How much does a license cost? $40 outside of New York City limits or $35 in NYC.

What documents are needed? The application is an affidavit where you and your prospective spouse must list your name; current address; city, state, ZIP code and country; country of birth; date of birth; name and country of birth of your parents; Social Security number; and marital history.

When you sign the affidavit, you are making a sworn statement that there are no legal impediments to the marriage.

Eight forms of identification are accepted. Expired identification is not accepted.

Driver License with photograph (from the United States of America or any of its territories)

Non-Driver Identification Card with photograph (from the United States of America or any of its territories)

Learner Permit with photograph (from the United States of America or any of its territories)

Active United States Military Identification Card

Passport

United States Certificate of Naturalization (good for 10 years after date of issue)

United States Permanent Resident Card

United States Employment Authorization Card

Are there residency requirements? No.

Is there a waiting period? Yes. A 24 hour waiting period after you and your prospective spouse obtain your license is required by New York State Law.

If you and your prospective spouse must marry before the 24 hour waiting period is over, you can request a Judicial Waiver from the County Clerk in the county (borough) where you obtained your Marriage License.

When both applicants are 16 years of age or older, the 24-hour waiting period may be waived by an order of a justice of the Supreme Court or a judge of the County Court of the county (borough) which either of the applicants resides.

If either person is under 16 years of age, the order must be from the Family Court judge of the county (borough) in which the person under 16 years of age resides.

How long is a license valid? 60 Days.

Where is a license valid for use? New York State.

What if someone has been married previously? If you were married before, you must list all prior marriages. You must include your previous spouse's full name; the date the divorce decree was granted; and the city, state, and country where the divorce was issued.

All divorces, annulments, and dissolutions must be finalized before you apply for a new Marriage License.

You may be asked to produce the final divorce decree.

If your spouse is deceased, you must provide such spouse's full name and date of death.

Documents must be originals or certified copies.

Are there any required tests? No.

Are proxy marriages allowed? No.

Can cousins marry? No.

Are common law marriages recognized? No.

How to Handle the Marriage License

Read and follow the instructions which come with the license on how to fill out your section, and ensure all other sections have been fully and correctly completed.

Celebrants must complete a marriage license and return it to the town or city clerk who issued the marriage license within 5 days after the marriage.

The Celebrant is not required to keep records of marriages.

North Carolina Wedding Officiant Regulations

Statute § 51-1. Requisites of marriage; solemnization.

A valid and sufficient marriage is created by the consent of a male and female person who may lawfully marry, presently to take each other as husband and wife, freely, seriously and plainly expressed by each in the presence of the other, either:

(1) a. In the presence of an ordained minister of any religious denomination, a minister authorized by a church, or a magistrate; and

b. With the consequent declaration by the minister or magistrate that the persons are husband and wife; or

(2) In accordance with any mode of solemnization recognized by any religious denomination, or federally or State recognized Indian Nation or Tribe.

Marriages solemnized before March 9, 1909, by ministers of the gospel licensed, but not ordained, are validated from their consummation.

§ 51-1.1. Certain marriages performed by ministers of Universal Life Church validated.

Any marriages performed by ministers of the Universal Life Church prior to July 3, 1981, are validated, unless they have been invalidated by a court of competent jurisdiction, provided that all other requirements of law have been met and the marriages would have been valid if performed by an official authorized by law to perform wedding ceremonies. (1981, c. 797.)

What You Need to Know

An Officiant must be over 18 years of age to perform a legal marriage.

In the state of North Carolina you are not required to register with the government before performing a marriage ceremony. However, you should be prepared to produce proof of ordination by a recognized body, in the event that this is ever requested. If you have any questions regarding the legality of your ordination in this state you should contact your local government office, or your ordination body itself. In a few counties in North Carolina, Ministers practicing under license from the Universal Life Church have been asked to provide further credentials to support their ordination status.

What Couples Need To Know

Where do couples apply for a license? Register of Deeds

What are the age requirements? All applicants, including those not present, must provide a form of identification.

Applicants 21 and over may use a valid driver's license, valid Military I.D, State ID, passport or certified birth certificate.

Applicants 18 to 21 must present a certified copy of their birth certificate.

Applicants 16 and 17 must present a consent form signed by the parent, individual, agency or institution having legal custody or serving as the legal guardian of the underage party. A certified copy of the birth certificate is also required. The consent form must be notarized.

Applicants 14 and 15 must provide a certified copy of the court order authorizing the marriage. A certified copy of the birth certificate is also required.

A marriage license may not be issued to applicants under 14 years of age.

How much does a license cost? $60. ($10 for a copy of the marriage certificate which can be pre-ordered)

What documents are needed?

Proof of Social Security number. Either the Social Security card, a 1040 or W2.

A current and valid government issued photo ID, such as a driver's license, passport, etc.

Are there residency requirements? No.

Is there a waiting period? No.

How long is a license valid? 60 Days.

Where is a license valid for use? The State of North Carolina.

What if someone has been married previously? If either the bride or groom has been divorced, he or she must know the month and year of the last divorce. If there has been a divorce within the last 60 days, the state requires a copy of the divorce decree signed by the judge.

Are there any required tests? No.

Are proxy marriages allowed? No.

Can cousins marry? Yes. (Not first)

Are common law marriages recognized? No.

How to Handle the Marriage License

Read and follow the instructions which come with the license on how to fill out your section, and ensure all other sections have been fully and correctly completed.

Ministers must complete the marriage license and return it to the register of deeds that issued it within 10 days or incur a $200 fine.

The Celebrant is not required to keep records of marriages.

North Dakota Wedding Officiant Regulations

Statute 14-03-09. Who may solemnize marriages.

Marriages may be solemnized at any location within the state by:

1. All judges of courts of record;

2. Municipal judges;

3. Recorders, unless the board of county commissioners designates a different official;

4. Ordained ministers of the gospel, priests, and clergy, authorized by recognized denominations; and

5. By any individual authorized by the rituals and practices of any religious persuasion.

What You Need to Know

An Officiant must be over 18 years of age to perform a legal marriage.

In the state of North Dakota you are not required to register with the government before performing a marriage ceremony. However, you should be prepared to produce proof of ordination by a recognized body, in the event that this is ever requested. If you have any questions regarding the legality of your ordination in this state you should contact your local government office, or your ordination body itself.

What Couples Need To Know

Where do couples apply for a license? Register of Deeds

What are the age requirements? If a person is between 16 and 18 years of age, a marriage license may not be issued without the consent of the parents or guardian. This requires a notarized statement.

A marriage license may not be issued to any person below the age of 16, notwithstanding the consent of the parents or guardian of said person.

How much does a license cost? $65. Some counties require cash only.

What documents are needed? Picture ID is required of each. Drivers License or certified copy of Birth Certificate.

Are there residency requirements? No.

Is there a waiting period? No.

How long is a license valid? 60 Days.

Where is a license valid for use? The State of North Dakota

What if someone has been married previously? If divorced, state law requires that they receive a certified copy of the Divorce Decree to keep with the Marriage License Application.

If widowed, law requires that they receive a plain copy of the Death Certificate of the deceased spouse.

Are there any required tests? No.

Are proxy marriages allowed? No.

Can cousins marry? No.

Are common law marriages recognized? No.

How to Handle the Marriage License

Read and follow the instructions which come with the license on how to fill out your section, and ensure all other sections have been fully and correctly completed.

Ministers must file a certificate of marriage with the county judge who issued the license within 5 days after the marriage. Certificates must also be given to the persons married.

The Celebrant is not required to keep records of marriages.

Ohio Wedding Officiant Regulations

Statute 3101.08 Who may solemnize marriages.

An ordained or licensed minister of any religious society or congregation within this state who is licensed to solemnize marriages, a judge of a county court in accordance with section 1907.18 of the Revised Code, a judge of a municipal court in accordance with section 1901.14 of the Revised Code, a probate judge in accordance with section 2101.27 of the Revised Code, the mayor of a municipal corporation in any county in which such municipal corporation wholly or partly lies, the superintendent of the state school for the deaf, or any religious society in conformity with the rules of its church, may join together as husband and wife any persons who are not prohibited by law from being joined in marriage.

What You Need to Know

The state of Ohio requires that all Celebrants wishing to perform a legal marriage ceremony register with the state. The current registration process is described as follows:

Consult an attorney or Ohio Revised Code Chapter 3101 for information on legal requirements.

Obtain the application (PDF) or contact our office at (614) 728-9200 to have the application mailed to you.

Complete the application:

The name of the minister provided on the application must match the name of the minister on the attached credentials.

Please provide the applicant's mailing address and an email address and/or telephone number which will be used to contact you if there are questions regarding the application.

Please provide the name of the Religious Society or Congregation. The religious society or congregation name on the application must match the name on the credentials.

Please attach a copy of the minister's credentials issued from the religious society or congregation. Credentials may come in the form of a certificate or a letter. The credentials must state the applicant is a regularly ordained or licensed minister of the religious society or congregation.

Enclose the required filing fee of $10.00 in a check or money order made payable to 'Ohio Secretary of State.'

Documents may be mailed or delivered personally to our office and will be processed within 2-3 business days.

Mail or deliver application to:

Ohio Secretary of State
Client Service Center
180 E. Broad Street, Suite 103
Columbus, OH 43215

You can download a copy of the application form here:
http://www.sos.state.oh.us/sos/upload/records/forms/8001.pdf
There is a shot list of Frequently Asked Questions here:
http://www.sos.state.oh.us/SOS/recordsIndexes/MinisterLicense/faq.aspx
The State also maintains a searchable listing of registered Celebrants here:
http://www2.sos.state.oh.us/pls/minister/f?p=241:1:16689814507812:::::

What Couples Need To Know

Where do couples apply for a license? Probate Court. You must apply in the county in which you want to get married.

What are the age requirements? If you are 18 to 21 years of age, you will need to show your birth certificate. Persons aged 16-17 must have consent to marry from parents or legal guardians and may have to contact the Probate Court. Additionally, the Jude ay require the minors to state that they have received marriage counseling that is satisfactory to the court.

How much does a license cost? $40+ depending on county.

What documents are needed? Government issued ID such as drivers license, visa, passport, state ID. You need to know your social security numbers.

Are there residency requirements? No.

Is there a waiting period? No.

How long is a license valid? 60 Days.

Where is a license valid for use? The State of Ohio.

What if someone has been married previously? Bring certified copy of divorce decree or a copy of deceased spouse's death certificate.

Are there any required tests? No.

Are proxy marriages allowed? No.

Can cousins marry? No.

Are common law marriages recognized? Yes.

How to Handle the Marriage License

Read and follow the instructions which come with the license on how to fill out your section, and ensure all other sections have been fully and correctly completed.

Ministers must send a certificate of marriage to the probate judge of the county which issued the marriage license within 30 days after the marriage.

The Celebrant is not required to keep records of marriages.

Oklahoma Wedding Officiant Regulations

Statute 43:7 Solemnization of marriages.

A. All marriages must be contracted by a formal ceremony performed or solemnized in the presence of at least two adult, competent persons as witnesses, by a judge or retired judge of any court in this state, or an ordained or authorized preacher or minister of the Gospel, priest or other ecclesiastical dignitary of any denomination who has been duly ordained or authorized by the church to which he or she belongs to preach the Gospel, or a rabbi and who is at least eighteen (18) years of age.

B. 1. The judge shall place his or her order of appointment on file with the office of the court clerk of the county in which he or she resides.

2. The preacher, minister, priest, rabbi, or ecclesiastical dignitary who is a resident of this state shall have filed, in the office of the court clerk of the county in which he or she resides, a copy of the credentials or authority from his or her church or synagogue authorizing him or her to solemnize marriages.

3. The preacher, minister, priest, rabbi, or ecclesiastical dignitary who is not a resident of this state, but has complied with the laws of the state of which he or she is a

resident, shall have filed once, in the office of the court clerk of the county in which he or she intends to perform or solemnize a marriage, a copy of the credentials or authority from his or her church or synagogue authorizing him or her to solemnize marriages.

4. The filing by resident or nonresident preachers, ministers, priests, rabbis, ecclesiastical dignitaries or judges shall be effective in and for all counties of this state; provided, no fee shall be charged for such recording.

C. No person herein authorized to perform or solemnize a marriage ceremony shall do so unless the license issued therefor be first delivered into his or her possession nor unless he or she has good reason to believe the persons presenting themselves before him or her for marriage are the identical persons named in the license, and for whose marriage the same was issued, and that there is no legal objection or impediment to such marriage.

D. Marriages between persons belonging to the society called Friends, or Quakers, the spiritual assembly of the Baha'is, or the Church of Jesus Christ of Latter Day Saints, which have no ordained minister, may be solemnized by the persons and in the manner prescribed by and practiced in any such society, church, or assembly.

What You Need to Know

By law, those performing marriage ceremonies in the State of Oklahoma must record their credentials with the Court Clerk's Office. Ministers who live outside Oklahoma who desire to perform a marriage ceremony in our State also must file their credentials with the Court Clerk prior to conducting the service. No fee is required.

The application procedure varies by county however all Court Clerk's offices require a signed document from the minister's church to be submitted with their application. The most commonly requested documents are:

Ordination Certificate

Letter of Good Standing

You should be able to obtain these documents from your body of ordination.

What Couples Need To Know

Where do couples apply for a license? The County Clerk.

What are the age requirements? If under 18 your parents must appear at the courthouse with the couple to sign a consent form. Minors must wait three days before the marriage license is valid.

How much does a license cost? $50. However, you can have this reduced to only $5 by completing an eligible premarital counseling program such as those offered by The Oklahoma Marriage Initiative.

What documents are needed? Drivers License, certified birth certificate, passport or his or her Social Security number.

Are there residency requirements? No.

Is there a waiting period? No. However, minors must wait three days before the marriage license is valid.

How long is a license valid? 10 Days.

Where is a license valid for use? The State of Oklahoma.

What if someone has been married previously? Bring certified copy of divorce decree or a copy of deceased spouse's death certificate.

Are there any required tests? No.

Are proxy marriages allowed? No.

Can cousins marry? No.

Are common law marriages recognized? Yes.

How to Handle the Marriage License

Read and follow the instructions which come with the license on how to fill out your section, and ensure all other sections have been fully and correctly completed.

Ministers must complete a certificate of marriage and return it to the clerk or judge who issued the marriage license.

The Celebrant is not required to keep records of marriages.

Oregon Wedding Officiant Regulations

Statute § 106.120 Who may solemnize marriage

(1) As used in this section, judicial officer means:

(a) A judicial officer of this state as that term is defined in ORS 1.210 (Judicial officer defined) and includes but is not limited to a judge of a municipal court and a justice of the peace.

(b) An active judge of a federal court.

(c) An active United States magistrate judge.

(2) Marriages may be solemnized by:

(a) A judicial officer;

(b) A county clerk;

(c) Religious congregations or organizations as indicated in ORS 106.150 (Form of solemnization) (2); or

(d) A clergyperson of any religious congregation or organization who is authorized by the congregation or organization to solemnize marriages.

(3) A person authorized to solemnize marriages under subsection (2) of this section may solemnize a marriage anywhere in this state.

§ 106.150 Form of solemnization

(1) In the solemnization of a marriage no particular form is required except that the parties thereto shall assent or declare in the presence of the clergyperson, county clerk or judicial officer solemnizing the marriage and in the presence of at least two witnesses, that they take each other to be husband and wife.

(2) All marriages, to which there are no legal impediments, solemnized before or in any religious organization or congregation according to the established ritual or form commonly practiced therein, are valid. In such case, the person presiding or officiating in the religious organization or congregation shall deliver to the county clerk who issued the marriage license the application, license and record of marriage in accordance with ORS 106.170

What You Need to Know

An Officiant must be over 18 years of age to perform a legal marriage.

In the state of Oregon you are not required to register with the government before performing a marriage ceremony. However, you should be prepared to produce proof of ordination by a recognized body, in the event that this is ever requested. If you have any questions regarding the legality of your ordination in this state you should contact your local government office, or your ordination body itself.

What Couples Need To Know

Where do couples apply for a license? County Clerk's Office.
What are the age requirements? Legal marriage is 18.

Anyone not yet 17 years of age cannot legally be married in the State of Oregon. A 17 year old can be married if they have the parent's or guardian's consent.

How much does a license cost? Between $50 and $60. Cash only.

What documents are needed? Drivers license or certified birth certificate or passport and his or her Social Security number.

Are there residency requirements? No.

Is there a waiting period? 3 Days from issue to use.

How long is a license valid? 60 Days.

Where is a license valid for use? The State of Oregon.

What if someone has been married previously? A license can be issued one day after the final date of a divorce. The final divorce date is required on the marriage license application.

Are there any required tests? No.

Are proxy marriages allowed? No.

Can cousins marry? No.

Are common law marriages recognized? No.

How to Handle the Marriage License

Read and follow the instructions which come with the license on how to fill out your section, and ensure all other sections have been fully and correctly completed.

The minister must send a marriage certificate to the county clerk who issued the marriage license within one month after the marriage.

The Celebrant is not required to keep records of marriages.

Pennsylvania Wedding Officiant Regulations

Statute § 1503. Persons qualified to solemnize marriages.

(a)   General rule.--The following are authorized to solemnize marriages between persons that produce a marriage license issued under this part:

(1) A justice, judge or magisterial district judge of this Commonwealth.

(2)   A former or retired justice, judge or magisterial district judge of this Commonwealth who is serving as a senior judge or senior magisterial district judge as provided or prescribed by law; or not serving as a senior judge or senior magisterial district judge but meets the following criteria:

(i)   has served as a magisterial district judge, judge or justice, whether or not continuously or on the same court, by election or appointment for an aggregate period equaling a full term of office;

(ii) has not been defeated for reelection or retention;

(iii) has not been convicted of, pleaded nolo contendere to or agreed to an Accelerated Rehabilitative Disposition or other probation without verdict program relative to any misdemeanor or felony offense under the laws of this Commonwealth or an equivalent offense under the laws of the United States or one of its territories or possessions, another state, the District of Columbia, the Commonwealth of Puerto Rico or a foreign nation;

(iv) has not resigned a judicial commission to avoid having charges filed or to avoid prosecution by Federal, State or local law enforcement agencies or by the Judicial Conduct Board;

(v) has not been removed from office by the Court of Judicial Discipline; and

(vi) is a resident of this Commonwealth.

(3) An active or senior judge or full-time magistrate of the District Courts of the United States for the Eastern, Middle or Western District of Pennsylvania.

(3.1) An active, retired or senior bankruptcy judge of the United States Bankruptcy Courts for the Eastern, Middle or Western District of Pennsylvania who is a resident of this Commonwealth.

(4) An active, retired or senior judge of the United States Court of Appeals for the Third Circuit who is a resident of this Commonwealth.

(5) A mayor of any city or borough of this Commonwealth.

(5.1) A former mayor of a city or borough of this Commonwealth who:

(i) has not been defeated for reelection;

(ii) has not been convicted of, pleaded nolo contendere to or agreed to an Accelerated Rehabilitative Disposition or other probation without verdict program relative to a misdemeanor or felony offense under the laws of this Commonwealth or an equivalent offense under the laws of the United States or any one of its possessions, another state, the District of Columbia, the Commonwealth of Puerto Rico or a foreign nation;

(iii) has not resigned the position of mayor to avoid having charges filed or to avoid prosecution by Federal, State or local law enforcement agencies;

(iv) has served as a mayor, whether continuously or not, by election for an aggregate of a full term in office; and

(v) is a resident of this Commonwealth.

(6) A minister, priest or rabbi of any regularly established church or congregation.

(b) Religious organizations.--Every religious society, religious institution or religious organization in this Commonwealth may join persons together in marriage when at least one of the persons is a member of the society, institution or organization, according to the rules and customs of the society, institution or organization.

(c) Marriage license needed to officiate.--No person or religious organization qualified to perform marriages shall officiate at a marriage ceremony without the parties having obtained a marriage license issued under this part.

What You Need to Know

An Officiant must be over 18 years of age to perform a legal marriage.

In the state of Pennsylvania you are not required to register with the government before performing a marriage ceremony. However, you should be prepared to produce proof of ordination by a recognized body, in the event that this is ever requested. If you have any questions regarding the legality of your ordination in this state you should contact your local government office, or your ordination body itself.

What Couples Need To Know

Where do couples apply for a license? Recorder of Deeds or Register of Wills.

What are the age requirements? A person must be at least 18 years old in order to get married without consent of an adult.

A child who is 16 or 17 can get married with the consent of a parent.

A child under 16 can get married with the consent of a judge and a parent.

How much does a license cost? Varies from county to county. Please call to confirm.

What documents are needed? A valid drivers license or official government issued photo identification as well as proof of Social Security number.

Are there residency requirements? No.

Is there a waiting period? 3 Days.

How long is a license valid? 60 Days.

Where is a license valid for use? The State of Pennsylvania.

What if someone has been married previously? If either party has been previously married, he or she must also bring proof that the previous marriage has ended, such as a divorce decree or the date on which the former spouse died, if a widower. If the document is in a language other than English it must be translated. If maiden name is re-adopted you may need to supply a Resumption of Maiden Name.

Are there any required tests? No.

Are proxy marriages allowed? No.

Can cousins marry? No, down to first cousins.

Are common law marriages recognized? No.

How to Handle the Marriage License

Read and follow the instructions which come with the license on how to fill out your section, and ensure all other sections have been fully and correctly completed.

The marriage document is in two parts. Ministers must provide a certificate of marriage to the bride and groom. Also, they must send a marriage certificate to the clerk of the orphans' court who issued the marriage license within 10 days after the marriage.

The Celebrant is not required to keep records of marriages.

Puerto Rico Wedding Officiant Regulations

Statute: Title 31. Subtitle 1. Part III. Chapter 31. Requisites Necessary to Contract Marriage

All regularly licensed or ordained priests or other ministers of the Gospel, Jewish rabbis, and the judges of the Supreme Court, judges of the Appeals Court, judges of the Court of First Instance, the judges of the United States District Court for Puerto Rico, may celebrate the marriage rites between all persons legally authorized to marry.

What You Need to Know

An Officiant must be over 18 years of age to perform a legal marriage.

In Puerto Rico you are not required to register with the government before performing a marriage ceremony. However, you should be prepared to produce proof of ordination by a recognized body, in the event that this is ever requested. If you have any questions regarding the legality of your ordination in this state you should contact your local government office, or your ordination body itself.

What Couples Need To Know

Where do couples apply for a license? The Demographic Registry Office.
(The third floor of the Plaza Las Americas Mall)
525 Avenida Franklin Delano Roosevelt
San Juan, 00918
Puerto Rico

Telephone: 1-800-866-7827

(Mon - Sat 9AM - 9PM | Sun 11AM - 7PM)

What are the age requirements? Anyone under 21 years of age must be accompanied by a parent or guardian.

Men over 18 and women over 16, but are under 21, require parent's permission.

Women under 16 and over 14 who have been seduced, with the consent of their parents or guardian, and if they denied it, with the consent of the Superior Court.

Men under 18 and over 16 who were accused of having seduced a woman over 14 and under 16 years, with the consent of their parents or guardian, and if they deny, with the permission of the Superior Court. It is necessary to prove the prosecution for the crime of seduction through the prosecution or the Sex Crimes Division of the Department of Justice.

Minors of both sexes between 18 and 20 years of age if it is proved that the woman has been raped or is in a state of pregnancy. In this case, parental consent for marriage is not required. It is necessary to prove the fact of the violation by the prosecution or the Sex Crimes Division of the Department of Justice.

Persons of 18 years and have been emancipated from their parents, or by order of a court against the will of their parents.

How much does a license cost? $150 (Fee for the I.R.S. stamp)

What documents are needed? Any person who is not a resident of Puerto Rico and wishes to get married on the island must present an affidavit, or sworn statement, certifying that they:

Are not residents of Puerto Rico

That the purpose of their visit to the Island of Puerto Rico is to get married

If a foreign citizen, that they will not stay in Puerto Rico for more than the duration specified in the permission documents to enter U.S. territory granted by the appropriate federal agency.

(An affidavit is valid for 30 days)

Medical certification that meets all the tests required for marriage in their place of residence. Such certificate will be valid for a period of ten (10) days from their expedition. After 10 days, the couple will have to get a new certification to get married.

Birth certificate copies (the names of the parties shall be recorded as they appear on the certificate).

Divorce decree (if applicable).

A couple that has a common child or children prior to marriage must bring the child(ren) birth certificate(s).

Are there residency requirements? See document and blood test notes.

Is there a waiting period? No.

How long is a license valid? 10 days.

Where is a license valid for use? Puerto Rico.

What if someone has been married previously? You will need to provide a copy of the divorce decree. If your former spouse is deceased, you will need to provide a copy of the death decree.

For women, if you want to get married before 301 days have elapsed since the divorce, you must bring a certificate from a gynecologist certifying whether you are or not in a state of pregnancy.

If either party or both were recently divorced, you may not marry within thirty (30) days of notification of the divorce becoming final and binding. The only exception is renounced to the term of 30 days at the time of divorce and a waiver is recorded in the divorce certificate. This exception does not apply when it comes to divorce by mutual consent, then, in that case the 30 day period cannot be waived.

Are there any required tests? If you are a Puerto Rican resident, blood and urine tests are required. These include tests for Syphilis, Chlamydia, and Gonorrhea, and they must be conducted by a Puerto Rican physician or Federally Certified Laboratory. If you test positive for one of these diseases, you will need to show that you are under a doctor's care and treatment. Bring original results, since copies are not valid. The cost for the laboratory test in Puerto Rico ranges from $66 to $70 per person.

If you are not a Puerto Rican resident you do not have to take the blood test. However, you will need to provide a sworn statement that you are not a Puerto Rican resident.

Are proxy marriages allowed? No.

Can cousins marry? One cannot marry the ascending and descending blood (grandparents and parents, children and grandchildren) and affinity (grandparents and parents, sons and daughters). They cannot marry collaterals within the fourth degree (uncles and nephews, cousins).

When the parties are first cousins may marry only if the Court of First Instance signs a waiver with just cause. For this purpose the parties shall file a sworn petition the Court for exempting them from the prohibition.

When cousins have lived together and as a result of that union they have children, or if one or both of them are in imminent danger of death, they may marry without dispensation from the Court of First Instance, giving the facts of the case to the Superior Court of First Instance by affidavit explaining the events.

Are common law marriages recognized? No.

Are same sex marriages legal? Yes.

How to Handle the Marriage License

Read and follow the instructions which come with the license on how to fill out your section, and ensure all other sections have been fully and correctly completed.

You will need two witnesses, each over twenty one years of age, at the time of the wedding.

The Celebrant will review all these documents and if they comply with the requirements of the Demographic Registrar's Office, must sign the certificate of marriage on all its parts, using permanent black or blue ink, or typewriter (not with a ball point pen), and officiate at the ceremony. Anyone under 21 must be accompanied by a parent, properly identified, who will sign the marriage certificate in the presence of the Celebrant.

The Celebrant shall deliver the certificate, and marriage license, with all attached documents to the Demographic Registry of the municipality where the ceremony took place, during the next ten (10) days after the marriage.

Rhode Island Wedding Officiant Regulations

Statute § 15-3-5 Officials empowered to join persons in marriage.

Every ordained clergy or elder in good standing; every justice of the supreme court, superior court, family court, workers' compensation court, district court or traffic tribunal; the clerk of the supreme court; every clerk, administrative clerk, or general chief clerk of a superior court, family court, district court, or traffic tribunal; magistrates, special or general magistrates of the superior court, family court, traffic tribunal or district court; administrative clerks of the district court; administrators of the workers' compensation court; every former justice or judge and former administrator of these courts; every former chief clerk of the district court; every former clerk, administrative clerk, or general chief clerk of a superior court; the secretary of the senate; elected clerks of the general assembly;, any former secretary of the senate; any former elected clerk of the general assembly who retires after July 1, 2007; judges of the United States appointed pursuant to Article III of the United States Constitution; bankruptcy judges appointed pursuant to Article I of the United States Constitution; and United States magistrate judges appointed pursuant to federal law, may join persons in marriage in any city or town in this state; and every justice and every former justice of the municipal courts of the cities and towns in this state and of the police court of the town of Johnston and the administrator of the Johnston municipal court, while he or she is serving as an administrator, and every probate judge and every former probate judge may join persons in marriage in any city or town in this state, and wardens of the town of New Shoreham may join persons in marriage in New Shoreham.

What You Need to Know

An Officiant must be over 18 years of age to perform a legal marriage.

In the state of Rhode Island you are not required to register with the government before performing a marriage ceremony. However, you should be prepared to produce proof of ordination by a recognized body, in the event that this is ever requested. If you have any questions regarding the legality of your ordination in this state you should contact your local government office, or your ordination body itself.

What Couples Need To Know

Where do couples apply for a license? Town Clerk
For Residents:
For marriages, if the bride lives in Rhode Island, the couple should apply for the license at the clerk office in the city or town of the bride's residence. If only the groom lives in Rhode Island, the couple should apply for the license at the clerk office in the city or town of the groom's residence.

For civil unions, if either partner lives in Rhode Island, the couple should apply for the license at the clerk office in the city or town of residence of either of the individual(s).

If at least one partner lives in Rhode Island, the marriage or civil union license is valid in any city or town and the ceremony may take place anywhere in Rhode Island.

For Non-Residents:
If neither partner lives in Rhode Island, the license must be obtained at the clerk office in the city/town where the ceremony will take place. If the ceremony is performed in a city or town other than where it was issued, the validity of the marriage or civil union may be in question.

What are the age requirements? For marriages where the bride is younger than 18 or if either individual is under the control of a legal guardian, a 'Minor's Permit to Marry' must be completed by the parent or legal guardian. Please note that men younger than 18 and women younger than 16 also need a court permission to marry.

Individuals must be at least 18 years of age to form a civil union.

How much does a license cost? $24

What documents are needed? Proof of birth facts and a valid form of identification.

Are there residency requirements? No.

Is there a waiting period? No.

How long is a license valid? 90 Days.

Where is a license valid for use? The State of Rhode Island.

What if someone has been married previously? If previously married or in a civil union, a certified copy of the final decree of divorce or dissolution of the civil union (with the raised or original stamped court seal), or a certified copy of the death certificate of the previous spouse / partner.

Are there any required tests? No.

Are proxy marriages allowed? No.

Can cousins marry? Yes. A man cannot marry his aunt, but can marry his cousin. A woman, by the way, may marry her uncle providing she is Jewish.

Are common law marriages recognized? Yes.

How to Handle the Marriage License

Read and follow the instructions which come with the license on how to fill out your section, and ensure all other sections have been fully and correctly completed.

Ministers must endorse and return the marriage license to the town or city clerk in which the marriage was performed.

The Celebrant is not required to keep records of marriages.

South Carolina Wedding Officiant Regulations

Statute SECTION 20-1-20. Persons who may perform marriage ceremony.

Only ministers of the Gospel, Jewish rabbis, officers authorized to administer oaths in this State, and the chief or spiritual leader of a Native American Indian entity recognized by the South Carolina Commission for Minority Affairs pursuant to Section 1-31-40 are authorized to administer a marriage ceremony in this State.

What You Need to Know

An Officiant must be over 18 years of age to perform a legal marriage.

In the state of South Carolina you are not required to register with the government before performing a marriage ceremony. However, you should be prepared to produce proof of ordination by a recognized body, in the event that this is ever requested. If you have any questions regarding the legality of your ordination in this state you should contact your local government office, or your ordination body itself.

What Couples Need To Know

Where do couples apply for a license? Probate Court.

What are the age requirements? If you are under the age of 18, parental consent can be granted for boys who are at least 16 years old and for girls who are at least 14 years old. All minor applicants must file an original birth certificate or a certified copy of their birth certificate, which becomes a part of their permanent application record. The parent or legal guardian of a minor applicant must appear at the same time as the minor to present identification and sign a form consenting to the marriage.

If you are 18 years old or older, you do not need parental consent. But you must provide proof of your age (or simply identification if you're over age 25) by presenting one of the following:

Valid driver's license;

Original birth certificate or a certified copy of your birth certificate;

Valid South Carolina identification card issued by the South Carolina Department of Public Safety; Current military identification card;

Current passport.

How much does a license cost? Varies from county to county. Please check with the appropriate probate court. Some locales charge extra for out-of-state residents.

What documents are needed? Drivers License or other valid government ID and Social Security card or other proof of social security number.

Are there residency requirements? No.

Is there a waiting period? There is a 24-hour waiting period after the application is filed before the license can be picked up and the marriage can take place. If you want to get married on a weekend, make sure you apply for a marriage license by Thursday so you can pick up your license by Friday.

How long is a license valid? No expiration date.

Where is a license valid for use? The State of South Carolina.

What if someone has been married previously? No proof of divorce is required.

Are there any required tests? No.

Are proxy marriages allowed? No.

Can cousins marry? Yes.

Are common law marriages recognized? Yes.

How to Handle the Marriage License

Read and follow the instructions which come with the license on how to fill out your section, and ensure all other sections have been fully and correctly completed.

Ministers must complete the marriage license and give one copy to the parties and the other two must be returned to the county judge of probate who issued it within 15 days after the marriage.

The Celebrant is not required to keep records of marriages.

South Dakota Wedding Officiant Regulations

Statute 25-1-30. Persons authorized to solemnize marriages.

Marriage may be solemnized by a justice of the Supreme Court, a judge of the circuit court, a magistrate, a mayor, either within or without the corporate limits of the municipality from which the mayor was elected, or any person authorized by a church to solemnize marriages.

What You Need to Know

An Officiant must be over 18 years of age to perform a legal marriage.

In the state of South Dakota you are not required to register with the government before performing a marriage ceremony. However, you should be prepared to produce proof of ordination by a recognized body, in the event that this is ever requested. If you have any questions regarding the legality of your ordination in this state you should contact your local government office, or your ordination body itself.

What Couples Need To Know

Where do couples apply for a license? Register of Deeds.

What are the age requirements? Applicants 16 and 17 must have parental consent. South Dakota law does not permit marriage of those under 16.

How much does a license cost? $40

What documents are needed? Drivers License or a certified copy of a birth certificate.

Are there residency requirements? No.

Is there a waiting period? No.

How long is a license valid? 20 Days.

Where is a license valid for use? The State of South Dakota

What if someone has been married previously? Proof of divorce may be required.

Are there any required tests? No.

Are proxy marriages allowed? No.

Can cousins marry? No.

Are common law marriages recognized? No.

How to Handle the Marriage License

Read and follow the instructions which come with the license on how to fill out your section, and ensure all other sections have been fully and correctly completed.

The minister must send a marriage certificate to the clerk who issued the marriage license within 30 days after the marriage.

Ministers must also keep a record book of all marriages they perform.

Tennessee Wedding Officiant Regulations

Statute 36-3-301. Persons who may solemnize marriages.

(a) (1) All regular ministers, preachers, pastors, priests, rabbis and other spiritual leaders of every religious belief, more than eighteen (18) years of age, having the care of souls, and all members of the county legislative bodies, county mayors, judges, chancellors, former chancellors and former judges of this state, former county executives or county mayors of this state, former members of quarterly county courts or county commissions, the governor, the speaker of the senate and former speakers of the senate, the speaker of the house of representatives and former speakers of the house of representatives, the county clerk of each county and the mayor of any municipality in the state may solemnize the rite of matrimony. For the purposes of this section, the several judges of the United States courts, including United States magistrates and United States bankruptcy judges, who are citizens of Tennessee are deemed to be judges of this state. The amendments to this section by Acts 1987, ch. 336, which applied provisions of this section to certain former judges, do not apply to any judge who has been convicted of a felony or who has been removed from office.

(2) In order to solemnize the rite of matrimony, any such minister, preacher, pastor, priest, rabbi or other spiritual leader must be ordained or otherwise designated in conformity with the customs of a church, temple or other religious group or organization; and such customs must provide for such ordination or designation by a considered, deliberate, and responsible act.

(3) If any marriage has been entered into by license issued pursuant to this chapter at which any minister officiated before June 1, 1999, such marriage shall not be

invalid because the requirements of the preceding subdivision (2) have not been met.

(b) The traditional marriage rite of the Religious Society of Friends (Quakers), whereby the parties simply pledge their vows one to another in the presence of the congregation, constitutes an equally effective solemnization.

(c) Any gratuity received by a county mayor, county clerk or municipal mayor for the solemnization of a marriage, whether performed during or after such person's regular working hours, shall be retained by such person as personal remuneration for such services, in addition to any other sources of compensation such person might receive, and such gratuity shall not be paid into the county general fund or the treasury of such municipality.

(d) If any marriage has been entered into by license regularly issued at which a county executive officiated prior to April 24, 1981, such marriage shall be valid and is hereby declared to be in full compliance with the laws of this state.

(e) For the purposes of this section, 'retired judges of this state' is construed to include persons who served as judges of any municipal or county court in any county that has adopted a metropolitan form of government and persons who served as county judges (judges of the quarterly county court) prior to the 1978 constitutional amendments.

(f) If any marriage has been entered into by license regularly issued at which a retired judge of this state officiated prior to April 13, 1984, such marriage shall be valid and is hereby declared to be in full compliance with the laws of this state.

(g) If any marriage has been entered into by license issued pursuant to this chapter at which a judicial commissioner officiated prior to March 28, 1991, such marriage is valid and is declared to be in full compliance with the laws of this state.

(h) The judge of the general sessions court of any county, and any former judge of any general sessions court, may solemnize the rite of matrimony in any county of this state. Any marriage performed by any judge of the general sessions court in any county of this state before March 16, 1994, shall be valid and declared to be in full compliance with the laws of this state.

(i) All elected officials and former officials, who are authorized to solemnize the rite of matrimony pursuant to the provisions of subsection (a), may solemnize the rite of matrimony in any county of this state.

(j) If any marriage has been entered into by license issued pursuant to this chapter at which a county mayor officiated outside such mayor's county prior to May 29, 1997, such marriage is valid and is declared to be in full compliance with the laws of this state.

What You Need to Know

An Officiant must be over 18 years of age to perform a legal marriage.

In the state of Tennessee you are not required to register with the government before performing a marriage ceremony. However, you should be prepared to produce proof of ordination by a recognized body, in the event that this is ever requested. If you have any questions regarding the legality of your ordination in this state you should contact your local government office, or your ordination body itself.

What Couples Need To Know

Where do couples apply for a license? County Clerk

What are the age requirements? If 16 or 17 years of age the parent or guardian must accompany in applying for license.

Custodial parent must bring custody papers (if applicable) to show proof of custody.

If 15 years of age or younger court consent must also be granted before license may be issued.

How much does a license cost? $93.50 - $99.50. Costs vary from county to county.

It is possible to receive a discount of $60.00. In order to do so, you must complete a premarital preparation course in the year prior to your application date. You will need to provide a Certificate of Completion in order to receive your discount.

According to Tennessee Statutes, non-residents in some counties can receive a $60 discount upon showing the county clerk proof that they are not Tennessee residents.

What documents are needed? Proof of Social Security number plus one of the following:

State certified birth certificate

Drivers License

State issued ID

For Legal Aliens who do not have a social security number:

Passport and American Visa or Resident Alien Card.

Please know the following:

Parents full name (including maiden name of mother)

Parents state of birth and address (if living)

Applicant's number of prior marriages

Date last marriage ended (if applicable)

Are there residency requirements? No.

Is there a waiting period? An underage application includes a 3 day waiting period, but may be waived by a Court of Record or the County Mayor.

How long is a license valid? 30 Days.

Where is a license valid for use? The State of Tennessee.

What if someone has been married previously? If previously married you will need to give the number of previous marriages and the date the last marriage ended.

Are there any required tests? No.

Are proxy marriages allowed? No.

Can cousins marry? Yes.

Are common law marriages recognized? No.

How to Handle the Marriage License

Read and follow the instructions which come with the license on how to fill out your section, and ensure all other sections have been fully and correctly completed.

Ministers must endorse the marriage license and return it to the clerk of the county court within three days after the marriage.

The Celebrant is not required to keep records of marriages.

Texas Wedding Officiant Regulations

Statute Section 2.202: PERSONS AUTHORIZED TO CONDUCT CEREMONY

(a) The following persons are authorized to conduct a marriage ceremony:

(1) a licensed or ordained Christian minister or priest;

(2) a Jewish rabbi;

(3) a person who is an officer of a religious organization and who is authorized by the organization to conduct a marriage ceremony; and

(4) a justice of the supreme court, judge of the court of criminal appeals, justice of the courts of appeals, judge of the district, county, and probate courts, judge of the county courts at law, judge of the courts of domestic relations, judge of the juvenile courts, retired justice or judge of those courts, justice of the peace, retired justice of the peace, or judge or magistrate of a federal court of this state.

(b) For the purposes of this section, a retired judge or justice is a former judge or justice who is vested in the Judicial Retirement System of Texas Plan One or the Judicial Retirement System of Texas Plan Two or who has an aggregate of at least 12 years of service as judge or justice of any type listed in Subsection (a)(4).

(c) Except as provided by Subsection (d), a person commits an offense if the person knowingly conducts a marriage ceremony without authorization under this section. An offense under this subsection is a Class A misdemeanor.

(d) A person commits an offense if the person knowingly conducts a marriage ceremony of a minor whose marriage is prohibited by law or of a person who by marrying commits an offense under Section 25.01, Penal Code. An offense under this subsection is a felony of the third degree.

What You Need to Know

An Officiant must be over 18 years of age to perform a legal marriage.

In the state of Texas you are not required to register with the government before performing a marriage ceremony. However, you should be prepared to produce proof of ordination by a recognized body, in the event that this is ever requested. If you have any questions regarding the legality of your ordination in this state you should contact your local government office, or your ordination body itself.

What Couples Need To Know

Where do couples apply for a license? The County Clerk.

What are the age requirements? If you are between 16 and 17 years old, you may apply for a marriage license only if you have written parental consent on an official form in the presence of the county clerk or if you have received an order from the Texas district court authorizing your marriage.

How much does a license cost? $31 - $71. Cash only. Fees may vary from county to county.

The license fee may be waived if a couple takes an 8 hour premarital preparation course that covers important marital skills and issues such as conflict management and communication.

What documents are needed?

One valid form of ID such as drivers license, certified copy of your birth certificate, US Passport, military ID card.

Your Social Security number.

Are there residency requirements? No.

Is there a waiting period? 72 hours. This can be waived for active duty military personnel.

How long is a license valid? 30 Days.

Where is a license valid for use? The State of Texas.

What if someone has been married previously? If divorced within 30 days, Texas requires that you show a certified copy of your divorce decree stating the 30 day waiting period is waived.

Are there any required tests? No.
Are proxy marriages allowed? Yes.
Can cousins marry? No.
Are common law marriages recognized? Yes.

How to Handle the Marriage License

Read and follow the instructions which come with the license on how to fill out your section, and ensure all other sections have been fully and correctly completed.

Ministers must complete the marriage license and return it to the county clerk who issued it within 30 days after the marriage.

The Celebrant is not required to keep records of marriages.

U.S. Virgin Islands Officiant Regulations

Statute 16-32 Persons solemnizing marriage

No marriage shall be valid unless solemnized by--

(1) a clergyman or minister of any religion whether he resides in the Virgin Islands or elsewhere in the United States; or

(2) witnessed by a Local Spiritual Assembly of the Bahai is according to the usage of their religious community; or

(3) any judge or any court of record.

What You Need to Know

An Officiant must be over 18 years of age to perform a legal marriage.

In the U.S. Virgin Islands you are not required to register with the government before performing a marriage ceremony. However, you should be prepared to produce proof of ordination by a recognized body, in the event that this is ever requested. If you have any questions regarding the legality of your ordination in this state you should contact your local government office, or your ordination body itself.

What Couples Need To Know

Where do couples apply for a license? The Clerk of the Court

For St. Croix:
Justice Complex
RR1 9000
1st Floor, Room 101
Kingshill, VI 00850
Tel: (340) 778-9750
For St. Thomas-St. John:
Superior Court of the V.I.
Family Court Division
5400 Veterans Drive
St. Thomas, VI 00802
Tel: (340) 774-6680

What are the age requirements? A couple must both be 18 years of age or older to marry without consent. For women only, if she is between 16 and 18 years of age, she must have proof of parental consent. Individuals under 16 year of age cannot marry in the U.S. Virgin Islands.

How much does a license cost? $200 (If the marriage is to be performed by the Judge of the Territorial Court, there is an additional fee of $200 for the marriage ceremony.)

What documents are needed? You must fill out and submit the application form. Each applicant will need to know:
Full name and age at last birthday
Social Security Number
Date of Birth
Nationality; Place of Residence
Name of Parents (present/maiden place of birth)
Previous Marital Status (widowed, divorced, marriage annulled)

If applicants have been divorced, it is required that a certified copy of their divorce decree be filed along with the application.

Applicants should attach a letter detailing: Date of visit; Length of Stay; Date of preference if desirous of having the marriage performed by a judge.

When you appear before the Clerk of the Court, you will need:
Some form of government issued identification

The Clerk will then notarize your application. Do not have the application notarized prior to appearing before the Court.

Are there residency requirements? No.

Is there a waiting period? Virgin Islands law requires that 'before any marriage license is issued, the application for such license shall be posted for public examination in the Office of the Clerk of the Court for eight (8) days.' The law contains an exception, however, for 'special cases.' If you will not be present in the Virgin Islands for eight (8) days preceding your marriage ceremony, you may be exempted from the posting requirement under the special cases exemption. Thus, applicants presenting these or similar circumstances may be granted a marriage license without having to comply with the posting requirement. If you need an exemption from the eight-day posting requirement, check the appropriate box on the application form and include a brief explanation of your reason for the request in the space provided.

How long is a license valid? Three months from time of pickup. While at the office of the Clerk ,awaiting pickup, the license remains valid for one year.

Where is a license valid for use? U.S. Virgin Islands

What if someone has been married previously? If applicants have been divorced, it is required that a certified copy of their divorce decree be filed along with the application.

Are there any required tests? No.

Are proxy marriages allowed? No.

Can cousins marry? Yes, though not first cousins.

Are common law marriages recognized? No.

Are same sex marriages legal? Yes.

How to Handle the Marriage License

Read and follow the instructions which come with the license on how to fill out your section, and ensure all other sections have been fully and correctly completed.

Either the Celebrant or the couple can return the completed license to the court house once it has been completed. The Celebrant is not required to keep records of the marriage.

Utah Wedding Officiant Regulations

Statute 30-1-6. Who may solemnize marriages

(1)Except for a county clerk, or a county clerk's designee, as provided below, the following persons may solemnize a marriage at that person's discretion:

(a) ministers, rabbis, or priests of any religious denomination who are:

(i) in regular communion with any religious society; and

(ii)18 years of age or older;

(b)Native American spiritual advisors;

(c) the governor;

(d) the lieutenant governor;

(e) mayors of municipalities or county executives;

(f) a justice, judge, or commissioner of a court of record;

(g) a judge of a court not of record of the state;

(h) judges or magistrates of the United States;

(i) the county clerk of any county in the state or the county clerk's designee as authorized by Section 17-20-4;

(j) the president of the Senate;

(k) the speaker of the House of Representatives; or

(l) a judge or magistrate who holds office in Utah when retired, under rules set by the Supreme Court.

(2) A person authorized under Subsection (1) who solemnizes a marriage shall give to the couple married a certificate of marriage that shows the:

(a) name of the county from which the license is issued; and

(b) date of the license's issuance.

(3) As used in this section:

(a) 'Judge or magistrate of the United States' means:

(i) a justice of the United States Supreme Court;

(ii) a judge of a court of appeals;

(iii) a judge of a district court;

(iv) a judge of any court created by an act of Congress the judges of which are entitled to hold office during good behavior;

(v) a judge of a bankruptcy court;

(vi) a judge of a tax court; or

(vii) a United States magistrate.

(b)

(i) 'Native American spiritual advisor' means a person who:

(A) leads, instructs, or facilitates a Native American religious ceremony or service or provides religious counseling; and

(B) is recognized as a spiritual advisor by a federally recognized Native American tribe.

(ii) 'Native American spiritual advisor' includes a sweat lodge leader, medicine person, traditional religious practitioner, or holy man or woman.

(4) Except as provided in Section 17-20-4, and notwithstanding any other provision in law, no person authorized under Subsection (1) to solemnize a marriage may delegate or deputize another person to perform the function of solemnizing a marriage.

What You Need to Know

An Officiant must be over 18 years of age to perform a legal marriage.

In the state of Utah you are not required to register with the government before performing a marriage ceremony. However, you should be prepared to produce proof of ordination by a recognized body, in the event that this is ever requested. If you have any questions regarding the legality of your ordination in this state you should contact your local government office, or your ordination body itself.

What Couples Need To Know

Where do couples apply for a license? The County Recorder.

What are the age requirements? You must be at least 15 years old to be married in Utah. If you are over 18, you do not need consent to get married. If you are 16 or 17, you need signed consent from a parent or guardian, which must be given in person to the county clerk before a marriage license will be issued.

If you are 15 years old, you need consent from a parent or guardian, and:

The juvenile court must approve the marriage, and must conclude that the marriage is voluntary and in the best interests of the minor.

The juvenile court may require premarital counseling.

The juvenile court may impose other conditions, such as requiring the minor to continue to attend school.

If you are under 18 but you have been married before, you do not need consent a second time.

How much does a license cost? $45+ in most counties.

What documents are needed?

Valid picture ID such as a passport, birth certificate, drivers license, or state ID card.

Either bring your Social Security card or know your Social security number.

If you want to use your maiden name on the license bring a certified copy of your birth certificate or a certified copy of your divorce decree that states name is to be changed to maiden name.

Are there residency requirements? No.

Is there a waiting period? No.

How long is a license valid? 30 Days.

Where is a license valid for use? The State of Utah.

What if someone has been married previously? If previously married, the date of divorce or date of spouse's death must be provided.

Are there any required tests? No.

Are proxy marriages allowed? No.

Can cousins marry? Yes. If both cousins are over the age of 65, or over the age of 55 and can prove sterility.

Are common law marriages recognized? Yes.

How to Handle the Marriage License

Read and follow the instructions which come with the license on how to fill out your section, and ensure all other sections have been fully and correctly completed.

Ministers must provide a certificate of marriage to the county clerk who issued the marriage license within 30 days after the marriage.

The Celebrant is not required to keep records of marriages.

Vermont Wedding Officiant Regulations

Statute § 5144. Persons authorized to solemnize marriage

(a) Marriages may be solemnized by a Supreme Court Justice, a Superior judge, a judge of Probate, an assistant judge, a justice of the peace, a magistrate, a Judicial Bureau hearing officer, an individual who has registered as an Officiant with the Vermont Secretary of State pursuant to section 5144a of this title, a member of the clergy residing in this State and ordained or licensed, or otherwise regularly authorized thereunto by the published laws or discipline of the general conference, convention, or other authority of his or her faith or denomination, or by such a clergy person residing in an adjoining state or country, whose parish, church, temple, mosque, or other religious organization lies wholly or in part in this State, or by a member of the clergy residing in some other state of the United States or in the Dominion of Canada, provided he or she has first secured from the Probate Division of the Superior Court in the unit within which the marriage is to be solemnized a special authorization, authorizing him or her to certify the marriage if the Probate judge determines that the circumstances make the special authorization desirable. Marriage among the Friends or Quakers, the Christadelphian Ecclesia, and the Baha'i Faith may be solemnized in the manner heretofore used in such societies.

(b) This section does not require a member of the clergy authorized to solemnize a marriage as set forth in subsection (a) of this section, nor societies of Friends or Quakers, the Christadelphian Ecclesia, or the Baha'i Faith to solemnize any marriage, and any refusal to do so shall not create any civil claim or cause of action.

What You Need to Know

There is a great deal of variation between practices in the different counties in Vermont. I would encourage all Celebrants to contact the district probate court in their location.

All Celebrants residing outside the state of Vermont, and wishing to perform a legal marriage ceremony within that state, must register with the local probate court before doing so.

The other option for all non-resident Celebrants is to make application for a Temporary Officiant License to the Vermont Secretary of State.

Temporary Officiant Registration in Vermont

As of July 1, 2008, Title 18 of Vermont law allows the Vermont secretary of state to authorize individuals to officiate at specific marriages in Vermont. To become a temporary Officiant, an applicant must fill out a registration form and return it with a filing fee of $100 (check or money order) to:

Office of the Secretary of State
Temporary Officiant Program
128 State Street
Montpelier, Vermont 05633-1101

The applicant will then receive written authorization from the secretary of state to officiate at a specific marriage. This authorization must be attached to the marriage license that is returned to the issuing municipal clerk. Officiants must be 18 years of age, or older. Please submit the registration form at least 10 days prior to the ceremony.

You can find more information, and download the application form here: https://www.sec.state.vt.us/temporary-Officiants.aspx

What Couples Need To Know

Where do couples apply for a license? Town Clerk's Office.

What are the age requirements? If you are at least 16, but under 18, you will need the consent of a parent or guardian. They will need to go with you to the town clerk's office to sign an affidavit giving you permission to marry. No person under 16 may marry in Vermont.

How much does a license cost? $45

What documents are needed? Besides basic information about yourselves (names, towns of residence, places and dates of birth), you must also provide your parents' names, including your mothers' birth (maiden) names, and their places of birth. (Certified copies of your birth certificates can supply most of this information). You will also require a valid government issued photo ID.

Are there residency requirements? No.

Is there a waiting period? No.

How long is a license valid? 60 Days.

Where is a license valid for use? The State of Vermont.

What if someone has been married previously? If your husband, wife or civil union partner has died, you are free to marry. The clerk will ask the date your spouse or civil union partner died. If you are divorced, you may remarry after the date on which your previous marriage or civil union was legally dissolved. If you are partners in an existing civil union, you are free to marry one another.

Are there any required tests? No.

Are proxy marriages allowed? No.

Can cousins marry? No.

Are common law marriages recognized? No.

How to Handle the Marriage License

Read and follow the instructions which come with the license on how to fill out your section, and ensure all other sections have been fully and correctly completed.

After the ceremony, the Officiant will complete the license, sign it, and return it to the town clerk's office within 10 days of the ceremony so your marriage may be officially registered.

The Celebrant is not required to keep records of marriages.

Virginia Wedding Officiant Regulations

Statute § 20-23 Order authorizing ministers to perform ceremony.

When a minister of any religious denomination shall produce before the circuit court of any county or city in this Commonwealth, or before the judge of such court or before the clerk of such court at any time, proof of his ordination and of his being in regular communion with the religious society of which he is a reputed member, or proof that he is commissioned to pastoral ministry or holds a local minister's license and is serving as a regularly appointed pastor in his denomination, such court, or the judge thereof, or the clerk of such court at any time, may make an order authorizing such minister to celebrate the rites of matrimony in this Commonwealth. Any order made under this section may be rescinded at any time by the court or by the judge thereof.

What You Need to Know

Here is an example of what is required by most counties in the state of Virginia.

1) The individual must appear in person at the Circuit Court Clerk's Office during regular

business hours (9:00 a.m. to 5:00 p.m., though hours may vary by county, Monday through Friday except holidays).

2a) The individual must produce

· proof of ordination

· and a document of recent date (less than 30 days old) from his/her superior or church board stating that he/she is in good standing with the church for which he/she is ordained.

OR

2b) The individual must produce

· a local minister's license

· and a document of recent date (less than 30 days old) from his/her superior or church board stating that he/she is in good standing with the church and that he/she is serving as a regularly appointed pastor in his/her denomination.

3) The individual must also produce literature that shows when and where he/she gathers their congregation to perform their ministerial duties.

The fee for authorization is $31.00 cash or money order payable to the Clerk of Circuit Court.

Note: Your ordination body will be able to provide you with the documents you need to satisfy the requirements listed above.

Authorizations are effective immediately and are valid for marriage ceremonies performed under

a Virginia Marriage License anywhere in the Commonwealth of Virginia. There is no expiration

on the authorization.

There is still a wide degree of variation, interpretation, and discrepancy between the counties in their views on the acceptability of online ordination.

One stumbling point is the notion of 'regular communion'. A reasonable definition of this could be that Celebrants must hold valid ministerial credentials, and contact their body of ordination at least one time each year, and if any contact information should change (name, physical address, or email) be notified within two weeks of the change. This would imply that your ordination is more likely to be accepted if you (a) obtained it via a process other than one solely based online, and (b) have an ordination which requires renewal rather than having no expiry date.

You do not need to register with your local County Clerk's office or the office that issues the couple's the marriage license. Authorization from any county grants you the authority to perform marriage throughout Virginia.

Once your application is accepted, the Clerk will provide you with documentary proof of your authorization. You should keep this safe for future reference.

What Couples Need To Know

Where do couples apply for a license? Circuit Court Clerk.

What are the age requirements? The minimum age for marriage in the Commonwealth of Virginia is sixteen (16) years for both the bride and groom; however, if either party is under eighteen (18), consent to the marriage must be given by the father, mother or legal guardian. This may be done in person by the parent or legal guardian before the person issuing the license or by written consent properly sworn to before a notary public. Special provisions are made in Virginia law to allow marriage for under age parties when the female is pregnant and for situations in which under age applicants have no parent or legal guardian. A pregnant bride under age may marry without consent if they are pregnant or have been within the last nine months, have a letter from a doctor to confirm this, and are a resident. All applicants under 18 must be resident in the state.

How much does a license cost? $30

What documents are needed? Each applicant will need a Photo ID.

Applicants must, under oath, furnish information required to complete the marriage record. These items are material and the applicant may be subject to prosecution for perjury for violation of the portion of the statutes which requires this information. For divorced persons, there is no statutory waiting period before marriage after the divorce is granted unless remarriage is specifically prohibited by a court. In some cases, clerks may require documentary proof of age or termination (and date of termination) of previous marriage.

Are there residency requirements? No.

Is there a waiting period? No.

How long is a license valid? 60 days.

Where is a license valid for use? The State of Virginia.

What if someone has been married previously? For divorced persons, there is no statutory waiting period before marriage after the divorce is granted unless remarriage is specifically prohibited by a court. In some cases, clerks may require documentary proof of age or termination of previous marriage.

Are there any required tests? No.

Are proxy marriages allowed? No.

Can cousins marry? Yes. (First cousins may marry)

Are common law marriages recognized? No.

How to Handle the Marriage License

Read and follow the instructions which come with the license on how to fill out your section, and ensure all other sections have been fully and correctly completed.

Ministers must complete the marriage certificate and return it to the clerk who issued the marriage license within five days after the marriage.

The Celebrant is not required to keep records of marriages.

Washington Wedding Officiant Regulations

Statute RCW 26.04.050 Who may solemnize.

The following named officers and persons, active or retired, are hereby authorized to solemnize marriages, to wit: Justices of the supreme court, judges of the court of appeals, judges of the superior courts, supreme court commissioners, court of appeals commissioners, superior court commissioners, any regularly licensed or ordained minister or any priest, imam, rabbi, or similar official of any religious organization, and judges of courts of limited jurisdiction as defined in RCW 3.02.010.

What You Need to Know

An Officiant must be over 18 years of age to perform a legal marriage.

In the state of Washington you are not required to register with the government before performing a marriage ceremony. However, you should be prepared to produce proof of ordination by a recognized body, in the event that this is ever requested. If you have any questions regarding the legality of your ordination in this state you should contact your local government office, or your ordination body itself.

What Couples Need To Know

Where do couples apply for a license? The County Auditor.

What are the age requirements? Applicants who are 17 years of age must be accompanied by one parent or legal guardian who can provide consent.

Applicants under the age of 17 must obtain permission from the Family Court.

How much does a license cost? $32 - $62+ depending on the county.

What documents are needed? You must have a current photo ID.

Are there residency requirements? No.

Is there a waiting period? There is a mandatory 3 day waiting period before your license is issued to you. In most states, the waiting period does not include Saturdays, Sundays or federal holidays. In some instances, the day the application is filed is not included within the waiting period timeline.

How long is a license valid? 60 Days.

Where is a license valid for use? The State of Washington.

What if someone has been married previously? Proof of divorce from a previous spouse, or death of a spouse, is not required to obtain a marriage license. It is the responsibility of the applicant to ensure that the final decree of divorce is filed before applying for a new marriage license.

Are there any required tests? No.

Are proxy marriages allowed? No.

Can cousins marry? No.

Are common law marriages recognized? No.

How to Handle the Marriage License

Read and follow the instructions which come with the license on how to fill out your section, and ensure all other sections have been fully and correctly completed.

Ministers must send two certificates of marriage to the county auditor within 30 days after the marriage.

The Celebrant is not required to keep records of marriages.

West Virginia Wedding Officiant Regulations

Statute §48-2-402. Qualifications of religious representative for celebrating marriages; registry of persons authorized to perform marriage ceremonies; special revenue fund.

(a) Beginning the first day of September, two thousand one, the Secretary of State shall, upon payment of the registration fee established by the Secretary of State pursuant to subsection (d) of this section, make an order authorizing a person who is a religious representative to celebrate the rites of marriage in all the counties of the state, upon proof that the person:

(1) Is eighteen years of age or older;

(2) Is duly authorized to perform marriages by his or her church, synagogue, spiritual assembly or religious organization; and

(3) Is in regular communion with the church, synagogue, spiritual assembly or religious organization of which he or she is a member.

(b) The Secretary of State shall establish a central registry of persons authorized to celebrate marriages in this state. Every person authorized under the provisions of subsection (a) of this section to celebrate marriages shall be listed in this registry. Every county clerk shall, prior to the first day of October, two thousand one, transmit to the Secretary of State the name of every person authorized to celebrate marriages by order issued in his or her county since one thousand nine hundred sixty and the Secretary of State shall include these names in the registry. The completed registry and periodic updates shall be transmitted to every county clerk.

(c)(1) Upon written request from the registrant, the Secretary of State shall designate the registrant as inactive on the registry.

(2) Upon written notice from the governing body of the registrant's authorizing body that the registrant has died or that the registrant's authority to perform marriages has been revoked, the Secretary of State shall attempt to notify the registrant of the change in the registrant's status by United States mail addressed to the registrant's last known address. If the registrant fails to provide the Secretary of State with proof of good standing with his or her authorizing body within thirty days, the registrant shall be designated on the registry as inactive.

(d) A fee not to exceed twenty-five dollars may be charged by the Secretary of State for each registration or reactivation of an individual designated as inactive on the registry received on or after the first day of September, two thousand one, and all money received shall be deposited in a special revenue revolving fund designated the Marriage Celebrants Registration Fee Administration Fund in the State Treasury to be administered by the Secretary of State. Expenses incurred by the secretary in the implementation and operation of the registry program shall be paid from the fund.

(e) No marriage performed by a person authorized by law to celebrate marriages may be invalidated solely because the person was not listed in the registry provided for in this section.

(f) The Secretary of State shall promulgate rules to implement the provisions of this section.

§48-2-202. Endorsement and return of licenses by persons solemnizing marriage; duties of clerk pertaining thereto.

(a) The person solemnizing a marriage shall retain the marriage license and place an endorsement on it establishing the fact of the marriage and the time and place it was celebrated.

(b) Before the sixth day of the month after the month in which the marriage was celebrated, the person who solemnized the marriage shall forward the original of the marriage license to the clerk who issued the license.

(c) In the event that the marriage authorized by the license is not solemnized within sixty days from the date of its issuance, then the license is null and void. If the county clerk has not received the original license within sixty days after the expiration date on the license, the clerk shall notify each of the applicants of that fact, by certified mail, return receipt requested.

What You Need to Know

State Registration

In 2001, the West Virginia Legislature adopted S. B. 59, establishing provisions for the registration of religious representatives to be authorized to perform marriages in any county in West Virginia. These provisions are under West Virginia Code §48-2-402.

Requirements for Registration:

Proof of Age. The registrant must be 18 years of age or older, and may show proof using a photocopy of a birth certificate, driver license, passport or military ID.

Proof of Authority:

The registrant must be:

duly authorized to perform marriages by his or her church, synagogue, spiritual assembly or religious organization; and

in regular communion with that group of which he or she is a member.

Registry

The Secretary of State established a registry of all persons authorized to perform marriages. County clerks in the 55 counties forwarded to the Secretary of State the names of persons authorized since 1960 to perform marriages for inclusion in the registry.

You can find the application form by visiting the link below:
http://www.sos.wv.gov/business-licensing/licensing/Documents/m-1.pdf

Complete the application form online and print. Be sure the application is properly signed.

Provide documentation required for proof of age and proof of authority. Proof of authority has be satisfied by providing a photocopy of your license or ordination from your religious organization and having a letter signed by two people stating that you attend church regularly or a letter of good standing from your religious organization.

Mail or deliver your completed application with a fee of $25 made payable to WV Secretary of State.

To search the registry, go to the link below and select 'Ministers'.
http://apps.sos.wv.gov/business/licensing/

What Couples Need To Know

Where do couples apply for a license? County Clerk's Office.

What are the age requirements? If either of you are under 18 years of age, you must have the consent (in person) of a parent or guardian. There will be a 3 day waiting period after you apply for the license. There may be special provisions for an underage bride who is pregnant.

How much does a license cost? $36. Cash only. Fees may vary from county to county.

What documents are needed? You will need to present photo identification such as your driver's license, state ID, or passport. You will also need to know your parent's full names, including your mother's maiden names, and the states where they were born.

Are there residency requirements? No. However, if you are a West Virginia resident, you must apply in the county where you live.

Is there a waiting period? No for those 18 or over. 3 days for those under 18.

How long is a license valid? 60 days.

Where is a license valid for use? State of West Virginia.

What if someone has been married previously? Most counties will require documentation to prove a previous marriage has been dissolved either through death or divorce.

Are there any required tests? No.

Are proxy marriages allowed? No.

Can cousins marry? No.

Are common law marriages recognized? No.

How to Handle the Marriage License

Read and follow the instructions which come with the license on how to fill out your section, and ensure all other sections have been fully and correctly completed.

Ministers must return the completed marriage license to the county clerk who issued it on or before the fifth day of the month following the marriage.

The Celebrant is not required to keep records of marriages.

Wisconsin Wedding Officiant Regulations

Statute 765.16   Marriage contract, how made; officiating person.

(1m) Marriage may be validly solemnized and contracted in this state only after a marriage license has been issued therefor, and only by the mutual declarations of the 2 parties to be joined in marriage that they take each other as husband and wife, made before an authorized officiating person and in the presence of at least 2 competent adult witnesses other than the officiating person. The following are authorized to be officiating persons:

(a) Any ordained member of the clergy of any religious denomination or society who continues to be an ordained member of the clergy.

(b) Any licentiate of a denominational body or an appointee of any bishop serving as the regular member of the clergy of any church of the denomination to which the member of the clergy belongs, if not restrained from so doing by the discipline of the church or denomination.

(c) The 2 parties themselves, by mutual declarations that they take each other as husband and wife, in accordance with the customs, rules and regulations of any religious society, denomination or sect to which either of the parties may belong.

(d) Any judge of a court of record or a reserve judge appointed under s. 753.075.

(e) Any circuit court commissioner appointed under SCR 75.02 (1) or supplemental court commissioner appointed under s. 757.675 (1).

(f) Any municipal judge.

(2m) An officiating person under sub. (1m) (a), (b), (d), (e), or (f) must be at least 18 years old.

What You Need to Know

An Officiant must be over 18 years of age to perform a legal marriage.

In the state of Wisconsin you are not required to register with the government before performing a marriage ceremony. However, you should be prepared to produce proof of ordination by a recognized body, in the event that this is ever requested. If you have any questions regarding the legality of your ordination in this state you should contact your local government office, or your ordination body itself.

What Couples Need To Know

Where do couples apply for a license? County Clerk's Office.

What are the age requirements? If either the bride or groom is 16 or 17 years old, parental permission is required. Parents or guardians are required to sign in the presence of a notary public before a marriage application is processed.

How much does a license cost? $60 - $135. Fees vary by county. Cash only.

What documents are needed? You must bring your Social Security Card, show proof of residence (WI Driver's License or WI State ID), show a certified copy of your birth certificate. You must know your parents full names, including mother's maiden name and the correct spelling of their names. Make sure you have the date and place of your marriage ceremony and the name, address and phone number of the Officiant.

Are there residency requirements? At least one of the couple must reside in the county where the application is made for at least 30 days. If both reside out-of-state, the application is made in the county where the ceremony will take place.

Is there a waiting period? There is a mandatory 6 day waiting period before your license is issued to you. In most states, the waiting period does not include Saturdays, Sundays or federal holidays. In some instances, the day the application is filed is not included within the waiting period timeline. A waiver for the 6 day waiting period may be obtained at the discretion of the County Clerk. The cost of the waiver is $25.00.

How long is a license valid? 30 Days.

Where is a license valid for use? The State of Wisconsin.

What if someone has been married previously? You must show proof of a divorce, death or annulment from your most recent marriage. A copy of the judgment of divorce (signed by a judge), legal annulment (signed by a judge) or death certificate is required. In Wisconsin, you need to wait six months after a divorce before remarrying no matter what state the divorce took place in.

Are there any required tests? No.

Are proxy marriages allowed? No.

Can cousins marry? Blood relatives who are first cousins must have proof of sterilization unless the female is 55 years of age or older.

Are common law marriages recognized? No.

How to Handle the Marriage License

Read and follow the instructions which come with the license on how to fill out your section, and ensure all other sections have been fully and correctly completed.

Ministers must complete the marriage certificates and give one to the bride and one to the groom. The original must be returned to the register of deed's of the county in which the marriage was performed or if performed in a city, to the city health officer. This must be done within 3 days after the marriage.

The Celebrant is not required to keep records of marriages.

Wyoming Wedding Officiant Regulations

Statute 20-1-106. Who may solemnize marriage; form of ceremony.

(a) Every district or circuit court judge, district court commissioner, supreme court justice, magistrate and every licensed or ordained minister of the gospel, bishop, priest or rabbi, or other qualified person acting in accordance with the traditions or rites for the solemnization of marriage of any religion, denomination or religious society, may perform the ceremony of marriage in this state.

(b) In the solemnization of marriage no particular form is required, except that the parties shall solemnly declare in the presence of the person performing the ceremony and at least two (2) attending witnesses that they take each other as husband and wife.

What You Need to Know

An Officiant must be over 18 years of age to perform a legal marriage.

In the state of Wyoming you are not required to register with the government before performing a marriage ceremony. However, you should be prepared to produce proof of ordination by a recognized body, in the event that this is ever requested. If you have any questions regarding the legality of your ordination in this state you should contact your local government office, or your ordination body itself.

What Couples Need To Know

Where do couples apply for a license? The County Clerk's Office

What are the age requirements? Applicants must be at least 18 years old or with written parental consent.

Applicants under 16 years of age can apply only with a court order.

How much does a license cost? $25. Be prepared to pay cash.

What documents are needed? A valid driver's license, and a certified copy of your birth certificate.

Are there residency requirements? No.

Is there a waiting period? No.

How long is a license valid? 1 Year.

Where is a license valid for use? The State of Wyoming.

What if someone has been married previously? If either applicant has been married before, you may be required to bring Proof of Dissolution.

Are there any required tests? No.

Are proxy marriages allowed? No.

Can cousins marry? No

Are common law marriages recognized? No.

How to Handle the Marriage License

Read and follow the instructions which come with the license on how to fill out your section, and ensure all other sections have been fully and correctly completed.

Ministers must give a marriage certificate to the bride and groom upon request and must return a certificate to the county clerk.

The Celebrant is not required to keep records of marriages.

Appendix B
Who Can Officiate Outside the United States?

The United Kingdom

In the United Kingdom, couples have a choice between choosing a Civil Ceremony or Religious Ceremony.

Statutory Vows in the U.K.

In order for a civil marriage to be legal, there some vows that are mandatory. These words must be said by both partners in the ceremony. However, you will also usually be allowed to add your own choice of vows before or after the statutory ones.

In England and Wales the statutory declaration is:
'I do solemnly declare that I know not of any lawful impediment why I, __may not be joined in matrimony to __.'

In Scotland the statutory declaration is:
'I solemnly declare that I know of no legal impediment why I, __, may not be joined in matrimony to__. I accept.'

In Northern Ireland the statutory declaration is:
'I know of no lawful impediment why I, __, may not be joined in matrimony to, __, to be my lawful wedded husband/wife.'

It is followed by these contracting words:
'I call upon these persons here present to witness that I, __do take thee, __, to be my lawful wedded husband/wife.'

There are also two legal alternative declarations:
'I know of no legal reason why I, __, may not be joined in marriage to __.'
Or by replying 'I am' to the question: 'Are you, __ free lawfully to marry__?'

These are followed by the contract:
'I, __, take you,__ to be my wedded wife/husband.'
Or
'I, __ take thee, __ to be my wedded wife/husband.'

Civil Marriage in the U.K.

You and your partner will be asked for certain information when giving notice of your intention to marry. Giving false information is a criminal offense. The information which may be required is:-

- evidence of name and address
- evidence of date of birth
- if one partner has been married before or in a civil partnership, documentary evidence that the marriage or civil partnership has ended, for example, a death certificate or decree absolute. Uncertified photocopies are not accepted. A certified copy of a decree absolute may be obtained from the court which decided the divorce. This can take about a week
- evidence of nationality.

A variety of documents can be used as evidence of the information required, but a passport, travel document or birth certificate is usually sufficient. You should contact the register office where you're getting married for more specific advice on what they will accept.

People from overseas may be asked to show their passports. There is no legal requirement to show a passport before getting married and instead, they can produce a birth certificate (accompanied by a certified translation if necessary), an affidavit or other personal identity document.

If you are traveling to the UK to marry either a British citizen or an EEA national, you will need a visa. This is called entry clearance. This will be either a fiancé(e) or proposed civil partner visa if you are not an EEA national or an EEA Family Permit if you are an EEA national.

People who wish to marry in the UK in a Register office in England and Wales must give notice at a Register Office. If you are subject to immigration control, you can only give notice at a Designated Register Office in England and Wales. In Northern Ireland, notice may be given in person or by post. Everyone wishing to marry in a Register Office must provide proof of their nationality.

You are subject to immigration control if you are not:

a British citizen (or someone with right of abode in the UK) or
an EEA national or
don't have any conditions attached to your stay in the UK because you are for example, a diplomat, or a member of visiting armed forces.

For more information on coming to the UK to marry, go to the GOV.UK website at www.gov.uk/marriage-visa.

If the registrar believes that a person is entering or has entered into a marriage for immigration purposes, the registrar has a duty to report this to the Home Office. The registrar must provide the Home Office with certain information, including the marital status and nationality of the person. The Home Office may wish to carry out investigations to ensure that the proposed marriage is not a 'sham'. It may extend the notice period to 70 days in order to carry out these investigations. If you don't comply with the investigations you may not be allowed to marry. You also risk being prosecuted and, if you are the person subject to immigration control, you will gain no advantage from the marriage and could be removed from the UK.

The marriage ceremony in the local Register Office or local authority approved premises will take approximately 10-15 minutes. The Superintendent Registrar or Registrar in Northern Ireland will make a short statement about marriage; you can ask the registrar beforehand to indicate what form of words will be used. It is not possible to use religious words in the civil ceremony. However, the ceremony may include readings, songs or music that contain reference to a god as long as they are in an 'essentially non-religious context'.

Each partner is required to repeat a standard set of promises. These may not be changed, but may be added to, as long as the additions are not religious. Rings are not required but can be exchanged if the couple wishes to.

After the ceremony, the marriage register is signed by both partners. Two witnesses, who must be over 16, must also sign at the time of the marriage. Witnesses must understand the language of the ceremony and have the mental capacity to understand the nature of the ceremony. Register Office staff are not allowed to act as witnesses.

Before signing the register, you should check the information in the entry is correct. It is possible to get incorrect information in the register on marriage certificates changed if there is proof that the errors were notified at the time of the marriage. When trying to correct information at a later stage, you will have to explain in writing how the incorrect information came to be recorded at the time of the marriage and may need to provide documentary evidence to prove any statements. The process may take a long time.

A fee must be paid for the ceremony. A certified copy of the entry in the register may be obtained at the time of the marriage for a fee. Additional copies may be obtained for a further fee.

For details of the fees, contact your local Register Office or in England and Wales, go to the GOV.UK website at www.gov.uk or in Northern Ireland, go to the nidirect website at www.nidirect.gov.uk.

(Source: Citizens Advice UK)

England

Religious Ceremonies

The Church of England and the Church in Wales are allowed to register a marriage at the same time as performing the religious ceremony.

You won't have to give notice of the marriage to the Register Office unless you or your partner are a non-EEA national. If this is the case, you will need to give 28 days notice to the Register Office.

For other religious marriages you'll need to give 28 days notice of the marriage to the

Register Office. Ministers and priests of all other religions can be authorized to register marriages and must have a certificate or license to do so from the local Superintendent Registrar. For Jewish and Quaker marriages, the authorization is automatic. For all other religions, if the official performing the ceremony is not authorized, either a Registrar must attend the religious ceremony or the partners will need to have separate religious and civil ceremonies.

Humanist Ceremonies are not yet allowed in England.

You can find an excellent guide to marriage laws in England at: https://www.citizensadvice.org.uk/relationships/living-together-marriage-and-civil-partnership/getting-married/

Scotland

Religious or belief marriage ceremonies

Opposite sex couples can marry in a religious or belief ceremony, conducted by someone who is an approved Celebrant. That Celebrant may be from a religion such as Christianity or Hinduism or from another belief system such as Humanism.

Same sex couples can have a religious or belief marriage ceremony if the religious or belief body has agreed to conduct same sex marriages and is authorized to do so. There is no legal obligation or duty on a religious or belief body to conduct same sex marriages. It is not unlawful discrimination for an individual Celebrant or a religious or belief body to refuse to conduct a same sex marriage.

You should be able to obtain a list of approved Celebrants in the area where you wish to marry from any district registrar.

It is possible for people over the age of 21 to apply to the Registrar General for temporary authorization to act as a religious or belief Celebrant if they are affiliated to a religious or belief body and are supported by the office bearers of that body to carry out marriage ceremonies on its behalf. This means for example, that you could be married by a member of your family or a friend as long as that person meets the necessary requirements about religious or belief affiliation. There is more information about applying for temporary authorization on the National Records of Scotland website at www.nrscotland.gov.uk.

Religious or belief marriages can be conducted anywhere by the religious or belief body concerned; they are not restricted to religious buildings.

For a religious or belief ceremony:-

you or your partner must collect the Marriage schedule in person from the district registrar and give it to the Celebrant before the ceremony
there must be two witnesses aged 16 years or over
the ceremony must follow the form recognized by the religious or belief body concerned
at the end of the ceremony, the Celebrant, you and your partner and witnesses must all sign the Marriage Schedule.

Civil Ceremonies in Scotland

Opposite sex and same sex civil marriages are conducted by district registrars, appointed by the Registrar General. The registrar will conduct the marriage in her/his district registration or any other appropriate place – see Where can a marriage take place.

You and your partner must provide two witnesses aged 16 or over who will be present at the ceremony and sign the Marriage Schedule.

The registrar will make a short statement about marriage; They should be asked beforehand to indicate what form of words they will use. You and your partner must say the statutory vows. You may wish to personalize your marriage ceremony by including readings, poetry, music or your own personal vows, in addition to the statutory vows. It is not necessary to have a ring.

If either or both of you cannot speak English, you must arrange for an interpreter to be present and are responsible for paying for her/his services.

At the end of the ceremony the registrar, you, your partner, and witnesses must all sign the Marriage Schedule.

Temporary Celebrant Licenses in Scotland

In Scotland a religious or belief marriage may be solemnized only by a minister, clergyman, pastor, priest or other person entitled to do so under the Marriage (Scotland) Act 1977. If it is a religious or belief marriage you are planning and your family friend is not already authorized to act as a Celebrant, the Registrar General can grant a temporary authorization for a particular marriage. A temporary authorization can only be granted to someone who is affiliated to a religious or belief body and who is supported by office bearers of that body to conduct a marriage ceremony on its behalf.

Please note that an application for a temporary authorization cannot be considered any earlier than 3 months before the date of a proposed marriage. Anyone applying for a temporary authorization should forward the following information on the first occasion they apply to Marriage Section at New Register House. The address of New Register House is on our where to find us page.

A copy of their religious or belief body's constitution or statement of faith, which should contain the aims and beliefs of the group together with details on the appointment of office bearers.

Details of membership, both locally and throughout the United Kingdom if applicable, and how often the local body meets for religious worship or to uphold or promote philosophical beliefs.

A copy of the wording of the proposed marriage ceremony.

Their full name and the designation they would use when signing the Marriage Schedule eg Minister, Pastor or Lay Preacher.

Letters from two office bearers of the religious or belief body supporting their application and testifying to their status within the group.

The full names of the couple, the date and place of the marriage.

A civil marriage may be solemnized only by a registrar or an assistant registrar who has been authorized by the Registrar General for the purpose.

(Source: National Records of Scotland)

Humanist Weddings in Scotland

A marriage ceremony can be conducted by approved Celebrants from the humanist belief system. The Humanist Society represents its members, who do not believe in any religion but believe in taking responsibility for their actions and base their ethics on the goals of human welfare, happiness and fulfillment. Several Humanist Celebrants have been authorized by the Registrar General for Scotland to carry out marriages in the same way as approved religious Celebrants. For further information, you should contact The Humanist Society of Scotland:

https://www.humanism.scot/humanist-ceremonies/become-a-Celebrant/

The address of the Registrar General is:-

National Records of Scotland
HM General Register House
2 Princes Street
Edinburgh
EH1 3YY
Tel: 0131 535 1314
Email: via contact form on website
Website: www.nrscotland.gov.uk

Staff at the National Records of Scotland can give addresses of district registrars and provide further information about all aspects of getting married. A Directory of Registrars in Scotland is available on the National Records of Scotland website at www.nrscotland.gov.uk PDF .

Local registration offices can be found in the phone book under Registration of births, deaths and marriages and can provide addresses of other district registrars, lists of approved Celebrants, marriage notices and information on all aspects of getting married.

You can find an excellent guide to Marriage Laws in Scotland at:
https://www.citizensadvice.org.uk/scotland/relationships/living-together-marriage-and-civil-partnership-s/getting-married-s/

Wales

You can find an excellent guide to Marriage Laws in Wales at:
https://www.citizensadvice.org.uk/wales/relationships/living-together-marriage-

and-civil-partnership/getting-married/

Humanist Ceremonies are not yet allowed in Wales.

Northern Ireland

You can find an excellent guide to Marriage Laws in Northern Ireland at: https://www.citizensadvice.org.uk/nireland/relationships/living-together-marriage-and-civil-partnership/getting-married/

Humanist Ceremonies are not yet legal in Northern Ireland.

The Republic of Ireland

In Ireland. You may choose a civil Registry Office marriage or opt for marriage by religious or secular ceremony. Marriages that take place in Ireland by certain specified religious or secular ceremonies or by civil ceremony (that is, in a Registry Office or other approved place) are equally valid and binding under Irish law. Whether you decide on a religious, secular or civil ceremony you will require a Marriage Registration Form which you obtain by fulfilling the notification requirements.

If you are getting married by civil ceremony in a Registry Office or other approved place, you should approach the Registrar of Civil Marriages for the district in which you intend to marry for information on how to proceed. If you are getting married by religious or secular ceremony, you should approach the authorities of the body concerned for advice on how to proceed. Since November 2007, the General Register Office maintains a Register of Solemnisers of Marriage and anyone solemnising a civil, secular or religious marriage must be on the Register. The Register can be inspected at any Registration Office.

For extensive information on the laws in Ireland you should visit: http://www.welfare.ie/en/Pages/Getting_Married.aspx

Marriage by Religious or Secular Ceremony in Ireland

Marriages by religious ceremony or secular ceremony are performed according to the beliefs, rites and ceremonies of the religious body or secular body which is carrying out the ceremony and a registered solemnizer may only solemnize a marriage according to the beliefs, rites and ceremony of a religious body or a secular body if he/she is a recognized member of that body.

It is important to recognize that a 'solemnizer' is recognized as different from a 'Celebrant' in Ireland. A solemnizer is the legal term applied to those registered by the state to perform legal marriage ceremonies.

However, all the civil requirements set out in Section 1 must first be complied with and the couple must have been issued with a Marriage Registration Form by a Registrar which they must show to the person solemnizing the marriage. The solemnizer must also be a registered solemnizer, nominated by his or her religious or secular body, and it is the responsibility of the couple to ensure that the person they wish to solemnize their marriage is on the Register of Solemnizers.

Temporary registrations of solemnizers of religious and secular marriages are possible for those who only wish to solemnize a specific marriage or to solemnize marriages for a specific period of time.

The venue for a religious or secular marriage is a matter for the authorities of the church or religious or secular body under whose auspices the marriage is being performed.

All marriages, civil, religious or secular, must take place at venues which are open to the public.

The ceremony must be performed in the presence of two witnesses who are both over 18 years of age. Both parties must make two declarations: - a) that neither of them knows of any impediment to the marriage; and b) that they accept each other as husband and wife.

At the end of the ceremony, the solemnizer, the couple, and the witnesses must all sign the MRF. The completed MRF should be given to a registrar (not necessarily the registrar who issued it) within 1 month of the ceremony, so that the marriage can be civilly registered. Please note that you will not be able to obtain a civil marriage certificate until such time as the MRF has been returned to a Registrar and the marriage is civilly registered.

Renewing your Wedding Vows in Ireland

Under the law in Ireland, someone who is already married cannot get married again (even if it is to the same person). This effectively means that you cannot renew your wedding vows in a civil ceremony in Ireland.

However, there is a long tradition of 'church blessings' in Ireland. This is where Irish people who have married in civil ceremonies abroad, marry in a religious ceremony the next time they are home. Sometimes, people living in Ireland have their marriage blessed in a religious ceremony, to commemorate a special anniversary or event.

Contact an appropriate local clergyman who should be able to put you in touch with a counterpart in Ireland. If you live in Ireland and would like to have your marriage blessed, you should get in touch with your local clergyman.

You can find an excellent guide to Marriage Laws in Ireland at:
http://www.citizensinformation.ie/en/birth_family_relationships/getting_married/different_legal_ways_of_getting_married.html

Canada

In Canada, section 92(12) of the Constitution Act, 1867 gives the provincial legislatures the power to pass laws regulating the solemnization of marriage.

In Ontario: For Religious ceremonies - A religious marriage is performed by a religious official of a recognized religious organization who has received authorization from the Office of the Registrar General to perform marriages in Ontario under the Marriage Act.

For Civil ceremonies - An Ontario judge, justice of the peace, or municipal clerk may perform a marriage under the authority of a marriage license. Each municipality will sets its own fees.

In Quebec: Clerks and deputy clerks of the Superior Court who have been specially designated for that purpose, and notaries authorized to execute notarial acts, may solemnize marriages.

Mayors, members of municipal or borough councils and municipal officers designated by the Minister of Justice may also solemnize marriages, but only within the territory defined in the instrument of designation.

Last, any person authorized by the Minister of Justice to solemnize civil unions may also solemnize a marriage. Some couples may wish to have their marriage solemnized by someone who is significant in their lives, but does not fall into one of the categories defined above. When this is the case, the intended spouses and the person they have chosen as Officiant must complete the form entitled Request for the Designation of an Officiant of a Marriage or Civil Union (http://www.justice.gouv.qc.ca/english/formulaires/mariage/Celebrant-a.htm). The completed form must then be sent, preferably three to four months before the date of the ceremony, to the Direction des services judiciaires of the Ministère de la Justice1.

The designated Officiant, after receiving the officially signed authorization, has full responsibility for the legal aspects of the ceremony. The Officiant will also receive an information kit (http://www.justice.gouv.qc.ca/english/publications/generale/Celebrant-trousse-a.htm).

More information about who is authorized to act as an Officiant, and the Officiant's obligations and duties, can be found in the document Officiants (http://www.justice.gouv.qc.ca/english/publications/generale/Celebrant-a.htm).

In Newfoundland and Labrador: Registration is required for all individuals wishing to solemnize a marriage, as defined and required under Statutes of Newfoundland and Labrador - Chapter M1.02 (http://www.assembly.nl.ca/legislation/sr/annualstatutes/2009/m01-02.c09.htm)

In Nova Scotia: All those wishing to solemnize a marriage in Nova Scotia must register with the Vital Statistics Office. For further information see: https://www.novascotia.ca/sns/paal/vstat/paal310.asp

Australia

Australian Celebrants must complete a specified level of training, at which point they can apply for official government registration. If you are interested in becoming a Celebrant in Australia you should start by visiting the government website:

https://www.ag.gov.au/FamiliesAndMarriage/Marriage/Pages/BecomingamarriageCelebrant.aspx

The Rest of the World

The Society of Celebrations (www.societyofcelebrations.org) is currently producing a guide to marriage and Celebrant laws across the world. This should be available in the spring of 2016.

Appendix C
Glossary of Wedding Terms

Aisle Runner. A long piece of fabric traditionally rolled out before the bridal procession to indicate the arrival of the bride.

All-Inclusive. A flat fee that covers a variety of wedding services. Most often associated with destination weddings at resorts.

Arbor. A shelter of branches under which a couple stands to exchange vows. Can also be made of latticework covered with vines.

Asymmetric. A dress neckline where one shoulder is covered and the other is bare, or a style that begins at the natural waistline and angles down to one side.

Basket Weave. An icing technique that mimics the look of a wicker basket, with piped lines of vertical and horizontal icing crisscrossing.

Biscotti. An Italian cookie often flavored with anise or nuts. Common as a wedding favor because of their long shelf-life. Traditionally oblong-shaped.

Black Tie. A semi-formal dress code; men wear tuxedos, while women wear cocktail dresses or gowns.

Blackout Dates. Dates unavailable for events, either due to holidays or a venue's lack of availability.

Blended Family. A family where members are not all biologically related. Typically, a result of a marriage when spouses and children from a former relationship or marriage form the family unit.

Block of Rooms. A group of rooms reserved at a hotel for guests, often at a discounted rate. The block is usually held in the couple's name, with guests paying for the reservations themselves.

Blusher Veil. A short veil worn over the bride's face while walking down the aisle that is lifted back to present her to the groom.

Bodice. The portion of a woman's garment that covers the upper part of a woman's body, above the waist.

Body Shapers. An undergarment used to mold the bride's body into a smooth silhouette.

Bon Bon. A type of candy that is covered in fondant or chocolate.

Bridal Boot Camp. A high-intensity workout regime for brides to lose weight and tone up before the wedding.

Brides Room. An area at the ceremony venue for the bride and her attendants to prepare for the wedding in private.

Budget. A list of planned expenses for a wedding that serves as a helpful guide to keep track of spending.

Buffet. A type of dining style where guests line up and either serve themselves or request food from the server.

Burlap Linen. A tablecloth made of or resembling burlap, a material of woven jute or hemp.

Bustle. When a wedding gown's train is gathered below the waist to prevent it from dragging on the floor, often done after the wedding ceremony but before the reception.

Butler Service. A type of catering service where servers offer food and drinks to guests on platters.

Cabana. A hut or a structure draped in fabric, typically found on a beach. Can be a relatively small 4-by-4 foot structure intended for shade or large enough to house an entire reception.

Candelabra. decorative candlestick that has multiple arms to hold multiple candles. Sometimes used as part of the unity candle lighting ceremony.

Candle Lighters. Members of the wedding party, often older children or young adults, who walk up the aisle with lit candles to light candles for the ceremony.

Capacity Charts. A chart that shows how many people a venue can accommodate.

Cardstock. A type of paper commonly used for wedding invitations. Thicker than normal printing paper and comes in varying colors and textures.

Carving Station. An area manned by catering staff who carve slices of meat, such as prime rib or chicken, in a buffet setting at the request of guests.

Cascade Bouquet. A bouquet style in which the flowers cascade downward from the bride.

Cash Bar. A beverage-service system where wedding guests pay for their drinks.

Cathedral Veil. The most formal of veils, also known as a royal veil. Standard length is 108 inches; the veil extends onto the floor.

Celebrant. An individual who officiates the ceremony. For weddings your Celebrant should be licensed to perform in your state.

Chafing Dish. A large dish that sits over a low flame to keep its contents warm. Popular at buffets.

Champagne Flute. A slim glass with a stem, designed to retain Champagne's carbonation.

Charger Plate. A plate, larger than a dinner plate, that is purely decorative and displays the meal's china.

Chartreuse. A bright yellow-green appropriate for a spring wedding

Chauffeur. A person responsible for driving a vehicle, such as a limo. Often the bridal party is chauffeured to the ceremony.

Chill Table. A table that can be filled with ice, over which food is placed to keep fresh.

Cocktail Hour. A festive gathering where guests mingle as cocktails and hors d'oeuvres are served, typically preceding dinner.

Comb. A decorative hairpiece attached to a comb that slides into the hair.

Common Law Marriage. When two people live together as if they are man and wife without going through the formality of marriage.

Crown. An ornamental, often bejeweled, headpiece that circles the head. Veils can be attached.

Cuban Cigars. A popular cigar for celebrations, rolled from Cuban tobacco leaves.

Day of Planner. A wedding planner enlisted to help only on the day of the wedding to make sure that all parts of the event run smoothly.

Destination Wedding. The term for when an engaged couple travels away from home for the wedding ceremony. A destination wedding may or may not include guests.

Down Payment Registry. A registry where the bride and groom request monetary contributions towards the down payment of a home.

Eggshell Blue. A greenish blue resembling the color of a robin's egg. Also called robin egg blue.

Elbow Veil. veil that extends to the bride's elbow, typically about 25 inches long.

Elopement. When a couple steals away to get married without notifying friends and family.

Emcee. An individual who moves the wedding reception forward by announcing speakers, songs and dances. Comes from the phrase Master of Ceremonies or MC.

Engagement Party. A party thrown at the beginning of the engagement, sometimes to announce the engagement to friends and family. Traditionally thrown by the bride's family but may be thrown by the couple.

Engagement Session. A series of photos taken by the wedding photographer during the engagement. Often used in wedding announcements, save-the-date cards or at the wedding.

Euro Tie. A long tie with a square bottom that is a cross between a regular necktie and the more formal ascot.

Favor Tags. A decorative label, sticker or hanging tag on a wedding favor. Usually printed with the couple's names or initials and the wedding date.

Final Guarantee. The final head count given to the caterer. The bride and groom will pay for this number.

Finger Sandwich. A small sandwich meant to be eaten in a couple of bites, often part of a buffet.

Fondant. A sweet icing that is rolled out and draped over a wedding cake for a smooth finish.

Food Stations. A style of dinner service that consists of multiple buffets set up at stations throughout the reception location. These stations are often chef-attended and may be themed by food type or cuisine style.

Frame Tent. A type of tent that can be installed without stakes or internal poles; these tents are typically small, no wider than 40 feet.

Full Service Planner. A wedding planner who assists the couple with every step of the wedding process, from selecting vendors to day-of coordination.

Garland. A full circle of flowers. Can be part of decor or worn in the hair.

Gerbera Daisy. A flower from the sunflower family that comes in many different colors; appropriate for a casual, spring wedding. Sometimes called Gerber daisy.

Gobo. A template attached to a light source to create a design, such as a monogram, that shines on the floor, wall or ceiling.

Gown Preservation. The method for preserving a dress after the wedding day. Typically involves a professional cleaning and boxing it to prevent damage over the years.

Green/Eco Wedding. A catchall term that can refer to different aspects of environmentally friendly weddings; can include serving organically grown food, using recyclable items, cutting down on waste, etc.

Groom's Cake. A secondary cake to the traditional wedding cake. Often masculine in design, reflective of the groom's interests or hobbies, and traditionally chocolate.

Head Table. A long, straight table set up for the meal during a reception. Typically the bride and groom sit at the center of the table, facing guests, with the bridal party and their dates flanking the couple.

Hen Party. The term used in some countries for a 'bachelorette party,' celebrating the last days of a bride-to-be's single life.

Honeymoon Package. A vacation package marketed to honeymooners. Usually includes accommodations and local or romantic activities.

Honeymoon Registry. An online service that allows couples to register for activities and upgrades for their honeymoon stay. This can be used instead of or with more traditional gifts and registries.

Honor Attendant. The attendant the bride wants by her side for the entire wedding process. Also called the maid of honor if the person is unmarried or matron of honor if married.

Hors d'oeuvre. French for 'outside of work,' referring to a food item served outside of the main body of the meal. Often used interchangeably with the word appetizer.

Hosted Bar. A beverage service system where the host pays for all drinks ordered by the guests. Also known as an open bar.

In-House Catering. Catering services supplied by the wedding venue. If a venue offers in-house catering, typically off-site caterers are not permitted.

In-Law. The parents of a spouse, such as a mother-in-law or father-in-law.

Jewelry Roll. A pouch used to transport jewelry when traveling. Often made of cloth and contains pockets that can be zipped. The pouch is then rolled and secured with an attached ribbon.

Jordan Almond. A candy-coated, often pastel almond that serves as a popular wedding favor.

Junior Bridesmaid. A female who is too old to be a flower girl and too young to be a traditional bridesmaid. Often participates in the bridal shower, ceremony rehearsal, rehearsal dinner and the ceremony processional but not the bachelorette party.

LED. A type of light popular for creating a dramatic event atmosphere; acronym for light-emitting diode.

Locally Grown. Items that are grown near the location they will be used; an encouraged element for eco-friendly weddings.

Luminaria. A decorative lantern most commonly made from a paper bag, then weighted with sand and lit inside with a candle.

Man of Honor. The title of the chief attendant to the bride when he is male.

Map cards. A card sent with the invitation that contains a small map and directions to the wedding ceremony and reception from the places that guests will likely stay.

Marquee Tent. A large tent used in place of a building at outdoor events. Almost always professionally installed.

Marquise. The shape of a diamond that resembles an oval with pointed ends, like a football.

Matron of Honor. The title of the chief bridesmaid when she is married, referred to as 'maid of honor' when unmarried.

Micro-Pave. A band with many tiny stones embedded in it, typically set around a larger diamond.

Milgrain Edging. A beaded or textured edge on a wedding band.

Minister. The individual who performs, or administers, your wedding or any other ceremony. A Minister need not be clergy or religiously affiliated but should be licensed to practice and experienced.

Mocktail. A mock cocktail that resembles a drink with spirits but contains no alcohol.

Monogram. The initials of a person's name, often appearing in an ornate, overlapping form and can be used on wedding invitations, piped on cakes as icing, etc.

Nosegay. A small, round bouquet of flowers wired together. Sometimes called a 'posy.'

Nuptial Blessing. A blessing by a priest occurring at the end of a Roman Catholic wedding ceremony.

Officiant. The person in charge of the wedding ceremony. They must be legally able to marry someone in their state but are not required to be a clergy member.

Online Proofing. An online service that allows a person to review print pieces, such as invitations or photography, before ordering them.

Organic Catering. Catered food grown without the use of pesticides or fertilizers. The food is often sourced from sustainable, local vendors

Organic Flowers. Flowers grown without the use of chemical pesticides.

Pages. A person who holds the train of a bride's gown when she walks down the aisle. This position is usually fulfilled by a boy under the age of 10 but older than the ring bearer.

Palladium. A silver-white pure metal; does not react with oxygen and will not tarnish, unlike silver or gold.

Parure. A matching set of jewelry, such as earrings and a necklace, sometimes intended to be worn at the wedding when presented as a gift by the bride.

Pashmina. A wrap of fine cashmere wool that women drape over their shoulders to keep warm when wearing formal attire.

Personal Vows. When the bride and groom express their commitment to each other with vows they've written rather than recite vows from the Book of Common Prayer.

Petit four. A small, individual cake covered on all sides with fondant.

Pew Vase. A container for flowers that is placed on or by a church pew.

Plantable Favor. A gift for guests that includes seeds, sometimes embedded in paper, that one can plant as a reminder of the wedding.

Playlist. The list of songs given to the DJ or band to play during the reception. Sometimes an iPod is used instead.

Plus-one. A notation on an invitation indicating that a guest can bring a significant other or date.

Prelude. Music played while guests are being seated for the wedding ceremony.

Premarital Counseling. Counseling that the couple receives before the wedding and specific to potential marital issues. Required by some religions before the couple can marry in the church.

Prenuptial Agreement. A contract where a bride and groom agree how property should be divided in the event of death or divorce. Also referred to as a 'prenup.'

Procession. The order in which the bridal party enters the ceremony. Differs depending on religion or style of ceremony, but generally begins with male attendants, followed by female attendants, and ends with the bride and her escort, if she has one. Or, male and female attendants walk down the aisle side by side, followed by the bride.

Processional. The song played as the bride walks down the aisle, traditionally 'The Bridal Chorus' or as it is more commonly known, 'The Wedding March.'

Proof of Residency. A document that proves residency of a country or state. Can be an electric bill, apartment rental receipt, etc. Often required to obtain a wedding license.

Pub Crawl. A party that travels to different pubs or bars within walking distance on the same night.

Push Pole Tent. A traditional style of tent where a series of poles and stakes hold up the fabric.

R.S.V.P. A request for invitees to accept or decline an invitation. French for 'Répondez s'il vous plaît,' meaning 'Respond, if you please.' An invitee should send an R.S.V.P. whether or not they can attend the event.

Recessional. Music that plays as the bridal party is leaving the ceremony.

Refundable Deposit. Money given to hold a venue or service that will be returned if the event is canceled due to extenuating circumstances.

Rehearsal Dinner. A tradition, typically held the night before the wedding, where the wedding party celebrates with dinner after practicing for the wedding ceremony.

Response Card. A card accompanying an invitation to a wedding that allows the recipient to accept or decline the invitation. It typically includes meal options. Sometimes called 'reply card.'

Responsive Vows. Answering 'I will' or 'I do' to a series of commitment questions asked of the bride and groom by the Officiant.

Ring Pillow. A small cushion carried by the ring bearer in the procession. Traditionally holds the rings for delivery to the Officiant, but now often holds decorative rings as a representation.

Roast. A type of toast that consists of poking fun at the honoree.

Save-the-date. An announcement of the date of the wedding, requesting guests to 'save the date' so they can attend the wedding; sent before the official invitation with the specific details.

Scavenger Hunt. An activity where teams compete against each other to find all the objects on a list.

Seating Cards. Cards propped up at place settings that indicate who sits where during a meal.

Secular Officiant. An official unrelated to a religion who can legally wed two parties, such as a judge.

Sheath. A dress style with a narrow fit that's ankle-length and hugs the bust, waist and hips.

Shoulder Season. Refers to the time between the high and low seasons of travel, often offering lower rates to travelers.

Site Coordinator. A venue staff member who serves as the contact person and coordinator for events in a role that is less extensive than the wedding planner.

Solitaire. A simple metallic band with one stone.

Spray. A single branch or stem with many blooms or leaves on it.

Stag and Doe Party. A combined bachelor and bachelorette party.

Stag Party. The term used in some countries for a 'bachelor party,' celebrating the last days of a groom-to-be's bachelorhood.

Stargazer Lily. A brightly colored, extremely fragrant flower sometimes found in bridal bouquets.

Stepparent. The parent of the child by marriage, not biologically.

String Quartet. A musical ensemble of four musicians playing string instruments, which typically includes two violins, a viola and a cello.

Swagging. A decorative element where fabric is draped to form a curve between two points. Often seen on the skirts of tables or as an effect to create the ceiling of a tent.

Tailcoat. A coat with tails. Seen primarily at weddings with white tie attire. May be a dress coat with a squarely cut away front or a morning coat with a tapered cut.

Tails. The two tapered extensions on the back of a formal tuxedo jacket.

Tension Tent. A parabola-shaped tent with clean lines, capable of withstanding winds up to 70 miles per hour. Contains few internal poles, making it a popular choice for large weddings.

Theme Wedding. A wedding centered around a specific theme that is not color or pattern focused, such as a winter wonderland.

Tiffany Setting. A traditional setting for a solitaire engagement ring that includes a plain band with a set of prongs that holds the diamond. Also called a Tiffany mount.

Toastmaster. The person in charge of introducing speakers and proposing toasts.

Topiary. A sculpture made out of shrubs or flowers. Floral topiaries can make colorful centerpieces.

Tossing Bouquet. A bouquet that is usually smaller than the more formal bouquet the bride carries down the aisle, specifically for throwing to single female guests during the customary bouquet toss.

Traditional Vows. Vows that a bride and groom repeat out loud to each other to express their love and commitment during the wedding ceremony.

Trellis. Latticework, often made of wood or metal, that supports climbing plants. Can provide a decorative backdrop to outdoor weddings.

Tribute Band. A band that plays songs entirely written by a popular band.

Trousseau. Historically refers to the bride's possessions that she brings to the marriage. Can also refer to the bride's gown or attire.

Trunk Show. A presentation of wedding attire, often by a designer, to bridal shops or brides, typically transported in trunks.

Tulle. A light, netted fabric used for veils, wedding gowns and decor.

Unity Candle. A large pillar candle the bride and groom light with two taper candles, symbolizing two individuals committing to each other.

Universal Registry. A single registry where brides and grooms can include gift preferences from many different stores.

Usher. Male bridal party member who show guests to their seats before the ceremony. Often also performs the role of groomsman.

Videographer. The person responsible for filming and editing a video of the wedding ceremony and reception.

VIEs. An acronym for 'Very Important Extras,' where family and friends can fulfill roles extending beyond the bridal party, from usher to soloist.

Waiting Period. The amount of time legally required between applying for a marriage license and being able to marry. Varies between states.

Wedding Arch. An arched structure commonly used at outdoor weddings that the bride and groom stand under during the ceremony.

Wedding Day Coordinator. A coordinator employed for the day of the wedding only; responsible for the execution of the wedding ceremony and reception.

Wedding Insurance. A policy that prevents financial loss from canceling a wedding due to natural disasters, medical emergencies, etc.

Wedding Planner. An individual an engaged couple hires to oversee every aspect of the wedding, including vendors, payment, decor, budget, etc. The wedding planner is on-site during the event to make sure things run smoothly.

Welcome Basket. A basket filled with items such as candles, guidebooks and other small luxuries, left for out-of-town guests in their hotel room or at the reception desk.

White Tie. The most formal dress attire. For men, this means white bow-ties and jackets with tails, while women should wear evening gowns. Also called 'full evening dress.'

Appendix D
Glossary of Funeral and Memorial Terms

Apportionment. This is when the cremated remains are divided into separate amounts. This can be done so some may be spread and the rest retained, or to distribute between members of the family.

Arrangement Conference. The meeting with the funeral director and staff to make the funeral arrangements.

Arrangement Room. A room used to meet with the family and conduct the arrangement conference.

Beneficiary. The person who is the recipient of the proceeds of the will or life insurance policy.

Bequest. Making a gift in a will.

Bereavement / Grief Counselor. Some funeral homes will have a member of staff qualified to provide counseling for bereaved family.

Burial. The act of burying the deceased underground.

Burial/Creation Permit or Certificate. A permit issued by local government that authorizes the burial or cremation.

Burial Garments. Clothes especially made for the deceased.

Burial Vault. The container placed inside the grave-site to hold the casket.

Canopy. A portable canvas shelter or marquee used to cover the grave-site during the burial service.

Casket or Coffin. The container generally made from steel, metal or wood for placing human remains in for burial.

Casket Veil. A transparent net that goes over the casket to keep flies off.

Catafalque. The stand that the casket rests on during a funeral service.

Cemetery. An area of land that is zoned for the burial or entombment of the deceased.

Cenotaph. A monument (sometimes an empty tomb) that is erected in memory of a person buried elsewhere, such as military cenotaphs.

Certified Crematory Operator. If the funeral home has an on-site crematory, they will have a member of staff trained and certified to operate the cremation equipment.

Certified Death Certificate. The legal copy of the original death certificate.

Chapel. A large room used for the purposes of conducting a funeral service.

Codicil. An amendment to a will that supersedes any original provisions.

Columbarium. A building that houses multiple niches.

Committal Service. The final part of the funeral service where the deceased is interred, entombed or cremated.

Community Liaison. This is a newer role in funeral homes and can be held by a member of staff who works to liaise with the community, providing outreach services and education for seniors about funeral planning. It is now an important role to move funeral homes into their changing role in culture in the 21st century.

Contest. The legal challenge to the validity of the will.

Continuing Care Coordinator / After Care. This is a role sometimes held by a member of staff who specifically provides after care service to a family once the funeral is conducted. It can often be the same member of staff who is trained in counseling.

Coroner. A public official whose role it is to investigate the cause of death if no physician was in attendance for a period prior to the death.

Cortege. The funeral procession.

Cosmetology. The use of make-up to enhance the appearance of the deceased.

Cremains. Another term sometimes used for cremated remains.

Cremation. The reduction of the body to ashes with extreme heat.

Cremation Urn. The container that the cremated remains can be stored in.

Crematory/Tort. The machine or furnace designated specifically for the cremation of human remains.

Crypt. A type of vault or room used for holding remains.

Death Notice/Obituary. The formal notice placed in the press that communicates the death and any funeral arrangements.

Deceased. The person who has died.

Disinter. This is when remains are dug up and removed to another place.

Display Room. A room set aside for the purpose of displaying funeral merchandise such as caskets, urns, prayer cards, etc.

Embalmer. The trained and certified person who can disinfect and preserve human remains.

Embalming. The method of preserving and sanitizing the deceased by circulating an antiseptic preservative through the circulatory system.

Eulogy. A speech given at the funeral in honor of the deceased.

Executor. The administrator of the estate, as outlined in the will.

Exhume. To dig up human remains, usually to conduct further tests to determine the cause of death or identity of the deceased.

Family Room. A special room where the bereaved family can convene in privacy.

Final Disposition. The final process for human remains.

Final Rites. The funeral service, can be considered in the faith aspect, rites of passage etc.

First Call. The initial and immediate visit by a funeral director to collect the deceased.

Flower Stand or Rack. Stands used to put floral displays on.

Funeral Arrangements. The conference between family and funeral director to arrange the funeral.

Funeral Assistant. This role is performed by a person not certified as a funeral director or mortician. They provide support services throughout the funeral arranging and funeral service processes.

Funeral Director/Mortician. This is the certified and trained professional who is licensed to perform the supervision and preparation of the deceased for burial or cremation.

Funeral Insurance/Burial Insurance. n insurance policy that covers the costs associated with a funeral or burial.

Funeral Procession. The procession of vehicles between funeral home and church, cemetery or crematory.

Funeral Service. The service or ceremony performed before the final disposition. Can be religious or non-religious.

Grave. he hole in the earth that the deceased is buried in.

Grave Liner. A receptacle made of wood, metal or concrete that lines the grave to give it some integrity.

Grave Marker, Headstone, Memorial Marker, or Monument. The above terms all refer to a marker placed upon a grave to identity the occupant of the grave. It can be constructed of marble, granite, stone, wood or other materials.

Green Burial. This refers to a burial conducted without any unnatural materials. i.e. no embalming and a burial in a wooden casket with no metal, or a shroud and buried directly into the earth without a grave liner.

Honorary Pallbearers. Friends or members of a fraternal, military or social organization who may provide a 'honor guard' but do not actually carry the casket.

Inquest. An official hearing if there are circumstances surrounding the cause of death.

Interment. The act of burying a body.

Intestate. When someone dies with no will.

Living Will. A legal document which details the wishes of an individual about his/her medical care should they become unfit to make decisions.

Lowering Device. This is the mechanism used to assist the funeral staff lower the casket into the grave.

Mausoleum. A building that houses above-ground tombs, crypts and niches.

Medical Examiner. Government official whose duty it is to perform an autopsy if one is required.

Memorial Service. A service or ceremony conducted in memory of the deceased, generally without the body present.

Memory Board or Memory Table. A display board where memorabilia about the deceased can be displayed.

Memory Book or Guest Book. A book that attendees can write their condolence messages in and any tribute to the deceased.

Minister's Room. A room for the use of a minister to prepare before a service and/or meet with family.

Morgue. A place where human remains are stored pending an autopsy or an official identification.

Niche. A small space designed to accommodate a cremated remains container.

Obituary. The notice of death published in a newspaper or online.

Opening and Closing Fees. The fees a cemetery charge for digging the grave and filling it, or for opening & closing an existing plot to inter a further occupant, or cremated remains.

Pallbearers. Family and friends who carry the casket during a funeral. This role can be performed by funeral home employees as well.

Perpetual Care Fund. A portion of funds set aside in trust for the ongoing maintenance of a burial plot.

Prayer Cards. Personalized stationery used during a funeral service.

Prearranged Funeral, Funeral Trust, and Preneed. These all refer to plans and contracts which involve preplanning funeral arrangements and prepaying before a death occurs.

Preparation Room. A room specially equipped for the preparation of the deceased. It is ordinarily where embalming, dressing and any cosmetology will take place.

Preplan Advisor / Advance Funeral Planner. This role is performed by a licensed funeral director or licensed preplan agent. They are specifically trained in the role of assisting families with the financial aspects of preplanning a funeral.

Probate. The court process to validate a will.

Reposing Room. The room where the deceased lies in state once casketed and awaiting the time of the funeral service.

Slumber Room. A room that contains a bed for the deceased to be laid in state prior to the funeral. This can be used for viewing or visitation purposes when a casket is not being used. i.e. for a cremation.

Testator. A person making a valid will.

Tomb. A chamber in the ground or above ground in rock or stone that houses human remains.

Trade Embalmer. A licensed embalmer who is not employed in a funeral home but provides embalming services as a trade service to funeral homes.

Transit Permit. The permit issued that enables the deceased to be transported to the burial site.

Trust. A monetary fund that is managed by one person for the benefit of others.

Viewing. When the deceased is laid-out for family and friends to visit before or after a funeral service.

Vigil. A Catholic service held on the eve of a funeral service.

Visitation. This is generally arranged as a private opportunity for family and friends to visit with the deceased before the funeral.

Visitation Room. room designated in the funeral home for the deceased to lie before the funeral so that people can view the deceased.

Wake. A form of death ritual where a watch is maintained over the deceased during the night before and after the funeral.

Will. A legal document stating the wishes of the deceased in terms of the disposal of their estate and their remains.

Appendix E
Online Resources

Professional Organizations

The International Association of Wedding Officiants
(iapwo.org)
The Society of Celebrations
(societyofcelebrations.org)
The Humanist Society
(thehumanistsociety.org)
The Universal Life Church
(themonastery.org)
American Marriage Ministries
(theamm.org)
The Church of Spiritual Humanism
(spiritualhumanism.org)

Community

American Association of Wedding Officiants
(figstreet.com/guesthouse/aawo.html)
Humanist Celebration Facebook Group
(facebook.com/groups/humanistcelebration/)
Funeral Celebrants Facebook Group
(facebook.com/groups/1463749080582393/)
Wedding Professionals of Facebook
(facebook.com/groups/Weddingprofessional247/)
American Wedding Professionals Facebook Group
(facebook.com/groups/AmericanWeddingProfessionals/)

For Business

Evolve Your Wedding Business
(evolveyourweddingbusiness.com)
Wedding Industry Law

(weddingindustrylaw.com)

Wedding Industry Rescue

(weddingindustryrescue.com)

Wedding Business Websites

(weddingbusinesswebsites.com)

Check your local Business Search Listing Status

(moz.com/local/search)

Off Beat Bride

(offbeatbride.com)

Wedding Wire

(weddingwire.com)

The Knot

(theknot.com)

Create a Facebook Page for your business.

(facebook.com/pages/create)

Create a Google+ Page for your business.

(business.google.com)

Create a Twitter Account for your business.

(twitter.com)

Create an Instagram Account for your business.

(instagram.com)

Create a Pinterest Account for your business.

(pinterest.com)

Create a LinkedIn profile.

(linkedin.com)

Start a blog.

(blogger.com)

Appendix F
Bibliography and
Recommended Reading

Alexander, Becky. The Complete Guide to Baby Naming Ceremonies. How To Books, 2010.

Berkun, Scott. Confessions of a Public Speaker. O'Reilly, 2010.

Black, Algernon D. Without Burnt Offerings, Ceremonies of Humanism. Viking Press, 1974.

Blum, Marcy. Weddings for Dummies. Hungry Minds, Inc, 1997.

Blum, Marcy & Kaiser, Laura Fisher. Wedding Kit for Dummies. IDG Books Worldwide, 2000.

Carr, Kelly. How to Write Wedding Vows. Franklin Publishing, 2012.

Collins, Herrick, and Pearce, ed. Seasons of Life. Prometheus Books, 2000.

Francesa, Lisa. The Wedding Officiant's Guide. Chronicle Books, 2014.

Hancock, Jennifer. Jen Hancock's Handy Humanism Handbook. Smashwords, 2011.

Hancock, Jennifer. The Humanist Approach to Grief and Grieving. Createspace, 2013.

Johnson, Judith. The Wedding Ceremony Planner. Sourcebooks, 2013.

Johnston, Sunny Dawn. The Wedding Officiant's Manual. Sunny Dawn Johnston Productions, 2013.

Jones, Karen. Death for Beginners: Your No-Nonsense, Money-Saving Guide to Planning for the Inevitable. Quill Driver Books, 2010.

Kubler-Ross, Elisabeth. Death: The Final Stage of Growth. Touchstone, 1986.

Lamont, Corliss. A Humanist Funeral Service. Prometheus Books, 1977.

Lamont, Corliss. A Humanist Wedding Service. Prometheus Books, 1972.

Long, Rev. Amy. More Weddings, Funerals and Rites of Passage. Self-Published, 2009.

Long, Rev. Amy. Weddings, Funerals and Rites of Passage. Self-Published, 2002.

Molander, Beverley & Savage, Dave. Heartfelt Memorial Services. Memory Keepers Publishing, 2015.

Moore, Faith. Celebrating a Life: Planning Memorial Services and Other Creative Rememberances. Stewart, Tabori & Chang 2009.

Morgan, Ernest. Dealing Creatively with Death. Upper Access Books, 2001.

Reid, Dayna. Do-It-Yourself Wedding Ceremony. Createspace, 2014.

Roney, Carley. The Knot's Complete Guide to Weddings in the Real World. Broadway Books, 1998.

Roney, Carley. The Knot Guide to Wedding Vows & Traditions. Clarkson Potter, 2013.

Van der Meer, Antonia. The Complete Idiot's Guide to Creative Weddings. Alpha Books, 1999.

Warner, Diane. Diane Warner's Complete Book of Wedding Vows. Career Press, 2006.

Willson, Jane W. Sharing the Future: Non-Religious Wedding Ceremonies. British Humanist Association, 1988.

Willson, Jane W. New Arrivals: Guide to Nonreligious Naming Ceremonies, Baby Naming Ceremonies and Poetry. British Humanist Association, 1991.

Wine, Sherwin. Celebrations. Prometheus Books, 1988.

York, Sarah. Remembering Well: Rituals for Celebrating Life and Mourning Death. Jossey-Bass, 2000.

Young, Barry H. The Funeral Celebrant's Handbook. JoJo Publishing, 2008.

Zorger, R. A. The Officiant's Manual. Church of Spiritual Humanism. 2nd Ed.

Appendix G
Example
First Enquiry Form

Celebrant Services Inquiry

Received on   /   /   @   AM / PM

Ceremony Overview

Date and Time of Ceremony: /   /   @   AM / PM

(Available?   Yes | No)

Type of Ceremony:

Location of Ceremony:

Expected Arrival Time:

Expected Departure Time:

Travel Time and Distance:

Contact Details:

Name of Contact:

Role of Contact in Ceremony:

How Did you Hear About Us?

Contact Telephone:

Contact E-mail:

Ceremony Details

Ceremony Details:

Approximate Number Attending?

Size of Party (if a Wedding)?

Is There a Rehearsal?

Rehearsal Details: /   /   @   AM / PM
(Check Availability)

Style of Ceremony?

Quoted Priced:

Quoted Travel:

Deposit Requested:

Notes:

Next Action / Action Date?

Inquiry Status: Active | Closed | Booked

Appendix H
Example Wedding Questionnaire

Wedding Ceremony Questionnaire

Completed on   /   /   @   AM / PM

Ceremony Overview

Date of Ceremony:

Time of Ceremony:

Officiant Arrival Time:

Inside / Outside?

Venue Address:

Venue Contact:

Venue Tel:

Venue E-mail:

Notes on the Venue:

The Rehearsal

Date of Rehearsal:

Time of Rehearsal:

Rehearsal Location:

The Couple

Name of **Partner A**:

Telephone #:

E-mail:

Occupation:

Addressed During Ceremony As:

Name of **Partner B**:

Telephone #:

E-mail:

Occupation:

Addressed During Ceremony As:

Do they have the license?

Place of license issue?

Will they be exchanging rings?

The Wedding Party

Bridesmaids:

Name of M.O.H:

Groomsmen:

Name of Best Man:

Name / Relationship of Escort:

Ring Bearer Details:

Flower Girl Details:

Who will hold the Rings?

Notes on Wedding Party:

Other Vendors:

Wedding Planner / Day of Coordinator:

Planner Telephone #:

Planner E-mail:

Photographer:

Photographer Telephone #:

Photographer E-mail:

Videographer:

Videographer Telephone #:

Videographer E-mail:

DJ / Musicians:

DJ / M Telephone #:

DJ / M E-mail:

Will a Microphone be provided?

Other Key Personnel?

Musical Plans:

Notes on the Style and Use of Music:

The Ceremony

Processional Description:

Will there be a formal **Hand Off/Question**?

Recessional Description:

Vows:

Recited   /   Repeated   /   Responsive

Notes on Vows:

Readings:

Details of Readings and Names of Readers:

Notes on Readings:

Unity Rituals:

Details of Unity Rituals:

Further Notes:

How many guests are expected?

How will the couple be presented?

Are there special instructions for the guests after the ceremony?

What style of ceremony will this be?

What are the ceremony colors?

Are there any special instructions or requirements?

Appendix I
Example Memorial
Questionnaire

Memorial Ceremony Planning Questionnaire

Completed on   /   /   @   AM / PM

Primary Contact Name:

Contact Telephone Number:

Contact E-mail:

Contact Address:

Ceremony Overview

Date and Time of Ceremony: /   /   @   AM / PM

Officiant Arrival Time:

Inside / Outside?

Venue Address:

Venue Contact:

Venue Tel:

Venue E-mail:

Notes on the Venue:

Deceased Details

Full Name:

Known To Others As:

Date of Birth / Age:

Date of Death:

Disposition / Committal Details:

Marital Status:

Relationship to Primary Contact:

Next of Kin:

Occupation:

Place of Birth / Hometown:

Family Details

Preferred Tribute

Description of Preferred Ceremony Style:

<u>Biographical Information and Notes</u>

Education:

Employment:

Awards of Achievements:

Hobbies

Clubs and Organizations:

Places Visited, Lived, and Loved:

Military Service:

Speakers and Readers

Speaker One:

Speaker One Description:

Speaker Two:

Speaker Two Description:

Speaker Three:

Speaker Three Description:

Speaker Four:

Speaker Four Description:

Speaker Five:

Speaker Five Description:

Speaker Six:

Speaker Six Description:

Speaker Seven:

Speaker Seven Description:

Music and Performance

Artist One:

Title and Description One:

Artist Two:

Title and Description Two:

Artist Three:

Title and Description Three:

Artist Four:

Title and Description Four:

Artist Five:

Title and Description Five:

Technical Requirements

Special Ceremony Components and Additions

Celebrant Pricing

Total for Ceremonies:

Total Travel:

Deposit Amount:

Date Balance Due:

Person Responsible for Payment:

Future Action Points

Appendix J
Celebrant Checklist

<u>Before the Day</u>

- o   Confirm exact time of arrival.
- o   Check travel time from base to destination.
- o   Check vehicle for gas, tires, etc.
- o   Pick up dry cleaning
- o   Lay out clothing and shoes for the day.
- o   Make any final changes to script.
- o   Create script for ceremony.
- o   Create any other materials needed for the ceremony.
- o   Confirm all legal paperwork will be made available on arrival.
- o   Confirm final payment.
- o   Charge all electronic items (phone, iPod, tablet, camera, etc.)
- o   Set alarm clock even if you plan to be awake.
- o   Check your Celebrant bag/kit/case.
- o   Make sure family, etc. are aware of your schedule.
- o   Get a good night's sleep and have a nice breakfast ready.

<u>On the Day</u>

- o   Check your script and kit.
- o   Confirm all is still as planned at the venue (no changes).
- o   Stay fed and hydrated.
- o   Leave on time, and travel safely.

<u>On Arrival</u>

- o   Connect with planner or coordinator.
- o   Obtain and process all legal paperwork.
- o   Ensure final payment is received.
- o   Walk the ceremony space to check layout.
- o   Check in with other vendors & get their contact info. Ensure they have yours.
- o   Check in with all party/family.
- o   Read through your script/notes briefly.
- o   Take five minutes to compose your thoughts.

- Warm up your voice.
- Remember you are terrific and perform wonderful ceremonies!
- Silence your cell phone.

After the Ceremony (at the venue)

- Take a moment to breathe. You did well!
- Congratulate the other participants.
- Thank all the other vendors and get their contact information if it was not available earlier. Ensure they have yours.
- Congratulate the couple (if a wedding)
- Get a picture with the couple (if a wedding)
- Ensure all paperwork is complete and safe.
- Ask if anyone has any questions.
- Thank and say farewell to participants.
- Check you have everything you need to take with you.
- Leave with a smile at a job well done.

After Returning Home

- Ensure all paperwork is completed, copied, recorded, and ready for the mail (if needed).
- Prepare "Thank You" cards for helpful vendors, and the couple or family.
- Put clothing in to be washed.
- Refresh your kit.

At a Future Date

- Request testimonial about two weeks after the event.
- Follow up with vendors for copies of photos and video.

Appendix K
Sample Contract

Contract for Celebrant Services

The Celebrant:
Address:
Telephone:
E-mail:

First Client:
Address:
Telephone:
E-mail:

Second Client:
Address:
Telephone:
E-mail:

Ceremony Type:
Ceremony Date:
Ceremony Location:

Ceremony Start Time:
Celebrant Arrival Time:
Celebrant Departure Time:

Is a Rehearsal Required?
Rehearsal Date:
Rehearsal Location:

Rehearsal Start Time:
Rehearsal Celebrant Arrival Time:
Rehearsal Celebrant Arrival Time:
Special Requirements and Conditions:

Fee for Ceremonies:

Fee for Rehearsals:

Fee for Travel:

Total Agreed Fees:

Deposit Required:

Balance Due Date:

Celebrant Signature:

Date:

First Client Signature:

Date:

Second Client Signature:

Date:

Terms of Contract

This Agreement: This agreement contains the entire understanding between the Celebrant and the Client(s) named. Where two clients are listed, both agree to be held fully liable for all matters of this contract, and any outstanding payments due at any time. Signature confirms that party has read, understood, and agreed to all parts of this contract without reservation.

Confirmation of Booking: A signed contract, and payment of the stated deposit, is required to confirm celebrant services.

Deposits: All deposits are non-refundable under all circumstances.

Final Payment: Final payment must be made on, or before, the balance due date stated in this document. If the client(s) prefer to make partial payments, they may do so as long as the full balance is received by the due date stated. Payments may be made by cash, check, or major credit cards.

Arrival and Departure: The Celebrant agrees to arrive within ten minutes of the stated arrival time. The parties agree that the Celebrant shall be free to leave after the stated departure time, unless late/overrun fees are immediately paid, as set out in this document.

Late and Overrun Fees: The Celebrant will stay beyond the agreed departure time only if additional payment is made, in advance, at the rate of $_____ per _____ minutes extra time required. All such payments are non-refundable under all circumstances.

Limit of Provision: This contract extends solely for the creation and performance of ceremony. The Celebrant is not responsible for the provision or supply of venue, furniture, structures, music, photography, or any other physical items or services desired or requested for the event.

Rehearsals: A rehearsal is considered a separate event from the ceremony, and total fee for that service is as stated in this document. If a rehearsal not listed in this document is later requested, a new contract reflecting this just be created and signed by all parties. Any such signed future contract automatically invalidates and supersedes this contract in all parts. All provisions for Celebrant arrival, departure, and overtime fees apply to rehearsal as in the case of a ceremony.

Special Requirements or Provisions: The scope of services for each party may only be made in the special requirements section of this document, and only before signatures are made. All requirements of the client must be met for the Celebrant to perform contracted services. The Celebrant agrees to all special requirements requested from them, as set out in that section before signatures are made.

Limit of Liability: If the Celebrant is unable to appear or perform for any reason, the Celebrant will make all possible efforts to supply a legally qualified replacement. If not Celebrant is available, liability is limited to the amount of any payments received.

Cancellations: All cancellations must be made at least _____ days before the date of the ceremony, as stated in this document, to avoid payment of the balance due. Cancellations made after such time shall require full payment to be made as set out in this document, as though the ceremony still took place. Client(s) agree to be fully responsible for all such payments, and to be held liable either together or separately for all outstanding amounts owed.

Date and Time Changes: All requested changes to the date and time of activities listed must be made, in writing, at least _____ days before the date of activity stated in this document. The Celebrant in no way guarantees automatic availability for alternate dates and times requested. Where changes to the ceremony date are made after the cancellation window is reached, and the Celebrant is unable to appear at such new time, all balances will remain due, as per this contract, as if the booking had been cancelled, and as stipulated in that clause. If the new dates and times are available, a new contract must be produced and signed by all parties. Any such later contract automatically invalidates and supersedes this contract in all parts.

Refusal of Service: Should it be decided any client(s) be intoxicated, or otherwise impaired in a way detrimental to the undertaking of the ceremony, the Celebrant maintains the right to cancel without notice, and with full entitlement to all fees outstanding regardless. Such determination of impairment shall remain exclusively the right of the Celebrant in all cases, and without appeal.

Consultation Availability: The Celebrant agrees to provide all required preparation prior to the ceremony. If the client has provided all required materials and information, the text and structure of the ceremony should be finalized at least a week before the stated ceremony date.

Photography / Use of Likeness: The clients agree to the use of all likenesses made electronically by the Celebrant, or furnished to them by other parties. The Celebrant may use such images for any promotional purposes without further permission of the client(s) or any other party contracted for the ceremony.

Travel and Parking: The client(s) agree to cover the costs of all travel, as stipulated by this document, as well as any parking, or unexpected travel expenses that the Celebrant may incur necessary to the fulfillment of their duties. All such additional expenses shall be payable immediately, and in full.

License Paperwork Availability: Where any legal paperwork or license is required for the Celebrant to fulfill their duties, it shall be the sole responsibility of the clients to obtain and furnish this prior to the ceremony, or the rehearsal if one is held. The Celebrant agrees to act on the requirements of all paperwork, as set out within the jurisdiction of the ceremony location, and by the issuing body.

Endnotes

While a great deal of time has been spent trying to ensure all the information in this volume is fully accurate, if you have an amendment, update, or suggestion, I would love to hear from you. Where I use a suggestion, I will give credit acknowledgement, and may even offer a prize for something truly outstanding.

You can submit information through the extra content section contact form, which can be reached by visiting hanhills.com/complete-celebrant/, and registering your email address for lifetime access to that area.

Thank you for taking the time to read this book, and I wish you the warmest success on your wonderful journey!

How to Get Extra Content

You can get extra content, including printable questionnaires, updates, resource lists, and more by visiting hanhills.com/complete-celebrant/. You will also find a contact form to submit questions to me personally. Simply register your email address for lifetime access to the extra content area for this book. I look forward to seeing you there!

Index

C

D

W

Y

Made in the USA
Middletown, DE
20 February 2022

61565220R00289